A HISTORY OF AMERICAN ART

Daniel M. Mendelowitz

STANFORD UNIVERSITY

A HISTORY

NEW YORK

OF AMERICAN ART

HOLT, RINEHART AND WINSTON, INC.

Chicago – San Francisco – Toronto – London

To the thousands of forgotten artists,
artisans, and craftsmen who have helped
shape the face of America

November, 1964

PREFACE

THE TITLE of this book demands some apologies and explanations. This is a history of the visual arts in the area which now constitutes the United States. Such a book is difficult to title. *A History of United States Art* not only sounds awkward but might logically exclude the arts of the original Indian inhabitants of the country and even the arts of the Colonial period. Thus, with apologies to our northern and southern neighbors, we are using the title A HISTORY OF AMERICAN ART knowing full well that the terms *America* and *United States* are not synonymous.

This volume has been designed to serve the need for a well-illustrated, broadly conceived introduction to the history of art in America. Both typical and distinguished examples of architecture, painting, sculpture, interior design, the household arts, and the crafts have been selected to characterize each of the major periods in our history, from the prehistoric Indian era to the present. In order to eliminate ambiguity and the need for supplementary illustrative material, all the works discussed in the text have been illustrated. Discussion has been focused around the illustrations, which have been considered both from an esthetic and historical viewpoint—that is, as objects of visual beauty and also as expressions of the life and thought of our rapidly developing society.

Insofar as possible, the individual works of art have also been presented in a biographical setting. In this way the role of the significant personalities as they established the characteristics of the various artistic movements can be revealed, and at the same time the way in which personal expression is shaped by the social forces dominating each period is made evident.

No one volume has previously introduced students to an all-encompassing survey of the development of the visual arts in America. A number of specialized histories of American architecture, painting, sculpture, and the individual crafts and household arts have been published. Oliver Larkin's ART AND LIFE IN AMERICA is general treatment; yet, though it presents a superb picture of the development of American culture through the arts, it demands a more thorough background in our cultural history than is possessed by the beginning student or the average layman. My hope is that this book will introduce our vigorous heritage in the arts to the interested reader so that he then may approach the many more specialized books with assurance and profit.

D. M. M.

Stanford, California
February 19, 1960

CONTENTS

vii

Seventeenth-century Painting · Eighteenth-century Painting ·
Prints · Sculpture

PART I

The Arts of the Indians

The Arctic,
Eastern Woodlands,
and Great Plains

TWO GREAT MIGRATIONS POPULATED THE WORLD OF THE
Americas. The first commenced between fifteen and twenty-five thousand
years ago. The ice which covered the continent during the last Ice Age
had receded enough to allow small groups of nomadic hunters from northeast Asia to enter northwest America across the ice, land, and shallow
water of Bering Strait. These hunters were following the animals who
moved north with the ice to regain their natural habitat. The descendants
of these original settlers formed the local native population when the
second of the great migrations started about five hundred years ago. Most
of its members came from northern Europe, though in later years people
came from all parts of the world. In an unbelievably short period the
Europeans conquered the older inhabitants of the country and introduced
the more elaborate social patterns of their homelands. This predominantly
European way of living, modified, of course, by the demands of the new
environment and the rapidly developing technology of the nineteenth

3

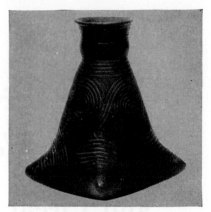

1-1 (*left*). Chanting warrior pipe, stone. Adena Mound. Ohio State Museum. Columbus, O. 1-2 (*below*). Clay bottle. Louisiana. Museum of the American Indian, Heye Foundation, New York.

century, created the brilliant and dynamic civilization which now covers the American continent.

Most historians of American art have overlooked the Indians, the descendants of the first migrants. However, tastes have broadened immeasurably in the past few decades and today the arts of the Indians have acquired a new significance. We now see universal relationships between the arts of all peoples. A stone pipe in the form of a warrior (1-1), carved long before the first European landed in America, is closer to the contemporary spirit than was most of the sculpture done in the early years of the twentieth century. By the same token, we tend to prefer a ceramic water bottle from a prehistoric mound in Louisiana (1-2) to the hand-painted vase left by our grandmother. In addition, the systematic archeological explorations of our day have revealed a much higher level of Indian culture than had formerly been known. We now realize that in almost all areas of artistic activity—architecture, sculpture, painting, weaving, ceramics, woodcarving, as well as a host of specialized native crafts—the Indians of America achieved superlative results. It is to these indigenous arts that we shall first turn our attention.

There are two conflicting theories concerning the origins of the American Indians and their culture. Both theories assume that man originated on a continent other than the Americas since no remains of a true primitive man, such as the Java or the Peking man, have been found here. Both theories agree that man first entered the continent between fifteen and twenty-five thousand years ago. The older theory assumes that the inhabitants of the Americas were of the protomongoloid stock—that is, that the inhabitants of Asia and the American Indians came from common ancestral groups. These ancestors of the Indians are thought to have migrated to America while in a stone-age level of culture and to have subsequently developed their elaborate ceremonial civilizations in isolation from the rest of the world. The other and newer theory is based on the premise of successive migrations of peoples of varying racial elements at different levels of development who brought with them varying patterns of culture. Today the second theory is receiving ever wider acceptance. These successive migrations are seen as part of a general diffusion of culture through the Asiatic-Oceanic-American orbit. Some of the late arrivals probably brought in highly developed ceremonial practices and crafts. It also seems probable that not all of the migratory wanderers came via the Northwest—some undoubtedly came by boat from the South Pacific. New evidence suggests that much of Polynesian culture may have come from South America and that in prehistoric times there were movements in both directions across the Pacific.

When the European settlers arrived in North America they found a thinly scattered population of native tribes of varying levels of development, even the most primitive of which performed admirably in some of the arts. In North America the areas of Indian culture were determined by the natural geographic and climatic divisions of the continent, and it is in relation to these areas that Indian art may be most meaningfully studied. A glance at a map (1-3) reveals the six chief areas. Starting at the north and moving clockwise, we see the following broad divisions: (1) Arctic, (2) Eastern Woodlands, (3) Great Plains, (4) Southwest, (5) California, (6) Pacific Northwest.

Each of these geographic areas had its particular climate, topography, fauna, and flora as well as its unique native materials; and in each area peoples adapted the local materials to their particular requirements. Clay, wood, stone, bone, sinew, shell, fur, feather, grass, stem, bark, and an endless variety of other natural materials were fashioned with ingenuity and skill to serve the needs of these primitive men. Much of the pleasure we derive from the arts of the Indians comes from observing the brilliant invention and skillful manipulation that characterized their creations.

If we enjoy these objects that have come down to us from the Indians only as works of art, we overlook much of their significance. To be fully appreciated they should be seen as functionally designed, beautifully

1-3. Geographic division of Indian culture in North America.

made objects with auxiliary religio-magical functions. We tend to look at a stone pipe or a mask (1-4) as a piece of sculpture, but the Indian, while deeply conscious of the visual qualities of these objects, was probably most concerned with their utilitarian and ceremonial effectiveness. The Indian's esthetic sensitivity is revealed first by the perfection of craftsmanship for its own sake, second by the intensive refinement of shapes and surfaces, and third by the use of applied decorations. Thin-walled ceramic vessels of elegant shape and decoration (1-2) and baskets with dozens of stitches to the inch are a tribute to that feeling for refinement for its own sake which we call love of beauty. At the same time, these beautiful objects functioned effectively in their utilitarian capacities. The tightly woven baskets are not only miracles of craftsmanship, but can often hold water; and the elegantly chipped spear heads and polished stone clubs were deadly in the hunt or in warfare. The decorative motifs which enhance household and ceremonial objects also served both an esthetic and utilitarian function. Carving an animal head on a hunting club was a magical act to insure success in the chase while the decoration of a garment with the sun motif procured the sympathy and protection of a powerful deity.

The most elaborate and refined objects were made for ceremonial and burial purposes, since the most exacting skills were devoted to supplicating or placating the gods. Such masks, burial and effigy jars, figurines, and ceremonial pipes please us visually much as they did the original maker and user, but our appreciation is limited to the visual aspects. While we may be aware that the decorations were used for their protective powers, the magic eludes us emotionally since, though we recognize this function intellectually, we cannot feel it.

It is important to remember, then, that these objects of long ago were not created just to be looked at, and certainly not to be placed in a museum or hung on a wall. They were made in response to the requirements of daily life, much like contemporary automobiles or sacred vestments, and are as complex and subtle as the civilizations which created them. They served utilitarian functions, pleased the eye and mind, and propitiated the gods. We see them out of context and so tend to appreciate only one facet of a multifaceted creation.

The subsequent discussion is organized in relation to the chief geographic areas of the North American continent, concentrating on the most noteworthy achievements in each area. Starting in the north and moving east, south, west, and then again north, we parallel, to a degree, the movements of the original migratory tribes as they filtered down and across the continent.

THE ARCTIC

The treeless tundra that stretches for thousands of miles, from the northwestern tip of Alaska across the northern fringe of the continent to Greenland, is the home of the Eskimo. One of the most noteworthy traits of the Eskimos is their amazing ingenuity in adapting themselves to their environment—or rather in adapting their seemingly uninhabitable environment to their needs. The snow house or igloo represents only one way in which these self-reliant and inventive people have shaped a way of living from their inclement and snowy wastes. The snow house, which has caught the imagination of the world because it represents the triumph of practical imagination over the hostile forces of nature, is not the typical Eskimo dwelling, for less than a fourth of the people of the Arctic live in igloos. For the most part they live in houses of earth raftered with slabs of stone, wood, or the bones of large animals. These dwellings usually consist of one large room, often semisubterranean, which is entered by a

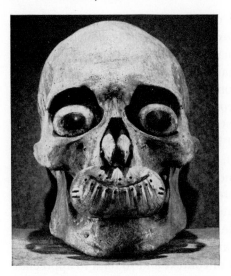 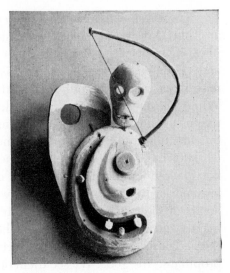

1-4 (*left*). Decorated skull, Ipiutak site, Alaska. Courtesy of the American Museum of Natural History, New York. 1-5 (*right*) Eskimo mask, wood. The Anthropological Museum, University of California, Berkeley, Calif.

covered passageway. This arrangement provides both protection and warmth.

The Eskimos have proved themselves equally imaginative and skilled in devising their clothing, boots, household gear, and hunting and fishing equipment. From the feathers, fur, bones, shells, mosses, sticks, and stones which constitute the raw materials of their economy they fashion the efficient and occasionally even beautiful objects that have enabled them to survive in what appears to the outsider to be an inhospitable if not an uninhabitable world.

The oldest strata of Eskimo remains, from around the beginnings of the Christian era, disclose beautifully carved objects of walrus ivory that reveal a fully developed artistic tradition. The surfaces of these objects are frequently engraved with realistic pictographs of hunting and fishing scenes or with abstract geometric patterns. One of the most striking and memorable objects to be unearthed from a tomb in an ancient Ipuitic town is a decorated human skull (1-4). The ivory eyes are inlaid with jet, the nostril cavities are filled with two delicately carved birds, and the mouth is covered with a curiously shaped and engraved ivory plaque. By sealing the orifices of the skull with precious materials and magic symbols, primitive man hoped to build a safeguard against the mystery of death and disintegration. Graves from this area also reveal beautiful linked-chains, combs, long-handled back scratchers, and realistic seals.

These objects were usually carved from bone or fine-grained richly colored walrus ivory.

Carved and inlaid wooden objects, pottery lamps, and clay cooking vessels have also been discovered at these ancient sites. The masks which the Eskimos of northern Alaska fashion from driftwood, bits of bone, feathers, and other curious odds and ends of materials are among the most charming and whimsical Indian creations (1-5). These are usually carved from light, thin, oval or circular pieces of wood. The features are indicated by carving or by coloring white, black, red, and blue. Appendages which dangle and sway like parts of a modern mobile indicate the animal, bird, or fish attributes of the mythical or fantastic creatures represented by the masks. Various human and animal parts are rearranged with amazing freedom, and the fanciful results equal the boldest imaginings of the contemporary surrealists. The ancient Eskimo skull and mask reveal certain qualities common to much Indian art—a delightful ability to manipulate environmental materials in an imaginative way, a high level of craftsmanship, a sense of humor, and the power to communicate the awe of primitive man before the mystery of life and death.

EASTERN WOODLANDS

Moving south and east, one comes to the most extensive area of Indian culture in North America. The Eastern Woodlands commence in the forests of northern Canada, sweep east and south, and cover the heavily wooded eastern half of the United States. The Indian tribes in the northern and northeastern parts of this vast region were the least developed of the area. In the Ohio and Mississippi River valleys and along the Gulf of Mexico, a higher level of culture existed, including some of the most elaborate ancient civilizations of North America. Of particular interest are the Mound Builders of the southeastern quarter of the United States, whose most spectacular achievements were the construction of vast ceremonial and burial mounds of earth, frequently shaped in the forms of birds and mammals (1-6). The Mound Builders were fine sculptors and potters—they also worked copper, mica, and a variety of other materials.

A detailed study of the Eastern Woodlands reveals over eighty related cultural units which flourished at different times in various sections of the area. The universal presence of chipped flint arrowheads indicates an archaic period of great antiquity, stretching back as far as 8000 B.C.

1-6. Snake Mound. Ohio. Photograph courtesy Lt. Col. Albert W. Stevens.

Between 1000 B.C. and A.D. 100 more differentiated local cultures developed. Copper tools appeared in the Great Lakes area (artifacts of a culture called "Old Copper"), and extraordinarily fine tools of ground slate were produced in New England. An Asian type of pottery marked with textures made by a mallet wrapped with cord appeared in widely separated areas.

Next came the earliest Mound Builders in the Ohio Valley. Estimates as to the dates of the early mound-building cultures vary; some contemporary judgments based on the Carbon 14 tests put them back almost to 1000 B.C. More conservative archeologists date the Adena and Hopewell cultures of Ohio, two of the most important mound-building cultures, between 350 B.C. and A.D. 100. Later the Mound Builders moved south into the lower Mississippi Valley along the coast of the Gulf of Mexico. The remains from this area have been dated between A.D. 900 and 1700 and this later phase of the Eastern Woodlands culture is frequently referred to as the "Temple Mound" period, since the mounds appear to have been substructures for ceremonial buildings. Beads and metal objects of European manufacture in some mounds indicate that the mound-building cultures were still flourishing when the first European settlers arrived.

Ceremonial Mounds

The most elaborate ceremonial structures erected by the Indians of North America were the great earth mounds, of varying heights and shapes, found throughout the Eastern Woodlands from Canada south into Florida. The custom of building mounds may be of Mexican origin, for the construction of large earth platforms as the base for ceremonial structures was general practice in Mexico and Central America. Mound-building was spread through many different tribes at many levels of culture, and the mounds appear to have been built for several different purposes. Three types of mounds were constructed—conical burial mounds, effigy mounds in the shapes of birds and animals, and pyramidal mounds which served as substructures for ceremonial buildings or the dwellings of chiefs. In general, the conical burial mounds and the effigy mounds are from earlier periods; the pyramidal mounds are later.

The effigy mounds were probably ceremonial constructions associated with burial practices and are shaped to resemble mammals, reptiles, birds, and other tribal totems. These effigy mounds frequently attain an impressive size. The Snake Mound in Ohio (1-6) is one of the most imposing, as is revealed by aerial photography. The carefully planned and laboriously built head, twisting body, and spiraled tail, which, following the curve, measure almost 1400 feet, or a fifth of a mile, in length, testify to the importance of the effigy in some remote and long-forgotten ceremonial activity. Monks Mound, the largest known, is the central unit of the Cahokia group near St. Louis; this group consists of over forty-five large mounds and many smaller ones. Monks Mound is over 1000 feet long, over 700 feet wide, almost 100 feet high, and covers an area of about 16 acres. This makes it larger than the Great Pyramid of Cheops in Egypt, which covers about 13 acres. One of the largest earthworks in the world, Monks Mound is composed of four terraces of diminishing height and size, placed one on top of the other, reminiscent of the platforms that formed the bases for the temples of the Mexican area. The sloping sides, now eroded by centuries of weathering, probably formed a ramp or stairway which provided access to the top. Monks Mound, like many of the later large flat-topped mounds, appears to have served as a platform for a ceremonial structure or a residence of a priest or chief.

Stone

The working of stone was the most ancient art of the Indian, and stone remained the material in which he created his most monumental

1-7. Bowl, diorite. Hale Co., Ala. Museum of the American Indian, Heye Foundation, New York.

work. The hunter who first crossed Bering Strait in search of reindeer and mastodon already knew how to shape the spear heads and stone axes which he used in warfare and the hunt. During thousands of subsequent years, the art of making spear points and arrow heads of pressure-flaked flint was perfected along with the art of shaping the ground stone implements of the neolithic age—the beautifully shaped celts, axes, gouges, knives, weights, ceremonial pipes, bowls, mortars, and pestles necessary for a semisedentary life. Chipped and polished stone implements and ceremonial objects of a high level of technical excellence have been found distributed throughout North America.

A diorite bowl 12 inches high from the late Temple Mound period in Alabama (1-7) provides a superb example of the skill and taste with which the Indian craftsman worked stone. Diorite is an igneous rock of unusual density and hardness. Cutting this smooth bowl with its even thickness of wall from a solid piece of diorite and allowing for the graceful projection of the bird's head, neck, and tail represents an amazing technical achievement; the Indian craftsman had no metal-cutting tools but had to shape the stone, smooth it, and polish it with other stone or bone tools and abrasives. The stone was first chiseled into the general required shape and next shaped by the picking away of smaller particles. The surface was then polished by abrasion with fine, hard, gritty materials, and the lines and details were incised by drilling with both solid and tubular drills rotated between the hands or with bow strings. The engraved lines of this bowl have been skillfully placed to reinforce the circular shape and then become formalized patterns suggesting the feathers and the anatomical forms of a duck. The skill involved in producing this vessel from the intractable stone is no more impressive than the restrained taste shown in designing the forms from which it is composed.

1-8 (*left*). Hawk pipe, stone. Tremper Mound, O. Ohio State Museum, Columbus, O. 1-9 (*below*). Pipe, stone, Miami, O. Museum of the American Indian, Heye Foundation, New York.

The richest deposits of stone ceremonial objects have been taken from the burial mounds of Ohio—from the famous Adena Mound and from the important Hopewell mounds, named after the owner of the lands on which the mounds were discovered. The tribes of the Hopewell culture constructed great effigy mounds in the shapes of birds and animals and buried their dead under elaborate funerary mounds. Carbon 14 tests now indicate that the Hopewell culture may be the older of the two, going back at least as far as 350 B.C. Both Adena and Hopewell appear to have been important centers of cultural diffusion and the influence of these two centers can be seen throughout the central Mississippi and Ohio valleys.

One of the most striking stone pipes from the Adena Mound is in the form of a standing human figure (1-1). The figure is about 8 inches high and has the large head, heavy limbs, and simplified anatomical forms with which the Indians achieved the sober monumentality so characteristic of their sculpture. A grave and somewhat ferocious grandeur emanates from the small figure, which probably represents a chanting priest or chief executing a ceremonial dance. The figure exhibits such decidedly Mexican qualities as the ovoid mouth and eyes, the formalized muscles, and the flat ribbonlike design of the loincloth. An admirable skill and certainty are communicated both by the techniques with which the stone is finished and by the vigor with which the sculptural form has been conceived. Such an assured projection of the planes of the head and body only accompanies a highly developed sculptural sense.

The stone pipes from the Hopewell mounds, usually representing birds or animals, were carved with flint tools from grayish Ohio pipestone, stone capable of taking a high polish. The bowl of the pipe is in the head or back of the creature represented and the mouthpiece is in the base of

1-10. Textured jar, ceramic. Miller Co., Ark. Museum of the American Indian, Heye Foundation, New York.

the pipe, which was held in the hands of the smoker. The hawk pipe (1-8) from the famous Tremper Mound is a fine example of the Hopewell style. While it is realistic in its essential concept, both the basic form and the incised feather patterns are formalized and simplified in much the manner of the monumental sculptured birds of ancient Egypt. The feet are particularly expressive of the ability to simplify a thoroughly understood anatomical form. A pipe from Miami, Ohio, is unusual in the strange variety of its form (1-9). A fantastic effect is created by the large human head, the bizarre long-necked animal, the worshiping seated figures, and the little white shell eyes. This pipe undoubtedly represents a ceremonial rite.

Ceramics

The early European settlers found that almost all the Indians except those of California and the Pacific Northwest made pottery. None of it, however, was as beautiful as the ceramics from the prehistoric sites.

Pottery making is one of the first crafts to be developed by a people becoming sedentary in its living habits. The seasonal ripening of crops creates the necessity for storage containers, as does the more elaborate preparation of foods that characterizes a settled way of life. Where and how the ceramic arts first developed in America remains conjectural. The wide distribution of pottery marked with cord pattern from sites dated as early as 1000 B.C. suggests that the ceramic arts may have been introduced from Asia, since similar cord-marked pottery was produced there at an early date.

The American Indian fashioned his pottery without the aid of the potter's wheel. The clay was built up by the coil method or pushed into shape from a lump. A number of early sites in the Eastern Woodlands

1-11 (*left*). Effigy jar, ceramic. Arkansas. Museum of the American Indian, Heye Foundation, New York.   1-12 (*right*). Effigy jar, ceramic. Arkansas. Museum of the American Indian, Heye Foundation, New York.

area reveal pottery that appears to be patterned after simple stone vessels as well as more sophisticated potteries marked by a wide variety of textures. These textural enrichments were achieved by punching, pinching, incising, and stamping, as well as by using the very ancient cord-marking techniques. A jar (1-10) from Miller County, Arkansas, illustrates a rich surface of textures. The first impression one receives upon looking at the jar is one of vigor and crudity, but more careful study reveals a sensitive feeling for relationships of shape and surface textures. The clay is used in a way that emphasizes massiveness and weight. The shapes are heavy, slightly angular, and almost awkward. The incised patterns appear to have been put on spontaneously, yet they not only emphasize the shapes, but also reinforce the effect of a fresh, unpremeditated creation. The horizontal engraved lines on the neck contrast effectively with the concentric swirls of texture on the body. Each swirl is centered by a raised rough area to create an accent. Similar handsomely textured pottery in which designs were pressed into the clay with wooden stamps has been found in Georgia. Carbon 14 tests indicate that these richly textured ceramics were produced prior to A.D. 500.

The most beautiful wares of the Eastern Woodlands area come from the lower Mississippi Valley mounds of the late Temple Mound period, between A.D. 900 and 1700. The elegant ceramics from this period include the beautiful, polished brown wares (1-2) from Ouachita Parish, Louisiana, which represent a very refined development of the early cord-marked patterns. The 5¾-inch-high water bottle pictured here is thin-walled and hard-fired. The handsome and subtle form is reinforced by a delicate pattern of logically placed rhythmic lines that emphasize the unique bottle shape in a most sensitive way. The surface texture has a handsome satiny sheen and the color is pleasantly muted. A number of pieces of this polished brown ware have been discovered. They vary considerably in shape, but they all reveal the technical skill and refined taste that places this small bottle in the front rank of American ceramic achievements.

A beautiful frog jar modeled from green clay (1-11) is typical of the ceramic effigy jars of reptile, bird, animal, and human form from the mounds of the lower Mississippi Valley. Curiously, these effigy jars resemble ceramics from ancient Peru more than products of any neighboring peoples. These jars were made for use in burial ceremonials and may have established clan relationships. Despite the fact that they are modeled as thin-walled vessels capable of holding liquids, they are essentially religious sculptures. The frog jar reveals its maker's feeling for the plasticity of hand-shaped clay through the rhythmic unity of its generalized shapes and the monumental character of its forms.

The front view of another effigy jar (1-12) reveals the simple forms and heavy proportions that characterize Indian treatment of the human figure. The head is large; the body forms are massive, generalized, and rhythmically unified. Anatomical detail and exactness of proportion are sacrificed to achieve a sense of weight, monumentality, and sculptural unity. The expressive power of such primitive art frequently appears to result from the presence of highly formalized elements together with naive and even crude expressions of deeply felt experience. Here one feels the direct communication of intense feelings and perceptions. The emaciated body is tellingly defined by the incised lines of the ribs, and the resigned, closed eyes, the thin arms, and the cross-legged, seated position all foretell death. A profile view reveals a hunched back, reminiscent of the Peruvian portrait vases, which frequently represented deformed and sick people.

Wood

Wood is one of primitive man's basic materials. Unfortunately, wood decays readily and consequently the mounds and similar sources of prehistoric art have revealed few ancient wooden objects. A very fine deer head which displays sensitive naturalism of a high order comes to us from the swamps of Key Marco in southeastern Florida (1-13). In this same area were found other fine naturalistic animal sculptures: pumas,

1-13. Deer mask, wood. Key Marco, Fla. University Museum, Philadelphia.

wolves, alligators, and birds as well as masks, statuettes, and wooden utilitarian objects.

Perhaps the most entertaining wood carvings created by the Indians were the masks which represent various mythical beings. Some very effective masks were made by the Iroquois, Seneca, and related tribes from New York and New England. These vigorous masks (1-14) are like sculptured caricatures with bold features, deeply grooved wrinkles, and strongly contrasting eye and mouth patterns. They are usually painted, red and black being the most frequently used colors. Long masses of horse hair were attached to the head. These masks are frequently boldly asymmetrical, with one eye or one side of the mouth going up while the other turns down or the nose twisting to one side. The result is both grotesque and humorous.

Wood was naturally the basic material from which the inhabitants of the Eastern Woodlands fashioned their ingenious and efficient shelters. A bark lodge from the Winnebago tribe of Wisconsin (1-15) illustrates one of the simpler types of dwellings they constructed. The Indian living unit usually had one room for a family, although the family concept was more complex than our present one. Most sedentary groups created multiple-unit dwellings which were frequently of impressive dimensions. These were really clusters of single-family dwellings under one roof. The long house of the Iroquois, one example of such a structure, was an elaborated development of the bark lodge. Located in a protected area of the forest, the rectangular long house frequently attained the length of 80 or even 100 feet. It had a simple pitched roof and was built over a structure of wooden poles which provided a frame for the covering of bark. A passageway ran down the center of the interior. The side areas were divided by partitions into room-sized stalls which were open to the center passageway. These were used for sleeping, eating, and storage. Fire pits were centrally located at regular intervals, and an opening in the roof above

1-14. Seneca masks, wood. Museum of the American Indian, Heye Foundation, New York.

1-15. Bark lodge. Wisconsin. Museum of the American Indian, Heye Foundation, New York.

each fire pit allowed the smoke to escape. Raised benches along the walls provided space for sleeping and storing tools and utensils. The two ends of the long house were closed by bark doors or hangings of animal skins.

The early settlers of New England patterned many of their first dwellings after the bark lodges and long houses of the Indians, for such structures were easy to devise from the materials at hand and provided some degree of privacy and protection from the elements. It is significant that wood has remained America's first choice as a building material for dwellings.

Metal and Precious Materials

There is ample evidence that the art of working metals was introduced to North America from Asia at a very early date, probably almost a thousand years before metallurgy was known in Central and South America. Archeological sites from the Great Lakes area as old as 1000 B.C. disclose tools of hammered copper sufficiently unique to have bestowed the name of "Old Copper" on the culture. Lances and knives were made with notched stems, and crescent-shaped knives, harpoon heads, and chisels have been found which appear to be replicas of similar metal objects from early cultures in Asia. The peoples of the Hopewell culture hammered nuggets of copper into thin sheets and cut them into bird, animal, human, and abstract shapes which were sewn on clothing and used as jewelry or as part of an elaborate headdress.

One such copper headdress (1-16), from the Citico Mound in Nashville, Tennessee, is almost 12 inches high. It is handsomely designed with a pleasant variety of shapes. A subtle use of indented grooves and slightly rounded edges separates and emphasizes the various parts of the design and creates an illusion of volume and richness despite the flat surface.

The peoples of the Hopewell culture carried on extensive trading activities with distant tribes, obtaining rare raw materials such as grizzly bear teeth, pearls, mica, and sea shells from the remote coastal areas and the Gulf states. The elegant silhouettes of mica which have been found in the burial grounds of the Hopewell culture have been shaped to emphasize the intrinsic beauty of this rare material. These artfully fabricated objects appear in a variety of strange motifs: headless human bodies, dismembered arms and legs, heads, hands (1-17), eagle claws, duck bills, spear throwers and replicas of spear heads. The fragile and flaky mica was cut with elegant precision into flawless forms with graceful flowing

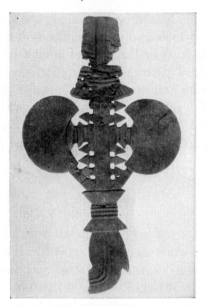 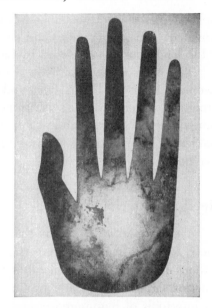

1-16 (*left*). Headdress ornament, copper. Citico Mound, Tenn. Museum of the American Indian, Heye Foundation, New York. 1-17 (*right*). Hand, mica. Hopewell culture, O. Chicago Natural History Museum, Chicago.

contours. These mica silhouettes were undoubtedly made from this precious material as votive offerings, precious substitutes for real objects made to be buried with the dead.

Pictorial Arts

The Mound Builders of the Eastern Woodlands left examples of pictorial art painted and engraved on the elaborate objects interred in the burial mounds. Particularly interesting are the engraved shell gorgets from the lower Mississippi valley. These flattish disks were cut from the side of a conch shell, polished into a smooth flat shape, and then engraved with human, bird, snake, and other motifs.

Similar but larger is an unusual flat brown sandstone disk (1-18) from Mississippi, about 8½ inches in diameter and 1 inch thick. This disk employs a Mexican motif—entwined rattlesnakes with feathered headdresses. The beautiful placement of the group of snakes in the circle, the clarity of the strongly organized border, the contrasts of eyes, rattles, and fangs all attest to the intelligence of the designer and the maturity of the artistic tradition in which he worked.

1-18. Disk, sandstone. Mississsippi. Ohio State Museum, Columbus, O.

The very early stages of primitive culture occasionally produce paintings and sculpture of such astonishing visual realism as the ancient cave paintings of Spain and France, but no such visual realism characterizes the arts of the Indians whose pictorial conventions conform closely to the schematic pattern of most neolithic art. Representational symbols were based on an idea about a form rather than on an analysis of its visual aspects. A few typical characteristics were hit upon—for instance the upright posture and two-leggedness of human beings—and these rather simple elements schematically rendered satisfied the needs of the artist. Such formalism characterized much of the art of the American Indian, whose pictorial expression can best be understood if it is considered as a system of graphic symbols designed to convey ideas. As we have seen in the sandstone disk from Mississippi, these ideographic symbols could be used with great distinction of decorative effect and even with expressive power.

Leathercraft, Bead and Quill Work, and Bark Baskets

Though there is ample evidence that textiles were produced in the Eastern Woodlands in prehistoric times, no true textiles were being woven in this area when the European settlers arrived. Instead, the arts of dressing and shaping leather were well developed. Deer hide and other large animal skins were made into light, soft garments as well as into pouches, baby carriers, parfleches, bags, and other useful objects. The skins of rabbits, squirrels, and other small animals were cut into narrow strips and woven into garments and blankets. Almost all leather goods were decorated with painted designs, feathers, shells, beads, and quills.

From very early times, the Indians of the northern woodlands and

1-19 (*left*). Shoulder bag, quill embroidery. Museum of the American Indian, Heye Foundation, New York. 1-20 (*below*). Algonquin buckets, birch bark. Quebec, Canada. Museum of the American Indian, Heye Foundation, New York.

plains decorated their skin garments and bags with a unique type of embroidery done with flattened porcupine quills. The quills were cut into short lengths, dyed, and sewn in place in bold geometric patterns. Porcupine quill embroidery has a shiny, smooth surface that contrasts very effectively with the soft mat surface of leather. Development of the skill necessary to achieve the even, fine surface texture of a Patamatomi shoulder bag (1-19) demands infinite patience. These elaborate and involved designs, though executed without patterns, have been distributed over the bag with no signs of crowding or distortion. The craftsmen appear to have improvised on traditional motifs, for no two designs are identical, yet despite the spontaneous nature of the procedure, no miscalculations mar the relationship between the designs and the surfaces to be decorated.

In the early nineteenth century, glass beads were introduced by the Europeans and thereafter were used alone or in conjunction with porcupine quills. Beaded decorations were executed in the traditional geometric patterns or in the floral, leaf, and curvilinear motifs of European textiles.

Baskets were woven by all the Indian tribes but the baskets from the Eastern Woodlands do not compare with those we shall see from the Southwest and California. Closely allied to basketry and perhaps representing a craft halfway between woodcraft and basketmaking are the birchbark boxes and baskets made by the Algonquins and other tribes from the northeast (1-20). The bark was carefully cut to the proper shape and sewn with fine root fibers. The patterns were made by scraping away the top layers of white, revealing the dark brown bark underneath. Conventionalized animal designs were frequently used, but the somewhat curvilinear floral designs used here are typical of the historic period when the influence of the European textiles became evident in the crafts of this area.

THE GREAT PLAINS

The third area in North America with a unique and specialized culture is the high prairie country bounded on the east by the Mississippi and Missouri rivers and on the west by the Rocky Mountains, extending from the Dakotas and Montana south to Texas. This was the home of the tribes who contested the nineteenth-century settlement of the plains. A large body of literature describing the westward movement and the spirited defense of their homelands by the Indians has familiarized us with the life of these tribes, and we have come to think that the costumes, weapons, and living habits from this period are typical of Indian culture. Actually the Plains Indian pattern of living with which we are familiar represents a violent distortion of an older and more civilized way of life, a distortion caused by contact with the Europeans. The introduction of the horse and the gun in the mid-seventeenth century and the later encroachments of white settlers on their territory encouraged the Plains Indians to give up their semisedentary life, follow the buffalo, and engage in warlike pillaging of other tribes and of white settlers. They developed a nomadic existence and abandoned their settled communities to live in portable tepees. As these Indians left their communities they also gave up the arts which characterize a sedentary pattern of living and developed a striking costume well-adapted to horseback riding and fighting. The nomadic way of life, so readily associated with this area, achieved its distinctive character during the early nineteenth century.

In the Great Plains, before migratory habits disrupted the more sedentary life of the earlier period, a common type of dwelling was the earth lodge. The appearance of a Mandan village of earth lodges has been recorded by the great painter of Indian life, George Catlin (11-21). The simplest type of earth lodge was a partially excavated pit, the sides of which were reinforced by a palisade of logs and the top covered by a layer of sod. Communities of these earth lodges were placed in a naturally protected cave, or artificial fortifications or ditches were constructed to protect the village. This simple earth lodge was elaborated by some tribes

1-21. Decorated tepee. Museum of the American Indian, Heye Foundation, New York.

into circular structures of considerable dimensions. The walls were then constructed of heavy wooden posts. Sometimes the posts, rafters, and beams were fitted together by skillful joinery; at other times the posts were held in place with woven cords. The lodge was covered with sod placed on a frame of branches and twigs. These earth lodges were entered by a covered entrance way, and were often partially excavated so that the structure had a semisubterranean character. The largest structures of this type would accommodate as many as a hundred persons and frequently measured 50 feet in diameter. Many variations of this basic structure still exist—the hogan used by the Navaho Indians of today is a simple one-family version of the earth lodge. Some Plains tribes, such as the Wichita, built very neat domed huts covered with straw thatch. Certain tribes in Utah lived almost without protection in poorly constructed brush shelters. Others, in the south, lived in circular or rectangular semisubterranean huts covered with grass.

The tepee or wigwam (1-21), so often pictured as the typical Indian dwelling, was originally used by most tribes only as a temporary shelter during the seasonal migrations that accompanied hunting and food-gathering expeditions. These tribes constructed more permanent abodes for use during most of the year. When the Indians of the Great Plains gave up their settled communities to follow the buffalo and deer, the tepee became the standard dwelling since it was easily transported. The tepee, was a cone of skins or cloth supported on a frame of from three to sixteen or more poles. Some tepees reached a height of more than 30 feet and required as many as twenty buffalo skins to cover them, while others were barely as tall as man. The tepee provides the prototype for the contemporary tent—a portable shelter, hard to surpass for sheer efficiency, in which a wooden skeleton supports a skin covering almost as in an organic form.

Tepees were decorated with a variety of designs, ranging from conventionalized geometric symbols to naturalistic depictions of birds and animals. The decorated tepees contributed a colorful and picturesque element to the plains landscape during the strenuous years of settlement and left a more vivid impression on the national memory than any other type of Indian dwelling.

Much of the artistry of the Plains Indians went into the making and decorating of their colorful costumes as well as of their dwellings. Feathers, embroidery, beads, bits of glittering metal, shell, and other decorative elements were used on their clothes, on the bridles and harnessings of their horses, as well as on their hunting and battle equipment. As the horse became more and more a part of daily life the Indians dressed to increase the effectiveness of their movements on horseback. The great feather headdresses, the bundles of quivering feathers attached to their bridles, their fringed and flowing costumes all were designed to increase the effect of ferocity and speed as they galloped across the prairies.

Contact with the Europeans stimulated an interesting development of painting in the late eighteenth century among the Plains Indians. All through the area painting appeared on wearing apparel, tepees, and shields. Two styles developed: one, practiced by the women, utilized abstract and

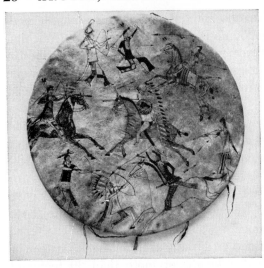

1-22. Sioux dance shield. Museum of the American Indian, Heye Foundation, New York.

decorative motifs of a traditional type. The men, apparently stimulated by the European tradition of representational art, employed a realistic style and usually pictured some military exploit or hunting scene. The Sioux dance shield (1-22) illustrates this realistic style in a battle scene distinguished by elegance of line and liveliness of pattern. The figures and horses are drawn with surprising accuracy, for realistic representation was foreign to the Indian and these artists were completely untrained in the western style of drawing. This composition is full of movement expressed by the skillful organization of the scattered figures around the central figure of the chief. Despite the absence of formal perspective and foreshortening, the forms are realized with force, and the general vitality of the delineation contributes to the total sense of exciting action and movement. These painted skins, recounting the stories of exploits and victories, provided a permanent record of prowess for all the members of the tribe to see and remember.

The tribes of the Eastern Woodlands and the Great Plains had achieved their most impressive developments long before the Europeans reached America. When the first settlers arrived, there was little to indicate the high level of development which subsequent archeological research has revealed. As the settlers moved across the continent they discovered a vital body of arts in the Southwest which was, in fact, the feeble afterglow of a brilliant earlier period. It was not until the end of the eighteenth century that contact with the Pacific Northwest revealed a flourishing culture in which the arts were at their zenith.

2

The Southwest,

California, and

Pacific Northwest

THE SOUTHWEST

The oldest traces of man in America are in the Southwest, centering in the canyon-eroded, high plateau near the convergence of Arizona, New Mexico, Utah, and Colorado. Stone spearpoints discovered in caves with the bones of extinct animals indicate that man lived and hunted here ten or even fifteen thousand years ago. The ancient way of life in this area changed very slowly. Around the beginning of the Christian era there appeared polished stone implements which, along with rude pottery and woven baskets, indicate a more sedentary way of life. By A.D. 500 the woven baskets were so fine that the culture has been termed "Basket Maker." The Basket Makers built settled communities and, in addition to weaving fine baskets, made decorated pottery, began to raise turkeys, beans, and corn, and wore ornaments of turquoise. After the Basket Makers the direct ancestors of the Pueblo Indians appear to have come from Mexico around A.D. 700 and introduced a number of Mexican traits into pueblo life.

27

Architecture

The most impressive development of domestic architecture achieved by the Indians in the United States is found in the cliff dwellings and pueblos of the Southwest. At the beginning of the Christian era, the inhabitants of the high plateau and desert areas, the previously mentioned Basket Makers, lived in caves modified by simple additions to make them more secure. Around A.D. 700 the new culture group from Mexico, who were physically distinguished by round heads rather than the long, narrow heads of the original inhabitants, introduced the more systematic construction of shelters. This cliff-dwelling, pueblo-building culture, called the Anasazi culture, reached its height between the eleventh and fourteenth centuries A.D. and received its most impressive physical expression in two types of complex community structures—the great communities built in the immense shallow caves which pit the canyon walls of this area and the pueblos in the plains beside the rivers.

Mesa Verde, in the southwestern corner of Colorado, contains the most extensive cliff dwellings. One side of Mesa Verde, or "green mesa," standing 1000 feet above the great highland plateau, rises to a height of over 8500 feet. The other side of the mesa slopes away in narrow gorges in which there are innumerable shallow caves, many bearing evidence of prehistoric habitation. There are a considerable number of communities in Mesa Verde, the Cliff Palace (2-1) and Spruce Treehouse being the most notable.

Few architectural monuments in the world have a more impressive site than does the Cliff Palace at Mesa Verde, and not many builders have so sympathetically integrated their architecture with the site and with their living pattern. Such a broad shelf of land standing securely above the plateau could be easily defended from intruders attacking from below, and a sheltering half-dome of rock gave complete protection from enemies above as well as from the extremes of Colorado weather. In this naturally protected, shallow cave, these early Americans built an imposing structure. Their site measures 425 feet in length, 80 feet in depth, and its greatest height is almost equal to its depth. In this huge cavern they constructed a complex of over two hundred rooms. The site was, of course, as irregular as nature often is. Participating happily in nature's laws and freedom from straight lines, these builders adapted their shelter with an innate sense of fitness.

They built with the materials at hand. The walls were of stones dressed to a generally rectangular shape and fitted together with clay mortar. Floors and ceilings were of heavy beams covered first with branches and twigs and then with packed clay to seal the surfaces. We do not know the exact date of this structure, but most of it appears to have been built in the twelfth century A.D. There are, however, evidences of earlier and cruder constructions which suggest that the same site served earlier generations. Lower stories at the front lead to a multistoried section at the rear in a series of irregular, steplike terraces which echo in man-made forms the topography of the local landscape. These communal dwellings were continually modified in terms of changing needs: chambers that were older, lower, and therefore less desirable as living space were walled off or used for storage. Entrances to the many chambers were provided through hatches in the roofs; wood ladders provided for passage from story to story. Pulling up the ladders and closing the hatches transformed this apartment house into a fortress.

The Cliff Palace is a great complex of living quarters, storage space, and the all-important sacred kivas, subterranean rooms used for religious ceremonies. The dramatic setting, the irregular terraces, the solid walls with only occasional small window openings, the rectangular and cylindrical towers and the circular kivas, made a memorable architectural mass, primitive and crude, perhaps, yet monumentally grand.

Perhaps the most beautiful of the ancient cliff dwellings are the ruins in the Canyon de Chelly, Arizona (2-2). The sheer pale mass of the cliff provides a dramatic background for the geometric patterns of the Casa Blanca. The sense of scale is overwhelming, partly because the total relationship of cliff dwellings can be seen at a glance. No other ruin conveys so forcefully the way primitive man adjusts to and improvises on nature. Here is functional architecture, literally growing from its carefully chosen site and from the precarious lives of its builders.

Characteristic features of both the cliff dwellings and the pueblos are the great semisubterranean ceremonial chambers, which are evident in Figures 2-1 and 2-4. A partially restored one, the Great Kiva (2-3) from Chetro Ketl, New Mexico, provides us with some idea of their original appearance. The kivas were covered by a flat roof made with huge beams which supported a ceiling of smaller poles and twigs plastered with adobe. The kiva was entered from a hatch which led to the antechamber and thence through to the main chamber. A low ledge ran around the wall of the circular main chamber, providing seating space. In the center were fire pits and an altarlike platform. The regular rectangular recesses in the main wall probably held ceremonial objects. A circular hole in the roof allowed air to enter and provided a chimney for

2-1 (*above*). Cliff Palace. Mesa Verde, Col. National Park Service photograph.
2-2 (*below*). Casa Blanca. Canyon de Chelly, Ariz. National Park Service photograph.

2-3. Great Kiva (restored). Chetro Ketl, N. M. Museum of New Mexico, Santa Fe.

the smoke from the fires. As can be seen from the seated figures, the Great Kiva at Chetro Ketl must have been well over 50 feet in diameter. Some kivas from the fourteenth century were decorated with elaborate frescoes picturing ritual symbols. Unfortunately, the adobe plaster walls have disintegrated, leaving only fragments of the original fresco decorations.

While certain tribes of the Southwest sought the protection of inaccessible cliff caves, others built their fortified communities on the plains close to the source of their food. The Spaniards called these communities pueblos, meaning villages.

The ruins of Pueblo Bonito (2-4) one of twelve communities in the Chaco canyon, New Mexico, provides a picture of the extensive nature of these prehistoric apartment houses. The pueblo is a great walled semicircular, or D-shaped, complex. The exterior walls reached a height of 40 feet on the curved side; the straight side, which faced the open floor of the canyon, was made up of one-story rooms. The encircling wall was built without a break except for a narrow entrance in front which was blocked by a boulder that permitted only one person to enter the compound at a time. In the interior of this enclosure was a huge court occupied by about twenty kivas. At the back the living quarters and storage areas rose tier upon tier to a height of four or five stories. Pueblo Bonito, over 650 feet at its greatest length and over 300 feet wide, contained more than six hundred chambers.

2-4. Pueblo Bonito. Chaco Canyon National Monument, N. M. Photograph courtesy New Mexico State Tourist Bureau.

A devastating drought of quarter-century duration occurred in this area at the end of the thirteenth century. At this time the cliff dwellers abandoned their inaccessible caverns and joined the pueblo dwellers who lived nearer to the sources of water. The abandoned cliff dwellings were never used again, but were held in awe by successive generations as the abodes of the spirits of their ancestors. Though there was a general decline in the culture of this area after the fourteenth century, a number of the pueblos have been inhabited continuously up to the present time.

The most dramatic of these ancient, but still occupied pueblos are Acoma, New Mexico, and Walpi, Arizona. Each of these villages occupies a promontory atop a steep mesa and is approached by a tortuous path up the cliff. Acoma, Zuni, and Taos (2-5) are more typical pueblos of today, multistoried, made of rich tan adobe brick with great projecting poles providing the horizontal supports. Each story is recessed behind the one below it to form terraces which lead to the various apartments. Ladders provide passage from story to story.

These more modern pueblos are finished with a smooth coat of adobe plaster. In certain lights the undulating, smooth wall punctuated by the extended ends of poles and beams and the wavering horizontals of roof and terrace, broken only by the Spanish-type chimney pots, stand out with dramatic clarity. These elements combine with the irregular rectangles of the varying sized rooms, the crude log ladders leading from story to story, and the round beehive ovens in front to create an almost magic illusion of an austere yet picturesque ancient way of life. At other times all illusion disappears. The harsh light of noon reveals the conflict between the stone-age Indians and the modern world—shabby doors, windows, screens, electric wires, metal pails, tubs, and mechanical devices catch the eye and introduce a jarring note. The modern pueblo, standing beside the highway in the clear desert air, exists as an architectural anachronism, partly prehistoric monument, partly contemporary slum.

Ceramics

The beautiful pinkish tan clay of the Southwest encouraged the development of an unusually high level of ceramic arts both in prehistoric and modern times. The Southwest is unique in that it exhibits an abun-

2-5. Taos pueblo. New Mexico. Santa Fe Railway photograph.

2-6. Bowl and jar, ceramic. Arizona. Museum of the American Indian, Heye Foundation, New York.

dance of both early pottery and deposits from subsequent periods, making it possible to follow the evolution of ceramic techniques in the area. There is some evidence that the first step from basketry to pottery occurred when the Basket Makers daubed their baskets with clay to make them waterproof. Certainly baskets preceded pottery, and some of the pots from this area, made between A.D. 500 and 1000, simulate the texture of the woven basket as a decorative device (2-6).

Toward the end of this same period, smooth, rather chalky pottery appeared in an exuberant variety of forms. Between the ninth and twelfth centuries these informal and vivacious ceramics were produced in great quantities. Unlike the later and more refined wares, they were unstandardized in form and decoration (2-7). Bold patterns of stripes, interlocking scrolls, stepped terraces, concentric meanders, checkerboards, fine parallel lines, and combinations of dots were freely painted in black over a white, or occasionally a red, slip. The geometric and frequently angular character of these suggests a textile or basket-weaving origin though many of the motifs appear to have originated as nature symbols. The same gay and lively attitude that characterizes the patterns pervades the forms; mugs, bowls, "Roman lamps," and fanciful shapes frequently suggesting humorous animals and birds give evidence of a gay and sensitive people whose creative spirit had not been stultified by formulas and conventions.

In the following century, technical perfection appears to have been stressed. A large 15-inch olla, or water jar, from the thirteenth century, suggests that at the height of the culture the taste shifted toward formal perfection and increased elegance of form and decoration (2-8). The beautiful fullness of form of this vessel is skillfully reinforced by the boldly conceived, precisely executed pattern that encircles it. The rhythmic movements of the great diagonal black and white zigzag patterns are striking. Diamond-shaped lozenges filled with small checkerboard shapes provide an effective contrast. Fine sets of parallel lines create a gray tone, thus adding subtlety and refinement to the already richly varied textures and tones of this water jar. The skill necessary to paint freehand the fine sets of parallel lines on the rounded surface of the vessel gives ample testimony as to the technical discipline of the potter. The surface of the vessel has been polished, and the luster, too, contributes to the general elegance.

In the mountainous southwestern corner of New Mexico, a pit-dwelling people with a generally low level of culture developed a particularly charming ceramic style between the tenth and twelfth centuries. This culture, called "Mimbres," was a localized offshoot of the earlier cultures of the Southwest. Large quantities of Mimbres pottery, chiefly bowls, were buried with the dead, and at the time of burial each bowl was "killed" by having a hole knocked in the bottom (2-9). Mimbres pottery was technically fine, light in weight, and decorated with freely

2-7. Ceramic shapes, 9th to 12th centuries. Socorro Co., N. M. Museum of the American Indian, Heye Foundation, New York.

2-8 (*left*). Pottery jar, 13th century. Laboratory of Anthropology, Inc., Santa Fe, N. M. 2-9 (*right*). Mimbres bowl. New Mexico. Buffalo Museum of Science, Buffalo, N. Y.

painted black designs on a white base. An unparalleled variety of motifs were used to decorate these bowls. Birds, insects, reptiles, animals, people, and mythological creatures predominate, but geometric designs, bandings, hatchings, and a variety of abstract patterns were also used. The Mimbres potters revealed endless powers of invention in varying the patterns on their bowls. In one site where over seven hundred pieces were excavated, no two were alike.

A general decline in the cultural level of the Southwest occurred after the fourteenth century. This was reflected in the coarsening of the later ceramics, but the techniques were not forgotten. A jar (2-10) 20 inches in diameter, from a modern Hopi potter, reveals the same disciplined taste and high level of craftsmanship that distinguished the finest prehistoric wares.

Wood and Metal

Though clay is the medium most frequently used in the arid Southwest, the Hopi Indians still carve charming Kachina dolls from the soft wood of the cottonwood trees. Kachina dolls, made in the images of masked ceremonial dancers (2-11), are created as playthings for children. Kachina is a term denoting spirits—the spirit of the dead, of rain, of local springs, and of many other natural phenomena. Masked Indian dancers represent the Kachinas on ceremonial occasions; in fact, the belief is that

2-10 (*below*). Hopi bowl. Arizona. Museum of the American Indian, Heye Foundation, N. Y. 2-11 (*right*). Hopi Kachina doll, wood. Museum of International Folk Art, Santa Fe, N. M.

the wearing of the Kachina mask transfigures the human dancer into a supernatural being. Fabrics, feathers, furs, and other materials are often used to enrich the Kachina doll costumes.

In the nineteenth century the Navaho Indians of New Mexico and Arizona developed the craft of making cast and wrought silver jewelry of an original and distinguished character. The techniques for working metal were acquired from Mexico along with the dies used to decorate the silver. The Navaho craftsmen adapted these dies, originally used for leather tooling, to the techniques of working metal and used them along

2-12. Navaho squash blossom necklace, silver. Lore Bloch photograph.

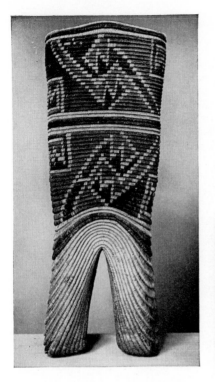

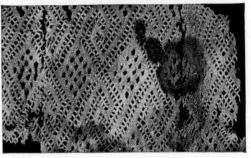

2-13 (*left*). Cradle basket, 11th to 14th centuries. Utah. University Museum, Philadelphia. 2-14 (*below*). Openwork textile, cotton, 14th century. New Mexico. Peabody Museum, Harvard University, Cambridge, Mass.

with the traditional turquoise to enrich their bracelets, rings, buttons, beads, buckles, necklaces, as well as to ornament bridles, halters, and stirrups. A squash blossom necklace (2-12) reveals the original and distinguished character of Navaho jewelry.

Basketry and the Textile Arts

It is difficult to determine the antecedents of the textile arts in North America. The mounds of the Eastern Woodlands and other prehistoric remains in North America reveal evidences of well-developed textile arts. Like wood, however, textiles disintegrate in the damp earth, and it is only in the dry caves of the arid Southwest that sufficient quantities of prehistoric weavings have been found to provide any substantial picture of the development of weaving in North America.

The Basket Makers of the Southwest were dependent upon the gathering of wild seeds, acorns, nuts, and roots, and this necessitated light, easily transported containers. The baskets from as early as A.D. 500 are highly developed in technique and tremendously varied in size and shape, ranging from great storage baskets in which a man could hide, to gemlike little baskets for storing precious small seeds. Some of the baskets are so tightly woven that they are waterproof. They were filled with water which was brought to the boiling point by immersing heated stones and could thus be used for cooking.

The ingenuity and skill with which the basket weaver of the Southwest developed his craft is illustrated by a cradle basket (2-13) from the cliff dwellers of Moki Canyon, Utah, produced between the eleventh and fourteenth centuries. The form of the object has been determined by its function—to carry a baby on its mother's back. The manner in which the twined technique has been adapted to create the complex shape of a cradle basket reveals an impressive command of the craft. The structural ribs have been spread on the outside and brought together in the crotch with consummate skill. Despite the complicated shape, the bold decoration is applied with clarity and logic to produce a handsome, animated, functional object.

By the eighth century A.D. cotton had been introduced to the pueblo peoples from Mexico, and this material and the contact with the highly developed textile tradition of the Mexicans stimulated an impressive flowering of the already well-developed weaving tradition. Through the successive centuries appeared textiles of an ever-increasing variety of weaves, distinguished both by technical and decorative excellence. Elaborate damasks employing contrasting colored threads were woven, as well as lacelike textiles with openwork patterns. An example of cotton openwork in an intricate fret and diamond-patterned mesh from fourteenth-century New Mexico attests to the sophistication of the textile arts at that time (2-14).

The Spaniards' introduction of sheep and goats and the standing loom in the sixteenth century stimulated the production of woven woolen blankets, saddle blankets, and in modern times, Indian rugs (2-15), particularly among the nomadic Navaho tribes who are the principal sheep owners of the Southwest. These beautifully woven blankets and rugs are decorated with typical abstract or formalized designs. While the designs used are traditional, each weaver modifies and combines the motifs according to individual preference so that an element of originality always exists and prevents the exact repetition of any pattern. Rugs and blankets were originally executed in natural wool colors: black, gray, brown, and white accented by a few bright vegetable dye colors. In the early twentieth century the introduction of brilliant aniline dyes cheapened the color schemes. Since 1940, the quantity of weaving done in the Southwest has dropped, but some that has been produced under the

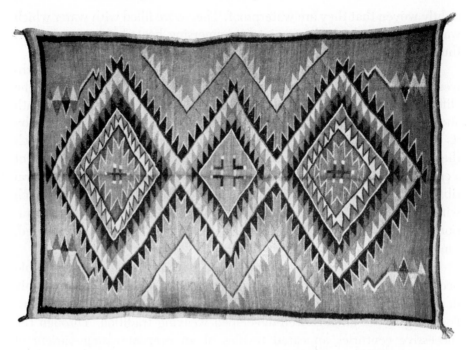

2-15. Navaho woven rug. New Mexico. Museum of the American Indian, Heye Foundation, New York.

guidance of the Federal Arts and Crafts Board is distinguished by a fine sense of design and by subtle vegetable dye colors.

Pictorial Arts

Curious symbols have been found pecked, painted, or incised on boulders and rocky walls of canyons in many parts of the continent, but most notably in the Dakotas, California, and the Southwest. Frequently, the symbols are geometric—triangles, zigzags, meanders, circles, dots, and parallel lines. At other times strange wavering, almost formless, motifs have been painfully engraved into the hard surface of the rock. The incised or pecked out patterns are often reinforced with color. Symbolic motifs which can be easily identified also appear in these cryptic murals. Human figures, animals, silhouettes of hands and feet are grouped in a way to suggest that some ancient ceremonial rite is being pictured. Some of the best preserved and largest rock engravings measuring many yards across have been found pecked into canyon walls in Utah (2-16). The

2-16. Pictographs. Glen Canyon, Utah. Photograph courtesy Gene Foster, University of Arizona.

random variety of the patterns, the curious scrambling of figures, mountain goats, and hands, and the many enigmatic, unidentifiable motifs suggest some infinitely patient and whimsical Paul Klee working to mystify later generations.

The Southwest remains one of the few areas in which the Indians have maintained a living tradition of pictorial expression in the twentieth century. A sand painting (2-17) depicting the Night Chant Ceremony shows four figures in black, blue, yellow, and white—the colors of the four points of the compass. The elongated, highly formalized symbols are typical of this elaborate ritualistic art, one of the few remaining forms of expression that reveal the magical background of much Indian art.

Sand painting is an old and unique art practiced by the Navaho tribes of the Southwest. Colored rocks are crushed to make the delicately colored sands used by the medicine men for the magic ceremonial pictures. The magic sand painting is supposed to banish the offending spirit from the body of the sick person. The various motifs are symbolic; each line, form, and color has its particular meaning. The medicine man works from memory, laying out the various colored patterns in their proper places with amazing certainty and skill. If a sand painting fails to effect a cure, the medicine man destroys it and continues to make new sand paintings until the patient recovers or dies. When a patient is cured, the sand painting is destroyed to insure his continued health.

Recently under the stimulus of the Indian Arts and Crafts a new

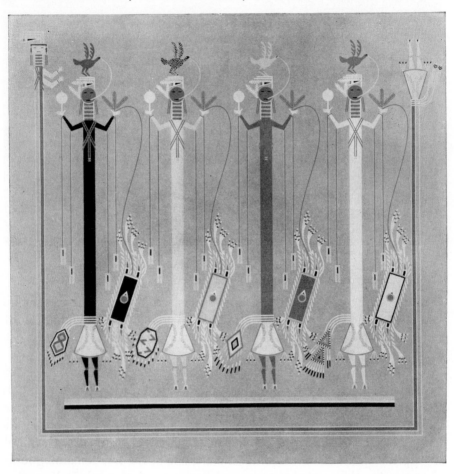

2-17. Night Chant Ceremony, sand painting. Museum of Navaho Ceremonial Art, Santa Fe, N. M.

school of easel painting by Indian artists has appeared in the Southwest. This school of painting started among the Pueblo tribes, but it spread to the Navaho, Apache, and even to some of the tribes of Plains Indians. The paintings are usually done on paper in watercolor, though a few artists also do oils. The subjects are drawn from Indian life and depict religious ceremonies, dances, genre subjects, and animals. *Apache Fire Dance* (2-18) by Al Momaday, a Kiowa Indian, illustrates the somewhat flat, decorative style of drawing and the vigorous rythmic sense of movement that characterize this contemporary school of Indian painters.

2-18. Al Momaday, *Apache Fire Dance*. Philbrook Art Center, Tulsa, Okla.

CALIFORNIA

The next geographic and cultural area is in the southwestern corner of the United States. The Indians in the narrow strip of California between the Sierra Nevada Mountains and the Pacific Ocean and from the islands off the southern coast were among the least developed on the continent. Despite their low level of culture, they produced what are perhaps the finest woven baskets in the world, and they also created out of soapstone charming fish and animals and handsome bowls and containers. Little is known of the prehistory of these people whose original way of life, modi-

fied at first by contact with the Spanish settlers, has completely disappeared.

Basketry

The timid and backward California Indians lived upon fish, shellfish,
acorns, seeds, and roots. Their habitations were extremely sketchy, and
when the Spaniards discovered them they exhibited no notable achievements except for their great skill in weaving baskets.

Most notable among the basket weavers of California were the
Pomo tribes. These Indians made baskets of incredible fineness—in some
one can count sixty stitches to the inch. Baskets produced in a great
variety of shapes were boldly decorated with designs which usually
moved diagonally across the surface. The characteristic stepped patterns
which develop naturally from the weaving process can be seen in a beautiful Pomo storage basket (2-19). Many of the patterns have identifying
names, like fish teeth, earth worm, arrowhead, or clouds, which may or
may not be related to the origin of the motif. The various natural-colored
materials, barks, roots, grasses, and other fibers, employed for the patterns
were reinforced with dyes to provide a greater range of tones. Black,
brown, and red were used most frequently, and they contrast effectively
with the pale straw-colored backgrounds.

Shell, feathers, and other precious materials were used for the splendid ceremonial baskets. A coiled gift basket (2-20) from the Wappo
Indians of northern California is richly decorated with colored feathers
arranged in a pleasant, but simple design supplemented by bead and
abalone shell pendants. Elegant baskets of this type were frequently made
as wedding gifts. The feathers from many species of birds were collected
for their bright colors and saved to make this laborious art possible.
Feather work of a similar type was practiced in the Southwest, in Central
and South America, and among the South Sea Islanders.

Sculptured Stone

The California Indians also left a group of small stone pipes, bowls,
and similar ceremonial objects designed to resemble whales, sharks,
other kinds of fish, animals, and insects. These charming sculptured
forms were carved in full plastic shapes from steatite, a kind of soapstone, and were enlivened with details of shell circlets. Three whale
pipes (2-21) from Los Angeles County are typical in their naturalism

2-19 (below). Pomo storage basket. California. Museum of the American Indian, Heye Foundation, New York. 2-20 (right). Wappo gift basket. California. M. H. De Young Memorial Museum, San Francisco, Calif.

and informal grace. The shell circlets create a sense of scale, provide a decorative touch, contribute animation and even humor. An unusual and very effective sculpture from this culture is in the form of a tarantulalike monster (2-22). This grotesque bowl, a little over 10 inches long, is larger than most of the sculpture from Southern California. These steatite sculptures were carefully finished and polished to produce a handsome sheen.

A curious group of steatite masks from Colusa County, in northern California, appears quite unrelated in both feeling and technique to the carved bowls and pipes from the Southwest. These masks are much less formalized than is typical of Indian sculpture, and while their asymmetrical arrangements of features and violent grimaces are reminiscent of Iroquois masks, their rough textures and rich plastic surfaces represent an unusual facet of Indian artistic expression (2-23).

THE PACIFIC NORTHWEST

The last area to be considered, the Pacific Northwest, is the home of one of the most exciting Indian cultures. Here a narrow strip of land is cut off from the rest of the continent by high mountains on one side and ocean on the other. This thousand-mile strip which runs south from southern Alaska to the Columbia River is a mountainous coast dotted with

2-21 (*above left*). Whale pipes, steatite. California. Museum of the American Indian, Heye Foundation, New York. 2-22 (*below left*). Bowl in form of spider monster, steatite. California. Museum of the American Indian, Heye Foundation, New York. 2-23 (*right*). Mask, steatite. California. Museum of the American Indian, Heye Foundation, New York.

thousands of islands. The area abounds in fish, game, and berries, and is heavily wooded. From these great coastal forests came first and foremost the cedar, but also the spruce, pine, cypress, fir, hemlock, yew, maple, and alder from which the Indians of this area created most of their material culture, for wood remained the material most frequently used for both practical and beautiful objects. With an unerring sense of their craft, these master carvers could shape a seventy-foot totem pole or make a tiny rattle from wood and achieve an equally fine sense of form and decoration.

The arts of the Northwest show puzzling similarities to those of many far removed areas, but are quite unrelated to the arts of the other Indians who inhabited the continent of North America. South Sea Island traits are frequent, and an affinity to the arts of the early Chinese as well as the Mayans and Olmecs of Central America has been noted. There is no evidence on which to base a chronology for the prehistoric developments in this area for little archeological exploration has been conducted here. When Captain Cook visited it in 1778 he found a thriving culture in which the arts were flourishing. Some students believe that the introduction of cutting tools by the Europeans stimulated the native arts, which came to their fullest development in the nineteenth century. Others believe that the culture was at its height when Captain Cook paid his famous visit. Cook noted that the Indians used metal tools of their own manufacture with great effectiveness, and the objects he and others of his time collected in this region are in no way inferior to later products.

The chief tribal names in this region, starting at the mouth of the Columbia River and going north are Salish, Nootka, Kwakiutl, Haida, Tsimshian, and Tlingit. While minor differences differentiate the arts of one tribe from another, the similarities are greater than the differences, and for our general purposes the entire area can be considered as one culture.

Both the objects used in daily life, such as fish hooks, oars, ladles, cooking vessels, and storage boxes, and the objects for ceremonial purposes are decorated with the characteristic carved and painted patterns that make the arts of this region so rich and fascinating. The largest and most elaborately decorated objects are the totem poles. Equally impressive are the many ceremonial objects that were made for the elaborate ritual which formed such a vital part of the life of these peoples.

Totem Poles

The unique product of the Northwest is the totem pole, a tall cedar column carved and painted with typical symbols. Totem poles vary in height from a few to seventy feet. The poles were used in various ways; some were attached to the front of the house, at times straddling the entrance, and indicated the totem and clan affiliations of the family living in the house. Some were erected in front of a house to commemorate the dead, and some shorter and heavier posts, called house posts, were placed in the interior of the house to help support the roof. Lastly, there were also mortuary columns which actually held the body or ashes of the deceased.

A house front (2-24) in Thunderbird Park, Victoria, British Columbia, was made by taking a number of parts from different houses, including a totem pole and two side posts, and assembling them in one building for display purposes. Houses of similar design provided shelter for most of the tribes in this area. Usually of cedar planks and frequently forty or fifty feet long, these rectangular structures with their moderately pitched roofs resemble houses of European derivation in their external appearance except for the totem poles and painted decorations.

The fecundity of imagination displayed by the sculptors who carve

2-24. House front. Thunderbird Park, Victoria, B. C. Photograph courtesy Canadian National Railways.

the totem poles appears endless, for no two are alike. Formalized though these symbols may be, this is no art of formula, for each artist modifies and combines the totemic symbols in a personal way. This is well illustrated by a totem pole in which a break in the vertical silhouette caused by the extending wings of a raven adds an unusual element of interest (2-25). The richly intertwined forms combine human figures, bird symbols, and the usual enigmatic eyes, feathers, and faces. The base of the pole is in the form of a frog with faces appearing at the tips of its

2-25. Totem pole. Near Ketchikan, Alaska. Steve Forrest photograph.

feet. An innate sense of design enabled the sculptor of the pole to establish focal centers in the design and thereby avoid an undue diffusion of interest. The powerful surmounting raven's head, the three curiously intertwined human figures, the central human face, the lower bird's head, and the great face of the frog provide a satisfying succession of accents. These focal centers are reinforced by rich variations in the depth of the sculptured forms and by bold color and tonal contrasts. The superb flow of movement mounts from the simpler forms at the base of the pole through a sequence of increasingly complex patterns to culminate in the bold projections of the wings, the staring eyes, and great raven's beak. There is not an uncertain form nor a weak pattern in the entire structure to mar the assurance with which the aboriginal sculptor established these complex forms. The result is a classic example of the style of this area—unself-conscious, intuitive, and sure, growing from the living habits, beliefs, and traditions of a people who were dedicated to an ancient way of life.

The decorative characteristics of the art so brilliantly developed in the totem poles can be summarized as follows: In general, the motifs are

2-26. Haida house post. Alaska. Museum of the American Indian, Heye Foundation, New York.

drawn from the birds, animals, and fish of the area and include, of course, the human form. Raven, hawk, eagle, owl, bear, beaver, wolf, seal, otter, salmon, octopus, shark, and whale are the most common totem symbols, for totemism is the motivating force behind the decorative arts of the Northwest. Totemism is the belief in the animal ancestors of the groups of people that made up a family or clan. It is this ancestral relationship that determines the social affiliations, degrees of kinship, marriage relationships, and ceremonial rituals of each individual. Totemism therefore determines the insignia, crests, and decorations that will be used to identify and enrich an individual's belongings. As new clan relationships are acquired through intermarriage and conquest, the totem is enriched by secondary motifs which indicate these new additions. The basic crests are raven, eagle, bear, and wolf, but there are countless subclan motifs extending even to starfish, the moon, and the rainbow. This is the basis for the involved combinations of fish, bird, mammal, and human form in a typical totem pole.

The Indians of the Northwest considered all living things to be spirit manifestations. Human characteristics were bestowed upon the various mammals, birds, and sea creatures, and both in mythology and everyday life they were endowed with supernatural powers. The totem animals were considered the guardians of the family and clan. Dances, ceremonials, the display of totemic devices, and certain taboos propitiated the spirit of the guardian animals and procured their protection. The motifs used in the totemic decorations represent natural forms abstracted, simplified, formalized, and then combined into bold interlacing curvilinear shapes, usually arranged bisymmetrically, or perhaps one should say bilaterally. These rich and involved arrangements were made even more effective by the free use of strong contrasts of tone and color to reinforce the various levels of relief carving.

The vigorous stylizations of anatomical form and the characteristic bold patterns are handsomely displayed in a Haida house post (2-26). The carved figures on this post have a typical combination of human and animal attributes; the eyes and brows of the top head appear human while the nostrils and protruding tongue suggest the bear symbol. This probably indicates that the figure represents a mythological creature or bear spirit. The bold staring eyes, the strange anatomical dislocations, and the placing of heads at both the top and bottom of the pole transform this 11½-foot post into a vivid sculptured form.

Ceremonial and Household Arts—The Potlatch

The large scale of much of the art of the Northwest and the boldness of the designs are in keeping with the spirit of the most typical institution, the potlatch. The potlatch was a ceremonial feast given by an important chief to display his wealth and power. The potlatch lasted for several days, and in the course of the celebration the host gave to his guests vast quantities of his most valued possessions—slaves, canoes, blankets, clothing, and household articles. The guests were obligated to accept the gifts, and custom demanded that they return the favors with gifts of even greater value. If this could not be done, the recipients were disgraced, to the point where some individuals who were unable to compete effectively committed suicide from shame. Thus, there existed a kind of obligatory parade aimed at self-glorification through the display of wealth and largesse and, as a corollary, the disgrace and humiliation of rivals. The tremendous quantities of goods exchanged in the course of the potlatch and the fact that richness and elaborateness of the ceremonial objects gave evidence of a host's influence and power provided a strong stimulus to artistic production.

2-27 (*left*). Bowl in form of seal, wood. Stanford University Museum, Stanford, Calif. 2-28 (*right*). Bowl, painted wood. M. H. De Young Memorial Museum, San Francisco, Calif.

In addition to the potlatch, there were religious ceremonies in the winter months in which special dances and elaborate performances took place under the direction of the medicine man to illustrate or commemorate events from the elaborate and complex mythology. Rich costumes and masks designed to represent the supernatural forces of the spirit world were worn by the participants in these ceremonies.

Wood Carving and Painting

A great variety of wooden objects, produced for the potlatch, for hunting and fishing expeditions, or for household purposes, exude the surging vitality so characteristic of the arts of this area. Two bowls reveal the typical blends of utility, magic, and display. An oil dish (2-27) with the head of a seal, enriched with crosshatched patterns, engraved lines, and mother-of-pearl eyes, nostrils, and teeth, is both a container and a rich, vivid, and refined sculptured form. In addition it insured its owner success in his hunt for the all-important seal. In the second bowl pictured (2-28), an enigmatic horned creature holds an infant in his front paws. The rounded forms are vigorously realized by means of a slight degree of abstraction and simplification. The glass eyes add a vivid contrast in texture. The directness and vigor of the forms in this bowl contribute an illusion of realism that is unusual in the highly conventionalized art of the Northwest Indians.

2-29 (*left*). Tlingit comb, wood. American Museum of Natural History, New York. 2-30 (*right*). Tsimshian headdress, wood. British Columbia Government photograph.

A charming little wooden comb (2-29) from the Tlingit tribes of Alaska displays the same vigorous sense of form that distinguishes the monumental sculptures. A bear, seated on his haunches, holds a chubby fish in his paws. The forms are effortlessly related by the alternation of vertical, horizontal, and curved movements. The shell nostrils, teeth, and eyes provide lively contrasts with the dark wood. The gay, almost humorous, quality of this lively sculptured comb is delightful.

The Indians of the northwest coast produced a great number of masks for use in the dances and rituals of the winter ceremonies. The masks represent various spirits, human, animal, and mythological.

An unusually handsome mask-type headdress (2-30) is made up of a large human face framed by eleven small faces. The squarish shape of the large head is rhythmically emphasized by the surrounding concentric planes of similar shape. The varied facets of the encircling border contribute an illusion of depth to the essentially flat surface of the mask. The effect of a fully developed three-dimensional form is intensified by skillful variations of the relief carving and by the firm definition of the planes of the face. The headdress is enriched with color and inlaid with abalone shell. The glittering eyes and teeth reinforce the almost hypnotic effect of the large staring head and create a mask of magic potency.

2-31. Bear partition screen, House of the Chief Shakes. Wrangell, Alaska. Denver Art Museum, Denver, Col.

In the art of the Northwest each animal is characterized by certain typical symbols. The beaver, for example, is identified by its hachured tail and large incisor teeth (2-35), the bear by its large nostrils and protruding tongue (2-26, 2-29), the eagle by its hooked beak (2-24), the killer whale by its large dorsal fin. These characteristics may be combined with human elements. These highly conventionalized symbols, modified according to the area to be decorated, are arranged in such complex, interwoven patterns that it is difficult to separate and identify the various elements of the design. The deliberate mystification of the onlooker by scrambling the parts of the totemic motifs seems to be part of the artist's aim, so that the art appears to be designed for the elite group of chieftains and medicine men who seek to impress and mystify the uninitiated. Probably only the artist who created a design could identify the symbols with

2-32. Haida sculptured group, black slate. Stanford University Museum, Stanford, Calif.

certainty. Other characteristic aspects of the style are the frequent use of a squatting human figure with the arms and legs extended frog fashion, and a curious custom of placing the eyes or human faces at the joints of the arms and legs of human, animal, and bird forms. These conventions can be seen in a carved and painted Tlingit partition screen (2-31) from the House of the Chief Shakes, Wrangell, Alaska. This great bear is seated frog fashion with extended arms and legs. Heads are placed at all of the joints as well as in the eyes and nostrils, full figures decorate the ears, and eyes appear in the ankles, chest, and abdomen. The hole between the bear's legs served as a door. This splendid screen is painted red and blackish brown.

Much of the painting on wood is carried out in a local type of true oil painting. With the ingenuity that characterizes so much of their art the Indians squeezed oil from salmon eggs and colors were applied in this oily base on the hand-hewn cedar logs.

Stone

The Indians of the northwest coast, most noted for their virtuosity in wood carving, were also expert sculptors in stone. Stone sculptures by the Indians of the Northwest were collected by Captain Cook during the

2-33. Skaouskeay, *The Bear Mother*, slate. Smithsonian Institution, Washington, D.C.

eighteenth century. The introduction of metal cutting tools by European traders stimulated a unique development among the Haida tribes of the Queen Charlotte Islands in the nineteenth century—the carving of handsome ornamental black slate ceremonial objects and totemic devices. Many of these richly designed slate objects provide amusing surprises. Human or animal forms spring up when the lids of vessels are removed and other movable parts reveal an unexpected sense of humor. These handsome slate sculptures are frequently enriched with mother-of-pearl, shell, and ivory inlays.

A remarkable level of skill was developed in carving this evenly textured black carboniferous shale and some of the striking designs acquire an added dignity because of the rich and severe character of the slate. A typically elaborate bas-relief group (2-32) combines human figures with animals, birds, and other characteristic motifs. The alteration of large and small shapes and of smooth and patterned areas and the clear articulation of the various planes produced a unified bas-relief distinguished by a fine sculptural sense.

The Bear Mother was carved in the late nineteenth century by a Haida Indian named Skaouskeay. This sculpture is based on a local legend, the story of a woman who married the bear king. Her child was born in the image of man, but with the instincts of the bear, and the human mother is shown grimacing with pain at the violence of the suckling infant (2-33). The forms are naturalistic and the composition is illustrative and expressive. In this respect the carving is unusual and

represents the intrusion of European artistic concepts with the consequent departure from the traditional symbolism and formalism. There is
almost no slate carving done today, because of a general disintegration
of traditional culture in the area.

Textiles and Leatherwork

The large fringed blankets made by the Chilkat branch of the
Tlingit tribes are an interesting textile development from the Northwest.
On important occasions, the leading members of a clan used these handsome blankets as capes to display the family crests. The designs, usually
symmetrical, are typical of the area—boldly patterned in contrasting tones
and colors with intricately intertwined symbolic motifs. In the blanket
shown here (2-34) a striking animal form is enhanced with spots and
human heads, and the background is filled with bold, enigmatic symbols
including eyes and large heads. The designs for the blankets were prepared by the men who painted them on boards, but the actual weaving

2-34. Chilkat blanket. Museum of the American Indian, Heye Foundation, New
York.

2-35. Painting on white buckskin.

was carried out by the women who wove these large blankets with their fingers in a simple tapestry technique without the aid of a loom. A surprisingly fine texture was achieved by this primitive technique. A strand of cedar bark formed the core of the thread and this core was covered with the hair of the mountain goat and dyed to provide a variety of colors. The color scheme is usually black, white, green, and yellow. Skirts, kilts, and leggings were also woven in this manner.

Painted buckskins are another product of the northwestern tribes. The supple white buckskin was decorated and then made into dance shirts and other articles of ceremonial apparel. A handsome painted buckskin with a striking beaver motif (2-35) has been enriched by the curious additions of eyes and faces which add to the decorative effectiveness of the whole. The brilliant pattern, made up of basically rectangular shapes with typically rounded corners, has been executed in fluid lines of great elegance and distinction.

A characteristic feature of northwestern art, seen in both the Chilkat blanket and the painted buckskin, is the bilateral representation of natural forms—that is, the tendency to split forms into halves laid open to show both sides. Animals are represented by having the profiles of the two halves placed facing each other to make a full mask; birds are united along the back with the two profiles facing away from each other. Frequently both internal organs and external anatomical details are represented in one form, the spine, stomach, or intestines making a pattern along with claws, eyes, ears, and so on. Elements from the underside and top are also transposed freely, apparently at the whim of the artist. The beaver motif used here, identified by the two large incisor teeth and the hachured tail, shows the face in full front view and the underside of the body. There is a face on the beaver's chest and at the base of the tail, while eyes are placed at the joints of the limbs.

As yet we have no clue as to the origin of the tribes of the Northwest and the antecedents for their art pose a number of enigmatic problems. Many of the elements appear to have been derived from the South Sea Islands and Asia. The great houses of wood with the central totemic posts strongly resemble those of the Maori of New Zealand and of the Bataks of Sumatra. Totemic posts with figures of animals and men arranged in series are found in New Zealand, New Ireland, and New Guinea. Heads or masks surmounting one another were also used in early China and among the Mayans of Central America. The principle of bilateral representation, the use of squatting figures with arms and legs spread frog fashion, and the use of eyes or human faces in the joints of the arms and legs can also be found in ancient China, Polynesia, and the cultures of Central America.

Fortunately for us, the arts of the Northwest Indians flourished throughout the nineteenth and into the early twentieth century. This enabled museums and collectors to make precious acquisitions before this original and vital culture disappeared and the magnificent wooden sculptures returned to the humus of the rain-sodden forests.

As our civilization becomes more complex and fraught with conflicts and responsibilities, there are an increasing number of moments when the more primitive ways of living appear to be less harried, and more healthy and happy. Though it carries only a faint echo of the past, contemporary Indian life and culture still appear colorful and have a real fascination. Yet it is almost impossible to reconcile the traditional Indian economy, even in a situation as stable as the pueblo community, with the standards of modern living. Basically the entire body of folklore, ritual, and living habits is in conflict with modern social institutions and practices. The Indian lives on his reservation, protected by isolation and government assistance, as a separate element in the social fabric, cut off from modern American life.

Yet, despite isolation and the anachronistic character of their craft activity, a high level of workmanship and design still distinguishes many Indian crafts. Much that is bad has been produced for the tourist trade, often under sweatshop conditions in a desperate attempt to adjust to modern economic patterns. Most of what is fine has been created by retaining traditional practices. Under the stimulus of the Indian Arts and Crafts Board of the Department of the Interior, the Indian craftsman has been encouraged to produce work for a discriminating clientele rather than for the more competitive tourist market. By producing the finest of which he is capable, the Indian can achieve a reassuring sense of inner worth. The Hopi potter, Seminole seamstress, Navaho rug weaver, the silversmiths, basket makers, fabricators of toys, beads, and leather-work are all continuing the practice of an earlier age in an attempt to work out a way of life in which ancient skills and values can be reconciled with the modern world.

SELECTED REFERENCES

for PART I The Arts of the Indians

Covarrubias, Miguel, *The Eagle, the Jaguar, and the Serpent*. New York, Alfred A. Knopf, Inc., 1954.

Davis, Robert Tyler, *Native Arts of the Pacific Northwest*. Stanford, Calif., Stanford University Press, 1949.

Douglas, Frederick H., and d'Harnoncourt, René, *Indian Arts of the United States*. New York, Museum of Modern Art, 1941.

Inverarity, Robert Bruce, *Art of the Northwest Coast Indians*. Berkeley, Calif., University of California Press, 1950.

Keleman, Pal, *Medieval American Art*. New York, The Macmillan Company, 1943.

LaFarge, Oliver, *A Pictorial History of the American Indian*. New York, Crown Publishers, Inc., 1956.

Vaillant, George C., *Indian Arts in North America*. New York, Harper & Brothers, 1939.

PART II

The Arts
of the Colonial Period

Architecture and the Household Arts, Seventeenth Century

THE SECOND OF THE GREAT MIGRATIONS WHICH PEOPLED the continent of North America started with a trickle of European explorers and adventurers early in the sixteenth century. They were joined by an increasingly steady stream of settlers from Europe during the seventeenth and eighteenth centuries, and in the following hundred years this stream swelled to a torrent of peoples from all parts of the world seeking political, economic, and religious freedom. By the end of the nineteenth century the continent was covered with peoples of varying colors, nationalistic backgrounds, cultural traits, beliefs, and ambitions who had conquered the Indians and created the dynamic and splendid culture of which we are the heirs and progenitors. Except for the few isolated situations where the Spanish and Indian cultures merged, the Indian way of life was rejected by the settlers from Europe. They methodically dispossessed the Indians of their lands and turned away from the Indian pattern of living, retaining only tobacco, a few foodstuffs, and building techniques.

The Spaniards arrived in the last half of the sixteenth century and built their first settlements in Florida and the Southwest. At the end of the sixteenth and during the seventeenth and eighteenth centuries, the French fur traders established trading posts and isolated communities along the St. Lawrence River in Canada, through the Great Lakes district, and down the Mississippi River to New Orleans. In the seventeenth century the Dutch settled in New York, the Swedes in New Jersey and Delaware, the Germans in Pennsylvania, and the English up and down the Atlantic seaboard.

Man lives by habit except when circumstances force him to do otherwise, and habit directed the colonist to attempt to recreate familiar patterns of living. Each of the national groups that settled America, as soon as the barest foothold had been established in the new land, tried to duplicate its former way of life. The settlers began to build houses and churches, make furniture and household utensils, and paint pictures as much like those they had left behind as was possible.

EUROPEAN INFLUENCES ON ARCHITECTURE

The first concern of the European settlers after they arrived in America was to provide themselves with shelters. They did this with whatever materials were at hand, according to whatever methods of construction they could remember, devise, or observe. The earliest shelters in all frontier situations were similar; caves were dug in hillsides, tentlike structures were made of tree branches and covered with sail cloths, or stakes were driven into the ground to form palisades which were roofed with rushes or branches woven into mats and covered with sod or plastered with mud.

The first step toward more permanent shelters were the "cottages" built by the settlers at Plymouth, Salem, and Jamestown within a year of their arrival, simple frame houses patterned after the crudest huts of shepherds and peat burners in England. The colonists brought axes, adzes, and similar tools with them, making it possible to hew the framing timbers which were then covered with broad boards laid flush. A reconstruction of such an early cottage from the Pioneers' Village in Salem, Massachusetts (3-1) provides us with a picture of these cabins. As rapidly as was feasible, the first rude shelters were replaced by more substantial dwellings patterned after the simplest and most familiar types of houses

3-1. Reconstructed cottage, 1630. Pioneers' Village, Salem, Mass.

in the homeland. In order to understand the colonial architecture of America, we must examine the building tradition which the settlers had known in Europe.

These people knew little of what we generally consider as the significant arts of Europe in the sixteenth and seventeenth centuries, for these were the arts of a small elite. By the seventeenth century the monarchies and aristocracies throughout Europe had adopted the elegant Renaissance mode of fifteenth- and sixteenth-century Italy for building and decorating their palaces and churches. This style—formal, splendid, and dependent largely on the use of carefully cut stone—was well established as the court style of France and Spain, and was becoming established in the aristocratic circles of England, Holland, and even Germany when the first settlers from Europe were landing in North America. However, very few of the settlers came from court circles and those who had would hardly have dreamed of attempting to build in this learned and pretentious manner during the initial years of colonization. Instead, they drew on the familiar, medieval building conventions of their homeland, not as developed in the construction of great stone cathedrals and fortress-like castles, but as they were employed in the tidy homes that lined the streets and squares of small villages.

Medieval construction in Northern Europe tended to be of two fundamental types: all-wood log and half-timbered. The first, native to the heavily forested areas of northeastern Europe—Scandinavia, Eastern Germany, and Russia—used carefully fitted unframed log walls and was the precursor of the log cabin. The other was common to most of the peoples that settled America, and it is to this tradition of construction that we shall first turn our attention since it formed the basis for most of the early building practices in America. Half-timbered construction was based on the use of heavy wooden posts and beams erected on a stone or timber foundation to provide vertical supports, horizontal cross-beams, and diagonal braces for the exterior walls, interior partitions, and the roof braces of a building. This heavy timber structure, pegged and notched at the joints, constituted the skeleton of the building. The spaces between the wooden posts and beams were filled with stone, brick, plaster, earth, rubble, or any other satisfactory material. The exteriors of the wooden half-timbered structures were finished in a number of ways. At first both the wooden frame and the material used to fill the spaces between the timbers were left exposed, creating the characteristic interesting pattern of wood contrasting with brick, stone, or plaster. However, in order to make the building waterproof, various kinds of surface sheathing were eventually added. A coat of hard plaster covered the entire structure or left only the heavy structure exposed; or a coating of horizontal boards called clapboards or a surface covering of slats, tiles, or brick sheathed the entire surface and protected it. A great chimney formed the heart of the building. The high-pitched roof was covered with thatch, sod, tiles, or, in areas where timber was abundant, shingles. It was to this common tradition that the first builders in America turned for their models.

In America, particularly in New England, the heavy structural timbers were usually of oak, an exceptionally sturdy wood. They were fitted together by various types of mortise and tenon joints which were in turn strengthened by a wooden pin, known as a treenail, which ran through the entire joint. The carefully fitted mortise and tenon joints, hand-cut with augers, chisels, and mallets, are wonderfully skilled pieces of carpentry. The clapboards were usually about 5 inches wide and 4 to 6 feet long. Cut from oak, cedar, or pine, they were wedge-shaped and placed to overlap. The shingles were hand-split and heavy, varying from about 14 inches to 3 feet in length.

Typical half-timbered construction as it was used in the villages of England, France, Germany, and elsewhere was not a formalized system of architecture but was an elastic mode of construction influenced by local tastes and materials and subject to infinite minor variations. The informal and elastic nature of this building tradition made it well-suited to the needs of the early settlers, and within a few years after settlement each community boasted a number of substantially built houses patterned after the familiar models of the homeland. No unsheathed half-timbered houses of the seventeenth century have survived to the present time;

3-2 (*upper*). Moravian Meeting House, 1743-1745. Berks Co., Pa. Courtesy Historical Society of Berks County, Pa. 3-3 (*lower*). Cahokia Courthouse, 1737, re-erected 1939. Cahokia, Ill. Library of Congress photograph.

however, two eighteenth-century models will serve to visualize this elementary kind of construction.

The Moravian Meeting House (3-2), built by the German settlers in Berks County, Pennsylvania, between 1743 and 1745, shows the typical supporting skeleton of timbers with the areas between the timbers filled with whitewashed plaster. The second example (3-3) is a reconstruction of one of the oldest houses in the Midwest, the Cahokia Courthouse, Cahokia, Illinois, originally built as a dwelling by a French settler around 1737. A stone foundation supported horizontal timbers which served as a sill into which were fitted vertical posts spaced within a few inches of each other. Doors and windows were framed by the vertical and horizontal timbers, and the spaces between the wooden posts were filled with crude rubble and hard clay plaster. English half-timbered construction resembled that employed in the Moravian seminary in its broad and irregular spacing of timbers more than it did the typically French construction of the Cahokia Courthouse. Since the early settlers had an abundance of wood, the practice of sheathing the half-timbered structure with wooden clapboards rapidly became standard practice among the English colonists. To our good fortune, a number of these seventeenth-century clapboard-covered houses have been preserved in New England.

NEW ENGLAND COLONIAL BUILDING

The wooden-sheathed heavy-timber-framed mode of construction that became characteristic of seventeenth-century New England cannot reasonably be classified by any of the traditional style names used in identifying European architecture; hence it is best described by the term "colonial." The more formal, decorated structures of the eighteenth century, even though they, too, were built during the colonial period, are best termed "colonial Georgian," after English architecture of the reign of the Georges. The colonial way of building left a permanent imprint on house design and construction in America.

An examination of three houses, commencing with one of the simplest one-room plans and continuing to more complex structures from the end of the century, reveals the development that occurred during these early years. The Paul Revere House in Boston (3-4) is thought to have been built in 1676. The façade typifies the earliest New England house. It is a simple rectangle of two stories topped by a high-pitched shingle

3-4. Paul Revere House, 1676. Boston, Mass. Reproduced by special permission from HOLI-DAY, copyright 1954 by The Curtis Publishing Company.

roof and a great chimney. The framing timbers have been sheathed with typical clapboards. The second story overhangs the ground floor, providing more space on the second floor and simplifying the waterproofing of the wall areas. The structural timbers of the second story and the eaves are carved into bulbous pendants, introducing an interesting decorative accent with a decidedly medieval flavor. The eaves of the high-pitched gables extend only slightly beyond the wall, producing a compact and unified profile. Shuttered windows, small because glass was scarce and expensive, are glazed with little diamond-shaped panes of glass. Doors were of heavy planks equipped with large wrought-iron locks and hinges.

The interior details indicate that the house originally had a one-room plan, but subsequently a kitchen was added in back and a chamber was added above the kitchen. A typical one-room house had the plan indicated in Figure 3-5. The exterior door opened into a small vestibule which contained a steep staircase crowded against the great chimney. This vestibule led directly into the main room which served as living room, dining room, and kitchen. The fireplace occupied almost all of one side of the "hall," as this main room was called. The staircase in the vestibule led to a second-story bedroom, which was under the sloping eaves of a story-and-a-half house or occupied the full height of a two-story structure.

The two-room plan was essentially a doubled one-room plan except

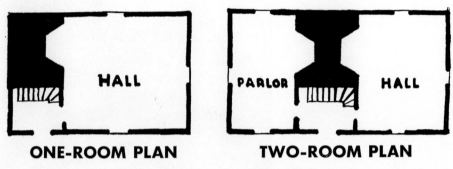

ONE-ROOM PLAN   **TWO-ROOM PLAN**

3-5. New England house plans, 17th century.

for the fact that a single vestibule provided access to both of the down-stairs rooms, one of which was called a parlor. The staircase led to two upstairs sleeping rooms, called the hall chamber and the parlor chamber depending on which room they surmounted. All the fireplaces in such a house opened directly off the great central chimney which formed the core of the house. The two-room plan, it is evident, would constitute a four-room house today.

The most familiar expansion of this basic plan in the seventeenth century was by the addition of a one-story lean-to at the back of the house. The roof of the lean-to frequently had a less sharp pitch than the original roof. The additional space was usually used as a kitchen, and the cooking was done in a fireplace added to the back of the central chimney mass. When not all the space in the lean-to was needed for cooking purposes, part of the additional area might be partitioned off into additional bedroom space. The garret of the lean-to provided closet space for the upstairs bedrooms or additional sleeping quarters. The two-room plan plus the lean-to became standard in the later seventeenth century and was called an "original lean-to" to differentiate it from the added-on lean-to. In constructing an "original lean-to" the builder employed con-tinuous rafters to cover the two-room width of the rear half of the house. This produced a house with a two-story façade and a one-story rear, the standard salt-box type of colonial house. The Whitman House (3-6) in Farmington, Connecticut, is a fine example of the salt-box type with its two-story façade and long slanting roof that descends to a one-story level in the rear.

As additional space was needed and the patterns of everyday life became more elaborate, house plans became more complex. The addition of large gables lighted by small windows in the already steep-pitched roof provided large attic rooms. Gambreled roofs—roofs with a double pitch,

3-6 (*upper*). Whitman House, 1664. Farmington, Conn. Samuel Chamberlain photograph. 3-7 (*lower*). Ironmaster's House, 1689-1700. Saugus, Mass. Massachusetts Department of Commerce photograph.

a short upper slope of low pitch and a long lower slope of steep pitch—
also increased the usable attic space. Other additions were made as necessity demanded, and by the end of the century houses of impressive dimensions graced many of the cities.

The late-seventeenth-century Ironmaster's House (3-7) in Saugus,
Massachusetts, represents such an expanded structure with an extending
porch in front surmounted by a porch chamber. The overhanging second
story and the introduction of a cross gable on the front side added much
bedroom and storage space. No one building speaks more eloquently than
the Ironmaster's House of the honesty and energy that characterized the
colonial tradition of building. The aggressive rectangular bulk of the
building, the great jutting triangles of the gables, the sharp, fresh textures
of sheathing and shingles, and the weighty, exposed structural timbers
are concrete architectural expressions of the intelligence, energy, and
dauntless optimism that enabled these settlers to conquer and make
habitable the formidable wilderness in less than a century. The rhythmic
sequence of the forms as they expand from the ground up, the sensitive
relationship of the windows to each other and to the wall surface, the
richly carved pendants which add a note of decorative elegance to the
exterior, all give evidence that a vigorous native tradition was rapidly
replacing the building habits brought over from Europe.

Though there was an abundance of stone available for building purposes in New England, and bricks were manufactured at an early date,
the general scarcity of lime made stone and brick construction expensive
and therefore much less common than wood. Lime made from oyster
shells was needed for the construction of fireplaces and chimneys, for
the wooden chimneys of early years were indeed fire hazards. Toward the
end of the century the number of brick houses increased rapidly, particularly in cities where the danger of fire was great. We shall delay discussion
of brick construction until our study of Maryland and Virginia, where excellent examples of seventeenth-century brick structures are still standing.

Colonial Interiors

The same forthright vigor and honesty that distinguish the exterior
of the New England colonial house also characterized the interior. The
hall, the central all-purpose room, was where food was prepared, meals
were served, and the family spent most indoor hours. The visual and work
center of the hall was the great fireplace, as can be seen in the Eleazor
Arnold House (3-8), built in 1687 in Lincoln, Rhode Island. As in most
seventeenth-century interiors, the ceiling is low, barely permitting a tall

3-8 (*upper*). Hall, Eleazor Arnold House, 1687. Lincoln, R. I. Library of Congress photograph. 3-9 (*lower*). Interior, Thomas Hart House, 1640-1700. Ipswich, Mass. Metropolitan Museum of Art, New York.

3-10. Old Ship Meeting House, 1681. Hingham, Mass. Wayne Andrews photograph.

man to stand erect. The copious fireplace, which almost fills one end of the room, is an exceptionally large one, over 10 feet wide, 5 feet high, and almost 4 feet deep. While the mantel tree or lintel that spanned colonial New England fireplaces were occasionally of stone, they were most frequently of oak, like the 12-foot beam used here. The fireplace in the Arnold house is made of fieldstone, shaped and laid in irregular courses. Above the mantel the great structural beams and heavy timbers provide dramatic evidence of the massive construction. Spanning the room above the lintel is the heavy chimney girt into which is dovetailed the summer beam, which bridges the middle of the room to provide an intermediate support for the floor joists of the second story. The floor boards are wide oak planks, sanded smooth and laid over a heavy subfloor which gives protection against cold air rising from the unheated basement. Exposed timbers frame the doors and windows, and the intervening areas are plastered. More elegant interiors sometimes had a wainscoting of carefully finished pine boards.

The character of a more substantial New England house of the late seventeenth century can be judged by an interior from the Thomas Hart House (3-9), built in the mid-seventeenth century in Ipswich, Mass., and later remodeled. Here, too, the low-ceilinged room is dominated by the structural timbers overhead. Well-laid courses of brick form the hearth and fireplace, and a cast-iron fireback protects the bricks from the heat and reflects warmth into the room. The end wall of the hall has been surfaced with a wainscoting of vertical pine boards, beveled at the edges to provide a craftsmanlike refinement of finish to the room, as do the chamfered edges of the summer beam. The side wall clearly shows the exposed structural beam that provides the support for the overhead structure. The beautifully laid floor planks, the clear sharp patterns of dark beams against smooth white plaster, the simple but well-made furniture with its sturdy proportion and vigorously turned decorations all convey the sense of thrifty, well-ordered living that characterized New England. The elaborate court cupboard, the gleaming pewter, brass, and ceramic bric-a-brac, the rug on the floor as well as the rich fireback and the handsome Turkish rug on the table might well have been found in the home of many successful colonial merchants or professional men at the end of the century. Trade with Europe was well established, and the finest wares of England, Holland, France, and Germany graced the homes of the prosperous colonists.

While the development of domestic architecture was the most noteworthy achievement of the New England colonial settler, other types of buildings were put up by the same general methods of construction used for homes. The Puritan meeting house was purposely kept plain, since the elaborate Gothic structures of England were anathema to the Puritans who thought that sculptured saints, shadowy vaults, and lofty spires distracted the eye and mind from God. It was not until the following century that the graceful elaborations of the Georgian, which we think of as typical of New England churches, were tolerated by the Puritans. In England the dissenters had used any house or hall that would accommodate them, and at an early date the settlers of New England proceeded to build large plain rooms which would suffice for both religious and community assembly (3-10). These meeting houses (the word "church" was avoided as smacking of Popery) were usually square in plan (the term "four-square" is still with us) and were furnished with a simple pulpit and hard benches. The plain square structure was usually surmounted by a hipped or pyramidal roof topped by a square platform carrying a belfry. Schools, town halls, the first colleges, stores, mills, taverns, and trading posts were also built in the little New England communities, but none of these still stand.

3-11. Fort Halifax, 1754. Winslow, Me. Library of Congress photograph.

Before turning our attention to building practices in the South, let us observe an example of all-wood log construction. The log cabin has often been erroneously considered the standard type of dwelling built by the first settlers, but it did not achieve its wide popularity until well into the eighteenth century. The Swedes who settled in the Delaware Valley in the mid-seventeenth century brought from their motherland a superb tradition of wood crafts. Their early dwellings and fortifications were made of round logs, notched to fit together at the corners, with protruding ends. At a very early date, the Swedish settlers also used a superior form of log construction in which hand-hewn rectangular logs with dovetailed corners were fitted together so carefully that they remained waterproof even without the usual clay chinking. After its introduction into Delaware by the Swedes and into Pennsylvania by the Germans, the log cabin became a standard frontier dwelling, particularly among the Scotch-Irish immigrants who arrived in great numbers during the eighteenth century and who settled in many of the inland frontier areas where timber was abundant. Curiously enough, the English settlers also were familiar with hewn log construction, as is revealed by their early block houses and fortifications, but they did not adapt it to the construction of simple dwellings until a later date. While no blockhouses have been preserved from the seventeenth century, Fort Halifax (3-11), built in Winslow, Maine, in 1754, illustrates the typical hewn log construction and rectangular design of the earliest fortifications. The most distinctive features of these blockhouses are the heavy construction, the height, the bold overhang, absence of windows, and presence of an occasional loophole to permit the firing of guns. The few examples of these early fortifications that still stand serve as a grim reminder of the dangers of frontier existence. Such heavy hewn log blockhouses were ordered built in all the early communities to provide protection for the townspeople in case of attack by the French or the Indians.

SOUTHERN COLONIAL BUILDING

Jamestown, located on an island in the James River in the heart of tidewater Virginia, was the first city in England's great colonial empire of the south, which stretched for 500 miles along the Atlantic coast from the Delaware Bay to the Savannah River. About one hundred colonists established Jamestown in 1607 and sheltered themselves in "flimsy cabins and holes within the ground." Despite the initial hardships that decimated their ranks, by 1615 Jamestown boasted two fair rows of houses of framed timber, each of two stories and an upper garret, and three substantial storehouses. The colonists who settled in Virginia, Maryland, the Carolinas, and elsewhere in the south had no quarrel with the Church of England nor with the king, and for the most part their society reflected the aristocratic ideals and aspirations of England. In contrast to New England there were few towns or villages. This great agricultural empire was made up of large plantations, isolated yet connected with one another and with England by continuous waterways. Because of its social and economic structure and the larger proportion of aristocratic colonists, the South retained the more elegant traditions of Europe. Certainly the commodious mansions built before the end of the seventeenth century in Virginia and Maryland appear aristocratically grand in comparison with the structures of New England built during the same period.

The settlers of New England came mainly from the southeastern counties of England where wood was relatively plentiful; those of the

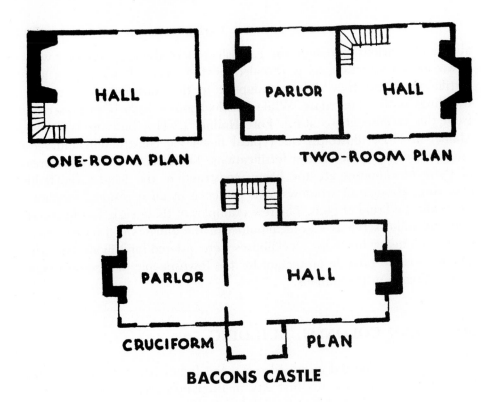

ONE-ROOM PLAN

TWO-ROOM PLAN

CRUCIFORM PLAN

BACONS CASTLE

3-12. Southern house plans, 17th century.

south more frequently came from areas where brick construction was traditional. Brick makers were among the first to settle Jamestown, and an abundance of fine clay and oyster shells from which lime could be made encouraged the construction of brick buildings.

The plans (3-12) of the first one- and two-room story-and-a-half and two-story houses built in Virginia and Maryland, whether of brick or wood, resemble those of New England except in one important respect. The chimney, which even in the one-room plan of New England was centrally located and entirely enclosed by the house, was incorporated into the end wall or projected from it, and the stairway to the second story was in one corner of the room. The typical two-room plan of the south had two chimneys, one at each end of the building, rather than the central chimney with the back-to-back fireplaces of the north. At rather an early date the staircase which led to the second story was placed in the center of the building, between the two rooms, on the side opposite the entrance. This stairway soon occupied a separate room, and the central section which housed the stairway was elaborated into an entrance hall which projected in front of the building; behind this were a central hall and a stairwell which projected from the back, making a cruciform plan. This plan is found in one of the most elaborate and impressive brick structures of seventeenth-century Virginia, Bacons Castle (3-13).

Bacons Castle, in Surry County, Virginia, was built around 1655 and is the earliest of the Virginia cross-plan houses still standing. Two large rooms, a hall and a parlor, run the length of the ground floor. A porch extending in front and a stair tower in the rear make the transept, or crossarm, of the cruciform plan. The second floor has two large chambers, and the garret encloses three additional bedrooms. Two great chimneys extend from the wall at each end of the building and serve the four main rooms of the house.

Each end wall was shaped at the top to terminate in impressive Flemish gables the rectangular steps of which alternate with curves to form a bold crested silhouette. Standing a few inches free of these gables were triple chimney stacks set diagonally and joined only at the top. These stacks rise from a capacious lower chimney, 4 feet deep and 10 feet wide. The English bond brickwork is skillfully done, and the elaboration of moldings at the tops of the gables and chimneys and around the windows is well conceived and executed. Bacons Castle is patterned after the great country houses that were appearing in England, houses in which such baroque elements as the crested gable were combined with such Tudor Gothic details as the great triple chimney stacks. Such an ambitious exterior speaks for the aristocratic temperament of the Virginian who fashioned his home after the manor houses of the English gentry.

The finest church to be built in America in the seventeenth century also stands in Virginia. The date of construction for the Newport Parish Church (3-14) of Smithfield, Isle of Wight County, is the subject of controversy. An inscribed brick in one wall has a worn numeral that could be a 3 or an 8. Modern study of the evidence places the date at 1682. The Newport Parish Church, often affectionately referred to as "Old Brick," was the handsomest duplication in America of the late medieval parish churches of England. The walls, over 2 feet thick, were skillfully laid in Flemish bond—a method of laying brick in which the lengths and widths of the brick alternate in a single course. A tower 20 feet square rises three stories to a belfry. The pointed arched windows with simple brick tracery, the sturdy pinnacled buttresses, the high pitched roof and stepped rear gable prove that the memory of Gothic churches was still alive and that the colonial builder was capable of handling these remembered forms with invention and vigor.

3-13. Bacons Castle, c. 1655. Surry Co., Va. Wayne Andrews photograph.

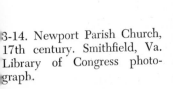

3-14. Newport Parish Church, 17th century. Smithfield, Va. Library of Congress photograph.

3-15. Old Dutch State House, 1642. New York. The Museum of Modern Art, New York.

DUTCH COLONIAL BUILDING

The Dutch West India Company was established in 1621 to found the colony of New Amsterdam. By 1626 a fort had been built and thirty bark-covered huts had been constructed. Within a short time thereafter, permanent homes, a church, an inn, and other necessary buildings were under construction. Though the Dutch ruled this area for less than fifty years, and though the city of New Amsterdam was noted for its cosmopolitan flavor, the architecture of southern New York, Long Island, and northern New Jersey retained its Dutch flavor for almost two hundred years. By the middle of the seventeenth century, New Amsterdam was in many ways a replica of Holland's Amsterdam with gently curving streets and canals lined with buildings whose quaintly gabled façades faced the main arteries of the city. A great fire in 1776 wiped out most of the original Dutch city but its appearance was recorded in a few old prints. One of the most informative of the early prints (3-15) shows the

3-16. Old Stone House at Gowanus, 1699, re-erected 1934. Brooklyn, N. Y. Library of Congress photograph.

character of the dignified five-story State House, as well as the more usual two-and-a-half- and three-and-a-half-story houses on either side of it. The most striking architectural features of Dutch architecture were the boldly stepped gables, facing the street, which rose through a series of stepped right angles to end in a chimney or rectangular crest. Framing and construction was of the heavy timbered type similar to that of New England. The windows, symmetrically placed on the front, had small panes, and the larger windows were divided into two parts by a heavy transom. The headers for the windows were often gently arched, and the space between the arch and the rectangular window frame might be ornamented with brightly colored tiles. Though houses were built in wood and stone, brick was the favorite material here as in the homeland, and the gay effect of the colored bricks and tiles was frequently commented on by travelers who contrasted the Dutch love of color with the drab sobriety of the villages of New England. Ordinary red bricks of fine quality were made, but monotony was avoided by the use of glazed bricks in pinks, yellows, oranges, and darks which ran to deep purples and blue

3-17. Hendrickson-Winant House. Rossville, Staten Island, N. Y. Staten Island Historical Society.

blacks. These shiny colored bricks were laid in a variety of bonds which were enlivened with diamond, herringbone, and other ornamental patterns. The warm colored tiles preferred for roofing also added color and texture. Travelers also noted the light, brightly painted interiors. The charm of the scrupulously clean Dutch rooms was enlivened by ceramics and pictures from Holland.

While the stepped gable was popular, it was not universal. In many rural areas the high-pitched, straight-edged gable was preferred. The "Old Stone House at Gowanus" (3-16) is a remarkably fine example of a Dutch colonial house with straight-edged gables. This structure, built at the end of the seventeenth century, stood until 1897. Subsequently it was demolished and then restored in 1934 in Brooklyn Park. This solidly built house has full two-story stone walls 2 feet thick, but, with true Dutch love of brick, the builder completed the tall end gables in brick handsomely laid in a complex pattern. Typical gently arched headers occur above the windows of the ground story.

During the seventeenth and eighteenth centuries, there appeared in certain rural districts of Long Island, southern New York, and northern New Jersey a type of house that departs radically from the tall gabled structures of New Amsterdam. The antecedents for this way of building appear to have been brought to Holland from Flanders by the Walloon and Flemish settlers who sought refuge in Holland during the Spanish occupation of Flanders early in the century. Finding Holland crowded,

3-18. Castillo de San Marco, 1672-1750. St. Augustine, Fla. National Park Service.

these refugees continued overseas to the New Netherlands, and since many were peasants, they settled in the rural areas. They introduced a type of house design common to northwestern France and Belgium. Usually a story-and-a-half, these houses are simple in plan, containing two or three rooms in a straight line, with narrow bedrooms in back opening off the main rooms. Shingle, clapboard siding, or fieldstone were the materials used most frequently on exteriors, and many houses combined them. The most distinctive feature of these dwellings was the roof which extended two or three feet beyond the wall in both front and back to create a graceful overhang with a gentle curve. The Hendrickson-Winant House (3-17) at Rossville, Staten Island, despite later additions provides an example of this kind of structure. The dormers and the farther section of the building were added in the following century, at which time the overhang was extended and supporting posts added. In the eighteenth century, this Flemish type of house, modified by the addition of gambrel roofs to create more space under the eaves and the enlargement of the front overhang to an entrance porch, produced a type of American house, called Dutch colonial, which persists into the twentieth century.

SPANISH ARCHITECTURE

The Spaniards were the first settlers and builders in America. The philosophy on which they built their empire is revealed by the sequence in which they constructed the buildings which marked their entry into a new country. First came the presidio or fort; second, the mission church, and last, the pueblo or village. The Spaniards came to conquer land for the king of Spain; to conquer souls for the church was also an ardent aim; to build villages and till the land and found a new way of life was farther from their purpose, although in time those activities followed as an inevitable corollary of the primary aims. To the building of the fort and the church then, the Spanish settler devoted his primary energies, and it is to these structures that we will turn our attention.

Spain and France fought for Florida in the sixteenth century, and Spain won. The Spaniards began settling in Florida, and by the middle of the seventeenth century they had established a chain of about forty missions, of which no sign remains. The one standing monument to Spanish rule in Florida is the great Castillo de San Marco (3-18) in St. Augustine. Commenced in 1672 and constructed over a period of more than seventy-five years, the Castillo de San Marco is the most impressive surviving example in the United States of the type of fortress that appeared in Europe in the late Middle Ages with the advent of gunpowder. Built of great blocks of gray-white coquina limestone, the fortress has an inner court, about 100 feet square, surrounded by heavy walls. In these walls are chambers with heavy vaulted ceilings, housing chapel, officers' quarters, arsenals, and cells. The entire fortification was surrounded by a great outer wall 25 feet high and 12 feet thick at the base, which sloped to a width of 3 feet at the top. A huge platform 40 feet wide faced the river, and this area was surrounded by a heavy parapet pierced for sixty-four guns. Except for this great bastion, a church, and a few houses of questionable authenticity, nothing remains in Florida from the Spanish builders except a tradition that remained dormant many years until its revival in the twentieth century.

New Mexico was the first part of the Southwest to be settled. Earlier expeditions from Mexico into New Mexico had come to nothing, but in 1609 Santa Fe was established as the administrative center of New Mexico, and the following year work was started on the Palace of the Governors (3-19). Completed in 1614, the building still stands—the oldest non-Indian structure in the United States. Typical of a presidio, this great rectangular enclosure, 400 by 800 feet long, once housed barracks, chapel, offices, storage facilities, and a prison. The most important building in the compound was the Governor's Palace proper, a long, low structure facing the open plaza, fronted by a covered porch. Indians provided the labor, and many traditional Indian building techniques were

3-19. Palace of the Governors, 1610-1614. Santa Fe, N. M. New Mexico State Tourist Bureau.

retained in constructing these buildings. Though the Indians used adobe bricks, a European improvement in the form of a box was used to mold the wet clay into uniformly sized and shaped bricks. The covered porch supported by wooden posts was also a Spanish feature as were the enclosed patio and the wooden-framed doors and windows. This manner of combining native materials and building practices with elements from the European tradition characterized Spanish building practices all through the New World; consequently the buildings erected under Spanish guidance seem less foreign, more in harmony with the original Indian culture of the area, than do those built by the English, Dutch, and French settlers.

Nowhere is this harmony between the traditional native style of architecture, the terrain, and the buildings of the Spanish settlers more evident than in New Mexico. Even today, as one travels through the little villages the peculiar rightness and charm of the low rectangular houses plastered with tannish orange adobe is inescapable. The small buildings, punctuated occasionally by the solemn bulk of a church, appear very little amid the endless vistas of mountain and mesa under the vast canopy of sky. The forms blend and become part of the earth, as related visually to their surroundings as the adobe is materially.

3-20. San Esteban Rey, probably 1642. Acoma, N. M. New Mexico State Tourist Bureau.

The mission churches, built during the seventeenth century, abandoned and then rebuilt during a period of intensive recolonization in the eighteenth century, are the major architectural achievements of the Spaniards in this area. In all Spanish colonies the church stands as the chief symbol of Spanish idealism, just as the private dwelling appears to express the aims, hopes, and ideals of the colonists of the Atlantic coast.

The great church of San Esteban Rey at Acoma (3-20) is probably the most impressive of the mission churches of New Mexico. It is estimated that the church was completed in 1642 after years of construction. The simple massive towers with their heavy, wavering, buttresslike forms frame the simple façade which is unbroken except for the entrance door and a window which lights the choir loft. The thick walls of adobe are narrower at the top than at the base, giving a weighty pyramidal character to the structure, and there are a minimum of windows, doors, or decorative enhancements. On the north side is the long, low convento, with its enclosed patio, living rooms, work rooms, store rooms, and picturesque

3-21 (*left*). Ranchos de Taos Church. Taos, N. M. New Mexico State Tourist Bureau. 3-22 (*below*). Interior of Ranchos de Taos Church. Library of Congress photograph.

balcony with irregular railings and curious corbeled capitals atop the columns. Impressive because of the sober monumentality of its forms, the handicrafted honesty of its surfaces and materials, and its magnificent location atop the mesa, San Esteban Rey stands as a tribute to the merging of two great building traditions.

Though it appears to have been built toward the end of the eighteenth century, the Ranchos de Taos Church (3-21) belongs stylistically to the seventeenth century. Not as large as San Esteban Rey nor remarkable in plan, nevertheless the church at Taos is the most frequently pictured of the New Mexico churches because of its rare charm. Two sturdy bell towers topped by simple crosses flank the entrance which is enhanced by simple wooden doors and a decorated tympanum, surmounted by a semicircular crest and a third cross. The forms of the buttresses, the central area, and the bell towers enfold one another with a rich sculptural unity, and the almost unbroken masses produce a handsome architectural composition of unique distinction. The interior (3-22) is of touching simplicity. The elaborately shaped corbels which support the heavy beams of the ceiling, the candidly crude braces, the simply constructed pews and altar railings were all the handiwork of the local craftsmen under the direction of the local priests. While a few sacred statues and paintings were brought up from Mexico, the Indians carved and painted most of their own images, and these simple, even crude figures, seen in the dim light against the whitewashed walls, convey the faith of these people with unusual directness and force.

FURNITURE

Furniture was scarce in seventeenth-century America, and the repertory was limited. Stools, benches, small tables, chests, and chest-and-drawer combinations were the pieces in most frequent use. A trestle board, a wide board which rested on light-braced saw-horses and could be dismantled and stored in a small space, served as a dining table. Side chairs, used much less frequently than stools, were reserved for old or distinguished persons. Settles, benches with high backs, were placed in front of the fireplace or surrounding the hearth; the high back held in the heat and kept out drafts. Small trundle beds on rockers provided protection for the babies. Beds hardly constituted a piece of furniture—a wooden frame supporting cross slats or ropes held a straw or feather mattress. At a later date, hangings were suspended from the ceiling or from a frame extended from the corner posts of the bed to provide increased protection from drafts, thereby creating the four-poster bed.

Little seventeenth-century furniture other than from the English settlers has come down to us. Most of that, like the architecture, was based on a simple medieval tradition in which sturdy utilitarian considerations were foremost. Square-framed construction was employed, with vertical supports connecting horizontal parts reinforced by vertical and horizontal stretchers. Much of the furniture was devoid of ornamentation, but in even the simplest pieces the headboards, arms, legs, and stretchers appear to have been shaped to increase the grace of the whole.

Turning was the most common decorative treatment in the seventeenth century. Turning is achieved by the application of cutting tools to a surface which is being rotated on a lathe. The most characteristic seventeenth-century turning is simple "bun" turning, such as can be seen topping the posts in Figure 3-23, or the sausage type made by repeating the bun profile. Late in the century, when the more pretentious court styles were introduced into America, elaborate designs were used—spiral turnings, baluster types (3-24), melon type (cupboard, 3-9), disc-and-spool (3-25), and many others. Turning was applied to legs, posts, feet, spindles, stretchers, and rungs, and turned spindles were split and applied as surface decorations. In addition to turned decorations, cabinetmakers decorated flat surfaces with shallow carvings of typical medieval folk motifs—formalized leaves, flowers, rosettes, and geometric patterns. These carved patterns were frequently reinforced by color or textural enrichments.

Chairs with straight posts and rush seats were common in all parts of Europe, and most of the chairs made in seventeenth-century America were of this type. When a chair of greater refinement was desired, the vertical supports were enhanced with simple turnings, and the back slats and arms were tapered and carefully shaped. Such chairs constituted unpretentious but pleasing pieces of furniture that were in harmony with the plain colonial interiors. A Carver chair (3-23), named after Governor Carver of Plymouth, is a fine example of such straightforward design. Small bun finials top the vertical posts, and turned spools and a double bar in the back-rest lighten the forms and provide a touch of grace to this serviceable piece of furniture.

Toward the end of the century American cabinetmakers began to copy the more elaborate and pretentious designs which were appearing in English court circles. The relatively light and simple early enhancements were replaced by the ornate and splendid carvings of the aristo-

3-23 (*below*). Carver chair, mid-17th century. Philadelphia Museum of Art. 3-24 (*right*). Wainscot armchair, late 17th century. Courtesy Metropolitan Museum of Art, Gift of Mrs. Russell Sage, 1910.

cratic Renaissance and baroque styles. An elaborate wainscoted oak chair (3-24) from the late seventeenth century provides us with a vivid, if somewhat naive, native version of the weighty and heavily ornamented English court furniture. The decorative motifs used on this chair are typical of Renaissance and the later baroque styles. Many are Classic, of Roman derivation—acanthus leaves, volutes, and ornamental moldings; many are of architectural origin—columns, arches, and balusters. Almost all of the surfaces except the seat and back legs are carved; the arms, legs, and back are particularly elaborate, and the carving is placed to emphasize the structural elements in the chair. The simple turned shapes of the earlier period have been replaced by baluster turnings which also have been carved.

At the end of the seventeenth century the English court furniture lost some of its massive rectangularity and the decorations became less ungainly. This more graceful manner first appeared in the Restoration styles, introduced into England from Flanders and France after the fall of the Cromwellian Commonwealth. Essentially baroque in style, Restoration furniture was rich, even flamboyant at times, but proportions were lighter, chairs were taller and more graceful, and decorations were more harmoniously integrated into the main structure. The character of this Restoration mode can be seen in a late-seventeenth-century maple chair

3-25. Chair, Restoration style, late 17th century. Courtesy Metropolitan Museum of Art, Gift of Mrs. Russell Sage, 1909.

(3-25) which was probably copied from an English import. The rake in the back of the chair, the irregular contour created by the crest and finials on the top of the back, and the shaped stretcher represent a departure from strict rectangularity. The high back of this chair, the luxuriant leaf and scroll pattern of the stretcher, crest, and back, the scroll foot and the complicated turnings all reflect the love of display which was the keynote of the baroque style. Pieces of furniture as elaborate as this were rare in the colonies in this century, but as wealth increased in the South and also in New England, a taste for opulence expressed itself in the most natural manner imaginable, by copying the modes and manners of the nobility and the wealthy mercantile class of England.

Chests and storage boxes were among the most useful pieces of furniture in the colonial household since they provided space for the household valuables. Though a few cupboards followed the styles of the English court, most of the cabinetmakers in the colonies drew the patterns of their wares from the folk crafts and evolved some interesting local versions of these humble traditions. On a chest (3-26) from Hartford County, Connecticut, the front is completely covered by bands of pattern carved in flat, shallow relief. The formalized leaf, flower, and tendril

3-26. Hartford chest, late 17th century. Hartford, Conn. Courtesy Metropolitan Museum of Art, Rogers Fund, 1908.

patterns based on the popular tulip motif are placed logically to enrich the drawer fronts and the frame. This clean craftsmanship and decorative patterning contribute an unpretentious charm which appeals to modern tastes more than do the heavily ornamented aristocratic styles. Though here the background in the carved section is separated from the front plane by a texture, the carved pattern was usually emphasized by staining or painting the background a contrasting color. So many similar chests have come from this area that they are frequently called Hartford chests.

An interesting type of chest from this period was the Bible box (3-27). This small boxlike chest with a hinged, slanting top, sometimes placed on long legs, was designed to hold the Bible and important papers. It was the precursor of the desk which, in the next century, was combined with the chest to form the high chest, or highboy. This Bible box from New York is decorated with rosettes, stars and other semigeometric motifs made by chip carving in v-shaped notches. The formalized floral patterns,

3-27. Bible box, late 17th century. New York. Index of American Design, National Gallery of Art, Washington, D.C.

rosettes, stars, and hearts, and the geometric all-over pattern-texture, like the floral pattern in the Hartford chests, were based on folk art patterns common to much of northern Europe. Pieces of furniture from the New York area, like this one, frequently have a Dutch flavor.

By the end of the century cupboards, like chairs, reflected the splendid Renaissance style that was popular at the English court. Such a cupboard can be seen in the interior of Hart House (3-9). A number of typical decorations have been combined to create this rich and dignified piece of furniture—heavy melon turnings, diamond-shaped inserts, carved moldings, and split halves of spindles applied as surface decorations.

Space was at a premium in the seventeenth century, for the crowded multipurpose rooms had to serve a great variety of family needs. Necessity coupled with Yankee ingenuity produced such interesting combination pieces of furniture as a chair with a back which folded down to make a table (3-28). The hutch tables of the day were similar, except that a third service was performed by including storage space in a chest incorporated in the base of the chair. Gate-legged tables (3-29) in a variety of forms, as well as butterfly tables—small drop-leaf tables whose leaves were supported by a swinging bracket shaped like the wing of a butterfly— also represented popular space-saving devices.

A variety of hard and soft woods was available to the colonial craftsman. Oak, birch, maple, and hickory were used when strength was the primary consideration. Pine was frequently employed when wide boards were needed or when ease of working was an important factor. A number of woods were frequently combined in one piece of furniture, oak or maple being used for the framing members while pine provided the paneling or the planking for chair seats or table tops. At the end of the century walnut became popular. Its fine grain was suitable for the more

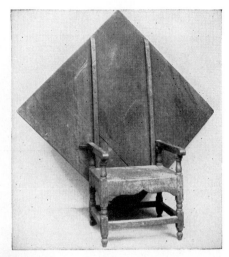

3-28 (*right*). Table chair, late 17th century.

3-29 (*left*). Gate-legged table, late 17th century. Philadelphia Museum of Art, Philadelphia.

elaborate turnings and carvings that were used in the furniture made for the rapidly expanding class of businessmen, planters, and traders. The wood was generally left raw; it gradually acquired depth of color and polish through simple friction and natural darkening.

HOUSEHOLD ARTS

Although the exigencies of settlement demanded the major energies of the people, within a surprisingly few years energetic craftsmen were busily producing the wares necessary for civilized living. Potters were making dishes and containers, brick and tile makers were at work, glaziers

3-30. Earthenware dishes, 17th century. National Park Service.

were making bottles and window glass, silversmiths, ironmongers, tinsmiths, and weavers—all were busy attempting to supply the needs of the colonists and augment the limited flow of goods from Europe. Unfortunately, few early wares survived the hard usage of colonial life. It is only in recent years that the excavation at Jamestown, Virginia, has provided enough household artifacts to give us a picture of the household arts in the seventeenth century.

Jamestown served as the capital of Virginia for almost a hundred years. After a century of prominence, it entered a long period of decline precipitated by the removal of the capital to Williamsburg in 1700. By the middle of the nineteenth century, the site of Jamestown had become farmland, but in 1934 the area was made a national park, thus permitting the extensive excavations that have enabled us to become familiar with the way of life that once flourished there.

Ceramics

The simplest and most abundant pottery uncovered at Jamestown, the essentially utilitarian glazed redware, is like that from seventeenth-century New England. This early redware was made from local glacial clays of the same type as were used in the manufacture of bricks and tiles. Pots, bowls, mugs, and pitchers were thrown on the potter's wheel, and their shapes were sturdy and full. Red lead or litharge was mixed

3-31 (*below*). John Hull and Robert Sanderson, caudle cup, silver, 1652. Museum of Fine Arts, Boston. 3-32 (*right*). Jeremiah Dummer, wine beaker, silver, 17th century. Museum of Fine Arts, Boston.

with sand or ground glass to provide a brilliant, shiny glaze, and pleasant variations of the glaze were obtained by the addition of manganese, copper filings, cobalt, and other materials. A photograph of ceramic wares (3-30) from Jamestown, which were probably from England but could have been from the hands of a local potter, reveals something of the variety of earthenware dishes that were used for baking, cooking, and the table.

The potters of Jamestown, like the potters of New England, employed various simple devices to decorate their wares. Some ceramics were enhanced by patterns of liquid slip made of white or pipe clays. This thin mixture of light-colored clay was trailed across the body of the darker base in thin lines to make zigzags, scrolls, dots, wavy lines, and other familiar patterns. Engraved parallel straight or wavy lines were also made on the body of a vessel before it was glazed by holding a sharp stick against the side while it was being turned on the wheel. An interesting ceramic find at Jamestown is English sgraffitoware, very similar in character to the sgraffitoware produced by the German settlers of Pennsylvania, even to the use of the tulip motif which was the favorite of the German craftsmen. Sgraffitoware was decorated by cutting through the covering slip with a pointed instrument and exposing the dark red pottery base.

Silver and Metal Wares

The accumulation of household silver presented a convenient way to store savings in the days before banks, stocks, and bonds. Con-

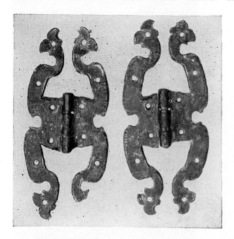

3-33. Hinges, wrought iron, 17th century. Courtesy Metropolitan Museum of Art, Rogers Fund, 1937.

sequently, there was a great demand for the services of the silversmith in the thriving colonies. The elaboration of social life in the late seventeenth century, the popularity of tea, coffee, and chocolate, and the general refinement of eating habits contributed to the demand for silver utensils for the home. Church ritual also demanded silver ceremonial plate. A number of silversmiths migrated from England, and while silverware was produced in Jamestown and other colonial cities, Boston became the chief center for the manufacturing of silver in the eighteenth century.

The English silversmiths working in America followed the English models but simplified them. Seventeenth-century English silver shows the baroque preference for heavy proportions, full rounded forms, and elaborate ornamentation. Floral and foliate patterns similar to those used on the furniture of the day provided the motifs for the engraved, embossed, and cast decorations. Colonial taste being conservative, the silver was devoid of excessive ornament and depended for its beauty on fine proportions and excellent craftsmanship. Most of the silver was rolled into sheets and hammered into shape, a method of production which creates a rich surface sheen. The pieces which were cast in molds or shaped over revolving wooden forms were also hammered and worked over until a fine surface was obtained, providing pleasure to both hand and eye.

The earliest Bostonian silversmiths of whose work we have records were John Hull (1624-1683) and his partner, Robert Sanderson (1608-1693). A caudle cup (3-31) from the workshop of Hull and Sanderson is dated 1652. The chubby full shape of this wine cup is enriched by a

3-34. Iron weather vane, reverse, 1673. Concord, Mass. Index of American Design, National Gallery of Art, Washington, D.C.

simply textured, engraved band of tulips and leaves and by the animated curves of the cast handles. The effect is gay and unpretentious. Jeremiah Dummer (1645-1718), an apprentice to Hull and Sanderson, was one of Boston's most productive silversmiths. His work is noted for its fine craftsmanship and simple elegance of form. A wine beaker (3-32), given to the Brattle Street Church, is distinguished by the restraint of the ringed base, the handsome gadrooned fluting, and the contrasting smooth top. The subtle relationship between the ornamentation and the beautiful chalice shape reveals Dummer's sensitivity as a designer.

The blacksmith, too, played a most important role in the colonial economy, as cast and wrought iron hardware and implements were in constant demand. The fireplace was the heart of the colonial home and the blacksmith produced tongs, shovels, warming pans, cast-iron firebacks, kettles, pots, skewers, and ladles as well as all kinds of knives, forks, and spoons. A pair of hinges (3-33) in a cockshead design are worth attention. They reveal the colonial ironmonger's delight in enriching the utilitarian necessities with ingenious and entertaining decorative touches. Such modest effects as the pierced, split, and shaped ends of the hinges provided charming enhancements to the rude and strenuous surface of colonial existence.

No more pleasing example of the gracious touches that appeared with increasing frequency in the course of the seventeenth century can be found than the graceful weather vane (3-34), dated 1673, which topped the First Church in Concord, Massachusetts. Recalling the heraldic devices of Europe, the iron standard, enhanced by four wrought-iron decorative arabesques, is topped by a gilded banner enriched with fleur-de-lis, the date of erection, and a gay pierced arrowhead. A shining finial tops the entire work.

Textiles

In the Colonial period most textiles were produced at home. Spinning yarn and weaving cloth were important parts of the housewife's responsibilities, and she and her family made cotton, linen, and woolen materials for clothing and all other household purposes. A knowledge of the various weaving processes as well as of the many kinds of decorative stitches formed an essential part of feminine education in both the Old and New World and this heritage was perpetuated by the daughters and grand-daughters of the first settlers well into later centuries. Every homestead was a textile factory; children helped with the carding and spinning, and when the men of the house were unable to pursue their regular duties, they also took a turn at the loom.

Though the production of workaday textiles was burdensome, the colonial housewife found time to indulge in her love of fancy work. As traveling journeymen and factories took over the task of producing the fabrics necessary for clothes and household linens, more time was available for weaving the elaborate bedspreads and for embroidering chair covers, bed curtains, and the samplers which were the pride of the colonial housewife.

The most popular early decorative needlework was done in crewel embroidery, which was used to decorate spreads, hangings for four-poster beds, chair covers, purses, and dresses. Crewel is a loosely twisted wool yarn, and this brightly colored wool was used to embroider on a cotton or linen twill base. A seventeenth-century chair seat (3-35) from Boston employs the typical birds, flowers, and landscape motifs. The fanciful designs were frequently taken from the Chinese embroideries that were being introduced into Europe, but they were freely adapted according

3-35 (*left*). Chair seat, wool embroidery on cotton and linen, 17th century. Index of American Design, National Gallery of Art, Washington, D.C. 3-36 (*right*). Sampler, embroidery, 1677. Philadelphia Museum of Art, Philadelphia.

to the tastes of the embroiderer. A great variety of stitches was used in crewel embroidery. The stem stitch, a large stitch on the surface with a shorter one in back, was popular, and small French knots frequently formed the centers of flowers.

Another form of stitchery to come down to us from colonial times is the sampler. In the early seventeenth century the sampler was a long strip of cloth which served as a source book of decorative stitching. It contained a collection of stitches adapted to various decorative needs and also reproduced popular decorative motifs. The housewife referred to the sampler when she needed direction or assistance or inspiration. By the end of the seventeenth century the sampler tended to be less a set of samples and more a vehicle for displaying embroidery skill. Verses and texts, alternating with borders, numbers, floral patterns, and other popular motifs, were carried out largely in cross-stitch, but samplers frequently included drawn work and other types of embroidery. A sampler (3-36) dated 1677 belongs to the earlier tradition; it presents a great variety of stitches and patterns rather than being composed around a Biblical text.

The seventeenth century in America was a period of gestation. Throughout the colonies the seeds of Europe's many rich cultures were sown. Some fell on fertile soil while others withered in the wilderness.

Men came and died by thousands; suffered, struggled against the cold, the wilderness, the Indians, and against one another, but by the end of the century a fruitful way of life had been established. From Florida in the South to the northernmost reaches of New England—from the great Mississippi Valley to the plateau of New Mexico—people were building homes, churches, and arsenals, shaping silver and iron, making furniture, glass, ceramics, and textiles. These first vigorous shoots of American culture grew from old memories and patterns of living modified by the raw materials, climate, and rigors of the new world. In the following century these vital shoots brought forth their first blossoms, and a new and unique way of life began to flower. It is to this more cultivated eighteenth-century mode of human existence that we will now turn our attention.

4

Architecture and Interiors, 1700-1776

THE PROGRESSIVE CHARACTER OF AMERICAN LIFE WAS evident early in the eighteenth century. While the seventeenth-century population had come largely from England, eighteenth-century emigrants came in increasing numbers from other parts of Europe. A restless energy infused the population. The mixture of various nationalities and religions served as a catalyzer in the raw frontier environment, stimulating a rapid social, economic, intellectual, and artistic development.

Though a few settlements along the Atlantic seaboard were predominantly German, Dutch, or Irish, the political dominance of England caused English cultural patterns to become all-pervasive at an early date. While the arts and crafts of seventeenth-century America seemed to reflect the patterns of rural England, the general culture of the eighteenth century in both England and America was predominantly an urban one. London set a common standard in matters of dress, literature, art, architecture, and home furnishings. Even Benjamin Franklin, with his genuine belief in the validity of colonial life, advised his wife to follow the latest London fashions in home furnishing and decoration. The finest products of London were imported and were intermingled with domestic wares. A Philadelphian in 1765, comparing goods produced in the colonies with those of England, declared that the household goods manufactured in Philadelphia were as cheap and as well made as those purchased in London. In surveying the churches, houses, furniture, and crafts of eighteenth-century America, one cannot help but be impressed by their amplitude, richness, and technical excellence. Experts today frequently cannot differentiate between colonial and continental products.

The Atlantic seaboard was, of course, but one part of colonial America. The French were moving into the limitless backwoods areas and building communities in the Mississippi Valley and around the Great Lakes. Their activity as traders and trappers was not conducive to a settled way of life, but New Orleans and the plantations and the few cities of the lower Mississippi Valley had a strong French flavor. The Spaniards continued building missions and settling in Texas, New Mexico, Arizona, and California. However, neither the French nor the Spanish traditions became an important factor in the mainstream of American culture until the nineteenth century.

Most eighteenth-century buildings constructed with no particular pretensions to elegance followed the pattern we saw established in the preceding period. However, the more splendid structures built between 1700 and 1776 on the Eastern seaboard were patterned after the Georgian style of the same period in England. The term "Colonial Georgian" best describes the architecture of the first three quarters of the eighteenth century in America. This term differentiates American architecture of the eighteenth from that of the seventeenth century, American Georgian from English Georgian, and also acknowledges the relationship between these periods and styles.

The Georgian style of England, named after the three Georges who ruled England during these years, is a very restrained, one might almost say domesticated, version of the continental baroque style which came to its most grandiloquent expression in the Louis XIV style of France. Georgian architecture appeared largely in great city and country houses constructed for the aristocracy and the wealthy mercantile families of England. The relatively modest character of the Georgian style can be partially explained in terms of the general restraint that has always characterized English taste in the arts. Also significant is the fact that by the eighteenth century the baroque style had lost its initial impetus. In both France and England the more extravagant baroque palaces had begun to be replaced by palaces and town houses with relatively simple exteriors and somewhat sensibly planned interiors. The eighteenth century was, after all, the age of reason! The baroque factor appeared principally in the embellishment of the entrances, the window areas, and the balustrades and pediments which capped the main façades of the exterior. Equally important was the elimination of high gables, pinnacles, and other Gothic irregularities. Inside, the overmantel, door, and window areas received the greatest attention.

The houses, churches, and public buildings built in America before the Revolution follow their English prototypes but are smaller and employ even fewer decorations. Most of the designs for the Colonial Georgian buildings were taken from the English books on architecture in which the work of the principal English architects were reproduced. The first English architect on whom the formal style of Italy made a substantial impact was Inigo Jones (1573-1652), whose most famous work, the severe and formal Banqueting House at Whitehall, introduced the manner of the late Italian Renaissance architect Palladio to England. The most influential architect to work in the Georgian baroque style was Sir Christopher Wren (1631-1723), whose greatest achievement was St. Paul's Cathedral in London. Wren designed many palaces as well as smaller but commodious middle-class residences for the expanding middle class. Another English architect whose influence was considerable in the colonies was James Gibbs (1682-1754). A number of the finest buildings erected in America in the eighteenth century were patterned after designs by these three men.

DOMESTIC ARCHITECTURE

The Eastern Seaboard

Among the most impressive architectural achievements in the Colonial Georgian style were the residences built by the mercantile princes of the North and the great landholders of the South. Three examples from this period are, in chronological sequence, Westover (4-1), the home of William Byrd, of Charles City County, Virginia, built around 1726, the Vassal (Longfellow) House (4-2), built by John Vassal but famous as the home of Longfellow in Cambridge, Massachusetts, 1759, and Mt. Pleasant (4-3), Philadelphia, built some time after 1761. Westover, the seat of an immense Virginia estate, is the most extensive of the mansions; Mt. Pleasant is the richest and most urbane, and the Vassal House comes

4-1. Westover, 1726. Charles City Co., Va. Library of Congress photograph.

closest to the traditional idea of the colonial house. As one might expect, Westover is brick, Mt. Pleasant is brick, stone, and plaster, and the Vassal House is wood.

The main mass of all three structures is symmetrical, though the smaller secondary additions on Mt. Pleasant and Westover depart from the strict symmetry of the main body of the building. Each building rests on a foundation which encloses a full basement; the main entrance leads to a central hall and stairway, on either side of which lie the various rooms. Large chimneys flank the sides of the main mass of the building to care for the fireplaces which originally provided the only source of heat. Colonial houses very frequently had four rooms to each floor, each room occupying one corner of the house. The windows, large as compared to those of the preceding century, provided a plentiful supply of light and air so that the interiors were bright, fresh, and serene, a quality commented on by continental visitors accustomed to the cramped and dingy houses of the crowded European cities.

The chief architectural feature of the exterior is the main entrance. In both the Vassal House and Mt. Pleasant, the entrance mass projects in front of the rest of the façade, thereby providing an effect of importance and adding to the three-dimensional movement of the façade. Columns and a triangular pediment, among the chief decorative devices of both Renaissance and baroque style, contribute an imposing dignity to each of the entranceways. In the Vassal House pilasters (attached columns) run the full two stories of the house and are topped by a bold

4-2 (*above*). Vassal (Longfellow) House, 1759. Cambridge, Mass. Library of Congress photograph. 4-3 (*below*). Mt. Pleasant, 1761. Philadelphia. Library of Congress photograph.

pediment. The same pedimental motif is repeated in the small dormer windows on each side, and pilasters indentical to those used at the entrance dignify the corners of the building. The bold dentil molding made up of small rectangular blocks, so characteristic of the fully developed Georgian style, enriches the cornice around the eaves and the pediments of both houses. The hip roof of each is topped by a strong balustrade and bold chimney masses.

As one approaches the Vassal House one is aware of its dignity in relation to its surroundings. The house is on a slight eminence. A balustraded fence and a sequence of steps lead up to the main entrance. Dark shutters create a pleasant accent that strengthens the window pattern. The typical horizontal siding provides an interesting texture and contributes to the unpretentious feeling of the house. The effect is serene, orderly, charming, and comfortable. Such a home could not be built until a stable way of life had been established.

The first of the three houses to be built, and the largest, was Westover. William Byrd was born to wealth and position, and a great mansion like Westover formed the proper setting for the elaborate social activities of a Southern gentleman. Westover has two almost identical façades. The one which faces inland to the north, pictured here, is approached by an impressive composition of entrance gates and an extensive forecourt. The southern façade tops a gradual rise of ground from the James River. The central building of two stories is topped by a high hipped roof punctuated with the third-story dormer windows. Four tall chimneys accent the end walls of the main structure. On each side a lower continuation of the building is set back from the front façade and lower chimneys accent the fore ends. The entire structure is imposing in its mass as well as in the bold contrast of white stone trim against the red brick. Westover has less exterior decoration than the Vassal house, but the main entrance is set off by a richly designed baroque composition of a scroll pediment resting on composite pilasters.

By Revolutionary times, Philadelphia, rather than Boston, had become the foremost metropolis of the new country, and the brilliance of Philadelphia's social life was reflected by the rich dignity of its homes and furniture. Mt. Pleasant was one of the grand mansions of eighteenth-century Philadelphia, in fact, of eighteenth-century America. The building is similar in plan to Vassal House and the same decorative motifs were used to enhance the façade. However, a more imposing over-all effect is produced by the richly formed character of the decorations; these have the weight and sculptural quality of stone, though the building was for the most part executed in rather crudely cut rubble masonry covered with

4-4. Stratford Hall, *c.* 1725. Westmoreland Co. Va. Library of Congress photograph.

stucco. Again, the central part of the façade containing the entrance projects in front of the main mass of the building to form a shallow pavilion. The entrance is traditional; a rather deeply inset doorway is topped by an elliptical fanlight. The door is framed by attached columns above which are a triglyph and metope molding and a pedimental triangle. The second story features a Palladian window group, an architectural device much valued by the Georgian designers, in which the arched central window is flanked by side lights each of which is framed by attached columns. Surmounting the whole is a bold pediment. The eaves and the pediment are finished with a heavy dentil molding. Contrasting stone quoins mark the corners with a strong pattern, and keystones and arches accent the windows. The dormer windows are arched and the chimneys are enriched with arched openings. The vigorous scale of the building and the decorative scheme, a certain authoritative certainty in the handling of parts, the suggestion of gracious affluence without ostentation, all mark the maturity of the Colonial Georgian tradition.

A view of some of the other houses built during this period may help to provide a sense of the variety in domestic architecture at this time. Stratford Hall (4-4), built in Westmoreland County, Virginia, around 1725, was the center of a 16,000-acre plantation. Its plan, a clear and bold H, was undoubtedly suggested by the palatial homes of eighteenth-century England. A handsome flight of stairs which narrow as they approach the doorway carries one's eyes to the main entrance. Here, an ingenious use of brick creates an interesting pilaster and pediment effect and provides a pleasing surface texture to soften the general austerity of the building. The symmetrical arrangement of all the parts, the monumental arched chimneys, the strong masses of the building, the fine craftsmanship exude a forceful air of vigor and self-confidence. The lack of applied ornament, which contributes to the severe dignity of the building, was either an expression of the taste of its builder or a reflection of the absence of local craftsmen to carve the sculptured ornamentation we have observed elsewhere.

The lovely Cowles House (4-5), in Farmington, Connecticut, built a few years after the Revolutionary War by the master-builder William Spratt, reveals a late New England interpretation of the Georgian style. Resourcefulness and imagination were used to modify the Georgian details to suit wooden construction. The animated moldings that frame the windows and the small-scale complexities of cornices, fluted columns, and pilasters convey an omnipresent sense of boards in harmony with the narrow clapboard sheathing. The increased lightness of scale carries a premonition of the Classical revival style which began to replace the Georgian within a decade.

Pennsylvania

In the early eighteenth century many German settlers immigrated to Pennsylvania and set up their prosperous communities in the interior valleys. Their word for "German," *Deutsch*, has frequently been corrupted to *Dutch;* consequently these peoples are usually referred to as Pennsylvania Dutch. The German settlers brought their crafts and modes of building with them and faithfully preserved many of their traditional practices in the communities they built in the new homeland. From one of these early communities comes the oldest example of half timber in America, the Moravian Meeting House (3-2), which we know, from the Oley Valley in Pennsylvania.

The German settlers established a number of religious communities, among which the most notable were the Cloisters near Ephrata, Pennsylvania, where the medieval-style buildings were constructed of heavy logs, and the Moravian Seminary at Bethlehem. The Pennsylvania Germans frequently turned to the abundant stone resources of the area for their building material, and the Sisters House of the Moravian Seminary (4-6), built in 1773, has the characteristic heavy stone walls and a great steep roof punctured by stories of dormer windows. An atmosphere of

4-5. William Spratt, Cowles House, 1780. Farmington, Conn. Wayne Andrews photograph.

weighty solemnity characterizes the interior, where heavy beams, unadorned walls, trestle tables, and simple benches create an atmosphere of cloistered dignity.

The Mississippi Valley

The French settlers of the Mississippi Valley built in a tradition stylistically far removed from the Georgian of the Eastern Seaboard. They combined elements from the medieval building traditions of France with features taken from the style of building which the Spaniards had evolved in the West Indies and in the humid ports of Central America. The Courthouse in Cahokia, Illinois, mentioned earlier (3-3), was built in the first half of the century by a French settler and later became a county courthouse and jail. Buildings of this type established the prototype for the plantation dwellings of a later period. The house had four rooms and a spacious attic. A gallery surrounded the house, and over it extended the double-pitched roof. Each end of the building boasted a heavy stone fireplace.

Very few structures built by the French in the Mississippi Valley survived to modern times, but the conventions the French established remained a most important element in the design of the plantation mansions of later years. Among these were a raised ground floor and the gallery that surrounded the entire house. This provided protection from the almost unbearable heat and humidity of the long summer. Parlange (4-7), in Pointe Coupee Parish, Louisiana, built around 1750, is one of the few classic examples of an eighteenth-century French plantation man-

4-6. Moravian Seminary, 1773. Bethlehem, Pa. Wayne Andrews photograph.

sion to come down to our day. The ground-story walls and the columns supporting the second-story gallery are of brick. The upper stories are of cypress timbers with a combination of clay and moss filling the chinks between the timbers. A great gallery extends around all four sides of the house, and the wooden posts of the second-story gallery extend up to support the high overhanging hipped roof, which is covered with heavy cypress shakes. Access to the second story is provided by a broad flight of outdoor stairs in front, and French doors surmounted by decorative transoms provide passage from the gallery to the inner rooms. The basic arrangement of plantation houses remained unchanged until the civil war.

Colonial Georgian Interiors

While the exteriors of the fine Colonial Georgian mansions are imposing and dignified, the interiors reflect to an even greater degree the newly found wealth and elegance of eighteenth-century colonial life. Three rooms that represent steps in the evolution of the Colonial Geor-

4-7. Parlange, *c.* 1750. Pointe Coupee Parish, La. Library of Congress photograph.

gian interior provide us with a picture of that style. The first (4-8), an interior from the Wentworth House in Portland, Maine, built in 1671 and paneled in 1710, shows the transitional stage between the low-ceilinged, informal seventeenth-century rooms and the fully developed eighteenth-century style. The ceiling beams and the low ceiling remain from the seventeenth century. The paneling of the fireplace wall—paneling one wall was probably all that the resources of the owner permitted—was patterned after the style of the late-seventeenth-century country homes of England. Regularly spaced panels divide the wall, each panel in turn being divided slightly below the center to create a dado below and larger panels above. In contrast to the preceding period, the panels in the Wentworth room are larger and are framed with more elaborate moldings. The fireplace is smaller than in seventeenth-century rooms. Whenever possible in this era, fireplaces were placed in the center of a wall. The moldings around the fireplace have a complexity and fullness of form that presages the baroque though the full elaborations of the later years are not yet evident. The woodwork is dark in color, waxed, and its polished surface conveys a feeling of gracious living and comfort. The furniture in this room also represents a transitional step between seventeenth- and eighteenth-century styles.

A handsome living room (4-9) from Patuxent Manor, a Maryland plantation house completed in 1744, reveals the character of the more developed Colonial Georgian interior. Coming almost fifty years after the

4-8. Interior, Wentworth House, 1671-1710. Portland, Me. Courtesy Metropolitan Museum of Art.

Wentworth House and in keeping with the more aristocratic way of life that characterized the South, the room is large and high-ceilinged, and the structural beams and framing timbers are hidden behind plaster and paneling. The tall double-hung sash windows reach almost to the ceilings; the fireplace and windows of the end wall are symmetrically composed. Beautifully finished paneling, divided as usual into a dado below and tall well-proportioned panels above, is disposed around the room with formal regularity, and the increased complexity of the paneling above the fireplace presages the handsome overmantels of the fully developed style. The architecture of the room provides a setting of quiet elegance and refinement for the rich furniture, the shining crystal and brass, and the handsome textiles of this Southern mansion.

In the two decades preceding the Revolutionary War the Colonial Georgian interior reached its full development. The great chamber from Mt. Pleasant (4-10) provides an example of the full-blown splendor of the Georgian style. As one might expect in the era which stressed formality and elegance, the end wall of the great chamber provided the chief

4-9. Living room, Patuxent Manor, 1744. Maryland. The Henry Francis du Pont Winterthur Museum, Winterthur, Del.

focus for the decorative scheme, and is symmetrically arranged about the fireplace. The fireplace area is emphasized by being projected slightly into the space of the room. Further emphasis is achieved through the thoughtful design of the overmantel, where the moldings frame an open space suitable for holding a painting and then culminate in a crest enriched by a pedimental scroll, rosettes, and crisp leaf patterns. The two side cupboards frame an arched double-door with pilasterlike moldings which take the eye up through the sculptured brackets and thence to the broken pediment which terminates the composition. Complicated moldings using a Greek fret provide a delicate transition from the walls to the ceiling. This refined and handsome architectural background formed the setting for the elegant furniture. The smooth plaster wall on the left provided the perfect background for the richly carved high chest with its flaming finials that was the special pride of the Philadelphia householder in the eighteenth century. Additional pieces of furniture and other appurtenances of everyday living formerly provided the animation and sparkle that distinguishes a lived-in building from even such a well-preserved historical mansion as Mt. Pleasant.

The Colonial Georgian mansions are among the most impressive achievements of colonial America. Their spacious and sensible elegance has made Colonial Georgian America's most popular revival style. Following close on the heels of the sturdy seventeenth-century homes, these houses provide concrete and tangible evidence of the remarkable economic and cultural growth of the colonies, a growth that made it possible and necessary to shake off the restraints of a colonial status and achieve the stature of an independent country.

4-10. Great Chamber, Mt. Pleasant, detail, 1761. Philadelphia. Philadelphia Museum of Art.

PUBLIC ARCHITECTURE

The flourishing colonial communities boasted a number of churches, schools, colleges, and government buildings which, like the houses, interpreted the Georgian mode with various degrees of provincial simplification and understanding. A few of the many public buildings, constructed before the Revolutionary War are still standing, seldom, of course, without having suffered some changes, renovations, and remodeling, but still retaining much of their original character.

Stylistically, the public buildings are similar to the private houses. They were symmetrically oriented around the main entranceway, which was decorated and accented to become the focal center of the design. Many of the motifs used to enrich and dramatize the important areas are already familiar—round arches, free-standing columns, attached columns, and pilasters, curved, triangular, broken, and scrolled pediments, as well as brackets, wreaths, balustrades, and various types of ornamental moldings.

4-11. Old State House, 1728. Boston. Courtesy The Museum of Modern Art, New York.

One of the earliest government buildings still in existence is the Old State House (4-11) built in 1728 in Boston, Massachusetts. After various vicissitudes of neglect and restoration, the exterior stands now very much as it appears in a late-eighteenth-century engraving. Its unbroken façade is reminiscent of the seventeenth-century English baroque, both in its use of red brick trimmed in white stone and in the undisciplined, even clumsy way in which motifs are combined. The balustraded central window, framed by Corinthian pilasters and capped by a curved pediment, breaks through the brick string course which marks the separate stories and carries the eye up to the clock framed by sculptured stone wreaths and swags. The crested gable which terminates the composition is flanked by sculptured heraldic figures which enliven the silhouette. The effect is vigorous, though awkward, for the window above the arched pediment crowds the center of the composition while the circular windows on each side are too small to fill the remaining area adequately. It is the work of an ambitious designer rather than a skillful one, anxious to build a town house for the leading city of the colonial empire in the latest and most splendid mode of London. The borrowing was enthusiastic rather than informed, the beginning of a long and frequently unsuccessful

4-12. Peter Harrison, Brick Market, 1761. Newport, R. I. Wayne Andrews photograph.

attempt to use the elaborate forms of European architecture without understanding their real significance.

Peter Harrison

By the middle of the seventeenth century, some American architectural designers were planning their buildings in a more enlightened and disciplined manner. That American designers of this period drew on English sources for direction and inspiration in no sense discredits them. Each stylish innovation from home, England, was eagerly followed to the degree permitted by the limitations of local craftsmen and materials, for the colonial settler at the time had no national identity independent of the motherland. Peter Harrison, one of the first architectural designers in America and creator of some of the finest churches and public buildings of his day, was active between 1748 and 1763. His old Brick Market (4-12) in Newport, Rhode Island, built in 1761, is a dignified design in the manner of Inigo Jones. The model for the Brick Market was the great gallery at Somerset House in London, but Harrison adjusted the design to meet the demands of brick construction, omitting the heavy rustication of the ground story, with its roughened surface and sunken joints. Originally the arcades of the ground floor were open, and this design of

4-13. Peter Harrison, Synagogue, Congregation Jeshuat Israel, interior, 1759-1763. Newport, R. I. Wayne Andrews photograph.

open arcades on the ground floor topped by an order of giant pilasters was one of the most formal and academically correct to appear in the colonies.

The handsome synagogue interior (4-13) Harrison designed for Congregation Jeshuat Israel, built in Newport between 1759 and 1763, was based on another Jones design, this time a galleried two-story hall in Whitehall Palace, London. The building is unpretentious on the outside, but the interior is richly decorated and ingenious in its successful provision for the requirements of a Sephardic Jewish congregation. Superimposed above the handsome Ionic columns which support the gallery is an order of beautifully carved Corinthian columns not visible here. An ornate pulpit is surrounded by a heavy balustrade, and another ornate balustrade taken from a design by Gibbs encloses the upstairs gallery. All of the devices of joiners' and carvers' art were lifted out of the latest books from England to create what for the day was a brilliant display of decorative virtuosity.

Williamsburg

Virginia was the wealthiest and most architecturally advanced of the colonies. The most impressive and fully realized group of public buildings in the Colonial Georgian style were constructed in Williamsburg, the capital of Virginia from 1699 to 1779, a span of time almost identical to that in which the Georgian style flourished in America. The city of Williamsburg was carefully laid out according to the precepts of eighteenth-century city planning, with streets and rectangular blocks oriented in relation to major avenues and vistas and minor reciprocal accents. The

4-14 (*left*). Governor's palace, *c.* 1720, restored. Williamsburg, Va. Library of Congress photograph. 4-15 (*below*). Capitol, 1751-1753, restored. Williamsburg, Va. Wayne Andrews photograph.

4-16. Independence Hall, completed 1753. Philadelphia. National Park Service photograph.

main avenue, the major axis for the city, was Duke of Gloucester Street, 99 feet wide, seven-eighths of a mile long, which was terminated by William and Mary College at one end and the imposing Capitol building at the other. Both the Governor's palace (4-14), completed around 1720, and the Capitol (4-15), originally built in the first decade of the century, then destroyed by fire and rebuilt between 1751 and 1753, depend for their effectiveness upon the bold massing of large forms rather than upon lavish decoration. In this respect they reveal the influence of Sir Christopher Wren, who caught the full spirit of baroque design in his rich relationships of three-dimensional masses, as distinguished from the work of minor designers who tended to remain dependent on surface ornament. In the Capitol building one sees, not an ornamented flat façade, as in the Old State House of Boston, but rather two great semicircular masses buttressing a deeply recessed entrance way. Even the entrance way is pierced on both sides so that a sense of all-pervasive space and of three-dimensional forms moving in space, along with a sense of fine scale and a vigorous variety of forms, contributes to the grandeur of the building. The view of the Governor's mansion also shows this conscious organization of three-dimensional forms moving into the distance. Even the garden is designed in terms of spheres, cubes, and other geometrically formed masses planned to be seen in perspective, moving into depth.

4-17. Hollis Hall, Harvard University, 1762-1763. Cambridge, Mass. Library of Congress photograph.

Another feature of the buildings at Williamsburg reminiscent of Sir Christopher Wren is the tall steeples or spires, which he developed as a baroque version of the medieval Gothic spire. These graceful steeples usually rise from a rectangular base and then step through a sequence of octagonal and circular drums to terminate in a dome or spire. Each story is smaller, more open, and usually more ornamented than the one below it. These steeples came to be the earmark of the colonial church, but in eighteenth-century America they graced government buildings as well. The familiar pediments, dentil moldings, balustrades and other baroque motifs are used effectively at Williamsburg, but with discretion.

In 1780 the capital of Virginia was transferred to Richmond, and from then on Williamsburg declined in importance and its buildings fell prey to fire and neglect. With the support of John D. Rockefeller, Jr., the restoration of Williamsburg as a complete eighteenth-century colonial capital was commenced in 1927. Since then more than three hundred buildings have been restored and reconstructed with scrupulous care for authenticity, making Williamsburg the most vivid "museum piece" in America today.

In 1731 the provincial assembly of Pennsylvania began the construction of a State House in Philadelphia. A number of talented men contributed their labors to the construction of the building which was not completed until 1753, but faulty construction made the great tower unsafe. It was removed a few years later, and the building stood without a tower until well into the nineteenth century when it was reconstructed according to the original design. Renamed Independence Hall after the Revolution, this handsome building (4-16), which witnessed both the adoption of the Declaration of Independence and the framing of the Constitution, has one of the finest towers in the fully developed Colonial Georgian style in America. The south façade is the most satisfying—the simple white-trimmed windows carry the eye along to the entrance and to the strong Palladian window which focuses the composition. Designed in the manner of Sir Christopher Wren's church towers, but certainly not copied from any one of them, the tower has as its base a strong rectangular brick mass; then rectangular wooden forms give way to octagonal and domed shapes. The tower is enriched with traditional baroque devices, used here with ingenious and sensitive variations of size and scale. White-framed openings of diverse sizes and shapes stand out against the red brick and reinforce the upward movement through their vertical alignment. Higher, the clock face and bell tower continue the rhythm. As the eye moves on up the differing widths of the cornices provide a continuous alternation of wide and narrow to animate the surfaces. Evolving ever upward from the solid and weighty brick base to the open arches of the cupola, the tower provides a continuous movement from stable base to lofty spire.

College halls remain among the few eighteenth-century buildings to come down to us relatively unchanged. Hollis Hall (4-17) at Harvard, built in 1762-1763, is very similar to contemporary halls at Princeton, Dartmouth, and Brown, all of which established the prototypes for college buildings in America. Hollis Hall is four stories high, with a hipped roof, many chimneys, and a central pavilion topped by a pediment. Here the Georgian mode is interpreted with New England restraint. Three modestly accented entrance doors on the front façade and a panel of tall thin windows in the center of the pavilion relieve the regularity and prevent the bare and forthright façade from becoming monotonous.

RELIGIOUS ARCHITECTURE

In America the church never became the dominating symbol of authority it had been in Europe and was in Latin America. Church and state were separate and the church stood as one of many focal centers

4-18 (*left*). Christ Church, 1727-1754. Philadelphia. Essex Institute, Salem, Mass. 4-19 (*below*). Christ Church, interior. Essex Institute, Salem, Mass.

of community life. This attitude found expression in the size and character of the church. Small communities frequently had simple one-room buildings which could be distinguished from a private dwelling only by the bell tower. The Puritans and other dissenting groups built austere meeting houses devoid of ornament. The wealthier Anglican congregations of the metropolitan areas, on the other hand built grand and richly ornamented edifices, designed to compete in size and elegance with the churches being erected in England.

Christ Church (4-18), the first Anglican Church in Philadelphia, is one of the largest, the most vigorously conceived in terms of the disposition of the main masses, and certainly the most ornate of the colonial churches. Patterned after contemporary English structures, its 28-foot square tower has brick-faced stone walls 4 feet thick which support a smaller tower and an octagonal wooden spire which rises 196 feet. The main mass of the church is heavily decorated in the fully developed Georgian style, with the chancel wall creating a particularly splendid effect. The great Palladian window which lights the chancel is topped by a richly carved keystone and a heavy projecting molding. Great spiral scrolls flank the crowning pediment which is topped by flaming bulbous urns. A heavy balustrade and similar flaming urns crown the eaves.

4-20. St. Michael's Church. Charleston, S. C. Wayne Andrews photograph.

The interior (4-19) is one of the few in America with a truly baroque disposition of parts. Seated in the spacious nave one senses the flow of space into the two storied side aisles and the deeply recessed chancel. Two great columns with bold and original capitals support the elliptically vaulted ceiling. The vigorous composition comes to a focus in the large Palladian window that lights the altar. Though some of the details may be gauche, there is a splendor about the total conception that makes the interior of Christ Church unequaled in eighteenth-century America.

There is a possibility that Peter Harrison also designed St. Michael's (4-20) in Charleston. The impressive two-story Doric portico was the first portico of such dimensions to be built in the colonies. The great 185-foot tower is unusually solid and simple in its continuous movement from a square base through diminishing octagonal drums to its graceful spire. The sides with their well-proportioned arched windows and two-story pilasters are handled with the same monumentality and dignity that characterize the façade and tower. St. Michael's Church, like the other great Colonial Georgian churches, reflects an exuberant and healthy community which expressed its pride through fine buildings.

By the time of the Revolution architectural design in America had traversed the long road from the mode of construction of the seventeenth century—vigorous, sturdy, but essentially unrefined and lacking in most decorative attributes—to the spacious, richly ornamented houses, churches, and public buildings of the Colonial Georgian style. In less than three quarters of a century American builders had spanned the range of styles from the Middle Ages to the baroque. The eighteenth-century housewife no longer looked at a medieval village through small diamond-paned windows, but instead looked out on orderly streets and handsome homes through the great Palladian windows which were the pride and signature of the Georgian designers. Much of the elegance which the colonial builder assumed was awkward and self-conscious, and many of the stylistic devices were used with little understanding, but such is the nature of growth. As America's physical resources and needs grew, its intellectual and artistic aspirations also expanded. Just as France, England, and Germany in earlier periods drew on the authoritative Italian sources, so American designers in this period went to the mother country, England, for inspiration, information, and direction. The concept of an indigenous art or of a native style was far beyond the aspirations of the colonies, who thought of themselves as outposts of the great mother country whose cultural ideals they shared. Artistic and cultural independence came, as would be expected, with maturity, and maturity only commenced after the link with the motherland was severed.

5

The Household Arts,

1700-1776

FURNITURE

The eighteenth century witnessed a brilliant flowering of all the arts in England. The growth of the colonial empire, the development of trade, and the acquisition of great wealth stimulated an elaborate social life which assumed its material form in splendid palaces and fine country homes furnished in a sumptuous and refined manner. Consequently, this was the great age of furniture design, and a succession of brilliant styles found expression during the last half of the century in the work of individual designers whose names are still household words—Chippendale, Sheraton, Hepplewhite, and the Adam brothers. In America, the household arts reflected the brilliance and sophistication of the motherland, partly because the colonies mirrored the style of the mother country, but also because like England, they were in a flourishing state of expansion. While the modes of London were faithfully followed, the colonial

129

craftsmen did not restrict themselves to what was done in that style center. Certain pieces of furniture developed here in a sufficiently unique way to become characteristically colonial—the Windsor chair, the block front chest, the double chest, and the case top desk or secretary. Brilliant styles followed one another in rapid sequence, first in England and then in America—(1) William and Mary, (2) Queen Anne, (3) Georgian, which received its richest formulation in the hands of the English designer, Thomas Chippendale, and (4) the Classic Revival. The Classic Revival styles, which began to appear in England soon after the middle of the century, did not arrive in America until after the Revolution and so need not concern us in this section.

William and Mary

The style in force at the turn of the century was named William and Mary after the English rulers. Good examples can be seen in the living room of the Wentworth House (4-8). The pair of chairs flanking the fireplace reveal such characteristics of William and Mary furniture as the essentially rectangular structure enriched with baroque elements—scroll feet, curved arms, crested backs, and scrolled and arched stretchers. Elaborate turnings such as decorate the gate-legged table and the various chairs in the room remained popular. Other characteristics of the style which can be clearly seen in the highboy standing against the plaster wall are the trumpet-shaped turnings on the legs and the use of Chinese-style lacquers and inlays. Walnut became the proper wood for fine furniture, and it was finished with a high polish. Caning and cushions contributed to increased comfort.

Queen Anne

Early in the century the William and Mary style began to give way to the Queen Anne style. The home-loving tastes of Queen Anne were reflected in furniture which stressed comfort, grace, and simplicity. The colonial preference for unpretentious lightweight furniture coincided most fortuitously with the emergence of the Queen Anne style when the settlers were building and furnishing their first fine homes.

In Queen Anne furniture, the characteristic rectangularity of the William and Mary style gave way to a curvilinear emphasis which established a rhythmic unity through the various parts of a piece of furniture. The single element which contributed most to the creating of this graceful unity was the consistent use of the elongated S curve. The cabriole leg,

5-1 (*left*). Queen Anne chair, walnut, 1725-1750. Philadelphia. Courtesy Metropolitan Museum of Art, Rogers Fund, 1925. 5-2 (*right*). Wing chair, mahogany, 1725-1750. Courtesy Metropolitan Museum of Art, Kennedy Fund, 1918.

the most obvious curvilinear feature of the Queen Anne style, was designed with a double S curve which moved gracefully from the heavier knee to the slender ankle and then in reverse curve swelled to a heavier slipper or especially in mid-century, to the popular claw-and-ball foot. A variety of pieces of furniture—chairs, tables, chests, desks, framed mirrors, and even grandfather clocks—were created in the Queen Anne mode, but the style received its most complete fulfillment in the side chair and arm chair (5-1). The cabriole legs, the horseshoe-shaped seat, wider at the front and narrower at the back, the vase-shaped back splat with its graceful curves and the continuous line running from the curved back through the raked back legs, all combined to create a unified and rhythmic piece of furniture with both simplicity and elegance. Philadelphia became one of the chief centers of fine furniture-making in the pre-Revolutionary period, and in the middle of the century, certain Philadelphia cabinet-makers used quite elaborate carving on their furniture. In general, however the colonial cabinetmaker relied for his effects on grace, lightness, fine proportions, and elegance of line rather than on rich decorations.

Toward the middle of the century, the double settee, the upholstered sofa, and the wing chair appeared. These elaborations of the simple chair retained the characteristics and shapes of the Queen Anne style although occasionally the cabriole legs were strengthened by the addition of stretchers (5-2). The tendency to upholster entire pieces of furniture

5-3. Piecrust tilt-top table, 1770-1780. Courtesy Metropolitan Museum of Art, Rogers Fund, 1925.

provides additional evidence of the increased elegance and comfort of household furnishings in the eighteenth century.

The elaborate social life of the eighteenth century necessitated a great variety of tables. Tray tables, card tables, piecrust tables, drop-leaf tables, dressing tables, and side tables all were in use, and many, such as the drop-leaf tables, had ingenious mechanisms that permitted them to be folded or collapsed and stored in a small space. Small tables such as the pie crust tables in which the top rested on a central baluster or column supported by a cabriole tripod remain charming examples of craftsmanship, ingenuity and taste. Two tables from this period can be seen in the great chamber at Mt. Pleasant, and a piecrust table (5-3) of the Revolutionary War period with claw-and-ball feet, cabriole legs, and an elaborately scalloped rococo rim provides an excellent example of this type of table from a slightly later period.

The Georgian Style—the Chippendale Influence

The three Georges ruled England from 1714 through most of the century. During the first half of the century the Georgian style developed from the relatively simple Queen Anne to a rich, highly ornamented style. These fully developed Georgian modes of the midcentury continued to employ the curvilinear construction that characterized the earlier Queen Anne style; the chief differentiating characteristic was a tendency toward greater magnificence, with florid decorations replacing the simple lines and light proportions of the earlier style. Too, a taste for mahogany replaced the earlier preference for walnut. In England the fully developed Georgian mode received its most handsome expression in the designs of

5-4 (*left*). Chippendale-style chair, mahogany, 1770-1780. Courtesy Metropolitan Museum of Art, Gift of George Coe Graves, 1932. 5-5 (*right*). Chippendale-style chair, 1765-1770. Boston. Courtesy Metropolitan Museum of Art, Fletcher Fund, 1944.

Thomas Chippendale, a designer with a unique gift for creating designs of great beauty in which the various Chinese, Gothic, and French elements of the rococo style were used in a manner acceptable to the English taste. In the two decades preceding the Revolutionary War, American cabinetmakers produced a number of pieces of furniture based on designs by Chippendale.

In the rococo style the baroque forms were lightened and relieved of their burden of weighty ornament. Shells, ribbons, leaves, flowers, rocks, fantastic and whimsical motifs frequently of Chinese inspiration, and many bucolic symbols were preferred to the Renaissance motifs on which the baroque was built. In general, rococo art is light, airy, and feminine in contrast to baroque which is heavy, bold, and masculine. A brilliant union of rococo charm and English restraint appeared in the furniture based on designs by Chippendale.

Chippendale's influence on chair design is particularly marked. The chair illustrated in Figure 5-4, compared with a typical Queen Anne design (5-1), reveals the way in which Chippendale modified the earlier models. In general, the Chippendale chairs are larger, more imposing, and more elaborately carved. Instead of the continuous flowing curves of the earlier style, straight lines and curves play against each other to provide an animated variety of line movements. The front and sides of

5-6 (*left*). Canopied bed, 18th century. H. F. Du Pont Winterthur Museum, Winterthur, Del. 5-7 (*right*). William Savery, double chest, mahogany, 1760-1780. Philadelphia. Courtesy Metropolitan Museum of Art, Rogers Fund, 1915.

the seat are straight rather than curved and the round back has been replaced by a somewhat rectangular back with elevated corners. The back splat of the Queen Anne chair has been pierced and elaborated into ribbonlike, interlacing forms designed with the graceful, flattened curves typical of the rococo. The vigorously formed cabriole legs terminate in the popular claw-and-ball foot. Judiciously placed carving enriches the surfaces and contrasts effectively with the smooth, beautifully shaped and proportioned, undecorated area. In a handsome arm chair (5-5) a Chinese feeling is established by the use of straight channeled legs which foreshadow the return to rectangularity that occurred at the end of the century. Chippendale's influence also appeared in a great variety of pieces other than chairs, such as chests (5-7), tables, beds (5-6), and mirrors.

William Savery (1720-1787), a Philadelphia cabinetmaker who worked in the highly ornamented Chippendale style, may well have made the uniquely American handsome mahogany double chest shown here (5-7). This imposing double chest shows the subtle refinements of design using Chippendale motifs that appeared in Philadelphia in the third quarter of the century. Measuring well over 7 feet from top to bottom and almost 4 feet in width, this chest could have looked oppressively bulky, even top-heavy, but for the skill with which the parts are related and the taste with which the ornamentation is distributed. Basically, this design consists of two rectangular chests resting on cabriole legs topped by a scroll pediment. The lower section, considerably shorter than the upper, acts as a subordinate, but horizontal base. The cabriole legs, a sturdy yet resilient support for the weight above, move up from the floor with a vigorous and energetic rhythm. This movement continues in the curved contours of the apron with its flowing lines of carved leaves, stems, and central shell, then continues up the sides to culminate in the great pedimental scrolls which continue and resolve the wavelike motion initiated by the legs. The surface carving provides a most effective unifying agent which reinforces and supports the rhythms of the major masses. On the legs, the fine carving animates the surface and intensifies the movement so that one is hardly aware of their weight. This rhythm is continued across the front and up the sides by means of the delicately carved corners to culminate in the fanciful flow of French rococo motifs which reach their climax in the dynamic interplay of carved leaves, stems, and flowers held in place by the powerful enclosing scrolls of the pediment. Other elements reinforce the upward movement in a most subtle way. The drawers in each section become progressively shallower from top to bottom. Even the handsome brass drawer pulls tend to take the eye continuously upward. In this piece one can see the union between the reasonable and the fanciful so aptly described by Talbot Hamlin when he wrote, "Over this bedrock of rationalism played the fantasy of the rococo imagination, as though to express the unconscious feeling of a world which was losing its old standards with amazing rapidity."

Many combinations of chests of drawers with china closets, tables, and writing desks appeared in the eighteenth century, and two characteristically American developments of the high chests and secretaries are particularly interesting. One was the tall double chest such as we have just discussed. The double chest appeared in England early in the century and then went out of fashion. In America the double chest, or high chest, remained an important piece of furniture all through the century. While the double chests from Philadelphia were famous for the splendor and elaboration of their carvings, many of these eighteenth-century highboys from other areas achieve an equal degree of distinction through their fine proportions and general restraint.

The second noteworthy local development of chests was the block front which was used on chests of drawers, desks, and secretaries (5-8). The block front appears to have originated with two Newport cabinet-

5-8. Peter Townsend, block-front chest, 1765. Courtesy Metropolitan Museum of Art, Rogers Fund, 1927.

makers, John Goddard and his nephew Peter Townsend, between 1760 and 1780. In the block-front chests, the front of the rectangular mass of the chest alternately protruded and recessed, the middle block being set back while the two front corner blocks protruded. The blocked masses were left undecorated except for a shell motif which was carved to make a convex ornament at the top of the protruding sections and a concave ornament above the recessed center.

During the eighteenth century many other pieces of furniture underwent elaboration. The bed emerged from its canopied obscurity to become a handsome object with reeded corner posts and carved cabriole legs. The simple wall clock became the grandfather clock, an important piece of furniture, housed in a tall case. Mirrors were framed with complex moldings and crests, and some of the mirror frames became veritable extravagances of rococo carving. Elaborately carved, gilded, and painted, they were used as important decorative accents over mantels or to enhance a bare wall.

5-9. Braced high comb-back Windsor chair. Museum of Fine Arts, Boston.

The Georgian age has been called the age of mahogany, and in both England and America this firm, hard-textured wood was preferred to any other for fine furniture. Contact with Cuba and with Central and South America insured an abundant supply. Mahogany was particularly admired for its soft warm color which gradually darkened to a rich tone. In the eighteenth century it was usually polished with red tinted beeswax to produce a lustrous satiny surface. The preference for mahogany lasted well into the nineteenth century.

Windsor Chairs

While the wealthy followed the fashions of London in their parlors, in many situations the folk traditions of the motherland were retained and furniture was made according to the older, simply carpentered handicraft traditions. The Windsor chair of English origin remained popular among all classes throughout the colonies. Of relatively simple construction, practical, and graceful, it developed its most refined form in America and came to be considered a characteristically colonial piece of furniture. Windsor chairs varied greatly in shape and size, depending upon the situations in which they were to be used. High comb-backed, with the center spindles extended at the back to support a shaped headrest, braced high-comb back (5-9), low-backed, double settee, high chairs for small children, and a great variety of other types of Windsor chair were produced. As it developed here, the original thick, crude, stool-seat was given a saddle shape. The legs, turned in slender baluster forms, were joined and strengthened by turned stretchers. A back of slender spindles, also housed in the seat, was held in place either by a hooped top rail returned and housed in the seat or by a horizontal rail extended into arms.

Like so many utilitarian objects which were developed in America to answer functional requirements, the Windsor chair achieved a lean elegance, a combination of lightness and strength, that contrasts interestingly with the ponderous design of European equivalents. All its parts were pared down to the minimum weight compatible with strength and were shaped primarily by function. The only decoration found on the Windsor chairs are machine turnings, used with craftsmanlike consideration and good judgment. Tables and stools of a similar type were also common. The thick seats of Windsor chairs were usually made of pine. Beech, hickory, birch, and ash were used in the bent parts, and maple, ash, beech, oak, and birch were all employed for turned parts. Windsor chairs and settees were frequently painted, dark green being a popular color, and lines and bands of gilt and bright color were used for added liveliness.

Dutch and Pennsylvania Dutch Furniture

Some of the German, Dutch, and Scandinavian groups in rural New York, New Jersey, and Pennsylvania retained the folk idiom of their native land and produced colorful, sturdy, and unpretentious furniture. Though the construction of such furniture was simple, the craftsmanship was excellent, and frequently the decorations were gay and charming. Of the various national groups that settled in the colonies the Dutch of New York and the Germans of Pennsylvania left the most vigorous heritage.

A wardrobe (5-10) from eighteenth-century New York shows the Dutch tradition both in its heavy rectangular construction and in its gay decoration. The great wardrobe, or "Kas," has an invigorating fresh handling of such traditional baroque decorative elements as the painted garlands of flowers and festoons of fruits, leaves, and ribbons which are handsomely massed against a strong background shaped and shaded to suggest a niche.

5-10 (*right*). Dutch wardrobe, or kas, 18th century. New York. Courtesy Metropolitan Museum of Art, Rogers Fund, 1909. 5-11 (*below*). Room from Millbach, 1752. Lebanon Co., Pa. Courtesy of the Pennsylvania Museum of Art, Philadelphia.

5-12. Pennsylvania-German bridal chest, pine and poplar, 18th century. Courtesy Metropolitan Museum of Art, Rogers Fund, 1923.

The most vigorous development of the North European peasant tradition occurred among the German settlers of Pennsylvania. The German emigrants who settled in Eastern Pennsylvania continued to create furniture and household objects in the traditions of their homeland with little change until almost the end of the nineteenth century. A mid-eighteenth-century room from Millbach in Lebanon County, Pennsylvania, reveals the character of the interiors and the furnishings (5-11). The low-ceilinged room has plain plaster walls, is uncluttered and un-crowded. Simple turning and contours sawed in scalloped or wavelike patterns animate the profiles. Rather flat moldings and such carpentered devices as simple beveled panels are used to relieve the plain surfaces. Geometrically patterned woven coverlets and curtains, and a variety of heavy, vigorously decorated ceramic and painted tin household wares provide spots of color in the room.

Bridal chests are perhaps the most charming and richly decorated pieces of furniture produced by the Pennsylvania Germans. The chest shown here (5-12) has two large drawers decorated with the very popular tulip motif as well as with handsome brass pulls. The top of the chest has three niches on the front, the center one featuring two dancing unicorns, while the narrower side niches are decorated with horsemen, birds, vases, spirals, flowers, and a number of geometric ornaments. The colors are as gay and bright as the patterns, and the entire piece is in an idiom which has great appeal to contemporary tastes, partly because of its intrinsic charm but also because we are still reacting against the Victorian preference for aristocratic styles and consequently prefer naive modes.

DECORATIVE ARTS

All of the decorative arts contributed to the gracious charm of the Georgian household. Ceramics, glass, textiles, silverware, pewter, wrought iron, brass, and copperware were greatly desired both for the conveniences they provided in the home and because the variety of their forms and colors and the luster of their surfaces added to the visual enrichment of the interiors. Though fine wares were imported from Europe in ever-increasing quantities, demand outstripped supply and ambitious settlers commenced to manufacture these various commodities. The first American glazed china was produced prior to the Revolution, and glassware, silver, pewter, pottery, and even brass fittings that were far beyond the utilitarian wares of the seventeenth century in design and craftsmanship appeared here early in the eighteenth century.

Silver and Metalware

Eighteenth-century silver was patterned after styles current in the capitals of Europe. Early eighteenth-century silver, like that from the preceding age, reflected the baroque taste for heavy rounded forms with a low center of gravity. By mid-century the rococo influence expressed itself in increased height and slenderness and in the elaboration of curves, particularly the characteristic playful reverse curves. In general, American silver like American furniture tended to be less heavily ornamented than that from Europe, and simpler in line. Coffee pots, tea kettles, sugar bowls and creamers, and trays provided the most striking examples of the silversmith's art. Cups, porringers, bowls, tankards and mugs, knives, forks, and spoons were the common pieces. Ecclesiastical silver, frequently of a very elaborate nature, was produced in limited quantities.

Three pieces from mid-century Boston illustrate the general character of New England silver where the English influence remained paramount.

5-13 (*left*). Paul Revere, Sr., porringer, silver, early 18th century, Boston. Courtesy Metropolitan Museum of Art, Bequest of A. T. Clearwater, 1933. 5-14 (*right*). Daniel Henchman, mug, silver, *c.* 1750-1775. Boston. Courtesy of the Newark Museum, Newark, N. J.

A porringer (5-13) by Paul Revere, Sr. (1702-1754), a fine silversmith, but less well-known than his famous son who will be discussed below, retains the familiar low porringer shape but displays a pleasant elaboration of the flowing lines of the handle. A mug (5-14) by Daniel Henchman (1730-1775) has a round full-bellied body, but the handle is enlivened with gay reverse curves. A silver sweetmeat box (5-15) by John Coney (1655-1722), one of the most versatile silversmiths of Boston and maker of many large and handsome pieces, provides a particularly splendid example of the elaborate decoration of which the colonial silversmith was capable. This particular piece is engraved with the legend "Gift of Grandmother Norton to Ann Quincy," and it was in the designing of such gifts that the silversmith displayed his skill and ingenuity. A full repertoire of decorative effects was used to enhance such special pieces. Floral and geometric ornament designed in medallions were used along with various elaborations of the simple gadrooning of the seventeenth century. Raised designs were embossed on the surfaces, and ornamental details, as well as the handles and the feet, might be cast in molds and applied. Chasing and other types of textures were used to vary the surfaces and contours and edges were cut and elaborated with rococo

5-15 (*left*). John Coney, sugar box, silver, 1719. Museum of Fine Arts, Boston.
5-16 (*right*). Cornelius Kierstede, snuffer stand, silver, *c.* 1705. Courtesy Metropolitan Museum of Art, Gift of Mr. and Mrs. William A. Moore, 1923.

5-17 (*right*). Simeon Soumain, salver, silver, *c.* 1750. Courtesy Metropolitan Museum of Art, Dodge Fund, 1935.   5-18 (*below*). Peter de Riemer, tea set, silver, late 18th century. Museum of the City of New York, New York.

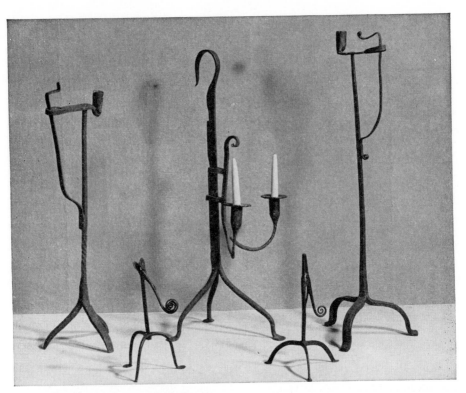

5-19. Candlesticks, iron, 1720-1750. Courtesy of the Art Institute of Chicago, Chicago.

curves. Cutout patterns created openwork effects, dies were used for stamping patterns, and bands, rims, and decorative moldings added to the sculptural enrichment of the form.

The Dutch tradition determined the forms and decorations of much of the silver produced in New York before the Revolution. A silver snuffer stand (5-16) by Cornelius Kierstede (1675-1757) shows the elaboration of form and decoration that characterized the more pretentious pieces wrought by the Dutch silversmiths. A succession of bold shapes with heavily wrought engraved and applied ornament makes this elaborately decorated stand appear much larger than its 8¼ inches. The Dutch influence also made itself felt in the preference for festoons of fruits and flowers and the use of much embossing and engraving.

A number of French Huguenot silversmiths, among them Paul Revere, Sr., had introduced French elements of design into the American tradition early in the eighteenth century. This French influence was apparent in New York and Philadelphia in a marked preference for the graceful rococo forms and decorations. Simeon Soumain (1687-1750) of

5-20. "The Highlander" fireback, cast iron, 18th century. Courtesy Metropolitan Museum of Art, Rogers Fund, 1916.

New York designed a silver salver (5-17) in which cabriole legs and fluted edges employed the reversed curves of the rococo style to contribute an element of grace, animation, and even frivolity to a simple design. An unusually handsome tea set (5-18) made by Peter de Riemer between 1763 and 1796 for Philip Schuyler Van Rensselaer is reputed to be the first silver service to have been made in New York. This silver tea service, adorned by the embossed garlands of flowers, leaves, and birds preferred by the Dutch silversmiths, displays the more slender proportions and the graceful flowing curves popular during the last half of the century.

The majority of the colonists could not afford to own silver service and used the more humble pewter ware. Less stylish than silver, pewter objects tended to keep the same forms over a long period, forms modeled on early-eighteenth-century silver objects. A wide variety of articles, including almost all standard kitchen and table items, were made of pewter.

The importance of the blacksmith in early American life has already been mentioned. Many iron objects were made for the stove and fireplace, but they also appeared in all the other parts of the house. Waffle and wafer irons, gridirons, lamps, trivets, tongs, shovels, andirons, candlesticks, stove plates, stoves, and firebacks for fireplaces were all produced in the colonial blacksmith shop and iron foundry. A group of iron candlesticks from the eighteenth century (5-19) reveals the varied forms and ingenious devices as well as the decorative touches that add a note of

5-21 (*left*). Shem Drowne, grasshopper weather vane, copper with glass eyes, 1742. Faneuil Hall, Boston. Index of American Design, National Gallery of Art, Washington, D.C.   5-22 (*right*). Shem Drowne, Indian weather vane. Massachusetts Historical Society, Boston.

grace to the simple utilitarian objects. The large central candlestick can stand by itself, or be hung from a wall bracket, while the notched standard provides for lowering or lifting the candles.

Eighteenth-century firebacks were usually cast in elaborate designs, contributing, along with the andirons, a decorative note to the fireplace. "The Highlander" (5-20), combining as it does human, fish, floral, and leaf motifs in a bisymmetric arrangement, is more elaborate and somewhat more formal in design than most American firebacks. The five- and six-plate stoves or jamb stoves which developed in America at this time represent an attempt to increase the effectiveness of the fireplace by extending the hearth into the room. From these jamb stoves Franklin developed the idea of the Franklin stove.

The elaborate exteriors of the Georgian houses also provided excellent opportunities for the ironmonger to display his skill and artistry. Knobs, latches, handles, key plates, bolts, and locks were given graceful enhancement whenever a surface or contour permitted. The impressive gates, stair railings, and fences which framed the entrances to the more imposing homes and estates were ornamented with the full vocabulary of wrought-iron effects as well as with cast-iron leaves, rosettes, and classical motifs. Foot scrapers were cast into fancy animal and plant forms as well as into geometric and architectural patterns, and weather vanes were ornamented with cutouts of birds, animals, fish, owner's initials, the dates when a house was built, and other relevant or whimsical motifs. Such weather vanes were frequently many feet across and created an elaborate and intriguing silhouette against the sky. The most famous weather vane in America is probably the great copper weather vane (5-21) which has topped Faneuil Hall in Dock Square, Boston, for more than two centuries. The great copper grasshopper with green glass eyes was hammered from one sheet of copper by Shem Drowne in 1742. Less famous but perhaps more amusing (5-22) is one in which Shem Drowne transmuted a ferocious Indian into a charming decoration.

Ceramics

The lead-glazed redware pottery described in the preceding chapter continued to be the standard household ware through most of the eighteenth century. Almost every town had its potters who provided vessels of this ware for the table, cooking, and storing food. Slip-decorated pottery was made by most early settlers; the vigor and variety of the Pennsylvania Dutch slip-decorated pottery makes it one of America's most charming ceramic wares. Pennsylvania pottery, like that produced in the English-speaking colonies, was both thrown on a wheel and made in molds. Two main types of decoration were employed: slip-painted (5-23) and sgraffito. The slip-painted ware was decorated with patterns painted on the cream-colored slip with various combinations of clay and color glazes. Sgraffitoware, as described before, was decorated by incising designs in the slip with a pointed instrument to expose the dark red pottery base beneath; sometimes both kinds of decoration were used on one piece (5-24, 5-25). In decorating the pottery, the cream-colored glaze was enlivened with a number of other colors; dark red, brown, green, and olive yellow were all used occasionally, although most of the potters contented themselves with color schemes limited to a few bright colors, red, green, and white being the most popular. In the final firing the glaze melted and filled the engraved areas; consequently the sgraffitoware presented an almost smooth surface. Slip-decorated pottery remained very much a folk art, carried on during slack seasons by farmers and other types of workmen who made the pottery almost as a lucrative hobby. The patterns and techniques remained unchanged over many generations.

5-23 (*left*). Pennsylvania-German shaving dish, slip-painted earthenware, *c.* 1768. Courtesy Metropolitan Museum of Art, Rogers Fund, 1953. 5-24 (*below left*). Pennsylvania-German dish, slip-painted sgraffitoware, late 18th century. Courtesy Metropolitan Museum of Art, Gift of Mrs. Robert W. de Forest, 1934. 5-25 (*below right*). Pennsylvania-German plate, slip-painted sgraffitoware, *c.* 1790. Courtesy Metropolitan Museum of Art, Gift of Mrs. Robert W. de Forest.

Platters, pie plates, jars and crocks, and cooking bowls were made in the greatest quantities but a wide variety of other pieces have been found. Many special shapes were made for particular individuals or for special occasions. The unique slip-decorated shaving dish (5-23) is a particularly amusing example of such a specialized piece. The motifs used to decorate this pottery are similar to those on the painted furniture from this area. Flowers, particularly the tulip, leaves, fruits, birds, animals, human figures, initials, writing, and many groupings of lines, dots, and simple geometric motifs were all popular, and as is so frequently the case in folk arts, while the same motifs were used many times, each potter modified them according to his own tastes.

Another handsome type of ceramic ware produced in the colonies was the gray or gray-brownstone ware used primarily as containers and for storage purposes. In the early years New Englanders, lacking a suitable clay, had to import their stoneware from England or from the other

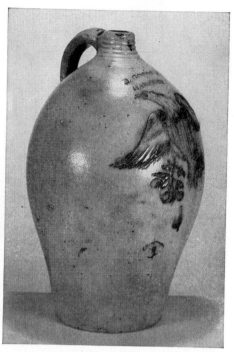

5-26 (*right*). Jug, glazed stoneware, 18th century. New England. Courtesy, Brooklyn Museum, Brooklyn, N. Y. 5-27 (*below*). Sauce boat, white earthenware, late 18th century. Philadelphia. In the Brooklyn Museum Collection.

colonies. At a later date the proper clay was imported from New York, New Jersey, and Pennsylvania, and the pottery works of New England produced fine stoneware (5-26). Pitchers, jugs, butter crocks, mugs, and pickle jars of fine simple shapes were made in this ware from the mid-eighteenth century up to modern times. Stoneware is a hard and dense type of pottery produced by firing the ware at a high temperature and glazing it with salt. It has a finely pitted surface texture similar to that of an orange peel. The gray and tan stoneware was frequently decorated with cobalt blue patterns which were either freely painted on the surface or run into shallow incised patterns before the entire piece was glazed. The most frequent patterns were floral sprigs, birds, or patriotic motifs. The Morgan potteries at Cheesequake, New Jersey, were famous for the fine quality of their stoneware.

Fine china tablewares were beyond the capabilities of the colonial potter. However, at the time of the Revolution a rather refined white earthenware (5-27) designed in a modified rococo form for the table was being manufactured in Philadelphia. This ware, decorated with an underglazed blue pattern of Oriental inspiration, was styled after and was produced in competition with the Oriental import china that graced the homes of the wealthy.

5-28 (*left*). Bottle, amethyst glass, late 18th century.   5-29 (*center*). Engraved bottle, white flint glass, late 18th century.   5-30 (*right*). Enameled bottle, blue glass, late 18th century. All courtesy Metropolitan Museum of Art, Gift of F. W. Hunter, 1913.

Glass

Glass manufacture commenced in America during the seventeenth century, and the first half of the eighteenth century witnessed continued attempts to manufacture the glass needed by the colonial settlers. The two best known eighteenth-century glass manufacturers were Caspar Wistar (1696-1752), who established his glass works at Wistarberg, West Jersey, in 1739, and "Baron" Stiegel (1729-1785), whose factory was located at Manheim, Pennsylvania, between 1760 and 1765.

Caspar Wistar is reputed to be the first man in America to manufacture flint glass though no glass can be attributed to him with certainty. Flint glass, now made with sand, was originally made with ground flint or flint pebbles and was a pure and lustrous glass of great beauty. Although his factory was set up primarily to make window glass and bottles, Wistar also made fine flint table glass in clear white and in a variety of colors. The so-called Wistar-style glass is fine in craftsmanship, simple but refined in shape; it achieves interesting decorative effects by superimposing waves, spirals, scallops, and similar shapes of colored glass on a plain or contrasting colored base.

Baron Stiegel was a German entrepreneur who came to Philadelphia in 1750 and embarked upon a series of ambitious business enterprises, one of which was a glass factory. Stiegel manufactured flasks, bottles, fine tableware, cologne bottles, goblets, tumblers, sugar bowls, creamers, and other pieces. His glass also was produced in many colors, but a very rich deep blue is the color of the glass most frequently associated with his name. Stiegel glass displays a variety of kinds of decoration. Engraving and enameling were both used extensively, and many variations of color and tone were produced by manipulating the molten glass in the blowing process.

A comparison of three bottles from this period shows the increased sophistication of form and decoration of eighteenth-century colonial glass as compared to that of the previous century. An amethyst bottle (5-28), a pure example of the glass blower's art, relies on its fine shape and on variations in the thickness of the glass for its decorative values. In contrast, a white flint bottle (5-29) has a lively engraved pattern of just the right weight and naïveté for the sturdy shape it decorates. A bottle (5-30) of deep blue glass is decorated with freely applied enameled patterns in bright colors. Any of these pieces of glass might have been produced by Stiegel, and they undoubtedly reflect his influence, but they cannot be positively attributed to his factories.

Textiles

The colonial housewife continued to spin yarn and to weave the sturdy textiles necessary for clothing and household linens throughout

5-31. "The Fishing Lady on Boston Common," petit-point picture, 18th century. Museum of Fine Arts, Boston.

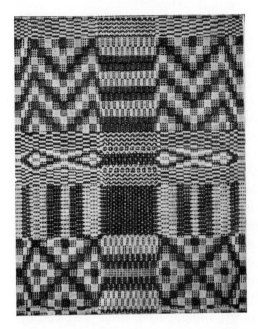

5-32. Coverlet, indigo wool and natural linen, *c.* 1779. Index of American Design, National Gallery of Art, Washington, D.C.

the eighteenth century. As the journeymen weavers relieved her of the more burdensome tasks and as importations became more numerous, she spent more time embroidering, weaving fancy bedspreads, and making the appliqué and patchwork quilts and coverlets which provided for her love of fancy work.

Fine needlework and embroidering constituted an important part of a young lady's education in colonial Boston, and the ultimate exercise in fine needlework was the needlepoint picture. A favorite subject for such pictures was a pastoral scene with a woman seated on a rock fishing in a small pond. The vogue developed of using the buildings and activities of the Boston Common as a background for such pictures. About a dozen of these elaborate needlepoint pictures (5-31) are extant today and they have the common title of "The Fishing Lady on Boston Common." Their decorative charm is enriched both by their quaint humor and by their exquisite craftsmanship.

No home craft was more universally popular than the weaving of decorative covers for the imposing bedsteads in which the colonial housewife took so much pride. Eighteenth-century bedspreads were usually woven in geometric patterns, since the hand looms of that period would not accommodate the more elaborate conventionalized floral and pictorial patterns popular in the nineteenth century. A detail of a bedspread (5-32) from New Hampshire, woven in the eighteenth century, shows the remarkable effects the colonial weaver could achieve within the limitations of simple basic geometric patterns. Chevrons, stripes, and squares combine here in a fascinating variety of sizes and shapes to achieve many different patterns and textures. The colors of this spread are those most frequently used, natural linen color and indigo blue. The effect is modest but certainly not dull. Cotton, linen, and wool were the fibers most commonly found in such spreads, with cotton and linen usually providing the foundation woof threads while colorful wools were used in the warp. Many of the dyes used to color the threads were made from native flowers, barks, and berries. Indigo provided the blue, sumac the orangish red that was so popular. The popular patterns were known by names, many of which have a quaint charm; "Checkers, Stripes, and Squares," "Sunrise," "Maid of Orleans," and "Nine Snowballs with Pine Tree Border" were familiar patterns to former generations.

Samplers remained popular in the eighteenth century, but they ceased to be a collection of stitches and became displays of embroidering prowess. Mottoes, texts, human figures, birds, beasts, flowers, and fruits were combined with great ingenuity. Framed and used as wall decorations, these elaborate inventions provided outlet for the housewife's embroidering enthusiasms and faith in uplifting maxims.

The architecture and household arts of the Georgian age are highlights in the history of American art. We have seen that the high roofs, the towering gables, and the bulbous pendants of an earlier period gave way to graciously decorated symmetrical façades, that low, dark, and crowded halls were transformed into high-ceilinged, spacious rooms, that great hand-hewn beams disappeared behind handsome wainscot paneling, and the heavy oak lintel above the fireplace was replaced by elegant pilastered and pedimented architectural composition. In like manner, the Bible box became a secretary, and from the sturdy chest sprang the great 7-foot-high chest on chest, replete with cabriole legs, carved apron, and towering pediments filled with rococo shells, leaves, and flowers.

By the time of the Revolution, America was well on its way toward competing with Europe in the elegance of its way of life and its arts. But the age of elegance in Europe was drawing to a close. The American Revolution was not an isolated event, but part of a great social change that was occurring all over the civilized world. This change eventually broke the power of the great monarchies of Europe, unseated the aristocrats, and brought to an end a whole complex of social institutions. The arts and crafts which were the chief expressions of those aristocratic institutions shared the same fate. France and then all the countries of Europe were caught in a maelstrom of successive disturbances, political, economic, and social. The arts reflected these disturbances through a series of shifting styles initiated with increasing rapidity all through the nineteenth century. Architects and designers revived earlier styles that were neither well understood nor logical for the political structure and technology of the age that was appearing.

The search for new forms to embody the forces of the new society continued well into the twentieth century. Now we look back upon the rich beauty of Georgian art as the flowering of an older way of life transplanted to our shores and we see the conflicting currents of nineteenth-century taste as the confused expression of a period of gestation. From the ripe beauty and wisdom of the one and the discoveries of the other, we are forging a new style that today promises another period of distinguished achievement in architecture, the household and industrial arts, and the handicrafts.

6

Painting and Sculpture
in Colonial America

UNLESS MEN REVERT TO A BRUTE LEVEL OF EXISTENCE, the home and its equipment are basic necessities. But man conquering the wilderness can hardly be expected to cultivate the arts. The hardships of colonial life left little time or energy for painting pictures or carving statues and the Puritan antagonism toward the arts as expressions of courtly extravagance and vanity did not provide an atmosphere conducive to artistic production. It comes therefore as something of a surprise to find artists working in America almost from the moment the continent was discovered.

The early explorers brought with them artists who played the same role as that of a photographer on a modern expedition of exploration, making records of new places, strange people, beasts, and plants. Among the conquistadors who accompanied Cortez were men who could make sketches of what they saw. During the sixteenth century in North America French, English, and Dutch adventurers also made drawings and water

155

6-1. Laurens Block, *New Amsterdam, 1650.* Courtesy of the New York Historical Society, New York.

colors which were taken back to Europe to inform the Europeans of the new continent.

SEVENTEENTH-CENTURY PAINTING

Laurens Block (dates unknown), a Dutchman, made a sensitive topographical water color (6-1) of New Amsterdam from the ship *Lydia* which was anchored in the harbor. The skill with which the boats in the foreground are silhouetted against the sky, the deft perspective, and the success with which the airy tones of the background recede into the distance indicate that Block was not without training. While the men who made the first sketches of America were in no sense artists of great distinction, they helped to establish a concept in the new world that had been long accepted in the old—that the activities of the artist were normal pursuits of civilized man.

In the seventeenth century, artists came to America in increasing numbers, not only as illustrators to parties of exploration, but as travelers and settlers. None of them were thoroughly trained or gave evidence of great talent, but they catered to the artistic needs of the colonizers, humble though these might be. They painted signs, decorated carriages, documents, and public properties with appropriate insignia, and painted likenesses. Many of the portrait painters appear to have moved from town to town to paint important personages and their families, probably carrying on most of this activity during the winter when cold weather made it impossible to work outdoors.

Few seventeenth-century portraits have come down to us except from New England and the New Netherlands, and consequently a discussion of seventeenth-century painting is confined to the areas around Boston and New York.

6-2. The Gibbs limner, *Margaret Gibbs*, 1670. Worcester Art Museum, Worcester, Mass.

The Limners

Little is known of the men who painted the earliest portraits in the Boston area but there are numerous references in the literature, letters, and documents of the day to the activities of "limners," as portrait painters were then called. The names of most of the limners are unknown; they are identified by the personages they painted, as the Davenport limner, the John Freake limner, the limner of the Mason children and the limner of the Gibbs children. The portrait of Margaret Gibbs (6-2) by the limner of the Gibbs children is both sensitive and stylistically typical and reveals characteristics that are common to a number of seventeenth-century portraits. The three Gibbs children, Margaret, Henry, and Robert, were all painted in the same manner by what was undoubtedly the same artist, and the two handsome portraits of members of the Freake family, *John Freake* and *Mrs. Elizabeth Freake and Baby Mary* are also similar in manner. It seems most likely that the Gibbs limner and the Freake limner are one and the same. In all of these portraits the poses reveal a full three-quarter face with the figure standing stiffly, as Margaret Gibbs stands here, with no body movement or foreshortening in the arms or body position. The backgrounds are dark and unbroken except for the occasional suggestion of a drapery and the bold tile patterns which establish the plane of the floor. The faces are similar in all of the paintings, small-featured with an almost heart-shaped fullness of cheek and smallness of chin. The modeling of the form is slight, yet though only enough contrast of light and dark is used to make the forms of face and body convincing, a grave, reverent, and poetic feeling for the wistful charm of the child is projected with surprising force. The details of costume, ribbons, lace, embroidery, bows, beads, and fan, as well as the treatment of the elaborate hairdo with its loops and curls, all reveal the same sensitive artist at work, an artist who delights in refinements of shape and decorative involutions of line. The limner who painted Margaret Gibbs, though limited in conventional skills when compared to the European masters of his day, was deeply poetic and able to project his sentiments and refined feeling for pattern and color into his work.

A portrait of Ann Pollard (6-3) reveals a very different talent. In the early eighteenth century, an unknown limner painted her as she approached the hundred-year mark. The sense of character and age is conveyed with direct force. Her sober and pious expression is established by strongly modeled forms executed with firmness and energy. The dark and light patterns animate the space of the composition with sufficient conviction so that awkwardnesses of drawing are overpowered by the vigorously painted shapes of face, hands, and costume. The limner who painted Ann Pollard may well have been acquainted with the work of some of the Dutch painters of his day, since the dark background and the sculptural modeling of the forms appear closer to the Dutch tradition of portraiture than to the English Tudor tradition.

To the limited degree that the work of the seventeenth-century limners was rooted in a tradition, it was based on a style of painting that had flourished in England through the Tudor period, coming to its full development during the reign of Queen Elizabeth. This style which lingered on in the rural areas of England and was still practiced by innumerable country painters in their painstaking portraits of country squires and their families, was essentially flat and linear. The sitter was painted in a full flow of light with only enough shadow modeling the edges of the form to establish a convincing sense of solidity. The sitter is usually seated full face to the front or in a three-quarter view, and the figure fills most of the area of the picture. There is little action in the pose and a minimum of background accessories. Details of costume are carefully and elaborately delineated, but no ideal of courtly elegance or sentiment softens the uncompromising observation of features and expressions. Colors tend to be pale and clear, the artist only attempting to render what he saw before him.

6-3 (*left*). *Ann Pollard, 1721*. Massachusetts Historical Society, Boston. 6-4 (*right*). *Thomas Smith, Maria Catherine Smith c. 1690*. Worcester Art Museum, Worcester, Mass.

By the end of the seventeenth century, in the court circles of England, this linear and detailed style of painting had been replaced by the suave and highly refined baroque tradition of painting practiced by Van Dyck and the artists who followed him. In this later style, broad masses of light and shadow reveal and envelop the sitter who is posed in deep space. Poses were casual and graceful; elaborate landscape and architectural settings as well as details of furniture and draperies created an atmosphere of elegance. An all-pervasive color harmony related the sitter, the background, and the details into a harmonious whole. Lastly, the application of the paint was dexterous and painterly, with skillful brush work and interesting variations of the density of the paint contributing an expressive variety to the painted surface.

Few of the painters working in seventeenth-century America revealed a familiarity with this tradition of court painting, and had they been competent to practice it, the populace at large would probably not have been sympathetic to a style which to them might symbolize an ideal of display, affectation, and sybaritic indulgence that was in conflict with their puritan ideals. One seventeenth-century painter, however, has left a few portraits which appear to have been influenced by this fully developed baroque tradition. Captain Thomas Smith (dates unknown), sailor and painter by profession, came to America from Bermuda, obtained a few portrait commissions, and left a portrait of himself and one of his daughter.

An increased sophistication of the artist's taste is reflected in the portrait of Maria Catherine Smith (6-4). Smith employed a number of devices that suggest a degree of familiarity with the tradition of the English court painters. The background is not a solid dark; but has a movement of tone so that one sees the figure as light against a dark background on the right side and as dark against a light background on the left. The costume and hair are painted with the rich swirling movements and the freely applied brush strokes of the baroque style, and there is a feeling of movement in the flowing draperies of the costume. There is also a suggestion of voluptuousness and physical beauty in the full features and the low neckline that is more akin to the worldly attitudes of the Restoration court than to the Puritan morality of the colonies.

The Dutch Tradition

A portrait of the artist's wife by Gerret Duyckinck (6-5) reveals the nature of the Dutch tradition from which the painters of New Amsterdam drew their sustenance. Evert Duyckinck, father of Gerret, came to New Amsterdam from Holland in 1638 and practiced the crafts of limner, painter, glazier, and glass manufacturer. His painting activities covered a wide variety of assignments, from signs, coats of arms on fire buckets and coaches, to portraits. Gerret (c. 1660-c. 1710) continued with his father's various activities. The portrait of the artist's wife reveals the plastic, three-dimensional emphasis of the Dutch tradition in New Amsterdam, as contrasted to the linear character of painting in New England. The circular movement of the shoulders in space, the relationship between the hands, the turn of the head, and the swirl of the draperies all indicate an awareness of volume and space. The modeling of the head and hands also suggests a systematic use of light, shadow, and reflected light that denotes a working knowledge of the space and form concepts of the mature seventeenth-century tradition in Holland. Like most portraits of Dutch burghers, the characterization is sober and factual. The artist had no desire to glorify or idealize his sitter but rather placed his emphasis on an honest presentation of appearances. Technical inadequacies, more apparent when an artist is attempting to work in the mature baroque manner rather than in the naive and linear style of the typical limner, kept Duyckinck from fully realizing his ambition. The foreshortening of the far eye is awkward, the hands are stiff, and the arm resting on the table is poorly related to the rest of the figure.

Inventories of the homes of the Dutch settlers indicate that they

6-5. Gerret Duyckinck, *Artist's Wife,*
late 17th century. Courtesy of The
New York Historical Society, New
York.

had a more developed taste for paintings than the English. A wide variety
of paintings were imported, but like the English, the local Dutch restricted their patronage to the commissioning of portraits. Hendrick
Couturier (died 1684), who moved to New Amsterdam from Holland in
1661, was recorded as a painter in the Leyden guild of painters, which
probably makes him the first professional painter to practice portraiture
in America. He obtained his burgher's rights in New Amsterdam by painting a portrait of Governor Peter Stuyvesant. Though it cannot be identified with absolute certainty as the portrait painted by Hendrick Couturier,
the portrait of Governor Stuyvesant (6-6), is by a trained artist familiar
with the tradition of Dutch portraiture. The drawing is accurate, the
compositional arrangement of the figure in the oval canvas is easy, the
value relationships bold and certain, and the paint is applied dexterously
and without pedantic fussing. Couturier moved from New Amsterdam
after a few years and became a trader and public official in a small Dutch
settlement on the Delaware River; consequently his career as an artist
was short-lived.

Not all of the painting produced among the Dutch settlers was in
the full-blown baroque tradition. In the Hudson River Valley between
Albany and New Amsterdam a group of forceful, naive portraits of Dutch
planters, burghers, and their wives and daughters was produced in the
late seventeenth and early eighteenth centuries. The painters of these
portraits, unlike those of New Amsterdam, show little interest in space
and form but painted with clearly defined patterns which are broad in

6-6 (*left*). Hendrick Couturier (?), *Governor Stuyvesant*, 1660's. Courtesy of the New York Historical Society, New York. 6-7 (*right*). *Girl with the Red Shoes*, c. 1729. The Henry Francis du Pont Winterthur Museum, Winterthur, Del.

conception, bold in execution, and often achieve a vigorous definition of character approaching caricature. In relative isolation, these painters appear to have developed a self-trained, native school out of an artisan tradition of decorative craftsmanship deeply rooted in the Dutch folk culture. *Girl with the Red Shoes* (6-7) as the popular portrait of Magdalena Douw is usually called, is a most charming work of the early eighteenth century. The color is clear and fresh and the shapes are animated and composed with an innate feeling for harmonious relationships of line and pattern. The relatively untrained and unknown author of the work accepted the baroque tradition of a richly costumed figure standing before a background of handsome architectural and landscape forms and translated this into the local idiom of flat patterns. The result is a most charming decorative painting—sprightly, fresh, and vivacious—that reflects the unpretentious but confident taste of this flourishing folk culture.

EIGHTEENTH-CENTURY PAINTING

The seventeenth century witnessed America's first attempts at painting; the eighteenth century saw the creation of an American school. By

6-8 *(left)*. Jeremiah Theus, *Isaac Motte* (?), *c.* 1740. National Gallery of Art, Washington, D.C., Mellon Collection.   6-9 *(right)*. Charles Bridges, *Maria Taylor Byrd*, *c.* 1735. Courtesy Metropolitan Museum of Art, Fletcher Fund, 1925.

the time of the Revolution a number of both foreign and native-born artists were at work in the principal colonial cities. Certain characteristics, a general simplicity of effect, a preference for fact over flights of fancy, and an emphasis on earnestness rather than style, permeate much of the painting done in America during the years immediately preceding the Revolution, giving it a common flavor of sufficient distinction to constitute an American school.

These distinctive characteristics did not result from any conscious sentiment on the part of the artists but rather were the inevitable result of the isolated colonial situation, the limited facilities that existed here for training artists, and the absence of major works of art which could serve as a guide to aspiring students of painting.

This absence of expert practitioners, schools, and works of art had both a positive and a negative aspect. The negative aspects are obvious. However, isolation also had its positive values. Copley, the most important painter of the colonial age, reveals the strength developed by isolation. His clear and objective vision of human character and his strong tactile sense might never had emerged had he spent his formative years learning the conventions of the eighteenth-century academies of Europe. The artist's vision of life established during his formative years was not limited

6-10. John Smibert, *Bishop Berkeley and His Family*, 1729. Yale University Art Gallery, New Haven, Conn.

by tradition and established conventions, <u>so while the artist frequently saw more naively, he occasionally saw more clearly, or at least saw aspects of reality that might be obscured by the dominating convention of his day</u>.

Imported Talents

Enough wealth had been accumulated by the eighteenth-century colonial planters, merchants, and professional men to attract the attention of ambitious or restless painters from Europe who had not achieved sufficient success in their homeland to satisfy them. No one of them was a major artist, and many of them were hardly more than amateurs. But they did bring some skill and knowledge with them which they passed on to the local practitioners, thereby making it possible for artists like Feke and Copley to develop without leaving the shores of America.

Of the many artists who came over before the middle of the century, only a few left enough identified paintings so that one can determine the nature of their work and influence. Jeremiah Theus (1719-1774), a Swiss, arrived in Charleston, South Carolina, in 1739, and spent the re-

6-11. Gustavus Hesselius, *Lapowinsa*, 1735. Historical Society of Pennsylvania, Philadelphia.

maining thirty-five years of his life doing somewhat decorative, vigorously painted portraits (6-8) of the people of that area. These portraits are not notable either as character studies or as incisive likenesses, but they are vigorously, if somewhat crudely, painted. Unlike the earlier limners, Theus employed the strongly massed lights and shadows, the richer colors, and the bold brushwork of the fully developed baroque court style. He helped popularize the gaily colored decorative portrait that was fashionable in eighteenth-century Europe and which contributed greatly to the decor of the interior.

In mid-century Charles Bridges (*fl.* 1730-1750) came to Virginia and spent some time painting planters and their families before he returned to England. Bridges handled the portrait formula of the eighteenth century with more refinement and assurance than Theus. His portrait of Maria Taylor Byrd (6-9) is firm in drawing, easy in movement, and has a poised elegance that suggests an artist of taste as well as skill. Peter Pelham (1695?-1751) is also worthy of mention. He was an English engraver, settled in Boston, who made mezzotint engravings (6-24) and taught drawing. He married Copley's mother.

The two painters who had the greatest influence on the emerging American school in the first half of the eighteenth century were John Smibert (1688-1751) and Gustavus Hesselius (1682-1775). John Smibert was born in Scotland and trained in Italy. He became Boston's leading

6-12. William Johnston (attributed to), *Thomas Mumford V*, 1776. In the Brooklyn Museum Collection, Brooklyn, N. Y.

portrait artist in those formative years. Gustavus Hesselius, a Swede, did the same for Philadelphia.

The most complex and ambitious painting of Smibert's that has come down to us is the large group portrait, *Bishop Berkeley and His Family* (6-10), frequently referred to as the *Bermuda Group* since both Smibert and Bishop Berkeley were in Newport, Rhode Island, en route to Bermuda when the portrait was executed. The composition, involved and carefully considered, indicates a rather thorough knowledge of the compositional concepts of the early eighteenth century. The figures on each side establish dignified vertical lines which are repeated in the shadowy colonnade in the background. The table top provides a stabilizing horizontal base for the central pyramidal group that constitutes the main mass of the picture. The eye enters the space of the painting through the flowing line of draperies on the lower left and moves up and back into the main pyramidal mass of the seated figures to the standing figures in the rear right. The gestures of hands, the directions of eye movements, and the rhythmic masses of draperies establish an arabesque of lines which animate the space of the picture. Well-rendered surface textures, rich color, and the effective dark and light pattern all attest to Smibert's competence. But his limitations are also evident. While the likenesses have a degree of differentiation, they do not communicate a strong sense of character; one senses an air of artifice dominating the gestures rather than an interplay of personalities. The application of paint is monotonous, careful finish substituting for spirited execution. It is a carefully planned and thoughtful piece of work, not a great group portrait but certainly the most complex and competent painting produced in America up to that time. Smibert was not only influential as a portrait painter but his copies of the Italian masters introduced Bostonians to the works of certain Renaissance painters.

Gustavus Hesselius played a similar role in Philadelphia. Coming to America from Sweden, he too practiced a competent kind of portraiture and also painted some classical allegories and other grand subjects. Like Smibert, as time passed, his style became less elaborate and courtly and more concerned with the realities of life in America. His portrait of Lapowinsa (6-11), one of the earliest paintings of an Indian subject, is distinguished by its searching truthfulness. No baroque glorification of the savage chieftain appears here. Instead the furrowed questioning face reveals the artist's interest in humans, not as symbols of elegance or power and glory, but rather as individuals. This concern with the individual as a unique personality rather than as a symbol of a social group became one of the chief characteristics of the American school of portrait paintings. Hesselius also painted elaborate mythological allegories which represent the first attempt in America to enlarge the scope of painting beyond factual statement. Later in the century John Hesselius (1728-1778), the son of Gustavus, followed his father's career as a portrait painter in Philadelphia.

Native Painters

The paintings by native artists from the early part of the eighteenth century echo those of the men who came from Europe. Joseph Badger (1708-1765) carried on as the principal portrait painter of Boston after the death of Smibert. One senses the deficiencies of these untrained but ambitious painters when one studies the portrait of Thomas Mumford V (6-12) painted by the American-born William Johnston (1732-1777) in the middle of the century. Johnston attempted a standard pose of a gentleman seated at his writing table, a pose that Copley was to handle with assurance and success a few years later. Johnston could neither foreshorten the legs and arms nor draw the hands fluently. The uniformly sharp edges of the forms destroy the sense of space, and the flat areas of color create an airless vacuum. Yet despite these limitations, a rather vivid sense of personality and appearance is conveyed. Johnson had none of the flourish of European trained painters, but one knows his characters

6-13. John Greenwood, *Sea Captains Carousing in Surinam*, 1757-1758. City Art Museum, St. Louis, Mo.

much more thoroughly than one knows the men and women portrayed by Theus or Bridges.

Another young Boston painter whose work is characterful and energetic despite its technical limitations is John Greenwood (1727-1792). Greenwood has left some portraits but the most original and interesting of his works are his satirical genre paintings. His *Sea Captains Carousing in Surinam* (6-13), a delightful piece of picaresque realism quite unlike the staid and proper pictures that have come down to us from colonial times, is undoubtedly the first genre painting done by an American.

Robert Feke

The most talented and fully realized talent to appear in America during the first half of the eighteenth century was that of Robert Feke (1705-1752, or 1767). This enigmatic figure, of whom little is known, produced his paintings in a limited period between 1741 and 1750 working largely in the cities of Boston, Newport, and also Philadelphia. Because of the assurance and taste with which he handled the baroque ideals of dignity and elegance, his paintings seem to summarize the aims of his time. His earliest work, *Sir Isaac Royall and Family* (6-14) is very similar to Smibert's *Bishop Berkeley and His Family* in conception and was undoubtedly influenced by it. Feke's lack of experience is evident. The faces are not strongly differentiated and the grouping lacks both

6-14. Robert Feke, *Sir Isaac Royall and Family,* 1741. Harvard University Law School Collection, Cambridge, Mass. Frick Art Reference Library photograph.

variety and a sense of interaction between the five sitters. The body of the baby is stiff and unconvincing in anatomy and proportion. But despite its awkward areas the painting has the air of poetry and grace that always distinguishes Feke's work. Each sitter painted by Feke seems to be endowed with the artist's personal concept of gracious dignity. Each painting radiates a serene and elevated mood. An innate painter's sense also keeps his pigments from being dead. The brush work is expressive, the paint flickers, and surfaces appear luminous. The colors are richly and harmoniously related. Somehow this artist, painting in America far from the schools of Italy and handicapped by a lack of knowledge and training, still could imbue everything he did with a dignified taste and impeccable painterly sense denied many a student of the academies.

The late *Self-portrait* (6-15) most fully reveals Feke's sensitivity as an artist. The intelligent face is made vivid and alive by a detailed treatment of the illuminated area, while the quiet simplification of the shadow plane provides relief and keeps the total effect from being factual and hard. The broad simplifications of form in the costume and in the

6-15. Robert Feke, *Self-portrait*, 1749-1750. Rhode Island Historical Society, Providence, R. I.

hand and the subtle diagonal movement created by the edge of the canvas on which the artist is at work indicate Feke's native artistry and his maturity of taste. The easy and broad application of paint reveals surprising skill. This portrait is indeed masterly in its restrained elegance and its power to suggest character, form, and space through airy and unlabored brushwork.

The Rococo

In the last half of the century the rococo style which was the dominant mode in the courts of France and England was imported into America. Joseph Blackburn (*c.* 1700-*c.* 1765) and John Wollaston (*fl.* 1750-1767) were the two men who played the most important role in popularizing the rococo style of portraiture in America. Joseph Blackburn arrived in Boston in 1753 and painted in the colonies for twenty years. John Wollaston arrived in New York in 1749. He too lived here for almost two decades and painted in most of the principal cities.

In *The Winslow Family* (6-16) Blackburn displays his facility in rendering the satiny surfaces of textiles and in endowing his sitters with an airy grace reminiscent of French court portraits. Wollaston painted with heavier brush strokes and larger simpler masses of color (6-17). A comparison of Blackburn's *Winslow Family* with Feke's *Sir Isaac Royall*

6-16. Joseph Blackburn, *The Winslow Family*, 1757. Museum of Fine Arts, Boston.

and Family reveals the change of emphasis that accompanied the rococo. Many devices were used to achieve the desired air of elegance: which was the ideal of the rococo painter. Poses were more animated, at times becoming frankly artificial and whimsical as can be seen in the little girl holding a skirt full of fruit. Much emphasis was put on the sheen of fine materials—on the undulations of ribbons, laces, and fluttering draperies. Such stabilizing compositional elements as the horizontal table top that plays such an important role in the Isaac Royall family portrait were eliminated in rococo portraits. Instead of stressing elements that contributed to compositional monumentality, the rococo painter emphasized curvilinear elements and sinuous line movements which produce grace and movement. Colors tended to be lighter: pale rose, turquoise blues, and clear yellows replaced the strong reds, blues, and golds of the baroque.

The influence of Wollaston on other American painters can be observed in the work of John Hesselius, the son of Gustavus. His paintings can hardly be distinguished from those of Wollaston; his *Portrait of Mrs. Richard Galloway, Jr.* (6-18) shows the same richly massed tonalities

6-17 (*left*). John Wollaston, *Mrs. Samuel Gouverneur, c.* 1750. The Henry
Francis du Pont Winterthur Museum, Winterthur, Del. 6-18 (*right*). John
Hesselius, *Mrs. Richard Galloway, Jr.,* 1764. Courtesy Metropolitan Museum
of Art, Maria De Witt Jesup Fund, 1922.

and solidly painted satins. In this portrait, however, the treatment of
the face indicates that John Hesselius, like his father, was more interested
in the character of his subject than was Wollaston, whose idealizations
frequently obliterate the individuality of the sitter.

William Williams (*c.* 1710-*c.* 1790) and John Durand (died *c.* 1820)
also reflect the influence of the rococo in the central colonies in mid-eighteenth century. William Williams followed the rococo conventions when he
painted his *Husband and Wife in a Landscape* (6-19). The handsomely
dressed couple are pictured strolling in the parklike setting of their estate.
The foreground is framed by a waterfall and a leafy bower. Though the
forms are delineated too sharply to create the mood of misty revery typical
of the rococo outdoor portrait and though the faces are too specific to
convey the rococo ideal, there is no question but that Williams's intention
was to portray his beautifully dressed couple *à la* Gainsborough. John
Durand, of Huguenot extraction, like most untrained painters, was unable
to envelop his sitters in the airy spaciousness so essential to the rococo
mood, but his gracious gestures, smiling faces, and splendid costumes
helped him to approximate his ideal.

Blackburn's influence in New England, particularly around Boston,
was comparable to that of Wollaston around Philadelphia. Blackburn

6-19. William Williams, *Husband and Wife in a Landscape*, 1775. The Henry Francis du Pont Winterthur Museum, Winterthur, Del.

came to Boston just when young Copley was first learning to paint and provided stimulation and example for the young man out of all proportion to his own power as an artist.

John Singleton Copley

In the years between 1760 and 1774, John Singleton Copley (1738-1815) created the most eloquent record left to us of colonial life. Copley was born in Boston, and grew up in the household of his artist stepfather, Peter Pelham, in what was an unusual atmosphere for an eighteenth-century Boston boy, surrounded by prints and paintings. This undoubtedly helped him to discover his vocation. Before he saw Blackburn's paintings, he had studied Smibert's portraits and copies of the old masters, and he had absorbed certain skills from the work of his stepfather as well as from Badger and Feke. From Blackburn he discovered how to make his color alive and his surface textures flash. In some of the work he painted immediately after being introduced to Blackburn's style he imitated the elegant artifice of the rococo style. As he matured, he moved away from the artificial and mannered aspects of the rococo and retained only those elements which suited his particular temperament. These were the use of vigorous rhythms, the strong sense of surface texture, and the practice established by the eighteenth-century French painters of portraying a subject in the setting of daily life.

In 1766 Copley, then twenty-eight years old, sent the portrait entitled *Boy with a Squirrel* (6-20) to an exhibition in London and asked Sir Joshua Reynolds and Benjamin West for criticism. Both men found the painting admirable and suggested that the author of the painting would gain greatly from study in Europe if it could be received before he was too old to profit from it. Reynolds found the painting a little hard, detailed, and meticulous, and consequently wanting in "atmosphere." If the mature baroque tradition is taken as an ideal, the criticism is justified, but the hard, meticulous realism of Copley's style constitutes strength as well as a weakness. This portrait displays the characteristics of Copley's mature style. The sitter is posed in a natural way, carrying on a normal activity in a familiar setting, and all the parts of the painting work together to communicate the character of the sitter and the mood of the moment. Copley seldom, if ever, painted only a head. He usually included much of the body, and the attitude of the body, the arms, and particularly the hands play an important role in providing a secondary source of insight into the temperament of the sitter. In every portrait by Copley the hands and what they are doing bear study. In *Boy with a Squirrel* the graceful hands, hesitating in their play, act in unison with the abstracted and thoughtful pose of the head, to establish the sense of a gentle and contemplative personality. The surface textures in the painting are triumphs of still-life rendering; the glass, chain, linen, hair, all are recorded with an unerring eye and amazing technical skill.

From a compositional standpoint also, we find Copley's mature style embodied in this painting. The eye moves into the painting at the bottom from a close front plane and carries back through diagonals into the main form which, placed in the mid-distance, turns rhythmically in space. The background closes the space and repeats the rhythms established below with gentle linear and tonal movements. The dark and light scheme is typically simple. The head is the chief center of interest, brilliantly lighted against the dark background, while hands, linen, and flashes of shiny material provide secondary lights. The color is clear, without being

6-20. John Singleton Copley, *Boy with a Squirrel*, c. 1765. Anonymous loan to the Museum of Fine Arts, Boston.

too sharp, and a greater range of hues is used than characterizes most of the American painters of that day. The entire painting is conceived and executed with astonishing consistency and technical brillance, and the level of maturity is doubly impressive when one remembers the scant opportunities for observation and training that existed in Boston at that time.

While the *Boy with a Squirrel* foreshadows Copley's mature style, his full power is not apparent. The characterization is satisfying, but not forceful; the very youth of the sitter mitigates against a powerful presentation of character. In the portrait of Mrs. Thomas Boylston (6-21) we see Copley displaying his powers at their fullest. The skill and subtlety of the linear, tonal, and spatial elements of the composition strike the observer immediately. The graceful interplay of rhythmic lines in the skirt, arms, body, and background draperies, the skillful increase in the boldness of contrasts as one approaches the focal points of the painting which come to a crescendo of lights and darks around the head, the forceful way in which the placement of the head dominates the entire painting while the hands become secondary accents despite the glitter of satin and the flourish of linen kerchief, all these factors are handled with amazing assurance and control. Each surface is painted with consummate skill so that an authoritative tactile quality is established throughout. The color is rich and fine.

But above and beyond Copley the craftsman with his skill, knowl-

6-21. John Singleton Copley, *Mrs. Thomas Boylston, 1766.* Fogg Art Museum, Cambridge, Mass.

edge, and control stands Copley the artist with his ability to perceive the character of the sitter and make it come alive. In the final analysis this is the source of Copley's greatness. Mrs. Boylston looks out of the painting and past us with quiet self-assurance and determination, kindly, patient, but with that core of firmness that must have been necessary for coping efficiently with the problems of colonial life. The face appears slightly isolated, not compositionally, but in spirit, from the elegance of the clothes, the furniture, and the sumptuous background, for the artist's New England morality inevitably made him more interested in the character of his sitter than in the sensuous beauty of the materials that surrounded her.

Copley spent the last half of his life in England where his efforts were rewarded handsomely. In London he continued to paint portraits but enlarged his repertoire to include the enormous historical genre paintings which constituted the chief basis of his fame abroad. The first important painting in this category which he exhibited in England was *Brook Watson and the Shark* (6-22), illustrating an incident in Havana Harbor. Brook Watson himself commissioned Copley to portray the event. The great historical canvases which established Copley's success in England had an important influence on historical painting in America during the early years of the young republic.

6-22. John Singleton Copley, *Brooks Watson and the Shark*, 1778. Museum of Fine Arts, Boston.

Copley was one of the many American artists to go abroad for study during the last of the eighteenth century. Almost every artist felt the need to take advantage of the superior facilities for training that existed on the continent, and an extended period of study abroad came to be considered a necessity. Copley commenced this exodus of art students to Europe. Benjamin West, Matthew Pratt, Charles Willson Peale, Gilbert Stuart, Ralph Earl, John Trumbull, and all the other major painters of the following period continued it. They succeeded in bringing the standard of American painting up to the general level of practice in Europe. This increase in technical excellence and refinement of taste was not accomplished without exacting its price. Something of the archaic strength of Copley's greatest works disappeared from American painting and did not reappear until almost the middle of the following century when artists like Cole painted the American landscape and artists like Bingham the folkways with the same freshness and assurance with which Copley had portrayed his sitters.

6-23. Paul Revere, *The Bloody Massacre*, engraving, 1770. Courtesy Metropolitan Museum of Art, Gift of Mrs. Russell Sage,1910.

PRINTS

A variety of prints and engravings appeared in the period before the Revolution. Some of the earliest engravings produced in America were the caricatures and political cartoons used to illustrate the handbills printed and circulated during the tempestuous conflicts which rocked colonial life. The appearance of caricatures, political cartoons, and topical sketches coincided with the development of American journalism, and they have remained vivid and important elements of our national life. The first example of the journalistic print based on a contemporary episode is Paul Revere's *The Bloody Massacre* (6-23). While its crudities are evident, the print manages to communicate both facts and feelings, and it established a precedent for recording the passing scene in a popular pictorial style. With the expansion of journalism in the nineteenth century, the various type of journalistic illustration constituted an increasingly original and lively body of pictorial material.

Peter Pelham had introduced the mezzotint early in the century, and his mezzotint portraits did much to familiarize a wide audience with

6-24. Peter Pelham, *Cotton Mather*, mezzotint. International Business Machines Collection, New York.

the appearances of the colonial leaders. His portrait of Cotton Mather (6-24) is one of his best known and earliest portraits and displays considerable technical facility in this difficult medium. The widespread popularity of such prints is indicative of a growing colonial consciousness of the independent and indigenous nature of colonial culture.

SCULPTURE

Monumental sculpture was not produced in America until after the Revolution, when the desire to commemorate great men, great deeds, and important events created a need for permanent and imposing memorials. However, from very early times wood and stone were carved to enhance buildings, boats, and pieces of furniture and to make signs, gravestones, weathervanes, and toys. Out of these simple crafts developed a rich and original tradition that came to fruition in the nineteenth century both on a folk-art level and in a more formal, learned, and traditional guise.

Just as portraits provided the most frequent opportunity for the painter to practice his craft in seventeenth- and eighteenth-century America, so did gravestones provide the stonecutter with his most frequent sculptural commission. Seventeenth-century gravestones were usually ornamented with motifs which symbolized the vanity of life, the omni-

6-25. Gravestone, 1681.

presence of death, and the glory of salvation. Skeletons with scythes, skulls, and hourglasses are the motifs most frequently encountered, for the puritan consciousness tended to dwell on death rather than life, but fig leaves, vine leaves, peacocks, the sun, moon, and stars were also used to symbolize the forces of good. The more austere symbols dominate the stone; but usually a graceful border of leaves implies that the deceased had achieved a state of grace by laboring in the Lord's vineyard. These few leaves and twining tendrils also provide a touch of decorative grace and reveal that our puritan forefathers had some feeling for the redeeming role of beauty in this harsh world.

An unusually rich carved gravestone (6-25) marked the burial place of John Foster, Bostonian painter, engraver, and printer. He probably designed his own gravestone and left its execution to some less imaginative stonecutter. A globe of the world supports the candle which symbolizes Mr. Foster's brief period on this earth. A skeletal death prepares to snuff out the candle, and Father Time, holding an hourglass, is unable to stop death's hand. Above all shines the sun, a symbol of God—benign, timeless, and omnipotent. The arched, rather handsomely shaped stone with its vigorous, but crude relief and its elegant lettering reveals a paradox of ambition, imagination, and inadequate technical skills, a paradox that grew inevitably out of the attempt to transport a rich old-world tradition to distant shores still without many of the craft skills necessary to give full expression to the elaborate social practices that make up tradition.

In the eighteenth century the dour skull and hourglass motif was frequently replaced or accompanied by an attempt at a bas-relief portrait. Crude though these grave portraits appear to be, they evoke a sense

6-26. Simeon Skillin, elder, *Mercury,* wood, *c.* 1750. Boston. Index of American Design, National Gallery of Art, Washington, D.C.

of sober urgency born of the desire to perpetuate an image of the deceased that could outlast time and man and serve to provide a landmark for a soul on some far distant judgment day.

In the eighteenth century almost every costal town had a wood carver who made handsome figureheads and the other carvings that enhanced the ships of that day as well as the Ionic and Corinthian capitals, fluted columns, wreaths, swags, garlands, crests, and other heraldic symbols which decorated the splendid interiors and exteriors of Georgian mansions and public buildings. Simeon Skillin (1716-1778) a famed wood carver of Boston, was such a master craftsman. To his hand has been attributed the wooden figure of Mercury (6-26) which is supposed to have stood before the Boston Post Office during the eighteenth century. This winged messenger has little of the grace of a classic symbol but rather resembles some sturdy New England boy decked out in a few borrowed classical properties.

In the days before shops were distinguished by a special type of architecture, the use of a figure in front of or above the door of a shop was common. In England, the use of figures to identify various kinds of shops

6-27. Figure of a felon, wood, *c.* 1775. East Greenwich, R. I. Index of American Design, National Gallery of Art, Washington, D.C.

was traditional, and this custom was continued in America, where public buildings, inns, and taverns, too, were marked by their special insignia and identifying figures. Sometimes classical, as with Skillin, they were more often picturesque and occasionally amusing. A stocky mariner using a quadrant might mark the shop of the seller of nautical instruments, a cluster of grapes that of a wineseller. These shop signs were painted in bold colors; the painting of sculptural forms remains one of the fundamental characteristics of folk sculpture. A 30-inch-high felon (6-27) identified the Kent County Jail, in East Greenwich, Rhode Island, during the last half of the eighteenth century. The carving is broad, almost crude, the texture of the tool marks revealing the activity of the carver with freshness and force. The face of the handcuffed wretch, with its great pleading eyes and tight lips, communicates in a direct and expressive way the tension under which the sad prisoner is laboring. Such a figure stood as an awesome warning to the lawbreaker, a perpetual reminder of the wisdom of righteous ways.

During the two centuries of colonial existence the painting and sculpture of America began to assume the attributes that were to characterize its maturity. Sculpture did not develop as early or as fully as painting, but much of the wood carving of the eighteenth century has an unpretentious charm that foreshadows the character of sculpture in the next century. Painting achieved a level of technical competence and then proceeded to reflect the fashionable currents of Europe, passing from the detailed and linear fashion of English Tudor to the more robust atmospheric character of the Dutch and English baroque to the animation and decorative splendor of the rococo. But American painting was not identical with that of Europe: it did not attain the power, eloquence, and sophistication of its European models. Instead it reflected the life of the colonial settlers, the way of life of an energetic, thoughtful, middle-class society that was sober, realistic, idealistic, and earnest. The art which appeared in America during these years was an art in which sensibility was balanced by sense, scientific objectivity by idealism, and a broad humanism was reconciled with practicality. These attitudes received their most forceful expression in the work of Copley where the objective approach of the scientist was accompanied by the ardor of the artist.

Architecture, sculpture, furniture and the crafts were infused by this same practical humanism. A Copley painting, a Georgian house, and a fine block-front chest are all of a piece in spirit. Each borrowed elements from a rich old tradition but only selected what could be meaningfully assimilated in the colonial environment. Each achieved a sturdy beauty through a harmonious relationship of necessary parts rather than through elaboration and enrichment. The Revolution interrupted the development of America's cultural life. The turmoil and economic disruption of years of war in a young nation left little time or energy for the arts. In the decade immediately following the Revolution, the country gathered its forces and renewed its energies, and the turn of the century witnessed a new florescence of our national culture. The arts of the young republic which followed the Revolution are our next concern.

SELECTED REFERENCES

for PART II The Arts of the Colonial Period

General References

La Follette, Suzanne, *Art in America*. New York, Harper & Brothers, 1929.
Larkin, Oliver, *Art and Life in America*. New York, Rinehart & Company, Inc., 1949.

Architecture

Andrews, Wayne, *Architecture, Ambition and Americans*. New York, Harper & Brothers, 1955.
Eberlein, Harold and Hubbard, Cortland, *American Georgian Architecture*. Bloomington, Ind., Indiana University Press, 1952.
Garvan, Anthony, *Architecture and Town Planning in Colonial Connecticut*. New Haven, Conn., Yale University Press, 1951.
Kimball, Sidney Fiske, *Mr. Samuel McIntire, Carver, the Architect of Salem*. Portland, Me., Southworth-Anthoensen Press, 1940.
Kubler, George, *The Religious Architecture of New Mexico*. Colorado Springs, Col., Colorado Springs Fine Arts Center, 1940.
Morrison, Hugh, *Early American Architecture*. New York, Oxford University Press, Inc., 1952.
Tallmadge, Thomas, *The Story of Architecture in America*. New York, W. W. Norton & Company, Inc., 1927.
Waterman, Thomas, *Mansions of Virginia, 1706-1776*. Chapel Hill, N. C., University of North Carolina Press, 1951.

Painting

Barker, Virgil, *American Painting*. New York, The Macmillan Company, 1950.
Drepperd, Carl, *American Pioneer Arts and Artists*. Springfield, Mass., Pond Ekberg, 1942.
Eliot, Alexander, *Three Hundred Years of American Painting*. New York, Time, Inc., 1957.
Flexner, James T., *First Flowers of Our Wilderness*. Boston, Houghton Mifflin Company, 1947.
Flexner, James T., *A Short History of American Painting*. Boston, Houghton Mifflin Company, 1950.

Flexner, James T., *John Singleton Copley*. Boston, Houghton Mifflin Company, 1948.

Foote, Henry, *Robert Feke*. Cambridge, Mass., Harvard University Press, 1930.

Hagen, Oskar, *The Birth of the American Tradition in Art*. New York, Charles Scribner's Sons, 1940.

Richardson, E. P., *Painting in America*. New York, Thomas Y. Crowell Company, 1956.

Interiors, Furniture, and Crafts

Aronson, Joseph, *The Encyclopedia of Furniture*. New York, Crown Publishers, Inc., 1938.

Christensen, Erwin O., *The Index of American Design*. New York, The Macmillan Company, 1950.

McKearin, George and Helen S., *200 Years of American Blown Glass*. New York, Crown Publishers, Inc., 1950.

Ormsby, Thomas H., *Early American Furniture Makers*. New York, Archer House, Inc., 1957.

Phillips, John Marshall, *American Silver*. New York, Chanticleer Press, Inc., 1949.

Ramsey, John, *American Potters and Pottery*. Clinton, Mass., Colonial Press, Inc., 1939.

Rogers, Meyric R., *American Interior Design*. New York, W. W. Norton & Company, Inc., 1947.

Winchester, Alice, *The Antiques Book*. New York, A. A. Wynn, Inc., 1950.

PART III

The Young Republic:
1776-1865

7

Architecture:

The Federal Style

and the Greek Revival

THE REVOLUTION ENDED AMERICA'S COLONIAL STATUS
and the dominance of the Colonial Georgian style of architecture. There
was little building in America for more than a decade after the Revolution, and when large-scale construction recommenced, the classic revival,
already well established in Europe, appeared here. The new mode revealed itself in a shift toward greater formality and a new reverence for
Roman, Greek, and High Renaissance precedent. The first phase of the
classic revival, or of neoclassicism (the new classicism) as the movement
is sometimes called, expressed itself largely as an enthusiasm for Roman
tradition. This Roman phase flowered here between 1785 and 1820, the
years during which the Federal government and its institutions became
established, and consequently has been called the Federal style.

The youthful republic of the United States was not a lone admirer
of the Roman style. The change in style of the public buildings of America was part of a change in architectural design that was also occurring

189

7-1 (*above*). Thomas Jefferson, Capitol, 1789. Richmond, Va. Virginia Chamber of Commerce photograph. 7-2 (*below*). Charles Bulfinch, Capitol, 1802. Boston. Library of Congress photograph.

in Europe. In the mid-eighteenth century Pompeii had come to light, and in 1763 systematic excavation was undertaken. The exciting discoveries revealed by the excavations of the dramatically buried city turned many minds again toward Rome. This was a time of political unrest, a time when the conflict between an increasingly powerful bourgeois class, an extravagant and irresponsible aristocracy, and an autocratic church was coming to a head in many countries and particularly in France. The excavations at Pompeii coinciding as they did with the political events reinforced the reawakened interest in the republican institutions of Rome as well as in rational philosophies of classical times. By association, almost by analogy as it were, the Roman style, particularly the columnar Roman style of Pompeii, became the official style of republicanism and of the nineteenth-century republics.

The chief characteristic of the early classic revival was, as the name implies, the attempt to duplicate Roman buildings. When this was not possible, elements from these buildings were used as "properly as possible," which meant, for the most part, as their use had been formulated by Palladio. Palladio, sixteenth-century Italy's great student of Roman architecture, had standardized the High Renaissance concept of Roman practice by establishing set proportions for the classic orders and setting down rules as to how they should be used. The ensuing baroque style had represented a bold departure from the academic Renaissance tradition. The eighteenth-century classic revival designers, when they did not go directly to ancient prototypes, again adhered rigidly to Renaissance formulations, and domes, vaults, arches, columns, and other elements of the Roman style were used in what was believed to be a correct duplication of ancient forms.

At the turn of the century, Greece was rediscovered and by the third decade of the century the second phase of the classic revival, the Greek revival, was at its height. The Greek temple then provided the pattern for architectural propriety, particularly the Doric or Ionic temple with a pedimented portico. All the elements of the Greek temple were duplicated to the degree that it was possible to reconcile them to nineteenth-century building needs. Since Greek temples were one-story buildings, every attempt was made to make buildings appear only one story high, albeit a rather tall one story. Greek temples had no windows, so windows were hidden or made as inconspicuous as possible. Greek temples were thought to have been of white marble, so many buildings were finished to look like white stone irrespective of their material. By 1840 the classic revival had passed its zenith but it left its permanent imprint on American architecture during the nation's formative years.

7-3. McComb and Mangin, City Hall (aquatint), 1803-1812. New York City.
J. Clarence Davies Collection, Museum of the City of New York, New York.

Before mid-century the Gothic revival, to be followed by a succession
of other revivals, was well under way.

As soon as the Revolutionary War was over and the reconstruction of
the exhausted nation had commenced, America faced the problems of
forging the new political institutions made necessary by its status as an
independent power. As state governments and in time a Federal government were brought into being, and as the various administrative agencies,
bureaus, and commissions necessary for government were formed, a pressing need developed for buildings to house them. The triumphant and
energetic nation wanted government buildings also to serve as monuments that would proclaim the pride, vigor, and independent status of
the new democracy and embody its ideals of freedom in concrete form.
By way of introduction to the Federal style, let us look at some of the
notable public buildings constructed during these years.

In 1785, at the request of the governor of Virginia, Thomas Jefferson,
who was traveling in France, drew up plans for a state capitol based on
the Maison Carrée, an old Roman temple in Nîmes. The Capitol in
Richmond (7-1) was completed in 1789, the first of a long succession of
buildings to abandon eighteenth-century models and to follow the pattern

7-4. Charles Pierre L'Enfant, plan for Washington, D.C., *c.* 1792. Library of Congress photograph.

of ancient Rome. In 1795 the architect Charles Bulfinch (1763-1844) laid the cornerstone for a new capitol building in Boston (7-2) which, completed by 1802, provided a handsome and monumental setting for the lawmakers of Massachusetts. A great dome, a colonnaded portico, arched arcades and windows proclaimed the glory of the young state. Again the borrowing was from Rome, but this time via English practice. Other states followed suit, and the spaciousness of the new capitol buildings and the rivalry as to the size of the domes and the length of the colonnades bore witness to the ambition and energy of the growing nation.

City halls of equally impressive design and scale were built in continuously increasing numbers after the turn of the century. In 1803 Joseph Mangin, a French architect, working with John McComb, began the construction of a city hall for New York (7-3). In its formal elegance it reflected the French background of the designer, as well as the desire of the young metropolis for a municipal hall as impressive as any of the great palaces or public buildings of the sister republic France.

Washington, D.C.—the Capitol

As the concept of a powerful Federal government evolved in the last decade of the eighteenth century, plans for the capital city of the nation and the new buildings for it took form. Under the general direction of George Washington and later Thomas Jefferson, a swampy site beside the Potomac River was selected, and the French military engineer, Major Pierre Charles L'Enfant (1754-1825), was commissioned to lay out the plans for the national capital.

7-5. United States Capitol. Washington, D.C. Library of Congress photograph.

L'Enfant's conception was a magnificent one, so grand in scale that only in the mid-twentieth century has the city of Washington, D.C., outgrown its original spacious plan (7-4). L'Enfant envisioned a series of broad avenues radiating from the Capitol, the White House, and other focal centers. This pattern of radial avenues was laid over a more typically American gridiron arrangement of parallel streets and rectangular blocks which ran north and south. As the modern city took form, the daring and breadth of L'Enfant's conception became evident. He had achieved the almost impossible feat of combining Versailles and the practical American city by superimposing radial avenues devised to provide glorious views of a palace over a gridiron of regular streets. The pattern resulting from this plan created the picturesque and irregular block shapes and building sites that characterized the charming older cities of Europe and at the same time introduced the regularity of arrangement that made American cities efficient and orderly. In addition, the points at which the broad avenues converged on one another formed open squares or circles suitable as sites for monumental sculptural groups while the intersections of the radial avenues with the parallel streets created open triangles of grass or park. L'Enfant's hope that at least half of the area of the city would be devoted to spacious streets, avenues, and parks has been maintained despite the repeated assaults of real-estate speculators and shortsighted engineers and builders.

The story of the Capitol (7-5) reveals the problems that were faced by the young republic in attempting to translate grand aspirations into concrete achievements. The design selected as the winner in a competi-

7-6. Benjamin Latrobe, corncob capital, U. S. Capitol, c. 1808. Museum of Modern Art photograph.

tion for the building was by Dr. William Thornton, an English gentleman born in the West Indies and by profession a physician rather than an architect.

Thornton's plan called for a central structure including a dome, not so high as the present one, flanked on each side by balancing wings. This basic concept has been adhered to despite subsequent additions and changes. The cornerstone for the original Capitol was laid in 1793 by President Washington. This building stood until 1814 when the two wings were gutted by a fire started by the British troops during the War of 1812. After the fire the building was reconstructed under the direction of Benjamin Latrobe, who had worked on the capitol building before the fire, and later Charles Bulfinch. Bulfinch did not contribute materially to the new structure, but Latrobe redesigned the portico on the eastern façade, added the domed roof and cupolas that can be seen topping each of the wings, and also redesigned the major interior chambers. Perhaps Latrobe's most popular innovations were the capitals of columns featuring ears of corn, tobacco, and other native plants which he designed for the Senate wing in an effort to create an indigenous classical column (7-6). Much to Latrobe's chagrin, the so-called "corncob capital" received more attention and approbation than many of his major architectural concepts.

By mid-century, the nation had outgrown its Capitol, and in 1851, Thomas Ustick Walter was commissioned to enlarge the building. He designed the present dome, which rises to a height of 268 feet, and also planned the two flanking wings. These two additions were completed by 1865. The new wings are of white Massachusetts marble, while the older central portion is of Virginia sandstone painted white. The grand structure, conceived by a number of America's best nineteenth-century architects and executed over a period of almost seventy years, expresses the architectural aspirations of the young nation—the desire to create a significant monument which would express the cultural aspirations and the political independence of the young democracy. To achieve this the United States in accordance with the fashion of the day had employed the architectural forms of ancient Rome—the forms through which Rome had proclaimed her power and grandeur.

The architecture of early America can best be discussed in terms of four geographic areas—the Middle States, New England, New York, and the South. The first area to be studied centers around Washington and Philadelphia. Both the Federal style and the later Greek revival flourished here. Thomas Jefferson and Benjamin Latrobe were the dominant figures, followed by Latrobe's two pupils, Robert Mills and William Strickland. The second area, New England, centering around Boston, adhered more closely to the eighteenth-century American and English traditions and achieved its most noteworthy architecture in the work of Charles Bulfinch, Samuel McIntire, and Asher Benjamin. The area around New York City seems to have been less dominated by individual personalities, but distinguished designs were produced by Mangin and Mc-Comb, who designed the previously mentioned City Hall, the firm of Town and Davis, and Minard Lafever. In the South, in the extensive coastal areas bordering the Atlantic and the Gulf of Mexico, and during the early years of the nineteenth century in the lower Mississippi Valley, the Greek revival style appeared in some unique and interesting local forms.

THE CENTRAL STATES

Thomas Jefferson and the Federal Style

The first and certainly a chief exponent in America of the new way of building was Thomas Jefferson (1743-1826). Jefferson was the product of an eighteenth-century classical education and the colonial environment. The result was a cultivated gentleman—a scholar interested in gov-

7-7. Thomas Jefferson, Monticello, 1770-1809. Albemarle Co., Va. Virginia Chamber of Commerce photograph.

ernment, philosophy, the arts, and the newly developing sciences, who was also a practical man of action deeply involved in affairs of state. His esteem for the arts is indicated by this epitaph; in it he did not mention having served twice as President of the United States but pointed with pride to having founded the University of Virginia where he planned the buildings to serve as an architectural handbook for builders.

Even before his travels abroad, Jefferson was dissatisfied with traditional colonial architecture. He found even the architecture of Williamsburg a sorry mess and bemoaned the "barbarous ornament" and the lack of symmetry and nobility. Too intent in his search for the noble grandeur of the ancient styles to feel the charm of the Colonial Georgian, he based his earliest architectural venture, his home, Monticello (7-7), on Palladian models.

What surprises us most about Monticello, which was constructed between 1770 and 1809, is the freedom with which Jefferson interpreted the Palladian rules and how uninhibited he was by his chaste models. While the projecting colonnaded porch and the low central dome reveal that the Roman temple served as an inspiration, such features as the octagonal projections at the sides show an independent and inventive designer who could admire the elegant restraint of Palladian architecture, retain the dignity and nobility of his models, and yet depart freely from precedent and established plans. Jefferson's inventive and practical turn of mind also found an outlet in many interior details. Here he developed and utilized double doors which worked simultaneously, dumbwaiters, cleverly concealed staircases, and many other novel and useful features.

The Federal style received its first formulation in Monticello. The most evident feature was the use of the projecting portico on the principal façade, colonnaded, capped by a triangular pediment, establishing a one-story effect. The careful proportioning of the classic orders, the maintenance of a rigid bisymmetric arrangement, the use of crowning balustrades, and along with them the elimination of all evidence of the high-pitched roof and irregular gables of early times, and lastly the use of domes on a circular or octagonal drum, all are characteristics of the Federal style apparent in Monticello.

In the capitol building at Richmond (7-1), all architectural elements are subordinated to that most characteristic feature, the imposing portico which formed the façade. Necessity in the form of a lack of skilled workmen forced Jefferson to substitute Ionic columns for the splendid Corinthian columns that ornamented the Maison Carrée, and necessity also demanded the two stories of windows in the main body of the building. But the public eye was distracted from these unauthentic details by the monumental temple façade with its free-standing columns surmounted by a pediment, which appeared here for the first time in modern times and gradually became the symbol of architectural respectability. The Capitol at Richmond was the first public building in this period to be patterned directly after an ancient temple.

The chief source of Jefferson's pride was the University of Virginia. This institution not only provided for Jefferson's ideal of state-supported education, but also served as a text on the Roman style. The chief building, the central library (7-8), is a small-scale replica of the Roman Pantheon. The series of professors' houses symmetrically arranged behind the library represents Jefferson's idea of the finest examples of the various classic orders; one building, for instance, employs the Doric order as used in the Baths of Diocletian, while another demonstrates the way the Ionic order appears in the Theater of Marcellus. Each building features one of the orders as used in a specific ancient prototype.

Equally important to Jefferson was the orderly and logical relationship of the various buildings to one another and the harmonious arrangement of buildings, gardens, and site. The symmetrical arrangement did not inhibit or restrict the plan. The variety in the sizes of the buildings and garden areas, the charm of the vistas, the sensible provisions for access to and from the various buildings, and the charming use of red brick with white stone trim all attest to the ingenuity with which Jeffer-

7-8. Rotunda, University of Virginia, 1822-1826. Charlottesville, Va. Virginia Chamber of Commerce photograph.

son reconciled his classical tastes with American building practices and the practical demands of an American university.

Jefferson's benign influence colored many phases of life in America during the post-Revolutionary period. Of prime importance was the influence he brought to bear by sponsoring certain architects of whose training and taste he approved. Benjamin Latrobe in particular received a number of commissions, both Federal and private, through Jefferson's influence, and Robert Mills and William Strickland prospered under his influence.

Benjamin Latrobe

Benjamin Latrobe (1764-1820) has already been mentioned in relation to the United States Capitol. He was, along with Jefferson, the most important architect practicing in the Philadelphia-Washington area. Latrobe was born in England, trained as an engineer in Germany, and was subsequently apprenticed to one of the first English architects to practice in the classic manner.

Latrobe came to America while still a young man and by 1800 he had settled in Philadelphia and received his first commissions. While he could admire with enthusiasm the "immense size, the bold plan, and arrangements of the buildings of the Romans," he found "their decora-

7-9. Benjamin Latrobe, Baltimore Cathedral, dedicated 1821. Baltimore, Md. Wayne Andrews photograph.

tions and details absurd beyond tolerance from the reign of Severus downward." While Latrobe built effectively in the Roman manner and through his work helped formulate the Federal style, his great love was Greek architecture and more than any other individual he helped launch the Greek revival. "My principles of good taste are rigid in Grecian architecture," he said, but his practice and understandings were less rigid than his taste. He found that "the forms and the distribution of the Roman and Greek buildings which remain are in general inapplicable to the objects and uses of our public buildings." Modern churches, government buildings, and legislative assemblies demanded plans that were very different from those used in ancient times, and certainly the severe winters of the Eastern seaboard necessitated a more protective architecture than the bland Mediterranean climate. Latrobe's greatness lay in his ability to provide plans to serve the needs of the aggressive young democracy and the evolving industrial age, to build the many specialized kinds of buildings demanded by the new society and yet to reconcile his solutions for these practical problems with his love for classic, and particularly Greek, architecture.

7-10. James Hoban, The White House, 1792. Washington, D.C. National Park
Service photograph.

Latrobe's work on the United States Capitol has already been mentioned. It is now difficult to separate Latrobe's contributions to the ·Capi-
tol from what went before and has been added since. While Latrobe is
remembered as the chief protagonist of the classic revival in America,
his own taste was more catholic than his influence. When he prepared
the original plans for his great cathedral in Baltimore (7-9), he submitted a Gothic design along with the Roman one that was accepted.
Two or three other ventures into the Gothic manner indicate that, like
most nineteenth-century architects, he sought through selective eclecticism to achieve a style which would serve the multifaceted diversity of
that dynamic age. The Baltimore Cathedral was the first great classic
revival church to be built in America. While Latrobe employed the
elements of the Roman style, he as usual adapted the ancient forms to
the tastes and needs of his own day and created an original and commanding church building.

The foremost Federal-style mansion of the Washington-Philadelphia
area is, appropriately enough, the White House (7-10). The design selected for the White House in a national competition held in 1792 was
by an Irishman, James Hoban. It was patterned after a Dublin mansion
and adheres to the formal Renaissance concept of the Roman manner.

7-11. Andalusia, 1833. Andalusia, Pa. Wayne Andrews photograph.

The dignity and formality of the main façade results largely from the great Ionic pilasters and free-standing columns which are spaced regularly across the entire façade. The handsome semicircular pavilion adds to the imposing and palatial effect, as do the regular repetition of arched and triangular pediments above the ground-story windows and the continuous balustrade which tops the profile of the buildings with the unbroken horizontal line preferred by the classic revival designers.

The Greek Revival

The Greek revival movement came to its height in the decades between 1820 and 1850, and its most brilliant examples first appeared in the Washington-Philadelphia area. By 1830 the Greek façade dominated the architectural world. Just as at the turn of the century Rome had provided the symbol for republican enthusiasm, now ancient Greece seemed synonymous with democratic ideals. The Doric order suddenly became the most popular of the classic orders because its severe character suggested a Spartan austerity pleasing to the Victorian idealist, while both the Ionic and Corinthian styles suggested oriental sensuousness. Perhaps no more handsome example of a mansion in the Doric style can be found than Andalusia (7-11), the Pennsylvania home remodeled in classic dress for Nicholas Biddle in 1833.

The Doric prostyle that forms the main façade of the building is a severe unadorned replica of the entrance to a Doric temple, even to the stepped stylobate, or platform that supports the great columns. A monumental portico dominates the building, overwhelming the two-story body of the residence. Pedimental triangles top even the side wings. The one-story effect is reinforced by keeping the second-story windows small and subordinate to those of the ground floor. The shutters and casements are regular, flat, and smooth, so that the entire structure suggests the austerity of masonry construction. The brilliant white trim recalls the mistaken Victorian concept of a pure, colorless, ancient classic world.

A comparison with the White House reveals some of the essential differences between the earlier Federal style and the Greek revival. First, the prostyle portico dominates the Greek revival façade. The similar portico in a Federal-style building is not so overwhelming, is not so heavy in its proportions, and is not apt to be in the Doric style. Slender Ionic columns and pilasters, curved pediments, and a semicircular pavilion grace the White House, while the Greek revival structure sedulously avoids both slender forms and curves. An elegant balustrade tops the Federal-style structure, and sometimes a dome is used, while the severity of the Greek revival skyline is unrelieved except for the great pedimental gables. Last, as can be seen in the White House, the Federal style is urbane and gracious, and while there is restraint and logic in the disposition of parts, the style is distinguished by a certain decorative splendor. The Greek revival, on the other hand, severe and unadorned, suggests the remote calm of antiquity rather than the animated nineteenth-century world.

Two of the principal architects of the Greek revival to practice in the Philadelphia-Washington area, William Strickland and Robert Mills, were trained by Latrobe. William Strickland (1787-1864), like his master, could design in the Gothic, baroque, or Greek revival styles, but the Greek revival was his favorite. There has been considerable controversy over whether Strickland or Latrobe himself designed the Second Bank of the United States (7-12) in Philadelphia, built in 1824. Latrobe is frequently credited with the original conception and Strickland with the final design of the building. Almost more than any other building, it established the Greek portico as a symbol of financial stability. In its day it was considered one of the most distinguished structures of the nineteenth century. James Fenimore Cooper said that while a hundred similar magnificent structures had been erected in Europe, not one could be found in which "simplicity, exquisite proportion, and materials unite to produce so fine

7-12. William Strickland, Second Bank of the United States, 1824. Philadelphia. National Park Service photograph.

a whole." Even today one is intimidated by this monumental façade with its broad flight of stairs, its great Doric columns, its severe symmetry, and the complete absence of ornament. Certainly there is nothing about the façade to reveal the commercial purposes to which this templelike structure was dedicated.

Robert Mills (1781-1855) is most frequently remembered for the disciplined, dignified, and severe buildings he designed for the Federal Government such as the Old Patents Office in Washington. A much more vivacious and interesting aspect of his personality is revealed in his handsome Bethesda Presbyterian Church (7-13), built in Camden, South Carolina, in 1820. One is more conscious of the charm of the slender Doric columns, the delicate proportions of the triglyphs, metopes, and cornice moldings and the tall slender arches than of propriety. The vivid contrasts of white trim, red brick, and dark doors and shutters, and the brilliant and original spire combine elegance and vigor in a structure of unusual distinction. Though most buildings by Mills are in the Greek revival idiom, they show no slavish adherence to the style.

While Washington and Philadelphia were leading centers of the Greek revival movement, Ohio, Kentucky, Missouri, Tennessee, and the other new states played the role of provincial outposts for the style. An examination of the areas settled between 1800 and 1840 reveals city after

7-13. Robert Mills, Bethesda Presbyterian Church, 1820. Camden, S. C. Wayne Andrews photograph.

city with Greek names: Athens, Sparta, and Troy were frequent, and each Athens, Sparta, and Troy boasted schools, city halls, churches, banks, and mansions that were elegant and Grecian—in front at least. If finances did not permit the entire façade to be designed as a prostyle portico, then at least the entrance way was framed by a pair of Doric columns, an entablature with triglyphs and metopes, and a pediment. If stone and brick were not available, wood and stucco sufficed, and many a master carpenter built his columns and walls of wooden boards fitted together so skillfully that even the most discerning eye could not detect the individual boards. America longed fervently to achieve the classic dignity and nobility befitting the concept of democracy, and each raw little village attempted to clothe at least its major institutions in time-honored appropriate garb.

NEW ENGLAND

Boston and the New England area remained conservative in architectural tastes—the Greek façade and the Roman portico never took over here as they had in the central states. Many elements of the Colonial Georgian mode remained in fashion, and the elements of classic tradition that did appear were via English precedent, particularly as they had been developed by the Adam brothers, England's most brilliant classic revival designers. The most obvious features of the Adam style were slender proportions and the very delicate scale with which they handled the niches, columns, balustrades, and molding common to the classic style as well as

7-14. Charles Bulfinch, Old Meeting House, 1816. Lancaster, Mass. Library of Congress photograph.

the garlands, fan patterns, and urns which were their favorite motifs. Elaborate molded stucco ceilings of fine scale enhanced their most exquisite interiors and contributed an effect of great elegance. They also introduced freer, more open, and more convenient floor plans, and they varied room shapes by the introduction of oval, circular, and octagonal rooms and niches. In New England, the tendency to restrict decoration to a few limited areas and to contrast decorated areas with extensive plain surfaces created a unique and charming effect of simple elegance. The delicate scale of the Adam style also coincided with the natural colonial tendency to reduce the weight of the architectural details being executed in wood from the proportions that had developed in Europe for forms originally conceived in stone.

Charles Bulfinch

The particular blend of the Colonial Georgian tradition and the English Adam style which flourished in New England at the turn of the century received its most mature and subtle expression in the work of Charles Bulfinch (1763-1844). Bulfinch came from a socially prominent family and received the advantages of a formal education and a trip abroad which provided an eighteenth-century gentleman's exposure to the arts. The handsome Old Meeting House at Lancaster, Massachusetts, (7-14) and the splendid capitol for the state of Massachusetts (7-2) reveal the character of his work.

The genius of Bulfinch appears in the originality and taste with which he combined the elements of both the Adam style and the older Colonial Georgian mode of building. This is illustrated with particular effectiveness in the state capitol. The design for the building combined vigor, stateliness, and refinement without any one of these qualities infringing on the others. The tall slender arches and columns, the recessed Palladian windows of the second story, the delicate proportions of trim and moldings throughout create an effect of great elegance but they do not detract from the strength of the massive structure. Even the great soaring dome seems almost weightless yet it adds a touch of majesty to the building.

The church at Lancaster, Massachusetts, is undoubtedly one of Bulfinch's masterpieces. At first one's attention is captivated by the elegance of the details—the slender height of the pilasters and arched openings of the porch and the crisp pattern of the fanlike forms that provide a transition between the rectangular front of the church and the vertical bell tower. The clear crisp carving of the swags, moldings, and columns, and the sparkle of white against dark brick and blue sky also catch the eye immediately. But more thoughtful examination reveals an unexpected strength that results from the clear statement given to the relationship of the various parts of the building. The porch, entrance hall, bell tower, and main auditorium are all clearly articulated, and yet they are held together and related by the vigorous and continuous movement from each part to the next. Rectangles, triangles, squares, and circles play against one another energetically, and one unconsciously feels these bold forms while noting the exquisite details. The elegance of English neoclassicism and the lean and logical clarity of New England, combined by the genius of Bulfinch, created an architectural gem. Bulfinch, more than any other architect of his day, formulated a style particularly suited to the moment of poised quiet at the turn of the century, the moment when the older tradition of eighteenth-century elegance and taste gave way to the dynamic mood of the nineteenth century.

Domestic Architecture

Contemporary with the construction of the grand public buildings of the Federal style, New England witnessed the flowering of a distinguished but relatively simple style of domestic architecture. As soon after the Revolution as shipping and business became re-established and prosperity returned, the merchants, bankers, and shipbuilders again began to build handsome houses along the main streets of such coastal cities as Salem, Providence, and Newport. The houses built in the last decade of the eighteenth and the first decade of the nineteenth century, though discreet in detail and style, were larger than those of the eighteenth century. The more imposing structures were three stories in height with flat or low hipped roofs hidden by cornices and balustrades. While in general they retained the traditional Colonial plan of four rooms to a floor, arranged around a central hall and staircase, variations of plan to provide for privacy, comfort, and ease of management began to appear. Rooms were varied in size according to their function, and circular and oval shapes were sometimes employed where an effect of particular elegance was desired.

The most subtle and refined interpretation of the Federal-style houses of New England appeared in the work of some of the master builders and wood carvers around Salem, of whom the most famous is Samuel McIntire (1757-1811). The Gardner-White-Pingree House (7-15) built in 1810 is a particularly fine example of McIntire's work. Comparison of the Gardner-White-Pingree House with those built before the Revolution makes evident the differences between the houses of the two periods. By the turn of the century the pitch of the gable and roof area was reduced and the roof was hidden behind the balustrade to create an effect of contained rectangularity of form throughout the entire structure. The façade is seen as a simple rectangular unit, the separate stories marked off by white stone divisions, the white balustrade and the white architraves above the windows relating all the parts of the building to the chief focal point, the entrance porch. The façade is smooth, and details of moldings, trim, and entrance porch are kept flat and project from the building as little as possible. All of the forms are slender, the columns delicate, the moldings thin, the fanlight over the door and the side lights designed with geometrically precise, delicate divisions. Essentially a craftsman, McIntire's work is distinguished by a fine sense of proportion and disciplined restraint in the use of ornament. Much of the most beautiful detail designed by McIntire is found in the interiors of his houses and will be discussed in the section on interior design.

A second house from Salem, Massachusetts, the Andrew Safford House (7-16), rounds out our picture of the New England Federal-style mansion. Again the entire structure is formal, self-contained, carefully proportioned, and discreet. Double balustrades, using a fan motif between

7-15 (*above*). Samuel McIntire, Gardner-White-Pingree House, 1810. Salem, Mass. Wayne Andrews photograph. 7-16 (*below*). Andrew Safford House, 1818. Salem, Mass. Library of Congress photograph.

7-17. Nichols-Sortwell House, 1807. Wiscasset, Me. Samuel Chamberlain photograph.

the balusters, crown the building, and a semicircular balustrade tops the entrance porch. A nichelike pediment accents the second-story hall window and repeats the curve of the porch roof. At the rear right a splendid three-story portico faces the garden. The Andrew Safford House is more splendid than the Pingree House, but even so one is more conscious of restraint than of splendor, since whatever splendor appears is of a proper and responsible kind, the expression of a conservative and secure propertied class whose inclination to cultivate its taste and live elegantly was counterbalanced by a sense of propriety and social responsibility.

Both the city mansions and the less elaborate small-town mansions of this period have beautifully designed entranceways as the chief focal point of the façade. The Nichols-Sortwell House built in Wiscasset, Maine, in 1807 has a particularly charming doorway (7-17). The approach to the house is through an open gateway in the gracefully balustered fence which curves in a semicircle to frame the walk. Very slender Corinthian columns support the light porch. A graceful semicircular fanlight and precisely patterned side lights flank the screened doorway. Above, the patterns of a latticed balustrade and a Palladian window framed with attached columns and fluted pilasters complete the composition.

The story of the development of building practices in America in the nineteenth century is not complete if one overlooks the influence of the books on architectural design from which many a modest builder took his plans. Such a book was Asher Benjamin's *The Country Builder's Assistant,* published in 1797, the first of many successful publications by Benjamin.

7-18. Lavius Fullmore, from a design by Asher Benjamin, First Congregational Church, 1806. Bennington, Vt. Wayne Andrews photograph.

Asher Benjamin (1773-1845) was a Massachusetts carpenter, cautious about abandoning the traditional ways of building yet willing to introduce the newer neoclassic styles when he felt that builders and the public were ready to accept them. All over the rapidly expanding country, carpenters, builders, and customers alike went to his publications for direction and inspiration. While Benjamin was not a powerful or very original architect, his designs have charm, and they helped raise the general standard of taste. The First Congregational Church (7-18) in Bennington, Vermont, built in 1806 by a carpenter-builder, Lavius Fullmore, is taken from a plate in Benjamin's *The Country Builder's Assistant*. Certain modifications were made, but the general design stays close to Benjamin's plan. We are again conscious of the sensitive development of wooden construction that occurred in America in the nineteenth century. While Benjamin took his inspiration for this building from English patterns, the scale and weight of all of the parts, the open and light character of the structure appear logical for wood. The two arched doors flanking the main entrance, framed by two receding moldings with the joint in the moldings capped by a light keystone block, reveal a refreshing sensitivity to the style potentialities of wooden construction. In grace, gaiety, and unpretentious charm, this façade is not unique; similar buildings appeared all across the land during the nineteenth century, thanks in large part to the designs of Asher Benjamin. From New England to California, narrow rustic siding became one of the standard materials for covering homes, schools, churches, and business buildings. The details of door, windows, eaves, pedimented gables, and bell tower were copied exactly or with slight modifications hundreds of times. Through Asher Benjamin's books, the New England pattern of building was spread across the land—the New England architectural idiom became the national tongue.

NEW YORK

The New York area abandoned the eighteenth-century models more readily than New England and, like Philadelphia and Washington, seemed more receptive to French influences. The elegant City Hall (7-3) already mentioned reveals its French origin both by the bold and clear relationships of its main masses and by the refined formality of such details as the suave groupings of pilasters, swags, and balustrades seen in shallow relief on the second story.

The architects of the New York area began to explore the possibilities of other styles of building while the Greek revival was in full swing. The first examples of Gothic revival structures appeared in New York almost contemporary with the Greek Revival buildings. Minard Lafever (1798-1854) worked in the Greek, Gothic, and even Egyptian styles. His Old Whalers Church (7-19) at Sag Harbor, New York, built in 1844, is an amazing building revealing an unusually ingenious integration of such divergent elements as Egyptian architectural forms and wooden construction. The influence of Lafever extended beyond his work and examples since he also published builders' handbooks which contained exquisite details ranging from Pompeiian to Gothic. The frantic searching through the architectural vocabulary of the ages had begun. Architects were looking for styles that would fit the varying needs of an age of increasing complexity and allow for new engineering and constructional methods. For the following hundred years elements from every historic style would be tested, and not always with the success that Minard Lafever achieved in his Egyptian church. The age of eclecticism was well under way.

7-19. Minard Lafever, Old Whalers Church, 1844. Sag Harbor, N. Y. Wayne Andrews photograph.

THE SOUTH

The landed gentry of the south continued to live in a lordly manner in the years after the Revolution and built accordingly, so that handsome examples of the classic revival also appeared in the southern cities. Latrobe himself worked in New Orleans; Robert Mills designed a number of buildings in his native city of Charleston and in Baltimore; Savannah and other southern cities boasted homes, churches, and public buildings of distinction in the Federal style. With the extension of the southern agricultural world through the purchase of the Louisiana Territory and the acquisition of Florida, the plantation system expanded, and the great cotton and sugar empires of the Far South developed. There were few cities, and the plantation seat became an almost feudal center where the mansion of the owner was surrounded by servants' quarters, shops, warehouses, and other buildings. The façades of the great mansions lined the shores of the Mississippi River as well as the other major waterways of the old South.

These vast plantation mansions with their great colonnaded porticos

7-20. Belle Grove, 1857. White Castle, La. Library of Congress photograph.

varied tremendously in design. Some are rambling and irregular, like Belle Grove (7-20), near White Castle, Louisiana, and show a free development of plans and details, free to the point where at times the houses appear to have grown merely according to the caprice and whim of the builder or owner. Belle Grove had seventy-five rooms. The florid exuberance of such mansions expressed the ambitions of their owners who aimed to achieve a level of splendor equal to that of ancient Rome.

In some of the Southern mansions a more authentic indigenous element characterizes the design. Belle Helene (7-21), at Beismar, Louisiana, utilized a plan developed by the French settlers. A two-story gallery around the house provided shade and protection from the heat. The large and high-ceilinged rooms inside were cool and shadowy. Great two-story columns made of plaster on a brick core supported the roof. The Greek revival taste for impressive simplicity and regularity was satisfied here, but there is no slavish copying of Greek stylistic details. Instead, an original and quite unique building was developed in response to the special demands of Southern plantation life.

The Greek revival reached the peak of its popularity in the northern

7-21. Belle Helene. Beismar, La. Library of Congress photograph.

and central state in the 1830's after which time it was gradually replaced by an enthusiasm for the Gothic style, but it remained the dominant style in the South until the Civil War. With the collapse of the southern economy the great plantation mansions were neglected and gradually fell into disrepair and ruin. In the first decades after the Civil War there was little building in the South, and by the time building activity was resumed the Greek revival was dead. Today the great porticoes and pediments of these old mansions constitute some of America's most romantic remains as they stand desolate amidst a sea of crumbling plaster and broken laths.

8

Architecture:

The Romantic Revival

THE NINETEENTH CENTURY EXPRESSED ITS BELIEF IN progress through an enthusiasm for science, education, new machines, and many types of social reform. It was a period of tremendous intellectual activity and exploration—of great social change and technological development. Nineteenth-century optimism concerning the future was accompanied by a reawakened interest in the past, in archeology, history, and religion, with the belief that lessons learned from the past would provide a guide to the future. While philosophers and scientists were forging new guiding concepts and patterns of social activity, architects were seeking forms of building to house adequately the expanding society with its banks, factories, schools, department stores, and millionaires' mansions. Architects were not only searching for solutions to the physical needs of the day; the search was also for styles that would express the humanitarian ideals and deep sentiments that guided the period. The enthusiasm for the styles of Greece and Rome which we have just wit-

216

nessed was the first of a long series of such enthusiasms, each of which tried to reconcile a genuine admiration for the achievements of the past with contemporary needs. First, as we have seen, the Roman and Greek manner flourished, then the Gothic; after, in rapid succession the styles of the Renaissance, the baroque, the rococo were revived. Later the modes of Oriental peoples, European peasants, and the various newly discovered primitive cultures provided new sources of inspiration.

Even while Greece and Rome dominated the world of style, the champions of the Gothic manner began to appear, first in England and to a lesser extent in France, then in America. The last phase of the classic revival, the Greek phase, contained elements that were out of harmony with the philosophic concepts of classicism, for classicism as an esthetic philosophy had within it much broader implications than the mere observance of Greek and Roman traditions and conventions in the arts. The use of the Greek temple as a façade to ennoble a building, a device to achieve grandeur by association, as it were, was a sentimental and romantic concept rather than a classic one. As such, it came closer to the tenets and practice of the newly developing romantic movement than to the older tradition of classicism.

Classicism as an esthetic philosophy had gradually come to describe an attitude in which rational elements provided the guiding philosophy, where artistic expression was controlled by a counterbalancing of the forces of tradition, logic, and emotion. Every artistic movement carries within itself the seeds of its dissolution. Because the urgencies of artistic expression grow from the entire range of potential human experience, each art movement, by its arbitrary limitation of expression, eventually sets up a current of opposition. Artistic expression in the classic revival period focused on the rational—the controlled, the balanced, and the reasonable. The deep springs of human emotion—mystical, inspirational, subconscious rather than conscious, often irrational—which were held in check by the classicists were gathering force. Gradually at first, and then in a torrential outburst, these forces began to break through the rigorous disciplines of the academies and the conventions of public taste to become the dominant forces in the artistic expression of the nineteenth century. The movement which gave artistic and philosophic expression to the deep feelings of the nineteenth century has been termed romanticism. As an artistic movement it embodies the tendencies which are opposed to classicism—the dominance of feeling over reason, reliance on personal taste and intuition rather than on tradition, an emphasis on content rather than on form. For inspiration the romantic artists turned first to the middle ages.

While at first glance only the differences between early nineteenth-century romanticism and classicism are apparent, closer examination reveals many common elements. Both movements tended toward the grand manner, orienting their expression around inspiring and grandiose concepts rather than around simple and familiar experiences. Both groups sought to achieve sublime and elevated modes of feeling. Both groups, antagonistic toward the scientific developments and the industrial technology of the day, tended to go to the past for inspiration, the romanticists merely seeking fresher and less codified sources than the classicists.

THE GOTHIC REVIVAL

The Gothic revival, the revival of the style of the middle ages, had appeared in England almost contemporarily with the advent of the Adam style. Even earlier, in the later furniture of Chippendale, Gothic motives had been featured, the quest for novelty, change, and a fresh source of stimulus already making itself felt. In the middle of the eighteenth century elements from the medieval style of building were appearing in England in a few country mansions, the most notable example being Strawberry Hill, the country home built for the romantic novelist Horace Walpole. At the same time there were other indications of the oncoming romantic movement. The construction of a picturesque bit of ruined medieval architecture in an English rustic wooded garden spot came into style, indicating a taste for something other than the symmetries of the classic mode, a desire for a melancholy note, an atmospheric detail.

America was not slow to follow. In 1829, young Alexander Davis, who was to become one of the chief practitioners of the Gothic revival style in America, sketched the buildings he saw about him on the streets of New York. He included in his notebook two structures with Gothic details. One was a synagogue in which a Gothic tower appeared above a Greek façade, the other a Masonic Hall which featured such Gothic details as pointed arches, tracery above the windows, and crenelated towers topped by medieval pinnacles. Gothic buildings had already been constructed elsewhere in America and by architects who were champions of the Greek revival. As we noted, no less a classicist than Latrobe had designed and built Gothic churches, one of his early designs for the Baltimore Cathedral being in the Gothic manner.

Some of the general characteristics of the Gothic revival architecture might be reviewed here. The symmetry so essential to the classic style gave way to a taste for irregularity, formality was replaced by informality, restraint in the use of decoration by exuberance. The horizontal moldings and low roof lines essential for creating an air of classic calm were replaced by a vertical emphasis. Round arches, domes, barrel vaults, and the classic columns and pilasters gave way to pointed arches, clustered columns, ribbed vaulting, and buttresses. The entire repertory of medieval architectural forms was used to satisfy the growing desire for a mood of romantic sentiment. Charming spires, towers, turrets, and pinnacles helped to create an uneven aspiring skyline; crenelated battlements and projecting machicolations suggested the romantic moods of knights in armor and of fair maidens in dark castles on remote moors. The bargeboards, the details of tracery in windows, and the flattened Tudor arch recalled the cozy rusticity of the Merry England of Queen Elizabeth and Shakespeare. In churches particularly, and to a lesser degree in homes, libraries, and public buildings, the high narrow rooms, the tall windows with their traceries and stained glass, the buttresses, spires, and mossy stones all contributed to a mood of religious exaltation, of the self being lost in a greater whole, of a mystic communing with an infinite good that quickened the Victorian sensibilities, reinforced their humanitarian convictions, and confirmed the belief that "God's in his heaven: All's right with the world."

The taste for visual picturesqueness and irregularity also coincided with a growing desire for more freedom in laying out the floor plans. The classical fetish for rigid symmetry had long restricted the development of efficient plans, and designers readily took advantage of the freedom which the new mode offered to introduce new and ingenious arrangements of interiors. This, in turn, produced greater variety in exterior appearances. Houses and public buildings lost the uniformity of the earlier periods, and a conscious striving for individuality and uniqueness became the order of the day.

Andrew Jackson Downing

The most influential spokesman for the romantic approach to architecture in early-nineteenth-century America was Andrew Jackson Downing (1815-1852). Downing was a writer, arbiter of taste, architect, and landscape designer whose books championed the new modes—the rustic, the informal, and particularly the medieval styles, Gothic, Romanesque, and Tuscan. In his writings, he frowned on the pretentious and pompous formality of the Greek mode in architecture and deplored the geometric

8-1. Alexander J. Davis, Rotch residence, 1845. New Bedford, Mass. Wayne Andrews photograph.

rigidity of the eighteenth-century formal gardens. He presented sound if sentimental arguments for the honest use of simple building materials, maintaining that stone should be used in such a way as to bring out its natural beauty and that wood should be treated as wood. The style of a building, he argued, should be related to its site, and he poked fun at battlemented castles in the midst of suburban meadows. He even championed the selection of building styles in terms of the personality of the owner, implying that a castle could make a mouse of a meek man. Probably more than any other individual, Downing helped bring to an end the reign of the Greek temple. He believed that the ideal dwelling would come from a creative adaptation of elements selected from the various architectural styles of the past, combined and modified according to the personality, needs, and tastes of the owner, and constructed soberly and with fine craftsmanship.

Believing in the salutary effect of natural surroundings on city dwellers, Downing championed the acquisition of great parks for our modern cities. It was through his agitation and vision that the plan for Central Park in New York City was first conceived and was later brought into being by Frederick Law Olmstead and Downing's pupil, Calvert Vaux. The gently curving walks and roads, the informal groupings of trees and shrubs, the outcroppings of rock, quiet pools of water, and graceful stretches of lawn all reflect Downing's principle of landscape gardening—to retain the feeling of nature, "refined and softened by art." Andrew Jackson Downing suffered an untimely death but he had already passed the approval of his patronage on to Alexander Jackson Davis.

Alexander J. Davis

Alexander J. Davis (1803-1892), probably the most successful builder of Gothic houses in nineteenth-century America, listed the following as the styles in which he could produce suburban dwellings—"American Log Cabin, Farm House, English Cottage, Collegiate Gothic, Manor House, French suburban, Swiss cottage, Lormbard Italian, Tuscan from Pliny's villa at Ostia, Ancient Etruscan, Suburban Greek, Oriental Greek, Oriental, Moorish, and Castellated." But his modern renown rests on his handsome mansions in the Gothic manner. Davis seemed particularly adept at selling great baronial castles to persons with newly acquired wealth, and the most extravagant of these were veritable mazes of rooms, hallways, and staircases topped by a forest of towers, turrets, balconies, great chimneys, and steep gables.

His achievements went beyond mere size and complexity, however. Davis had a genuine ability to adapt the Gothic manner to the needs and tastes of his day and create a visually charming, informal building. These talents can be seen to advantage in the Rotch residence (8-1), built in New Bedford, Massachusettts, in 1845. Using elements from the English Tudor style, but by no means restricting himself to this idiom, Davis created a charming house. The eaves of the steep roof are decorated with bargeboards, pendants, and finials, combined to suit his fancy but beautifully related in size and shape to the area in which they are located. The lacy trellises that support the porches, topped by pretty brackets enclosing quatrefoils, have little historic precedent but contribute unerringly to create a light open veranda. The low Tudor arch of the ground-floor window has been combined with rectangular windows and with windows framed by high pointed arches, yet each window shape is so logical for the area in which it is placed that the final effect appears harmonious. The Rotch home presents an arbitrary combination of elements of the Gothic style, a practice frowned on by the devotees of authenticity at a later date, but the final effect is fresh, vivacious, and pretty. It is easy to understand the attraction of the style for a public long restricted to the formal propriety and almost finicky refinement of the classic revival.

James Renwick, Jr.

James Renwick, Jr. (1818-1895), was another early nineteenth-century architect who did much to popularize the Gothic style. He was renowned as the designer of great mansions, of Grace Church in New York,

8-2. James Renwick, Jr., Smithsonian Institution, 1846. Washington, D.C. Wayne Andrews photograph.

and of the massive Smithsonian Institution (8-2) in Washington, D.C. This great structure of dark red sandstone, built between 1846 and 1855, might best be described as Anglo-Norman; certainly its round arches and clearly marked stories places it more in the Romanesque category than in the Gothic. This 500-foot-long maze of towers, turrets, gables, and chimneys is also distinguished by the inventive capacities of the designer rather than by authenticity. The crisp vigor of the detail, the dramatic effect of the crenelated rooflines, the forbidding machicolations and towers reflect the tastes of a strong and energetic personality searching, as would Henry Richardson a generation later, for a style appropriate to the expanding and energetic young America. Renwick's dark and dramatic achievement is particularly impressive when seen against the background of white-columned architectural propriety that characterized nineteenth-century Washington.

Richard Upjohn

Perhaps the best-known Gothic edifice in the United States, and probably the finest, is Trinity Church (8-3), New York, which today

8-3. Richard Upjohn, Trinity Church, 1846. New York City. Wayne Andrews photograph.

nestles amidst the skyscrapers at the foot of Wall Street and Broadway. Richard Upjohn (1802-1878) was probably the most distinguished practitioner of the Gothic revival style in nineteenth-century America, and Trinity Church is undoubtedly his masterpiece. Upjohn came to the United States from England in 1829, and though originally trained as a cabinetmaker, he went to work after his arrival here as a draftsman, teaching and working for various architects. His first architectural assignments were Gothic villas and he designed these with sufficient distinction so that he was called in to repair the sagging roof of the old Trinity Church of New York. Upjohn took advantage of the opportunity inherent in the situation and prepared a design for a new church so persuasive that the idea of repairing the old church was abandoned and the new church was completed by 1849. Its merit was soon recognized. No less a critic than Downing declaring it as superior to the other churches of its day as a Raphael Madonna was superior to a painted sign. It is difficult today, because of the neighboring skyscrapers, to see the building from a sufficient distance to appreciate the relationships of the main masses, but the unobstructed length of Wall Street still provides a superb view of the façade and of the towering spire that is the dominant feature of the building. The direct and unified movement of the great tower, the powerful way in which all of the details are held within one continuous upward sweep, the uninterrupted receding scale of the arches, windows, buttresses, pinnacles, and finials reveal Upjohn's power as a designer. His

8-4. John Haviland, Eastern State Penitentiary (engraving), 1829. Philadelphia. Courtesy of the New York Historical Society, New York.

background as a craftsman stood him in good stead for he planned and supervised the ornamental details in person. The clear, crisp, stone cutting and wood carving pay tribute to his early training as a cabinetmaker and contribute a masculine and incisive flavor to the detail. While the great office buildings surrounding Trinity Church may soar far above it in space, they do not overwhelm it visually or spiritually.

Early nineteenth-century architects were not so concerned with style as to be indifferent to the need for new plans and new building materials. Early in the century there began experiments with iron columns and roof trusses which were to bear abundant returns in the last half of the century. America revealed its progressive nature in a readiness to experiment. Prisons, for instance, were still medieval dungeons in most parts of the world—great thick-walled, windowless, foul caverns where human beings were confined under inhuman conditions. John Haviland (1792-1852), another Englishman who came to America to find an outlet for his abilities, specialized in the design of penal institutions which were sufficiently original and satisfactory to attract study from the major European capitals. He preferred the Gothic style for his institutions although he executed designs in other styles also, most notably an Egyptian exterior

8-5. Dome, Capitol, 1880's. Baton Rouge, La. Clarence John Laughlin photograph.

for The Tombs in New York. His design for the Eastern State Penitentiary (8-4) in Philadelphia, built in 1829, presents an unusually imposing exterior in which great crenelated towers and austere masses of unbroken wall suggest some unassailable medieval fortress, a suggestion appropriate enough for its function. The Eastern State Penitentiary also reflected a new concept of prison design in its plan. Cell blocks were arranged along corridors which radiated from a central point of observation, and each prisoner had his own bit of solitary garden as well as cell. The development of such revolutionary answers to an age-old problem represented a genuine optimism about society, a belief that human conditions could be bettered by new designs, plans, and arrangements. This deep optimism stimulated the changes in house plans, the development of kitchen equipment, the improvement of agricultural tools, and the thousand and one inventions that altered the character of nineteenth-century America.

The popularity of the Gothic style spread all across the country, and even the sacrosanct state capitols succumbed to the flattery of the new style. The old state capitol in Baton Rouge, Louisiana, reveals an interesting adaptation of the Gothic mode to the world of civil administration. Fire destroyed the original building during the Civil War, and it was reconstructed with its present dome (8-5) in the 1880's. The dome employed the cast-iron construction that was to contribute so much to the evolution of new building techniques in the last half of the century. The great cast-iron central column rises 80 feet above the floor before it unfolds into a cataract of ribs, pointed arched windows, and traceries. These all converge to form the great dome, revealing the taste for open space

8-6. Morse-Libby House, 1850. Portland, Me.

and light construction that became a major architectural preoccupation for the next hundred years.

The Tuscan Villa

As the nineteenth century progressed, a succession of other building styles were discovered and exploited. In 1835, the firm of Town and Davis designed what it called a Tuscan villa, in New Rochelle, New York. It is not surprising that as artists, writers, and sculptors rediscovered Italy architects too would be attracted to the charming villas scattered through Tuscany. The informal floor plans and profiles, the bold contrasts of irregular rectangular masses, the warm-colored stone or stucco walls with broad extending eaves appealed to the eye. The unformulated and essentially picturesque combinations of arches, columns, pediments, balustrades, and urns which characterized the style provided a new source of pictorial delights for the romantic designer nostalgic for a warmer and sunnier place than the chill gray world of northern medieval Europe.

The Morse-Libby House (8-6) of Portland, Maine, presents a mid-century interpretation of the Tuscan villa. Its richly bracketed, curved and triangular pediments, its Ionic columns, its pilasters, balustrades and textured quoins, reflect a growing taste for the splendors of the High Renaissance, even baroque, phases of the Tuscan style. The stern towers and the dignified, guarded approach suggest that as wealth accumulated and social discord increased a need was felt to reconcile the romantic mood with an air of authority.

DIVERGENT CURRENTS

Not all of the architecture of nineteenth-century America was based on the revival of historic styles, classic or romantic. The story of architecture in America went beyond the dominant culture with its imposing monuments and grand mansions. Religious mystics who sought to escape any worldly corruption of the spirit, simple working people, and the scattered settlers from other than English-speaking countries also contributed to the fascinating complexity of American building practice. These groups built their essentially utilitarian structures unaware of the sequence of revivals we have been studying, modifying the traditions of their motherlands in terms of new patterns of living.

Shaker Architecture

Far removed from the worldly concerns of the thriving business community were the Shakers, a dissident offshoot of the Quakers, who came over from England in the last half of the eighteenth century and, after a few desultory attempts to settle elsewhere, established the community of New Lebanon in New York. New Lebanon remained the chief center of Shaker life until the twentieth century, but in the early nineteenth century, a number of communities were established in New England, upstate New York, Pennsylvania, and farther west. Each of these settlements was almost self-sufficient, but certain commonly held attitudes, such as the conviction that "true Gospel simplicity . . . naturally leads to plainness in all things," created a homogeneity in the wares produced in all the Shaker communities. Using the simple materials at hand, the Shakers retained the basic forms of eighteenth-century architecture and furniture but modified them freely when they could thereby be made more efficient. A great circular stone barn (8-7) with a twelve-sided wooden superstructure topped by a hexagonal cupola at Hancock, Massachusetts, shows how far the Shaker builders could depart from their usual strict rectangularity when greater efficiency could be achieved. This great

8-7. Circular stone and wood barn. Shaker Colony, Hancock, Mass. Index of American Design, National Gallery of Art, Washington, D.C.

barn permitted the driver of a hay wagon to enter, unload directly into the copious loft, and leave with a minimum of waste motion. The direct use of the vigorously textured materials, the simplicity of the forms, and the sharp clarity of the doors, windows, and eaves reflect the same honesty of design and craftsmanship that distinguished the Shaker furniture, which will be discussed later.

The Cottage

The romantic nineteenth century was also a very practical age—its problems grew from its attempts to reconcile sentimental enthusiasms, humanitarian ideals, and technological developments. Accompanying the expansion of industry and the fantastic growth of the cities came urgent need for housing. Planners planned ideal communities, real-estate promoters made fortunes from building far from ideal housing, and somewhere between these two groups evolved the various typical American cottages. While the row houses of the city degenerated into airless and dark flats, the small-town, rural, or suburban cottages, standing free on

8-8 (*above*). Milltown house, 1846. Graniteville, S. C. Wayne Andrews photograph.   8-9 (*below*). Octagonal house. Watertown, Wisc. Library of Congress photograph.

their own lots and open to light and air, remained, on the whole, superior to their equivalents anywhere in the world. A milltown house (8-8) built in South Carolina in the 1840's typifies the small-town or country dwellings. Built of wood on a brick, or later a concrete, foundation, the plan followed the precedent of the colonial house. The front door opened directly into a parlor or a hallway flanked by a parlor, dining room, and kitchen. Following both the older colonial houses and the fashionable Gothic mansions of the day, a high-pitched gabled roof sheltered the second-story bedrooms. A front porch provided protection from the weather and a place for enjoying the outdoors. The shed roof in back covered whatever could not be comfortably included under the main roof. These modest cottages were frequently enhanced by stylish decoration; in this case a modest jigsaw cut-out trimmed the eaves, a faint echo of the splendid bargeboards which might be found decorating the mansion of the mill owner.

Not everyone concerned with developing a pleasant and comfortable home for the average man thought in such conventional terms. Americans had always shown an inventive turn of mind and a concern with practical matters, and as might be expected, these talents were applied to improving home design. Inventions to lighten housework, to improve ventilation, heating, plumbing, and lighting appeared in quantities during these years. Books of house plans assisted builders to design comfortable and efficient homes. In mid-century, Orson S. Fowler wrote A Home for All and presented the octagonal house, his solution to the problem of providing an inexpensive home for the average man. The octagonal house (8-9) contained no dark corners or long hallways and provided the maximum amount of enclosed living space with the minimum of construction. The book went into a seventh printing, and octagonal houses appeared all over America, the first of a number of radical housing concepts to appear here.

The French—New Orleans

We have already been introduced to the initial architectural ventures of the French settlers of the lower Mississippi Valley and of the Spaniards in the south and the southwest. During the last years of the eighteenth century and in the first half of the nineteenth century, there were further developments of these two traditions, far removed in spirit from the fashionable revivals of the north and east.

Except for a very few buildings, such as the Cahokia Courthouse and the plantation houses previously mentioned, little evidence remains of the long French domination of the Mississippi River valley except in the city of New Orleans. Remaining French through the early part of the eighteenth century, New Orleans fell into the hands of Spain and then reverted to France until it was purchased by Jefferson in 1803. During the period of Spanish occupancy, fires obliterated most of the old city except for the section around the main square. Most of what is now called the old city was built in the nineteenth century.

The Cabildo (8-10), or Old City Hall, built during the period of Spanish domination, retains much of the formal dignity that distinguished Spanish monumental architecture in the baroque style. At the same time, it displays qualities that characterize French architecture—a feeling for the logical proportioning of parts, a strong emphasis on structure, and a delicacy of detail. The increased lightness of the parts from the bold arcades of the ground floor to the delicate dormer windows of the mansard-roofed third story, the bold way in which the pedimental triangle, attached columns, and dome establish the central axis of the building, the delicacy of the decorative details, all speak for the rich tradition of building that formed the architectural heritage of the two mother countries.

The homes (8-11) in the surrounding area may be of more significance to the evolving American tradition than the imposing municipal buildings. Less European and more Creole, these houses combined French, Spanish, and local elements in a unique way that created a lively indigenous style. In the nineteenth century two- and three-story houses became frequent. Broad balconies, sheltered in the eighteenth century by high-pitched roofs and in the nineteenth by low-pitched ones, extended over the full width of the sidewalk and provided both access to the outdoors and a shaded walk. Windows were shuttered, and the balconies, in the eighteenth century held up by colonnades, were supported in the nineteenth century by ornamental iron grilles. Originally made of delicate hand-wrought iron, these ornamental grilles were supplanted by elaborate cast-iron trellises and railings in the last half of the nineteenth century.

The plans of these houses are as interesting as the façades. The typical plan featured a large room on the front with windows facing the street. This room was entered from a side hall or driveway which also provided passage to a courtyard in back. The courtyard served as an area for family activity. It also provided a space in which servants could carry out tasks not suited to the indoors and served as a passageway from such rooms as the kitchens, service rooms, and slaves' quarters which

8-10. Old City Hall, 1795. New Orleans, La. Bureau of New Orleans News photograph.

8-11. Le Prete mansion, 19th century. New Orleans, La. Library of Congress photograph.

opened off the court. This plan, common to Latin countries, in which rooms are arranged around an open court, gives a unique and exotic flavor to New Orleans houses.

The Spanish Styles

In the mid-eighteenth century, the Spanish colonial world entered a period of unparalleled prosperity due to the discovery of tremendous deposits of gold and silver in Mexico. The communities of the Southwest shared in this outburst of energy and experienced a period of expansion and building. New churches were put up in an area extending from eastern Texas to California. Two fine examples of these churches are still standing—San Jose and San Miguel de Aguayo, in San Antonio, Texas, and San Xavier del Bac (8-12), in Tucson, Arizona. Built between 1784 and 1797, after that final phase of the Spanish baroque style, the Churrigu   esque, found its most complete expression in the extravagant churches of Mexico, San Xavier del Bac represents a remote provincial echo of the Mexican style, a style with such a wealth of flamboyant ornament that even a remote provincial echo of it remains impressively rich. As in most of the Mexican churches of this type, two relatively simple side areas of the front façade carry bell towers which frame a richly ornamented central panel of baroque decorative motives. Scrolls, volutes, pilasters, crests, leaves, flowers, and the shell, the particular symbol of the Franciscan order, are all executed in a soft dark brick color that contrasts effectively with the light-colored surfaces that surround it. San Xavier del Bac probably boasts the most richly decorated façade in North America, an exciting contrast to the general restraint that characterizes our colonial heritage.

San Xavier is not splendid only on the outside. The interior (8-13), covered by five low domes made of brick with a high dome resting on an octagonal drum marking the crossing of the transept and the nave, is elaborately ornamented with carved stone, molded plaster, gilded woodwork, and painting. An immense richly gilded and polychromed altar occupies the entire end wall of the apse, and each of the transepts has a profusion of decoration.

The California missions, built between 1769 and 1823, the last mission churches to be established, are probably the most familiar examples of Spanish colonial architecture in North America. Architecturally, the

8-12 (*left*). San Xavier del Bac, 1784-1797. Tucson, Ariz.   8-13 (*right*). San
Xavier del Bac, interior. Library of Congress photographs.

California missions stand half way between the simple structures of New
Mexico and the elaborate churches of Texas and Arizona. Like the
mission churches of New Mexico, the California mission church was the
center of a group of buildings enclosed by walls and usually grouped
around one or more open patios. The church, the most imposing unit in
this complex of buildings, usually formed one side, or a part of one side,
of the main patio. Close to the church and usually attached to it were
auxiliary buildings which held living rooms, a kitchen, cells, offices for
the keeping of records, and quarters for travelers. Opening off the enclosed patio, fronted by covered arcades, were other buildings: dormi-
tories for the unmarried Indian neophytes, shops for all the craft activities
carried on within the mission, and rooms for storing food and the products
made and used by the mission community. Within easy reach were such
subsidiary buildings as barns, corrals, and a tannery. A short distance
away lay the Indian community, called the *rancheria*, usually an assemblage of crudely constructed huts.

San Carlos Borromeo (8-14) at Carmel was the administrative center
for the California missions, and in 1793 Father Lasuen began to construct
a new mission church worthy of its position. Since building in stone repre-

8-14. <u>San Carlos Borromeo Mission Church, 1793. Carmel, Calif.</u> Lee Blaisdell photograph.

sented the ultimate hope of the mission founders, a mason was brought in to instruct the Indian workers. An unusual wooden tunnel-vaulted ceiling supported by three transverse stone ribs provided an impressive interior to match the elaborate façade. In order to withstand the outward thrust of the vaulted ceiling, unusually heavy walls and thick reinforcing buttresses were used.

The façade of the Carmel mission is vigorous in its bold massings of form. A tall bell tower on the south has two openings on the front and one on the south side. Baroque finials crown its four corners, above which an octagonal drum decorated with eight finials carries the eye to the tall dome surmounted by a slender iron cross. A small tower with only one arched opening and a modest crest marks the north corner. The main portal, impressive in size, is framed by weighty pilasters and moldings. Above the door, a bold star and quatrefoil window and a strong arched pediment surmounted by a weighty finial terminate the composition. The combination of sturdy forms, of contrasts between the decorated areas and broad expanses of smooth wall, and the rich difference between the

8-15. Veranda of the de la Guerra House, 1819-1826. Santa Barbara, Calif. Library of Congress photograph.

cream-colored stone and the darker stucco makes the Carmel mission the most impressive monument left by the Spaniards in California. Neglected along with the other missions in the last part of the nineteenth century, San Carlos Borromeo has fortunately been restored with great care so that it appears now very much as it did in the early nineteenth century.

Municipal and residential architecture in Spanish colonial California followed the general pattern that characterized the mission churches. Adobe walls enclosed rectangular rooms which opened onto covered arcades. The arcade, formed by continuing the slanting roof beyond the façade of the building, was supported by either wooden posts or adobe piers. When there were enough rooms, buildings were arranged around a rectangular open patio. The adobe walls were given a heavy coat of whitewash, sometimes tinted with colored pigment, and the roof was covered with red tiles or, if tiles were not available, with heavy wooden shingles. This mode of building provided the basis for the modern California ranch house.

In southern California the one-story adobe ranch house was most common. The typical ranch house ranged from a few rooms, with or without an arcade, to a commodious structure with a dozen or more rooms opening onto spacious arcades which framed an orderly patio

8-16. Larkin House, 1834. Monterey, Calif. Wayne Andrews photograph.

(8-15). The patios, with flowering plants and paved walks, potted flowers, and sometimes a fountain, formed the heart of these houses in the same way that the great hearth served as the focal center of the New England home.

Further north, the two-story adobe was more frequent. Fine examples of the two-story adobe house are sufficiently numerous in Monterey so that the style is frequently called the Monterey style. A long veranda usually extends across the façade of the building, supporting a second-story balcony. In the famous Larkin House (8-16), residence of the first American consul to Alta California, the veranda and balcony extend across the front and down the two sides of the house. The verandas are supported on slender wooden posts which continue through second-story supports to the roof. A simple but graceful railing encloses the balcony. Though the walls of the ground floor in the Larkin House are 3 feet thick and those of the second story are 2 feet thick, the effect is graceful and light, the slender posts of the verandas and balconies and the graceful low slope of the pitched hip roof creating an open and airy feeling. The plan of the typical Monterey style colonial house was simple. The ground floor housed the living, dining, and service rooms and the kitchen. The stairway to the second floor was outside, at one end of the veranda, and led to the balcony which provided access to the bedrooms.

The buildings constructed for civil and administrative purposes by the Spanish settlers followed the same general pattern as has just been

8-17. Old Customs House, 19th century. Monterey, Calif. Rey Ruppell photograph.

described. The Old Customs House (8-17), also in Monterey, is similar in style to the Larkin House, but is less regular; it has a base of boldly cut limestone blocks and a heavy tile roof. Its picturesque irregularity creates an interesting contrast with the serene, almost classic regularity of the Larkin House. This was not the result of conscious planning, for the building evolved through the combined efforts of Spanish, Mexican, and later American builders who added to the structure and created changes according to differing needs. The result is charming, as is frequently the case with buildings which have grown over many years.

In the seventy-five years between the Revolutionary War and the Civil War, the United States emerged from colonial dependency to become a full-fledged sovereign nation. During these years the American builder abandoned the Colonial Georgian style of building and embarked on a series of revivals of earlier styles in an attempt to find ways of building suited to the tastes, institutions, and techniques of the new century and the new country. The early classic revival found expression here in the Federal style in which the modes and manners of ancient Rome were borrowed to provide a dignified garb for national and state capitols as well as for many other buildings. A particularly charming style combining elements from the earlier Georgian and the classic revival appeared in the Federal style of New England. After 1830 there was a rapid succession of revivals, led by the Greek revival and then the Gothic. This "trying on" of various modes of the past continued with unabated vigor in the years following the Civil War. Another quarter of a century would have to pass before the new style of the emerging industrial age would define itself with any degree of assurance and clarity.

The architecture of the French and Spanish settlers and of certain dissident religious groups in our midst constituted separate and independent elements of our architectural heritage. Not until the twentieth century would their unique flavor be incorporated into our rich architectural tradition.

Interiors and the Household Arts

FEDERAL-STYLE INTERIORS

When one compares a room in the Derby House (9-1) in Salem, Massachusetts, one of Samuel McIntire's masterpieces, with an equally splendid Georgian interior (4-10), the changes which characterized the Federal style are very apparent. The most striking difference is the diminished weight of the ornamental details. The scale of the decorations is more delicate; moldings are lighter, door jambs, mantel, and window details project only slightly into the room, and the carving, in very shallow relief, appears almost etched into the surface. The extensive wall paneling so characteristic of the earlier period has been eliminated and the walls are smooth and unadorned except for the chair rail which runs around the room on a level with the bottom of the window sills. The rich pedimental decorations have disappeared along with the elaborate sculptured brackets, the complex moldings, and the broken curves of the

240

9-1. Samuel McIntire, room from Derby House, 1799. Salem, Mass. Courtesy of the Pennsylvania Museum of Art, Philadelphia.

baroque style. Quiet horizontal and dignified vertical lines dominate the room. The ceilings in the more splendid homes were decorated with delicate molded stucco patterns which tended to be centered single designs rather than the continuous all-over patterns favored in the earlier period. The rich full-bodied colors of the Georgian interior have given way to pale tones with white predominating. The furniture, which will be discussed in detail later, is rectangular in structure, light in scale, with extreme refinement of detail. Rooms remained lofty and large with tall and imposing doors and windows. Door jambs frequently were topped

9-2. Samuel McIntire, mantel in Peirce-Nichols House, started 1782. Salem, Mass. Essex Institute, Salem, Mass.

by a broad carved panel to give an illusion of increased height. The decorative motifs used in the interior, like those on the exteriors, appear to have been inspired by discoveries at Pompeii and Herculaneum.

McIntire's talents were essentially those of a craftsman and decorator rather than those of an architect; consequently the refinement and charm of his work is most apparent in such interior details as the exquisitely carved woodwork seen in the mantel and above the doors in the Derby House interior. These areas are enhanced by cameolike swags, urns, flutings, and moldings. The delicately molded stucco ceiling contributes greatly to the elegance of the house, which featured a great oval drawing room on the garden side. Whenever possible, rooms in the Federal period were symmetrical, with oval, semicircular, and octagonal ends, niches, and bays providing stately variations of room shape when an effect of unusual distinction was desired. The Peirce-Nichols House in Salem is not so elaborate as the Derby House, but a close-up view of the fireplace and overmantel area (9-2) reveals the exquisite precision and delicacy with which McIntire treated the classic revival motifs.

Interiors of the Federal style were much alike throughout the states, but minor regional differences are evident. Restraint characterized New England, a continental splendor predominated in New York and the central states, and an air of aristocratic elegance distinguished the beautiful mansions in the South. A comparison of the New England interiors we

9-3. Duncan Phyfe room, 1807. The Henry Francis du Pont Winterthur Museum, Winterthur, Del.

have just seen with the Duncan Phyfe room (9-3) based on a New York room from around 1807 and with the stairwell from Montmorenci (9-4), a famous mansion near Warrenton, North Carolina, reveals minor differences in emphasis. The basic framework of the Duncan Phyfe room, named after the maker of its fine furniture, is similar to that observed in the Derby House. The room is large and high-ceilinged. The walls are plastered and without extensive paneling. The only moldings are the mop boards, chair rail, and cornice moldings. The paneling of the doors and window casements is rectangular, regular, and projects only slightly from the wall. The tall windows reach almost to the ceiling.

Other aspects of the room, however, reflect the oncoming Empire style, newly arrived from France. The Pompeiian and Roman motifs in the furniture and the design of the draperies, cut-glass ceiling chandeliers and wall sconces all have a Continental flavor. Though still airy, open, and graceful, the forms and line movements suggest a more formal and dignified manner. The designer of the Phyfe room aimed for a style that was more imposing than that which flourished in the restrained New Eng-

9-4. Stair hall in Montmorenci, 1822. Near Warrenton, N. C. The
Henry Francis du Pont Winterthur Museum, Winterthur, Del.

land atmosphere. Much of the bric-a-brac—the mirrors, vases, and bowls—
features lyres, urns, eagles, swags, and other Pompeiian and Greco-
Roman motifs. Even the pale colors so typical of New England taste have
disappeared. Clear, strong blues, yellows, and deep reds contrast boldly
with the dark mahogany furniture and the light walls. In the following
decades the more imposing manner featured in the Duncan Phyfe room
replaced the earlier and more discreet manner even in New England.

One entered Montmorenci from a two-story columned veranda and
looked across the spacious entrance hall to the back hall out of which
the stairway rose in an elliptical curve. The splendid sweep of the stairway is matched by the spaciousness of the hall and the elegance of the
graceful molded stucco ornamentation over the window and in the cornice
moldings. The handsome mirrors, the Oriental porcelains, and fine textiles
were imported to satisfy the distinguished tastes of the owners of Montmorenci. The furniture was made by skilled European craftsmen who
settled in America. The airy elegance and spaciousness of the Montmorenci stairway suggest that the older patterns of life still prevailed in
the South.

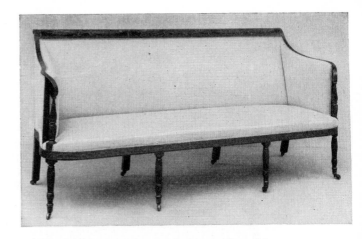

9-5 (*left*). Sheraton-style chair, late 18th century. Courtesy Metropolitan Museum of Art, Gift of Mrs. Faneuil S. Weisse in memory of her husband, 1941. 9-6 (*right*). Duncan Phyfe, Sheraton-style sofa, 1805. Courtesy Metropolitan Museum of Art, Gift of Mrs. Harry H. Benkard, 1942.

Furniture

The classic revival, like the preceding Georgian age, is one of the great periods in the history of furniture design. Such designers as the Adam brothers, Sheraton, and Hepplewhite in England and Duncan Phyfe in America established certain basic furniture styles of such vigor that the styles as well as the designers' names persisted well into the twentieth century. The Adam brothers, Hepplewhite, and Sheraton, in that sequence, published between 1760 and 1800 books of designs that were widely used by a host of superb cabinetmakers both in England and America. Taste and practice in America lagged behind that of England and the Continent; modes that began to appear in England around 1760 did not appear in America until after the Revolution.

9-7. Hepplewhite-style chair, 1790-1799. Courtesy Metropolitan Museum of Art, Lee Fund, 1937.

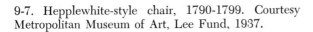

9-8. Hepplewhite-style chest, 1796-1803. Index of American Design, National Gallery of Art, Washington, D.C.

The furniture produced in America from the period between the Revolutionary War and 1810, inspired largely by the designs of the Adam brothers and Hepplewhite, and the early designs of Sheraton, is much lighter in weight than the preceding Georgian. A Sheraton-style chair (9-5) from late in the eighteenth century illustrates the characteristics of the period. Parts tend to be slender, at times even spindly, and the decorative enhancements are few and delicate in scale, thereby contributing to an effect of great refinement and elegance. Rectangular contours are most characteristic with vertical supports and horizontal lines dominant, although curvilinear elements are retained in minor areas. The manner in which curved lines are combined with straight can be seen in the graceful arm rests and ends of a Sheraton-style sofa (9-6) from around 1805, as well as in the shield-shaped back and shaped seat of a Hepplewhite-style chair (9-7) from the end of the eighteenth century. Restraint and a touch of formality replaced the vigor of Georgian furniture. Diminutive inlay patterns, marquetry, and painted decorations augment the fine-scale carving which was preferred to the bold sculptured decorations of the earlier style. Reeding and simple turnings reappear. These elements contribute to the smooth continuity of line that was desired by the classic revival designers. Classical decorative motifs were predominant; urns and swags can be seen on the Hepplewhite-style chair, although Hepplewhite and, to a lesser degree, Sheraton also used other motifs—the three-feathered crest of the Prince of Wales, wheat, ribbons, and formal garlands of leaves and flowers. In America, patriotic motifs were popular.

A chest of drawers (9-8) in the Hepplewhite manner, from between 1796 and 1803, effectively pictures the combination of straight lines and fluid simple curves that gives the Hepplewhite designs their particular charm. The essentially rectangular profile of the chest is relieved by the swelling front and the curve of the blocked legs which flow gracefully into the apron. This mahogany chest also shows the use of satinwood inlays, the delicate scale of the detail, and the fondness for patriotic motifs which characterized the period here. The American eagle decorates the top drawer and the brass pulls are enriched with an eagle motif. The furniture in the Derby House, the Duncan Phyfe room, and Montmorenci, all display the slender grace and formal elegance so characteristic of the style. No period in history has left us a more gracious legacy of beautiful furniture than the Federal age.

EMPIRE-STYLE INTERIORS

Created at the edict of Napoleon to provide the proper setting for his dreams of empire, the Empire style is the equivalent, in the decorative arts, of Greek revival architecture. By the third decade of the century, the Empire mode, foreshadowed in the Duncan Phyfe room, dominated the centers of fashion.

Stimulated by the grandiose ambitions of Napoleon and by the emerging Caesars of industry and commerce, as well as by the wonders being revealed through methodical archeological exploration, designers combined Pompeiian, Greek, Roman, and Egyptian elements to create imposing and grand interiors. The Rufus King parlor (9-9), from a mansion built in Albany, New York, around 1840, is a fine example of the Empire style in America.

The first characteristic to be observed is the increased weight of all the parts. The delicacy of proportion which distinguished the turn-of-the-century decor was gone, replaced by heavier proportions in the massive pilasters, moldings, and mantel. Chair railings were eliminated, creating an unbroken expanse of wall that provided a severe background to set off the imposing objects in the room.

Moldings framing the doors and windows were broad and flat, suggesting the stone-framed portals of antiquity, and the number of moldings was reduced in an attempt to recapture the grand austerity of masonry construction. The large scale of the interior proportions required massive and monumental furniture. The incorporation of such architectural forms as the classical columns in the pier table and the caryatids flanking the fireplace, the combination of marble and brass or ormolu with the wood, the use of ancient composite animal and human forms—sphinxes, phoenixes,

9-9. Room from Rufus King House, 1840. Albany, N. Y. The Henry Francis
du Pont Winterthur Museum, Winterthur, Del.

claw feet, and eagle heads—in conjunction with the larger size and heavier
proportions of Empire furniture, combine to contribute to an imposing
and imperial effect. An increased number of small objects was incorporated into the decorative scheme of the room. Mirrors, wall sconces,
oil lamps, candelabras, urns, pitchers, vases, elaborate clocks, and other
objets d'art were introduced to enrich the room and to increase comfort.
Colored marble, gleaming varnished mahogany, and shining brass added
splendid textures and color effects. Gilt as well as color was applied to

chair backs, lamp shades, and even to the marble tops of tables. Metallic embroidery shone in the curtains, metal fringe glittered on the valances, and gilded plaster enriched picture frames and mirrors. Heavy colors replaced the bright, even sharp, colors of the previous years.

Furniture

In the second and third decades of the century, fashionable American furniture designers adopted elements of the Empire style in response to the general wave of enthusiasm for the new fashion. While certain designers like Duncan Phyfe showed remarkable taste in the way in which they used elements of the Empire style, in the hands of lesser men the grace of the early classic revival gave way to a Greco-Egyptian solidity and a mistaken archeological exactitude. Roman, Greek, and Egyptian chairs, tables, and benches, were copied or adapted to nineteenth-century needs. For those articles for which the ancient world provided no precedent, archeological enthusiasm devised substitutes—bookcases were designed to suggest temple façades, couches were made from Roman beds, and console tables were inspired by ancient altars.

Duncan Phyfe

Duncan Phyfe (1768-1854), America's most distinguished cabinet-maker, worked in the Empire mode but is equally well known for his interpretations of earlier classic revival styles.

Duncan Phyfe arrived in New York City from Albany around 1790, and from that time until his death produced furniture of exquisite workmanship and design. During his first thirty years in New York City he produced a tremendous quantity of furniture based on Sheraton designs and French Directoire models which he interpreted with unsurpassed beauty and grace. After 1830, the heavier and more ostentatious aspects of the Empire mode characterized Phyfe's production. His early work was done in mahogany, but in later years he also used much rosewood.

The pieces of furniture in the Duncan Phyfe room are exquisite examples of his early work. They combine lightness of scale and grace of form and movement with surprising comfort and strength. Some of his favorite motifs are exemplified in the pedestal-based table with outsweeping tripod legs enhanced with fine-scale carved acanthus patterns. Chair backs are low and gracefully shaped, with slender diagonal cross braces.

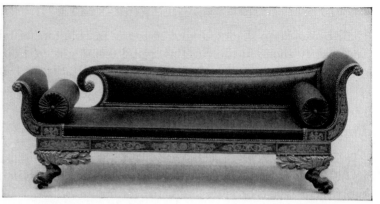

9-10 (*left*). Duncan Phyfe, Empire-style chair, 1805-1815. Courtesy Metropolitan Museum of Art, Bequest of Maria P. James, 1911.   9-11 (*right*). Duncan Phyfe (attributed to), Empire-style sofa, *c.* 1815. Courtesy Metropolitan Museum of Art, Gift of Mrs. Bayard Verplanck, 1940.

Another characteristic Duncan Phyfe piece is the lyre-back Directoire chair (9-10) with the typical incurved front legs which achieve continuity of line by joining the backposts, the side rails, and the front legs in one flowing movement. A third fine example of Duncan Phyfe's furniture is the Sheraton-style sofa (9-6) in which the subtly used straight lines, curves, and delicate flutings combine to produce an effect of rare elegance and distinction. A Duncan Phyfe sofa in the Empire style (9-11) provides an interesting contrast with the earlier Sheraton-style sofa. The proportions are heavier throughout the later work, most noticeably in the framing and the legs. Straight lines and gentle curves characterize the earlier model, while in the Empire sofa the long sweeping curve of the back and the bold reversed curves at the sides of the sofa predominate. Gilded ornamentation, bold metal mounts, animal claw feet, combined with bits of naturalistic carving, replace the simple reeding, turning, and delicate carving of the earlier style. Stunning as a design, this awesome piece of furniture seems far beyond the mundane uses of a household.

Not all of the furniture manufactured in the Empire style was designed for grand mansions. A chair (9-12) from around 1822 shows the character of Empire design translated into a more modest vein. The broad, flat back rail and central splat retain the formality and weight of the grander pieces, but the smooth unornamented surfaces contribute an effect of dignified simplicity. This is augmented by the continuous flow of line that moves from the back supports down through the side rail into the front legs to create a remarkably unified design. Stripped of its load of pompous ornament, Empire furniture often had a sober elegance and distinction.

9-12. Empire-style chair, c. 1822. Courtesy Metropolitan Museum of Art, Rogers Fund, 1926.

To round out our picture of Empire-style furniture, we might glance again at the room from the Rufus King House (9-9). The center table and sideboard illustrate the use of marble with wood and of gilded and brass ornaments. The heavier proportions and the use of architectural columns on a piece of furniture to convey a ponderous monumentality are also evident. The increased freedom with which various materials are combined in one piece of furniture; the combination of naturalistic and highly conventionalized motifs, the awkward convolutions of heavy forms all foreshadow the decline of taste evident in the furniture produced after the middle of the nineteenth century.

THE GOTHIC REVIVAL

By 1850 interior and furniture design also reflected the increased popularity of the Gothic, Tuscan, and other styles. Gothic architectural details similar to those used on the exteriors of the buildings appeared in interiors. Wooden paneling reappeared on the walls of living rooms, libraries, and dining rooms—frequently ornamented with linen-fold carving or with trefoils, quatrefoils, pointed arches, and other Gothic motifs. Windows became tall and narrow and were filled with colored glass and traceries. The curious mid-nineteenth-century translation of Gothic detail into an elaborate wooden pattern of brackets, vaults, and pendants reached its most astonishing development in the elaborate steamboats which served

9-13. Library of D. S. Kennedy mansion, 1847. Museum of the City of New York, New York.

as pleasure palaces on the rivers of America in the decade before the Civil War.

The library of the D. S. Kennedy House (9-13) in New York, dated 1847, has been attributed to Alexander Davis. In this unusually elaborate Gothic revival interior, the molded stucco ceiling was shaped to imitate Gothic ribbed vaulting. Typical Gothic motifs fill the spaces between the ceiling ribs, and the characteristic pointed arches were introduced wherever possible. The mirror over the mantel is tall, and the top, like the bookcase beside it, is carved in detail patterned after the elaborately decorated choir stalls of the middle ages. The geometrically patterned stained glass, which became popular for windows and transoms, can be seen at the far right.

The Gothic revival had little influence on furniture design. Since there had been almost no household furniture used in the middle ages, there was little authentic Gothic furniture to copy except for altars and choir stalls. Linen-fold patterns, trefoils, and quatrefoils, pointed arches,

9-14. Gothic revival bed. Bernard Rudofsky, *Behind the Picture Window* (New York, 1955).

interlacing rib patterns, and crockets and finials grafted on to the standard furniture forms of the mid-century constituted Gothic-styled pieces (9-14), frequently with grotesque effect. Machine-made cut-outs of a vaguely medieval character were used on heavy, awkwardly proportioned frames in the sixties and seventies. Probably the chief impact of the Gothic revival on furniture design was indirect; it was largely the interest in medievalism that stimulated Charles Eastlake and, later, William Morris in their attempt to combat machine developments through their revival of medieval handicraft practices.

The decline in taste that characterized furniture design in the decades before the Civil War was the result of a number of factors. A most important one was the development of elaborate mechanical lathes for shaping wood and jig saws for cutting patterns in it. These tools encouraged elaborate decorations, and furniture makers reveled in substitutes for the older and more expensive handicraft skills. Accompanying this development of new manufacturing techniques came a shift in social leadership. A new elite, born of the unprecedented opportunities that accompanied the economic and geographic expansion of the age, began to dominate both the settled eastern communities and the frontiers of the West. Social and economic power went to the cunning and the strong. The cultured gentlefolk of the eighteenth century and their standards of taste were lost in a flood of change. Handicraft production for a small clientele with cultivated tastes gave way to machine production for large numbers of uneducated people who preferred pretentious elaborateness to refinement of detail and proportion. Taste characterized the finest designs of the earlier period; ingenuity the best of the ensuing age. Many years were to pass before simple elegance and fine craftsmanship would again be the hallmark of distinguished furniture.

9-15. Hitchcock chair, 1830-1840. Index of American Design, National Gallery of Art, Washington, D.C.

DIVERGENT TRENDS

A native development of considerable charm is seen in the side chairs made by a number of companies but most notably by Hitchcock, Alford and Company of Riverton, Connecticut, and therefore, usually called Hitchcock chairs. These were inexpensive factory-made chairs based on Sheraton designs, with machine turnings and joinery replacing the more subtle molded shapes and the carved ornaments of the chairs made by fine cabinetmakers. The typical Hitchcock chair (9-15) was painted black and ornamented with bands, lining, and stenciled floral and geometric decorations applied in gilt, bronze, and color. Hitchcock chairs and the popular Boston rockers, in which a high back was topped by a broad, flat splat and legs set into rockers, were designed for mass production. The parts, made separately, were easy to assemble; the machine turnings and stenciled decorations could be applied by inexperienced workmen.

While the furniture and household wares designed for the dominant aristocracy of wealth each day became more elaborate and cumbersome, the Pennsylvania Germans continued to make their gaily decorated household furnishings and certain dissident religious groups and utopian communities developed their own simple and functional furniture and household equipment. The products of the Shakers, as in architecture,

are most noteworthy. For the most part, the Shakers retained the simple forms of eighteenth-century furniture. That which had been tried and proved serviceable was duplicated with little change. Simple trestle tables, drop-leaf tables, Windsor chairs, and various types of chests constituted the chief items of manufacture. While the Shakers retained many traditional pieces of furniture, much ingenuity went into increasing the comfort and efficiency of these familiar household items. Comfort and cheerfulness were not frowned on, though luxury was.

The rocking chair (9-16), supposedly a Shaker invention, although its use became widespread, is a modification of the older splat-backed chair designed for increased comfort. Like all Shaker furniture, this rocker reveals its structure in a straightforward manner; a glance shows how it was put together. Its charm is the result of the sensible and orderly relationship of the necessary parts, the quietly modulated shapes of spindle, splats, and rockers, and the solid and unhurried craftsmanship.

The Shakers were not averse to a gracious form although they de-

9-18. Spanish colonial chair, late 18th century. California. Index of American Design, National Gallery of Art, Washington, D.C.

cried elaboration for its own sake. "Put your hands to work and your hearts to God"—from this basic philosophy came the direct shapes that functioned so well, the beauty that was synonymous with utility, the conviction that superfluous ornament was only conducive to vanity. No where is this more clearly evident than in the corner of a room (9-17) with a stove and built-in closet, from early-nineteenth-century New Lebanon. The beautifully crafted efficiency of a Shaker interior is evident in every detail. The sparse, honest, clean shapes of the stove, like so much of Shaker manufacture, foreshadow the direct clarity of the functional designs of the twentieth century. This simplicity contrasts most effectively with the misplaced decoration which disfigured most of the early mass-produced cast iron. The orderly built-in wall closet, wide, flat mop board, pegged coat rack, and beautifully laid pine flooring create an air of sensible serenity.

Almost no furniture of American manufacture has come down to us from the French settlers. The trappers and traders rarely established a sufficiently settled mode of life to necessitate much in the way of household furnishings, and the plantation owners imported furniture for their handsome houses from Europe. The Spanish also imported much of their fine wares from Mexico and Spain, but in the mission communities the Indian neophytes were trained in all the crafts necessary for civilized living—potting, blacksmithing, stonecutting, carpentering, cabinetmaking. A chair (9-18) from the late eighteenth century was probably made for the priest in one of the California missions. Both in structure and decoration this chair is patterned after the furniture of the Spanish Renaissance. The severity of the essentially rectangular structure is relieved by somewhat flat, carved, allover patterns. The character of these carved patterns recalls the ornamented silver of the Spanish Renaissance period; consequently the architecture and furniture of this style are often termed "Plateresque," from "plata," the Spanish word for "silver." Most of the furniture and household wares made by the Indian craftsmen in the mission communities was simple and serviceable and, like this chair, had the strength that usually characterizes unpretentious handicrafts.

THE HOUSEHOLD ARTS

Silver

The making of fine silver remained in the hands of individual workmen through most of the nineteenth century, and the high standard of craftsmanship that distinguished the earlier silver was maintained despite changing tastes. The shift from baroque and rococo designs to the classic revival manner was clearly reflected in both the shapes of individual pieces and the typical decorative motifs. A sugar bowl and creamer (9-19) by Paul Revere reveal many characteristics common to the furniture and architecture of the Federal style. The individual pieces are taller and more slender than heretofore and some parts, like the handle of the creamer, are very attenuated. Chaste forms and restrained curves were preferred to the complex rococo shapes. The urn of classic antiquity became a source of continued inspiration. Urn shapes and the lines of Greek vases were adapted to coffeepots, teapots, creamers, and sugar bowls, while small urns were used as finials on the domed covers for tureens and teapots and coffeepots. Urn-shaped vessels frequently had a square base. The straight sides, the fine scale of the engraved designs, and the logical placement of the bands of decoration also reveal the rational tone of classicism as opposed to the whimsical rococo.

Paul Revere (1735-1818), famous as a patriot, was one of America's finest silversmiths. We have already seen an example of his father's silversmithing. Paul Revere, Jr., commenced his career when he took over his father's shop at the age of nineteen. His ability as a silversmith was

9-19. Paul Revere, creamer and sugar bowl, silver, 1770-1810. Boston. Courtesy Metropolitan Museum of Art, Bequest of A. T. Clearwater, 1933.

equaled by his versatility and ambition, for he was not only a silversmith and active politically, but was also one of the first manufacturers of brass in America.

While New England tended to remain conservative in its silversmithing tastes, New York and Philadelphia enjoyed a vigorous expression of the later classic revival tendencies. A teapot (9-20) made by William Heyer, one of many fine silversmiths who worked in New York in the first half of the nineteenth century, reflects the turn of the later classic revival styles toward heavier proportions and bolder curves. The oval base resting on ball feet, the full forms of the bowl and lid, the weighty finial, all suggest that the turn-of-the-century simplicity was giving way to formality and artifice.

A sugar bowl (9-21) made in Philadelphia during the third or fourth decade of the century further illustrates the Empire influence on silver. The florid decorations on the basic urn shape strike a pretentious, even pompous, note. Such traditional Empire motifs as the Greek key and the conventionalized acanthus leaves are combined with stylistically unsuitable details—for example, the naturalistic garlands of fruit and flowers

9-20 (*left*). William Heyer, teapot, silver, early 19th century. New York.   9-21 (*right*). Robert and William Wilson, sugar bowl, silver, 1825-1846. Philadelphia. Both courtesy Metropolitan Museum of Art, Bequest of A. T. Clearwater, 1933.

which encircle the body of the bowl and the shepherd which tops the cover. Though a high level of technical skill is evident, this striving for effect by combining a multitude of decorative devices suggests that in silver also the great eighteenth-century tradition of restraint gave way to a desire for pretentious elaboration.

Ceramics

Lead-glazed redware, slip-decorated potteries, and the sturdy gray and brown stonewares continued to be the staple output of most American potters throughout the nineteenth century. While a decent-looking white earthenware had been produced in Philadelphia in the 1870's most of the fine table china used on American tables in the nineteenth century was made in the Orient for export or imported from Europe. Though fine china and porcelains seemed beyond the capacity of American manufacturers, various potteries provide a charming expression of the popular tastes of the day. One of the largest centers of pottery manufacture was Bennington, Vermont, where a fine deposit of buff clay encouraged the manufacture of many popular decorative ceramics, notably the Rockingham and Parian types of ware.

Rockingham wares were popular all-purpose nineteenth-century ceramics made from a fine, cream-colored clay which, in its plastic state, could be easily and quickly pressed into molds. This permitted it to be fashioned by modern factory methods thereby eliminating the laborious

9-22 (*left*). Hound-handled pitcher, 1840-1845. Brooklyn Museum, Brooklyn, N.Y. 9-23 (*below*). Poodles, mid-19th century. Courtesy Metropolitan Museum of Art, Gift of Dr. Charles W. Green, 1948.

use of the potter's wheel. Pottery manufactured in molds was thin, light, and attractive. All types of table and kitchen as well as finely modeled ornamental wares in both low and high relief were manufactured in quantity. Rockingham wares were glazed with a mottled, shiny glaze that resembled tortoise shell, which varied from dark, almost blackish, brown, to light cream and tan tones, giving a tortoise-shell effect. Among the popular items manufactured in Rockingham ware were the hound-handled pitchers (9-22). The pitcher shown here combines the characteristic hound-handle, a bas-relief hunting scene, and the popular grape and grapeleaf motif. The pitcher is sturdy, and its mélange of naturalistic decorative motifs reflects the popular tastes of the time. Parian ware was one of the most noteworthy developments in decorative ceramics at Bennington. Parian ware, an unglazed porcelain named for its lovely surface texture which suggests Parian marble, originated in England. It was usually white or cream-colored, but vases, pitchers, and figurines were also produced in blue, buff, and green. A pair of amusing poodle dogs (9-23) have a characteristic combination of sentimental charm, humor, and decorative effectiveness. The clever way in which the various textures have been delineated—smooth clipped surfaces, crinkled fur, and woven basket—indicates a delightful exploitation of the beautiful mat surface of the unglazed porcelain.

Glass

Two basic types of glass appeared in America in the early nineteenth century. One, which relied for its decorative values on effects that grow

9-24 (*left*). Pitcher, South Jersey glassware, early 19th century.   9-25 (*right*).
Sugar bowl, green swirled glass, 1815-1845. Zanesville, O. Both, Yale University
Art Gallery, Courtesy of the Mabel Brady Garvan Collection, New Haven, Conn.

naturally out of the blowing process, has been termed South Jersey type
glass. The other, in which patterns imprinted on the molten glass by a
mold are expanded in blowing, is termed Stiegel type glass. After the demise in the late eighteenth century of Caspar Wistar's New Jersey factory,
his men settled throughout New Jersey, New York, and New England.
These men maintained the South Jersey tradition of allowing individual
workmen to make hand-blown pieces from the tag ends of molten glass
prepared for manufacturing windows and bottles. These pieces made at
the blower's pleasure vary greatly in shape, and much of their charm
results from their informality and the simple decorative devices that are
a natural outgrowth of the glass blower's techniques. The typical decorative effects of South Jersey glassware can be seen in an early nineteenth-
century pitcher (9-24). The generally sturdy proportions, the lily pad
decorations superimposed in a heavy swirl of glass over the body of the
pitcher, the crimped, applied foot, and the threaded neck are common
to the pitchers, bowls, and bottles produced in these small factories.

Baron Stiegel's factory had been set up to manufacture bottles and
fine glassware for the table and for decorative purposes. With this in
mind, Baron Stiegel imported workmen trained in the fine glass factories
of England. With the dissolution of the Stiegel enterprises many of his
former workmen went west to Pittsburgh and Ohio. A green swirled sugar

9-26 (*left*). Pitcher, blown three-mold glass, geometric type, 1810-1850. Courtesy Metropolitan Museum of Art, Rogers Fund, 1910.   9-27 (*right*). Compote, pressed lacy glass, 19th century. Courtesy Metropolitan Museum of Art, Gift of Mrs. Charles W. Green, 1951.

bowl (9-25) reveals the complexity and refinement of form and color found in the Stiegel type mold-formed glass. Such glass was shaped while molten in a mold incised with ribbings, flutings, and diamond-shaped patterns. The glass was then expanded by blowing, and subsequent twisting, turning, and other manipulations produced the desired shapes and surface textures.

The most distinctive development in American glassmaking came around 1820 with the invention of the full-sized three-piece mold which enabled American manufacturers to meet the competition of European cut glass at a much lower price. Hot glass was blown into a mold in which designs were engraved. As the mold was closed, the air pressure forced the glass into the patterns as well as the shape of the mold (9-26). The patterns on blown-mold glass are not so sharply defined as those on the pressed glass which came later, but because both the inner and outer surfaces of the glass are faceted, blown-mold glass reflects the light with great sparkle and brilliance. Blown-mold glass was occasionally fashioned with two- or four-piece molds, but the three-piece molds were most common.

In the late twenties, machines were invented for pressing glass into molds by means of mechanical power. The resultant designs are sharp-edged and clear, as distinguished from the softer and more fluid patterns of the blown-mold process. The most popular pressed glass in the first half of the century was the distinctive "lacy" glass (9-27), which at first imitated hand-cut glass but rapidly acquired a character of its own with fine textures replacing the more clearly defined patterns of wheel-cut glass.

While many American companies produced pressed glass, lacy and otherwise, the most famous company was the Boston and Sandwich Glass Company of Sandwich, Massachusetts, which made fine glass from 1825 to 1888. The fame of this company is such that all nineteenth-century pressed glass has often been called Sandwich glass, irrespective of its origin.

Textiles

The early years of the republic witnessed the full flowering of the craft of weaving, but in the 1780's the automatic loom was patented in England, and the machine-powered automatic loom followed soon after. The first Jacquard loom was set up in Philadelphia in 1826 and the day of machine weaving in America had begun.

Hand-weaving persisted side by side with the new industrial developments for a time, but the machine rapidly replaced the home weaver except in a few very poor and isolated communities like those in the mountains of Kentucky and Tennessee. Here handicraft weaving remained traditional into the early years of the twentieth century.

A woven linen double-cloth coverlet (9-28) from Indiana is dated in the first half of the nineteenth century. Geometric patterns of this type, characteristic of the eighteenth century, continued to be popular in the frontier communities. This pattern, called "Nine Snowballs with Pine Tree Border," is vigorous, crisp, and clear, with straight lines and rectangular shapes which are an unforced outgrowth of the weaving process. There is a pleasing variety in the sizes and shapes of this lively pattern so that though the effect is direct and uncomplicated it is neither dull nor lacking in interest. Double weaving—the pattern shows blue against white on one side and white against blue on the other—flourished in the early years of the century. The spread shown here is all linen, but usually in double-cloth, colored wool was combined with white cotton or linen. With the introduction of the Jacquard looms the simple geometric patterns dropped from popularity. A detail from a woven coverlet (9-29) from the mid-nineteenth century reveals the complicated leaf, flower, and bird patterns in flowering lines and interlacing rhythms that became popular in Jacquard weaves.

As hand-weaving disappeared, the housewives of America poured their enthusiasm for needlework into the making of elaborate appliqué and pieced quilts. An appliqué quilt (9-30) from Virginia combines a

9-28 (*left*). Double-cloth coverlet, woven linen, early 19th century. Indiana. Index of American Design, National Gallery of Art, Washington, D.C. 9-29 (*right*). Jacquard-weave coverlet, wool and cotton, *c.* 1850. Indiana. Index of American Design, National Gallery of Art, Washington, D.C.

number of characteristic motifs in a charming manner. An American eagle and stars form a medallion of patriotic motifs in the center. Above are the initials of the maker and below the date of manufacture. A bold border of quilt-blocked oak leaves frames the more delicate central motifs. A lovely leaf and star pattern in the quilting stitch and the small-scale patterns of the appliqué calico contribute to the total effect. In some quilts extra cotton was stuffed into the more important motifs to build them up, thereby creating textiles of unusual sculptural richness.

Candlewick bed spreads were also popular. To make the candlewick patterns, threads were worked over a roll to form looped knots which were left uncut or cut, depending on the texture desired. While braided rag rugs continued to be made throughout the century, elaborate hooked rugs provided an outlet for the weaver whose ambitions went beyond the purely utilitarian level. Most hooked rugs from this period were designed by the person who wove them, and their vigorous patterns and colors provide a refreshing contrast to the standardized designs that came into vogue toward the end of the century.

Pride of stitchery was great among nineteenth-century housewives, and while most of them found an adequate outlet for their skills in em-

9-30. Appliqué quilt, 1853. Virginia.
Index of American Design, National
Gallery of Art, Washington, D.C.

broidering pillows, furniture covers, and samplers, a few intrepid individuals embroidered elaborate pictures. Mourning pictures provided the
means for enshrining both the memory of loved ones and the maker's skill
in needlework. A mourning picture (9-31) from the first decade of the
nineteenth century, embroidered on silk in colored yarn, displays an
astonishing variety of stitches, a nice sense of design, and an unusual
ability to express genuine sentiment in what to our day appears to be a
medium somewhat unsuited to such sober purposes.

In the period following the Declaration of Independence, interiors,
furniture, silver, and other fashionable articles designed for the home
reflected the influence of the classic revival. Between 1790 and 1810 this
influence expressed itself in a preference for straight lines, light clean
surfaces, fine-scaled details and an orderly and logical disposition of parts.
Such typical classic motifs as swags, urns, and garlands replaced the
whimsical and fanciful rococo motifs, and slender and attenuated parts
were preferred to the heavier proportions of the Georgian style. Starting
around 1810 with the Greek revival, there was a return to massive, even
pompous, effects. Broad, flat moldings, the use of imposing architectural
forms on furniture and *objets d'art,* and bold, sweeping reverse curves
were characteristic of the Empire style, as the interior equivalent of the
Greek revival was called.

9-31. Embroidered mourning picture, 1808. Museum of Art, Rhode Island
School of Design, Providence, R. I.

The Empire style was followed by a succession of revivals, but by
mid-century the disintegration of the older handicraft tradition was becoming apparent. Furniture design and the traditional crafts showed the
effects of industrialization. The beauty of line and graceful proportions
which had distinguished fine furniture at the turn of the century gave
way to an endless elaboration of turned spools and cut-out ornaments.
Textiles, glass, ceramics, and metal wares were also elaborated to the
point of vulgarity. Much of the new purchasing public came from social
elements with little background in the arts.

Seen in perspective, the vulgar proliferations of nineteenth-century
mass production served their purpose. Through a long apprenticeship the
true potentials of machine design were discovered. Modern designers
learned from the mistakes of the Victorian age, and we owe thanks to
them for whatever dignity and restraint characterize machine production today.

Portraiture and

Historical Painting

THE REVOLUTIONARY WAR ENDED THE PERIOD IN
American painting when the untrained or partially trained artist was
typical. Thereafter, an increasing number of artists revealed an intimate
knowledge of the mature tradition of painting in Europe. Hands that had
been trained in the established academies and minds that had been
refined by contact with great works of art took over the leadership.

PORTRAITURE: THE LONDON SCHOOL

Benjamin West

The single individual who contributed most to the increased technical
and esthetic sophistication of the American artist was Benjamin West.
Benjamin West (1738-1820) was born in Philadelphia and in his youth

10-1. Benjamin West, *Penn's Treaty with the Indians*, 1771. Pennsylvania Academy of the Fine Arts, Philadelphia.

modeled his paintings after those of John Hesselius and other painters of the Philadelphia area. Like Copley's, his youthful efforts outshone those of his teachers. Unlike Copley, he left the colonies to study abroad before his considerable talents had an opportunity to mature at home; when he was twenty-one a group of Philadelphia merchants collected funds to send him abroad so that he might study, return, and shed glory on Philadelphia. West went to Rome where he studied for three years, after which he settled in England where he became a leader in English and Continental art circles.

When Benjamin West arrived in Italy the classic revival was in the air. Classic revival painting had a number of specific precepts most of which were closely related to the characteristics of classic revival architecture and household arts. Since the classicists held rationalism as an ideal, they proceeded in a rational way to create a style which would summarize and combine the finest from the past. The sculptural forms of Greece and Rome and the lucid and considered compositional devices of the High Renaissance, particularly of Raphael and the Venetians, provided the principal stylistic sources. Themes were drawn from history, both classic and contemporary, were of a didactic nature, and usually empha-

10-2. Benjamin West, *Robert Fulton*, 1806. New York State Historical Association, Cooperstown, N. Y.

sized some heroic act. Compositions were stable—strong vertical, horizontal, and pyramidal elements were introduced to replace the sinuous curves of the rococo. Line and form were given precedence over color. Painterly elements like spontaneity of execution and variety of brushwork were abandoned for an enamel-like smoothness of surface.

The precepts of this school were not clearly defined at the time West arrived in Rome, but were being formulated. His paintings were among the first to embody them, and when he arrived in London as a disciple of the new school of painting, his success was immediate. He proclaimed his American heritage by including subjects from the history of the new world as well as of the old. Both his *Death of Wolfe* and his *Penn's Treaty with the Indians* (10-1) treat incidents from American history with monumental dignity and force. *Penn's Treaty with the Indians* is worth examination as an example of the rational compositional concepts of the neoclassic painters. In each of the two lower corners of the canvas there is a triangular group of figures which carry the eye to the central group of actors. This group of principal characters forms a semicircle in the middle space of the painting, open in front and surrounding the kneeling figure displaying cloth to the Indian chief. Penn himself stands in back of the kneeling figure, and both the gestures of his spreading hands and the subtle spacing of the figures around him make his figure one of the principal focal points of the composition. The background establishes the setting for the action and provides stabilizing vertical and horizontal lines. The drawing throughout the painting is skilled and proper, textures are well simulated, the color is bright and clear, and the somewhat histrionic gestures insure narrative clarity. While the compositional arrangements and the groupings of the figures were traditional, West made innovations of his own. Costumes and background were drawn from life, and the choice of subject matter was unique. In its day, the painting stood as a marvel of dignified and monumental narrative realism.

In some of West's later works one feels his desire to enlarge the domain of classic revival painting by intensifying the emotional elements. His portrait of the inventor Robert Fulton (10-2) foreshadows the portraiture of the oncoming romantic school in the moody and contemplative pose of the inventor, whose pale face and dark eyes stand out in theatrical brilliance against the shadowy and ominous background. The manner of the painting, however, is still that of the classic revival. The stable composition, moving upward in a continuous sweep from the horizontal thigh and arm, is logical in its line movements and distribution of light and dark. West's skill is evident in the precise delineation of contours and the enamel-like smoothness of the surface. There are no ambiguities of form or space, no awkwardnesses of drawing. But control and technical skill seem almost to inhibit the free expression of perceptions and feelings, to stiffen gestures and confine the eye. One is left feeling that the painter's vision could only record the outward appearances—that West could not go beneath the smooth surface to discover the character of the sitter.

Both by direction and example West exerted a tremendous influence on the art of his homeland. Almost every important American painter of the late eighteenth century visited him in London and was inspired by his example. A number of these men—Charles Willson Peale, Gilbert Stuart, Ralph Earl, and John Trumbull—determined the character of much American nineteenth-century painting.

Gilbert Stuart

Probably no painter has left a more indelible impression on American life than Gilbert Stuart (1755-1828). Stuart not only created the image of George Washington which has been imprinted on the national mind, but he also painted almost every other important American during the forma-

10-3. Gilbert Stuart, *Athenaeum Portrait of George Washington*, 1796. Museum of Fine Arts, Boston. Courtesy of the Boston Athenaeum.

tive years following the Revolutionary War. His first portraits, executed in Newport during his teens, caught the attention of a Scotch migrant painter who took him to Edinburgh to study. Stuart eventually spent twelve years in London studying with the English masters and developing his own mature style. Here he achieved success and honors but his extravagant mode of living and the consequent debts finally forced him to flee. He returned to America where he spent the remainder of his years in productive activity.

Gilbert Stuart painted Washington many times, but the image of Washington that remains most vivid in the national consciousness is the unfinished portrait in the Boston Museum of Fine Arts—the *Athenaeum Portrait* (10-3). Here is no mere record of a man's appearance; instead Stuart created a symbol of a great leader, dignified, contemplative, and assured. This portrait reveals Stuart's particular ability to see beneath the gesture and expression of the moment to the basic physical structure and the fundamental character of the sitter. The form is built solidly by means of the most subtle modeling. The paint is applied with a direct certainty to reveal the sculpture of the skull, the strong jaw, the clear thoughtful eye, and the firm mouth. The virtuosity of the brushwork leaves a fresh and unlabored crispness of surface that almost denies the monumental nature of the form it describes. Most of Stuart's portraits, like this one, are without any supplementary devices. The head stands out against an

10-4. <u>Gilbert Stuart, *Mrs. Richard Yates, c.* 1793</u>. National Gallery of Art, Washington, D.C., Mellon Collection.

airy background, dignified and immobile. The sculpture of the form is revealed by the quiet flow of light over the features, creating a timeless and significant symbol of personality. Stuart had observed the work of Reynolds, Gainsborough, and others, and they had contributed to this direct, dignified, yet decorative style. The suave golden color harmonies and the luminous shining textures reflect the English masters; this was no shallow imitation of their skillful style, however, but rather a timely flowering of a great talent.

Stuart was at his best with a sitter who combined patrician distinction with a certain vigor of personality. <u>His *Mrs. Richard Yates* (10-4) is a masterpiece of subtle understanding, sharp observation, skillful brushwork, and harmonious tone. The light flows across the surfaces, revealing forms and textures with lucidity and elegance. The effortless depiction of the gesture of the hands, the sudden turn of the head, and the contained, knowing, and patient expression of the face are achievements of a master.</u>

While Stuart was certainly no doctrinaire classicist, <u>his attitude toward his subject was essentially a classic one.</u> He was concerned <u>not with the mood of the moment nor with fleeting expressions nor with momentary gestures but rather with the timeless aspects of his subjects, the contained and monumental elements of their character.</u> His subsequent influence resided largely in the high standard of taste and skill he established through his work.

like Copey

10-5. Charles W. Peale, *Timothy Matlack*, c. 1795. National Gallery of Art, Washington, D.C., Mellon Collection.

The Peale Family

For the most part the esthetic doctrines of classicism seem remote from the concerns of the portrait painters. The aristocratic ideals of the past had been swept aside by the great political movements of the age. A belief in the dignity of each individual had replaced older ideals of birth and position. The vigorous and positive personalities look out from nineteenth-century canvases full of optimism and self-confidence, and the artists who portray them seem to share the common fund of energy and assurance. No painter illustrates this outgoing and vigorous personality better than Charles Willson Peale (1741-1827). Born in Maryland, the son of a poor schoolteacher, Peale first thought of being a painter at the age of twenty-one. Subsequently he studied under West in London for two years, returned home, and then moved to Philadelphia where he spent the remainder of his life. The story of Peale's life is essentially that of an intelligent, optimistic extrovert, full of energy and enthusiasm, who could translate his ambitions into concrete achievements. The story of these achievements is an important chapter in the annals of American art. Peale not only produced some of the finest portraits and genre studies painted in the early years of the republic, but he also organized the first museum in the United States. His portrait of Timothy Matlack (10-5) reveals his particular gifts. Timothy Matlack looks out at us, thoughtful,

10-6. Charles W. Peale, *Peale in His Museum*, 1822. Pennsylvania Academy of the Fine Arts, Philadelphia.

clear-eyed, and resolute—his form defined by a clear full flow of light over the face and body. Neither the artifice of bold brushwork nor the evocative mystery of shadow obscures the homely familiarity of the face. We see what is essentially a thoughtful statement of fact by a sensible skilled craftsman. Yet this is no cold and disinterested delineation of form but an expression of the wholesome humanity of the artist. The warmth of

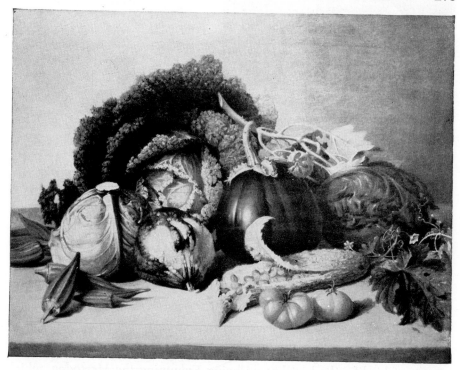

10-7. James Peale, *Balsam Apple and Vegetables*, n.d. Courtesy Metropolitan Museum of Art, Maria De Witt Jesup Fund, 1939.

Peale's regard for his sitter, his respect for the integrity of the man is conveyed with surprising force. The use of color in his portrait is typical of Peale. A generally warm tone pervades the canvas, grayed browns in the background providing a foil for the warmer tones of the coat and vest which in turn build up to the clear flesh colors. It is not a subtle and sophisticated color scheme such as Gilbert Stuart might have used, but is pleasant and satisfying.

Peale's self-portrait in his museum (10-6), painted when he was eighty-one, shows the artist lifting a curtain to display one of the great achievements of his life, the Peale Museum. In the foreground are the symbols of his accomplishments—the stuffed turkey and taxidermists' tools, the great bones of the mastodon, and the artist's palette suggesting in turn the craftsman, the scientist, and the artist. Beyond the raised curtain can be seen the exhibits of stuffed birds and animals, surmounted by the portraits of the great men of the American Revolution painted by the artist and his sons. The artist welcomes the spectator with a calm and

10-8. Raphael Peale, *After the Bath*, 1823. William Rockhill Nelson Gallery of Art, Atkins Museum, Kansas City, Mo.

inviting glance and gesture. The tone of the painting is one of quiet pride, the satisfaction of a sensible man in the considerable achievements of his lifetime. Peale painted a number of pictures depicting significant aspects of his life, the best-known being *Exhuming the Mastodon,* which pictures the excavation of the bones of the mastodon, and the *Staircase Group,* a life-sized portrait of his two sons, Raphael and Titian.

The influence of Charles Willson Peale extended far beyond his immediate accomplishments. His energetic devotion to the cause of the arts helped make Philadelphia a leading center of the intellectual and artistic life of the country. Under the stimulus of his example and training, a number of members of his immediate family became painters. His brother James Peale (1749-1831) achieved considerable distinction as a painter of still lifes. *Balsam Apple and Vegetables* (10-7) is typical of his work. The skillful rendering of the colors and surface textures of familiar objects creates a work of quiet charm.

After the Bath (10-8), by Raphael Peale (1774-1825), is far more unusual, both because of the unconventional subject and because of the startling effectiveness with which it is painted. A towel hangs on a line in front of a painting of a girl, presumably nude, drying her hair. Not only does this provide an unusual and brilliant *trompe l'oeil,* but it also constitutes an amusing conceit that suggests the gentle and whimsical personality of this talented, but not too successful son of Charles Peale.

Another son, Rembrandt Peale (1778-1860), became a portrait painter of considerable consequence. His handsome painting of Thomas

10-9. Rembrandt Peale, *Thomas Jefferson*, 1805. Courtesy of the New York Historical Society, New York.

Jefferson (10-9) displays his particular forte. The pose is quiet, the background simple, the movement of the fur collar and the turn of the head suggesting the thoughtful but active man. The quiet brush strokes that seem to describe the movements of the artist's eye over his subject are reminiscent of Charles Peale's *Timothy Matlock*. But the quiet harmony of tone provides a touch of poetic sentiment that is absent from the father's stalwart prose. The portrait is gentler, and though the perceptions are no less acute than those of the older Peale, they are presented with more grace and charm. Rembrandt had felt the oncoming tide of romanticism.

Ralph Earl

In many somewhat isolated areas of the country the awkward strength of the colonial style still persisted. Ralph Earl (1751-1801) is the most impressive example of a post-Revolutionary artist whose work gained in strength and power because of its indigenous and naive character. Earl was born in western Connecticut, an isolated rural area, and executed his earliest work with little or no training. He fought in the Revolution and then sailed for England, where he spent six years. Though he studied with West, his style always retained some of the awkward and monumental gravity that characterized it before his period abroad. On his return to America he settled in western Connecticut, where he spent the remainder of his life painting the local gentry, frequently in

10-10. Ralph Earl, *Roger Sherman,* 1775-1777. Yale University Art Gallery, New Haven, Conn.

the setting of their homes, fields, and village streets. Earl's portrait of Roger Sherman (10-10), painted before his sojourn in England, reveals the power of his severe style. Except for the light hands and face the painting is somber and dark, brown, black and dark red being the predominant colors. The forms, delineated with a direct severity, create from the black stockinged legs of the sitter and the black painted legs of the Windsor chair a pyramidal base which then builds up through the thighs, hands, arms and body to the strongly structured dominating face. No graceful supplementary forms, no flickers of deftly painted textiles, no flashing brush strokes relieve the angular grandeur of the sitter, whose movements were, as John Adams noted, "stiffness and awkwardness itself." Earl's severe but certain notations of form suggest an intense, even ardent, artistic personality restrained by the rural New England puritan tradition but still able to give expression to that graceless, severe, but forthright and courageous way of life.

PORTRAITURE AND ROMANTICISM

Though nineteenth-century portrait painters were primarily interested in the facts of appearances, they too were affected by the oncoming

10-11. Thomas Sully, *Mother and Son, 1840.* Courtesy Metropolitan Museum of Art, Bequest of Francis T. S. Darley, 1914.

tide of romanticism. Even Benjamin West, as revealed in his portrait of Robert Fulton, had become concerned with the realm of highly wrought emotions and exciting visions that were the particular province of the romantic. The romantic mood asserted itself in portraiture in a way particularly compatible with the American temperament, for the romanticism that flourished in America was not the most extreme or imaginative form. Romanticism in America was a kind of pragmatic romanticism, its head occasionally in the clouds, but its feet usually firmly rooted in reality.

That the portrait painting of the day reflected the romantic attitude was inevitable; the warmth of sentiment and the deep humanitarian impulses of romanticism were central to the human concerns of the portrait painter. The artist could achieve an exact and literal likeness and at the same time, by gesture and expression, and even more by the use of color and tone, could suggest such romantic attributes as a deep capacity for emotion, inner tumult, dreams, visions, compassion, and heroism. But the romantic tendencies were kept firmly in leash; the dominant desire was for a fine likeness.

Thomas Sully

Thomas Sully (1783-1872) was the leading portrait painter in Philadelphia and the central states during the third and fourth decades of the century. Immensely popular, Sully painted a remarkable number of por-

10-12. Thomas Sully, *The Passage of the Delaware*, 1819. Museum of Fine Arts, Boston.

traits as well as a great variety of landscapes and historical and genre paintings. His *Mother and Son* (10-11) provides a brilliant example of his ability to achieve a romantic portrait of mood. The sheer elegance of tone—flashing lights, rich darks, and melting grays—would be difficult to surpass. The sweeping line of the child's body forms a graceful opposing line to the mounting movement of the main compositional mass. Starting at the feet of the seated figure, the forms build up to the graceful urn on the upper right, creating a rhythmic and graceful flow of broadly massed oppositional movements which accord with the romantic love of grace, animation, and a sense of resolved conflict. The facial expressions are pensive and thoughtful, with a hint of a sad sweet smile, the sweet melancholy of popular poetic sentiment. The idealized and pretty features suggest elegance and breeding. The brushwork is broad and facile. This masterpiece of decorative romantic painting is so skillfully executed and charming that one hardly notices the absence of any incisive analysis of character.

While Sully is best known as a portrait painter, his historical compositions merit more attention than they customarily receive. In his *The Passage of the Delaware* (10-12) the handsomely conceived tonal

10-13 (left). Samuel Waldo, Andrew Jackson, 1817. Courtesy Metropolitan Museum of Art, Rogers Fund, 1906. 10-14 (right). Chester Harding, Amos Lawrence, c. 1845. National Gallery of Art, Washington, D.C., Gift of the Children of the Late Rt. Rev. William Lawrence.

pattern culminating in the focal figure of Washington on horseback concurs magnificently with the wave of movement that, starting in the lower left, rises to a crest in the form of Washington and the mounted rider behind him. The action is projected without effort; the handsome forms of men and animals are depicted with fluency and force. The ease with which all the elements of the painting are composed in a continuous movement of line, color, and tone reveals an ability to control and orchestrate all the parts of a complex narrative painting that no American painter of Sully's day, except perhaps Trumbull, ever surpassed.

Samuel Waldo (1783-1861) painted Andrew Jackson (10-13) in the romantic manner, but not the romantic manner of the Byronic gesture. Instead the deeply emotive device of the transparent shadow is explored. The soft brush strokes barely define the surfaces; the warm background seems vibrant, like some deep sonorous musical note. A reverent sentiment pervades this sober portrait, and yet the Andrew Jackson that looks out at us is no sentimental conception; a masculine character of surprising strength emerges from the canvas. After long years as a professional por-

10-15. George P. A. Healy, *President James Buchanan*, 1859. National Gallery of Art, Washington, D.C., Mellon Collection.

trait painter in New York, Waldo lost some of the evocative subtlety that distinguished his early work, but his portraits were always painted with sensitive honesty and strength.

Most typically a child of the new era of Jacksonian democracy was Chester Harding (1792-1866), farmhand, woodsman, saloon keeper, and peddler, who, though he had hardly seen a painting before the age of twenty, became a sufficiently successful portrait painter to have supposedly taken eighty sitters from Gilbert Stuart in a six-month period.

In the course of his long and successful career in the Boston area, Harding painted innumerable portraits of America's great and celebrated. His handsome portrait of the New England philanthropist Amos Lawrence (10-14) reveals his particular forte. Amos is seated in a comfortable chair, dressed in a handsome Paisley dressing gown. The atmosphere is relaxed and intimate. The background may suggest regal splendor, but this is the only concession to imagination or sentiment. The rest is clearly observed and brilliantly stated fact. The fine features of the face, the lively eyes staring out from beneath the bushy brows, the various surface textures—velvet, wool, wood, damask, and skin—the forms of the body and the spaces in the room are all described with startling fidelity. This is the work of an intelligent skilled man who saw clearly and objectively. No deep lyric feeling, subtlety of mood, or psychological insight distinguishes the work. It is a positive and energetic reflection of a positive and energetic age, completely knowing and certain.

George P. A. Healy (1813-1894) made his home in the new metropolis of Chicago though his successful career kept him continuously on the move both here and abroad. Healy's life was a nineteenth-century American story of rags to riches. Born of a poor Boston family, his rise to success was meteoric. At eighteen his portraits of Boston's celebrities had brought him renown. Before he was twenty he was studying with Gros in Paris, and in the course of his life he painted over six hundred of the famous people of Europe and America. From Gros, Healy learned the importance of varying the weight of the oil paint; American painters were apt to work in a thin manner that left a monotonous surface. By varying the paint from a thick impasto of great carrying power in the lights to thin transparent darks, Healy achieved the brilliant range of tone that is one of the most notable elements in nineteenth-century academic painting. The effectiveness of his light and dark contrasts distinguishes his handsome portrait of President James Buchanan (10-15). Healy was probably at his best communicating the physical energy and dynamic personalities of the vigorous and successful men who dominated his age.

Though portrait painting flourished, not all of the portrait painters enjoyed the worldly success of Harding and Healy. Two men from early in the period, John Vanderlyn (1775-1852) and Samuel F. B. Morse (1791-1872), produced some fine likenesses in the process of making a living but they considered portrait painting a prosaic task. Their ambition was to father more important works: great historical canvases or inspiring allegories. Unfortunately, their aspirations did not coincide with the opportunities in America; disappointment dulled their ardor, and their inability to realize their cherished ambitions made them bitter and frustrated men. The story of their struggle will have more significance in relation to the development of historical and genre painting and will be told more fully later. Suffice it for the moment to observe a portrait by each. John Vanderlyn, born in Kingston, New York, studied with Gilbert Stuart and then spent five years in Paris, probably the first American to study there. In Paris, under David, he absorbed the skilled draftsmanship and the firmly disciplined style of modeling that characterized the French neoclassic school. His *Self-portrait* (10-16) reveals this sober control of hand and eye. The form is observed dispassionately and calmly and is recorded with dignity and force in the manner of the neoclassic realists who followed the French master.

Samuel F. B. Morse, like Vanderlyn, dreamed of doing great canvases which would recall the grandeur of the Renaissance and looked with disdain on painting likenesses for his livelihood. The portraits of Morse, coming almost two decades after those of Vanderlyn, are romantic rather

10-16 (*left*). John Vanderlyn, *Self-portrait*, n.d. Courtesy Metropolitan Museum of Art, Bequest of Ann S. Stephens in the name of her mother, Mrs. Ann S. Stephens, 1918.   10-17 (*right*). Samuel F. B. Morse, *The Muse, Susan Walker Morse*, 1837. Courtesy Metropolitan Museum of Art, Bequest of Herbert L. Pratt, 1945.

than classic in atmosphere. A portrait of his daughter, *The Muse, Susan Walker Morse* (10-17), remains charming despite the sentimental idealizations of form. While there is much about the painting that reminds one of Sully, Morse did not abandon himself to lyric sentiments to the same degree. A gracious blending of fact and fancy modulates his style.

FOLK ARTISTS

All through the nineteenth century a multitude of untrained men and women in all walks of life painted more for pleasure than for profit. To the degree that they followed any conventions or traditions, they followed those of folk painting, far removed from the lessons of the academies and from both romantic and classical concepts and devices. In this folk tradition, forms were clearly defined but as flat decorative patterns rather than as three-dimensional entities. Compositions were conceived in terms of a flat picture plane rather than spatially. The traditional conventions for achieving depth, particularly the use of perspective and foreshortening, were largely ignored. Details of pattern and texture were carefully observed and as carefully described. Because these nonprofes-

10-18. L. Sachs, *The Herbert Children*, 1857. National Gallery of Art, Washington, D.C., from the Collection of American Primitive Paintings given by Edgar William and Bernice Chrysler Garbisch.

sional painters were frequently artists of sensitivity, they often revealed a singular capacity not only to describe their perceptions with clarity and a fine decorative sense but also to convey their emotions with enviable directness and force. Their forms, patterns, and textures assault our eyes more directly than they would had they been embedded in the matrix of familiar conventions.

Folk artists are seldom inventive about what they paint. Landscapes, still lifes, illustrations of Biblical texts, genre studies, and, of course, portraits were the most popular subjects and it is the portraits that interest us here. *The Herbert Children* (10-18) is signed by L. Sachs and dated 1857. It is evident that the artist is not completely naive. Some training is revealed by his systematic use of light, shade, and most important, reflected light to build a sense of form. The conventions of posing children were carefully observed; the children are seated in front of a partially drawn curtain which reveals a charming bit of landscape with flowering shrubs, a lake with sailboats on it, and a sky with floating clouds. The

10-19. Joseph H. Davis, *James and Sarah Tuttle*, 1836. Courtesy of the New York Historical Society, New York.

children are playing with their dolls and toys, one child rests her hand on the shoulder of the other. Reynolds and his followers would have been charmed with the group.

Here the similarity to fashionable portraiture ends. The composition is almost formally bisymmetric, the swirls of skirts balancing one another as do the patterns of sofa and flowering shrubs. There is no interest in such intangibles as air or space, but the surface facts fascinate the artist. Each fold of cloth is carefully described. Each anatomical detail, the hollow below the temples, the serious questioning eyes, the compressed lips are depicted with scrupulous honesty. And because the leaves on the rose bushes have been seen one at a time and the patterns of the sofa have been described as the artist knows they are, rather than as he sees them, we share his fresh enthusiasm and unjaundiced vision. His fact becomes our fancy.

In 1836, Joseph H. Davis painted a watercolor of James and Sarah Tuttle (10-19) which reveals to an unusual degree the peculiar strengths of the naive artist. Unlike L. Sachs, Joseph Davis was probably without any formal training. The faces, details of costume, and furniture give ample evidence of the artist's unerring eye. James and Sarah Tuttle sit in dignity, reading the Bible in their parlor. The picture on the wall, the pattern of the rug, the grain of the table, the cat, the fruit, and the hat are all noted with due seriousness. The symmetrical arrangement of the seated figures is both a formal compositional device and a subtle statement of human relationship. Such a painting provides a refreshing and delightful direct insight into the manner in which an artistic intelligence reacts intuitively to the familiar world. Training might have enabled Joseph H. Davis to portray forms with more illusion of depth, weight, air, light, and shadow. But training would probably not have enabled him to recreate the mood of Mr. and Mrs. Tuttle sitting in their parlor reading the Bible either more vividly or more delightfully.

Over America, all through the century, nonprofessionals painted their portraits of men, women, and children. This body of anonymous painting transmits the impression that there existed among the people deep reservoirs of sentiment and creativity sufficient to provide sustenance for a rich and continuous development of the arts in America.

HISTORICAL PAINTING

While many a painter was content to devote his life to recording the faces and figures that came to sit for him, not all were happy with such prosaic fare. Among the dreamers in this age of dreamers and visionaries were many ambitious painters. All about them a great nation was developing. New states and young cities were springing up; great city halls and greater state capitols were being built, and artists had visions of another Renaissance when artists would be entrusted with the glorious task of painting their noblest visions on the walls of public buildings. The new buildings exposed their expanses of bare wall and the artists had their dreams and noble sentiments, but it seemed difficult to reconcile the artists' ambitions with the facts of American life.

John Vanderlyn

John Vanderlyn was one of the first artists to face this dilemma. His self-portrait (10-16) has already been mentioned. Vanderlyn had spent five years in Paris where he had been sent to study by Aaron Burr, who had great faith in his talent. In France, he absorbed the precise drawing, the firm modeling, and clear color of the neoclassic school, but unfortunately he also became imbued with the idea that only didactic historical

10-20. John Vanderlyn, *Ariadne of Naxos*, 1814. Pennsylvania Academy of the Fine Arts, Philadelphia.

canvases or classic allegories were worthy of a great artist's talents. After his initial period of study abroad, Vanderlyn returned to America, spent a discouraging period at home, and on the receipt of another stipend from an American admirer, he returned to Europe for three more years of study, this time in Rome. It was during this last stay in Europe that he painted his best-known work, *Ariadne of Naxos* (10-20).

This large and brilliantly painted nude represents Vanderlyn at the height of his powers. The idealized figure, beautifully composed in relation to the spacious background, is like a quiet reflection of the great Venetian masters. Clear, lucid, and controlled, Vanderlyn's *Ariadne* is probably the finest example of the classic idealized nude in America, but the very nature of its subject matter reveals how far Vanderlyn's life as an artist in Paris and Rome had taken him from the tastes of American life.

Not until he was in his sixties did the great opportunity for which he had waited all his life come through. In 1838, he was commissioned to paint a *Landing of Columbus* for the Capitol in Washington. The commission came too late. Vanderlyn was unable to bring the project through to a successful state of completion. Though he went to France to carry out the work, most of it had to be executed by his assistants. The circumstances of American life had defeated Vanderlyn. His was one of the first and most noteworthy of the many nineteenth-century artistic careers that came to naught because they were not based on a realistic estimate of American needs and tastes. There was neither the tradition nor the institutional patronage here to insure the commissions which were part of the official pomp of Europe. Equally important, America still had no great collections of paintings and sculpture which could nourish the artist, when, lacking commissions, he might need to sustain his faith in the validity of his dreams by communing with the glorious examples of the past.

John Trumbull

John Trumbull (1756-1843) was the youngest son of Jonathan Trumbull, governor of Connecticut during the Revolution. Intellectually precocious, he was sent to Harvard at an early age where his tutor called his father's attention to the boy's "natural genius and disposition for limning," a talent which his father found not particularly useful. After graduation Trumbull returned home where he painted a group of portraits which reveals both his abilities and his lack of training. In 1784 he set out for London to study with West.

After a year in England, Trumbull returned to America with a grand project in mind, the depiction of significant scenes from American history in a series of great murals. During the next decade he painted eight small dramatic compositions as studies for the projected murals. He also executed a number of excellent miniature portraits of the notables in this drama so that his project would be both a work of art and an authentic record. These small studies reveal a genuine gift for narrative painting in the grand manner.

In 1817 Congress commissioned Trumbull to paint a group of his Revolutionary subjects as mural decorations for the rotunda of the new Capitol in Washington. These murals remain handsome and impressive paintings although Trumbull was unable to transfer the full fire and plasticity of his smaller sketches into the larger works. The wonder is that over the many years of inactivity Trumbull's talents had not atrophied from disuse.

To appreciate Trumbull's full gifts one must see his earliest studies. His *Battle of Bunker's Hill* (10-21) reveals his ability to organize a tremendous number of figures into a unified composition and at the same

10-21. John Trumbull, *Battle of Bunker's Hill,* 1786. Yale University Art Gallery, New Haven, Conn.

time to establish the complex currents of action and the different individual personalities in a clear and forceful way. The scene pictures the moment when the Americans had expended their ammunition, allowing the British troops to become master of the field. In this crisis, General Warren was killed by a musket ball through the head. The main group of figures shows General Warren dying. A kneeling soldier supports him and at the same time wards off the bayonet of a British grenadier. Colonel Small is shown grasping a musket and stopping the fatal blow, while directly behind him Colonel Pitcairn, mortally wounded, is shown falling into the arms of his son. A continuous diagonal line sweeps up from the lower right carrying the eye through successive waves of movement to this central group of figures which is boldly projected into a full burst of light. A countermovement is set up by the figure of Lieutenant Grosvenor and the other figures in the lower right, and this countermovement is sustained by the ominous line of the upraised sword and the rifle which is about to be plunged into the supine body of General Warren. As in all great dramatic painting, the narrative creates the composition and the composition, in turn, brings the narrative to life. Each head is an incisive portrait, a forceful character study full of life and individuality.

10-22. Samuel F. B. Morse, *The Old House of Representatives*, 1823. In the collection of The Corcoran Gallery of Art, Washington, D.C.

The broadly conceived tonal pattern is beautifully realized; from its fluid depths the forms emerge into light and sink back into darkness. There is an amazingly varied use of pigment from heavy impasto to thin fluid washes of transparent paint.

The late years of Trumbull's life witnessed a sad decline in his fortunes. He was made head of the American Academy of Fine Arts in New York, and through mismanagement and poor judgment he contributed to the financial ruin of the institution. Instead of providing much-needed leadership to the young painters of his day, he became a bitter and tyrannical old man.

Various episodes from the Revolutionary War, particularly those which pictured Washington's exploits, continued to fascinate painters. None of the many treatments of this theme were handsomer than Sully's *The Passage of the Delaware* (10-12), which we have already seen. The most popular picture of this type, however, was by a German, Emanuel Leutze, who painted the much-reproduced *Washington Crossing the Delaware*, in Düsseldorf, Germany.

Samuel F. B. Morse also dreamed of a Renaissance in America. His ambition, he wrote his father, was "to rival the genius of a Raphael, a Michelangelo, or a Titian." Morse was a forceful and effective realist. His scenes in Italy and his large genre paintings, like *The Old House of Representatives* (10-22), surprise us with their originality of conception, rich color, and sensitive observation. *The Old House of Representatives* combines a big conception with startling accuracy of detail. It is forcefully realized and is dramatic without being melodramatic, a real achievement for an age of romantic sentiment and melodramatic posturings. There is little evidence, however, that Morse had the temperament to create the great historical canvases and profound allegories of which he dreamed. After his invention of the telegraph he gave up his career as an artist.

11

Painting: Allegory, Landscape, and Genre

ALLEGORY

Washington Allston

While Vanderlyn, Trumbull, and Morse dreamed of immortalizing American history in great paintings, another artist, Washington Allston (1779-1843), concerned himself with the world of imagination and reverie that was the particular concern of the romantic age. Born in South Carolina, Allston was educated at Harvard, spent two years in London studying painting, and then visited Paris and Rome. His tour of the Continent introduced him to the Venetian masters and he was greatly impressed with their use of color and tone to create a pervasive mood or atmosphere, addressed, to quote his own words, ". . . not to the senses merely, as some have supposed, but through them to that region (if I may so speak) of the imagination which is supposed to be under the

293

exclusive domination of music." Allston introduced the romantic movement into America through both the highly emotionalized visionary painting of his early years and his later poetic landscapes, which reconciled his
romantic mood with the current of realism than ran through the middle
years of the century.

The nightmarish *Deluge* (11-1) illustrates the vivid and intense
emotionalism of Allston's earlier paintings. It is a vision of strange intensity, filled with mystery and terror. A great flood has spread its devasta-
tion, leaving only death and desolation. Man, one small element in the
cosmos, is the helpless victim of the overpowering forces of fate. Nature,
ominous, powerful, and cruel, is magnificent only in her strength. It is
significant of the contemplative nature of Allston that the moment he
depicted is not one of intense action, but the moment when the fury is
spent, when from the tragedy a philosophic comment can be made. Life
is conceived as terrifying but it achieves significance through contemplation—from terror man can create grandeur by casting the life of the inner
mind in monumental forms. Allston, like many of the painters of his day,
was inspired by a number of literary sources, including the Bible. From
the world of the Old Testament, of myth and prophecy, he created a
vision of divine omnipotence and supernatural mystery. "The Deluge"
appears part dream, part Biblical illustration.

In his later years Allston's dreams became gentler and more lyrical.
Moonlit Landscape (11-2) is a small and very lovely landscape painted
around 1819. The tone is one of peaceful reverie. Man still seems only a
small part of the scheme of things, but he is no longer overwhelmed either
physically or spiritually by the cosmos. The dream now seems to encom-
pass a peaceful and harmonious reconciliation of the force of nature with
human aspirations and activities. Allston, undoubtedly more than any
other artist, took American painting from a narrow concern with fact into
the realm of the imagination and introduced into the creation of a poetic
mood a subtlety of color and tone that was unknown before his day.

No American from mid-nineteenth century seems more concerned
with the world of inner fantasy than William Rimmer (1816-1879).
Although he is best known as a sculptor, his powerful drawings and his
strange and visionary paintings also deserve mention here. *Flight and
Pursuit* (11-3), though painted a few years after the confines of this
chapter, is in the contemporary allegorical vein, but this is not the allegory of sweet sentiment and noble rhetoric. Instead, as the surrealists
were to do a half-century later, it draws on the nightmare for its symbols.

11-1 (*above*). Washington Allston, *The Deluge*, 1804. Courtesy Metropolitan Museum of Art, Gift of William Merritt Chase, 1909.   11-2 (*below*). Washington Allston, *Moonlit Landscape*, 1819. Museum of Fine Arts, Boston.

11-3. William Rimmer, *Flight and Pursuit*, 1872. Museum of Fine Arts, Boston.

Man relentlessly pursues his illusions and is as relentlessly pursued by them. In *Flight and Pursuit* the palatial vistas recede to infinity, as in a strange and disturbing vision, peopled only by shadows and the silent obsessed dreamer. Rimmer drew on his own inner world for sustenance and in his isolation he created some of the most disturbing images of his day.

LANDSCAPE

The nineteenth century was the great century of landscape painting, and America provided the painter with materials of a seemingly endless variety. Mountains, lakes, rivers, deserts, and oceans were here for those challenged by space and grandeur. Woods, ravines, inlets, fields, and brooks provided more intimate and gentle aspects of nature. There were the cities, villages, farms, and frontier for those who preferred to include man. For many, the landscape of America symbolized the nation's greatness and its potential for human happiness. There was room for all in the

11-4. *Meditation by the Sea,* 1850-1860. Museum of Fine Arts, Boston, M. and M. Karolik Collection.

limitless expanses of the virgin continent, and the variety of opportunity was as great as the variety of climate and topography.

The landscape was not only a patriotic symbol but also served as a vehicle for expressing the deep religious and romantic feelings of the age. For those who could no longer believe in a religion of miracles and myths, the grandeur of nature symbolized the benign power of the Almighty. It was no wonder that in *Meditation by the Sea* (11-4) the unknown artist painted a small figure overwhelmed by the limitless expanse of sky, sea, and shore. Or perhaps one should say threatened, impressed, but not overwhelmed; for nineteenth-century man, despite his moments of questioning, remained optimistic as to his fate.

The role of Allston in the development of landscape painting has been mentioned. Through his later landscapes he encouraged the subsequent generation of painters to use the landscape as a vehicle for expressing the full range of their imagination and feelings. Certainly this ability to infuse the landscape with sentiment and grandeur constituted the particular strength of Thomas Cole (1801-1848) and the Hudson River school of painters.

Thomas Cole and the Hudson River School

Cole was born in England, but when he was a small child, his family came to the United States and settled on the frontier of Ohio. He commenced his professional life as a wandering self-taught artist, and his early pictures depicted the wild grandeur of the frontier. These early landscapes reveal the mood of solemn wonder that the seemingly endless expanses of wilderness aroused in the young man. The popularity of his youthful works enabled him to go abroad for three years of study and travel in England and Italy. On his return he settled near the village of Catskill and commenced to paint the Hudson River valley and the neighboring mountains. During his frequent sketching trips he made notes that could be composed in his studio, particularly when winter made travel difficult. Working at home, he let his imagination play over what he had seen, and he depicted the grand wilderness in its most dramatic and awesome moods. Though some of his pictures recall the works of Salvador Rosa, the wilderness he painted was the lonely back country of America, not picturesque Italy. *The Oxbow* (11-5), painted in his middle years, reveals Cole in a factual mood, depicting the pleasant cultivated valley of the Connecticut River. Despite the accumulation of detail there is a sense of space and bigness. The soft veil of rain-washed light in the middle distance, the rich pattern of cloud shadows, the energetic angle of the twisted oak in the foreground keep the painting from being a mere inventory of landscape forms. In paintings like *The Oxbow*, Cole showed himself able to reconcile his own taste for drama and sentiment with his clients' more prosaic tastes.

Cole's travels in Europe had quickened both his patriotic sentiments and his strong moral and religious propensities. In Europe he saw, to use his own words, "both the ruined towers that tell of outrage, and the gorgeous temples that speak of ostentation," and he found America, by contrast, "to be the abode of virtue." He returned from Europe deeply impressed with the great sweep of history and the fugitive nature of man's achievements. He saw the great architectural monuments of Europe as a setting for the endless pageant of civilization and the ancient ruins as God's judgment on the iniquitous nations that had abandoned Him. This vision of the past inspired a series of allegorical paintings picturing the theme of man's destiny and the passage of time. These comprised the major productions of his later years. Each of these allegories, the most notable of which were *The Course of Empire* and *The Voyage of Life,* was composed of a sequence of panels, each panel depicting one episode

11-5 (*above*). Thomas Cole, *The Oxbow of the Connecticut*, 1836. Courtesy Metropolitan Museum of Art, Gift of Mrs. Russell Sage, 1908.   11-6 (*below*). Thomas Cole, *Expulsion from the the Garden of Eden*, 1828. Museum of Fine Arts, Boston, M. and M. Karolik Collection.

11-7. Asher B. Durand, *A Catskill Stream*, 1867. Brooklyn Museum, Brooklyn, N. Y.

in a continuing theme. Engravings made from these paintings were widely circulated and provided the basis for much of Cole's popularity. These didactic illustrative paintings were deeply meaningful to the early nineteenth century. History, archeology, and science were providing new tools for exploring the past, and civilized man questioned the mystery of man's destiny and the meaning of life. *Expulsion from the Garden of Eden* (11-6) is in the manner of these historical allegories. In a visionary landscape of precipitous gorges, towering crags and eerie trees illuminated by a mystical radiance, the infinitesimal Adam and Eve commence their tragic wanderings. The minute figures and the low eye-level of the painting establish an effective grandeur of scale, and though the tendency to develop the form in undue detail detracts from the monumentality of the whole, an effect of tragic immensity is forcefully communicated.

Cole was undoubtedly the leader of the Hudson River school of landscape painting, but another artist in the New York area also contributed to the renown of the group, Asher B. Durand (1796-1886). Durand began his professional career as an engraver. The plates he engraved from Trumbull's *Declaration of Independence*, Vanderlyn's *Ariadne*, and the landscapes of Cole and others, had brought him considerable fame before he started painting in oils. Durand painted nature meticulously and sensitively with no other conscious aim than to convey

11-8. John Frederick Kensett, *Paradise Rock, Newport, c.* 1865. Newark Museum, Newark, N. J.

its sensuous beauty. Though, like Cole, he loved to depict the wilds of the Catskills, he preferred a more intimate scale than Cole. He saw nature not as an ominous force but as beneficent, a pleasant setting for human activity. Sometimes the human factor is only implied, as in his charming *A Catskill Stream* (11-7). Here no human figure obtrudes itself, but the poetic spirit of the artist contemplating the scene is felt and it infuses the woodland with a wealth of human sentiment. Durand's long discipline as an engraver appears in his trenchant use of line and the crisp clarity of his detail as well as in the fine sense of tone by which the dim and diffused light of the woods has been suggested.

Thomas Doughty (1793-1856) was another popular artist who painted upstate New York and the Catskills in the first half of the nineteenth century. Like Durand, he preferred the pastoral landscape. Doughty usually pictured figures—hunters, fishermen, or travelers—carrying on their activities in a quiet outdoor setting.

John Frederick Kensett (1816-1872), like Durand, became a painter after serving an apprenticeship as an engraver. In harmony with the dominant mood of the mid-century, he, too, endowed a friendly nature with delicate poetry. His most distinguished works are those in which a tranquil and slightly melancholy mood is imparted to a scene through a quiet sequence of horizontal lines that move through subtle gradations of

11-9. George H. Durrie, *Winter Landscape: Gathering Wood*, 1859. Museum of Fine Arts, Boston, M. and M. Karolik Collection.

texture, tone, and color into the far distance. *Paradise Rock, Newport* (11-8) illustrates this vein most effectively. The luminous tone of this painting works with the dominant horizontals in establishing the subtle mood of a quiet stretch of marsh land on a gray day. The particular quality of diffused light has been most sensitively observed; the gray sky illuminates the top planes of the landscape and brings out the sharply etched details of patterns and textures against the prevailing tone. Kensett is at his best in his paintings of water; a quiet stretch of river, a tranquil bay, or a moody expanse of marshland. His concern with the particular qualities of light establishes him as one of the first and leading of the nineteenth-century tonalists, that group of mid-century artists whose special concern was the study of outdoor light, particularly the modulated light of twilight and dawn or the diffused and misty light of the sea shore.

The artistic success and renown of the Hudson River school of New York tended to overshadow the achievements of landscape painters elsewhere. Alvin Fisher (1792-1863) in Boston and Thomas Birch (1779-1851) in Philadelphia painted pleasantly if without distinction. Almost every small town had its local artist, many of whom, popular in their own day, have been almost forgotten. Such a man was George H. Durrie (1820-1862), born in Connecticut, who tried portrait painting and then shifted to landscapes. He painted in both the New York and the New Haven areas. Many of his paintings were reproduced as prints by Currier and Ives and thus achieved extensive circulation. *Winter Landscape: Gathering Wood* (11-9) reveals the elements that made for his popularity. Durrie was not an artist of subtle perception nor were his technical methods far beyond those of popular illustration, but he operated effectively within the limited scope of his ambitions. His unerring sense of the gray tone and color of winter, of the scraggly texture of bare branches and snowy brush made his winter scenes particularly popular with rural America for whom winter with its enforced quiet and inactivity was a period of contemplation and delight in nature.

Topographical and Marine Paintings—Cityscapes

Maps, topographical views, and the painting of cities, harbors, fortifications, and gentlemen's estates had preceded landscape painting in America, and such paintings continued to be popular. A number of the artists who specialized in these subjects came from England in the last decades of the eighteenth century; among them were William Birch and his son Thomas, mentioned above, who settled in Philadelphia where they practiced painting and engraving. Thomas Birch specialized in marine views and naval battles, traveling all through the country for subjects. As the century progressed and the landscape tended to be painted as visual spectacle rather than as fact, the city, the harbor, and the life of the sea also became objects of esthetic contemplation.

Fitz Hugh Lane (1804-1865) was born in Gloucester, Massachusetts, a shipping and fishing center of New England and a community where the movement of tides and the moods of weather were a matter of daily concern. He moved to Boston where he was trained and worked as a lithographer, but later returned to Gloucester where he painted both landscape and marine subjects. *Ships in Ice off Ten Pound Island, Gloucester* (11-10) reveals the elegance of his crisp clear drawing, the subtle tonality and the fine sense of scale that distinguishes his painting. The discipline of his training as a lithographer had its effect in the precision of detail and the play of the small black accents against the pale and delicate

11-10 (*above*). Fitz Hugh Lane, *Ships in Ice off Ten Pound Island, Gloucester,*
1850-1860. Museum of Fine Arts, Boston, M. and M. Karolik Collection.   11-11
(*below*). Francis Guy, *Winter Scene in Brooklyn, c.* 1817-1820. Brooklyn Museum, Brooklyn, N. Y.

grays. Unlike earlier painters of similar subjects, his concern was not so much with the facts—though the paintings reveal an amazing ability to adhere to the factual aspects of his subjects—as with the mood of the weather, the color of the light, the pale distances, and the cold dream-like clarity of the winter day at sea. This sensitivity to atmospheric effects and the spacious grandeur of the open expanse of ice and sky suggests a refined and poetic temperament expressing itself through the discipline of exact observation and factual description.

Francis Guy (1760-1820), too, came from England between 1790 and 1800. While he painted country estates, harbor scenes, and views of cities, and, when he felt so inclined, could turn in a conventional and gentlemanly performance, his preference was for a more colorful genre. His street scenes of Brooklyn, New York, and of Baltimore constitute by far the most lively visual commentary on the folkways of America's young cities that has come down to us. A *Winter Scene in Brooklyn* (11-11) inevitably reminds one of Breughel; there is the same affectionate delight in the antics of men and animals, the same sharp eye for the patterns of buildings and the gleam of white snow against gray skies, the same ability to create a unified composition out of an infinite number of details. Guy's skill and imagination in organizing this entertaining pattern is worthy of our attention. The flow of movement projected by the imaginatively composed figures is as continuous and varied as the life of the community itself. The skillful alternation of lights and darks are in constant contrast, and snowy surfaces provide a quiet relief from the complex textures of the buildings and trees.

Guy had an enviable capacity to assimilate each fact and from it create an animated pattern imbued with wit and charm. He also has the distinction of having held what was probably the first one-man exhibition of landscapes to be shown in America. The show was held the year of his death, 1820.

Not all of the painters who created charming cityscapes had Guy's skill. The artist who painted *American Landscape* (11-12) reveals his naïveté both by the style of his work and by the charming signature, L. Whitney Pt.—Pt. undoubtedly signifying painter. The gay pattern of houses, a church, and a barn stretches across the front of the canvas, and houses mount the steep hill behind. Clouds fleck the sky, and bare trees and evergreens provide dark accents. Tiny figures and other details furnish a sense of scale and contribute animation to the scene. No element of technical skill blocks this folk artist's direct expression of his delight in folkways.

11-12. L. Whitney, *American Landscape*, n.d. Newark Museum, Newark, N. J.

GENRE PAINTING

Genre painting concerns itself with depicting everyday life and as the artist descended into the city streets he inevitably focused on man, his antics, and habits. Genre painting flourished in America between 1830 and the Civil War and displayed an engaging warmth and gentle humor, whether the subject was the life of the city, the quaint ways of country folk, or the bold adventure of the frontiersman.

Richard Caton Woodville

One of the most talented of the young nineteenth-century genre painters was Richard Caton Woodville (1825-1856), whose early death kept him from realizing his full promise. Woodville was born and spent his youth in Baltimore. A collection of Dutch genre painting which he saw there, combined with his own temperamental fondness for depicting the humor of character and situation, directed him toward the painting of picturesque anecdotes; consequently he departed for Düsseldorf, the particular center at this time for the study of anecdotal painting. He spent

11-13. Richard Caton Woodville,
Politics in an Oyster House, 1848.
Walters Art Gallery, Baltimore, Md.

most of his life abroad. He returned to the United States before his pre-
mature death and produced a small number of paintings that reveal his
unusual gift for the incisive depiction of personality and place.

Politics in an Oyster House (11-13) provides an excellent example
of his skill at vigorous narrative and at creating a convincing illusion of
realistic form and texture. The rendering of surface textures, the particular earmark of the Düsseldorf School, is not overstressed here as it
frequently was in the hands of lesser men. Woodville's primary concern
was to describe personality, the personality of people and places in interaction with one another. Woodville was one of those fortunate artists
whose ambitions coincide with their talents. His compositions appear
completely unpremeditated, yet examination of *Politics in an Oyster
House* reveals a thoughtful organization of the pictorial elements. Typical of his compositions is the limited space within which the figures are
composed. The tone builds up from grayer tones around the edges of the
canvas to more brilliant contrasts of dark and light around the focal
areas, creating a handsome and logical pattern. The way in which the
shining white pitcher focuses attention on the gesturing hand is masterly.
The faces, working with the hands, bodies, and clothes, give evidence
of vivid appreciation of personality just as the accessories reveal a quiet
delight in the character of things.

Each area of the painting has its element of interest. No part is
dull and yet the taste of the artist allows no part to become overly elabo-

11-14. William S. Mount, *Bargaining for a Horse*, 1835. Courtesy of The New York Historical Society, New York.

rated, and no objects appear to have been introduced merely to display the painter's virtuosity. The entire painting suggests a modest man of intelligence, capable of viewing the world with affection and good humor, delighted with the color and flavor of everyday life. Master of the immediate and the specific, Woodville provided a refreshing antidote to the pretentious symbolism and the didacticism of some of the more ambitious talents of the day.

William Sidney Mount

Another painter whose modest aims frequently resulted in an underestimation of his abilities is William Sidney Mount (1807-1868). Mount was a Long Island farm boy, one of three brothers all of whom were practicing artists. After a period of apprenticeship to his brother and a stint at the National Academy of Design, he started his professional life as a painter of portraits and religious subjects in New York. Illness forced him to return to the country and there he discovered that his forte was portraying the life of the farm and country folk. Mount settled at Stony Brook, Long Island, and spent the rest of his life painting anecdotes of rural Long Island. *Bargaining for a Horse* (11-14) reveals his particular talents—an ability to create a story from the quiet interplay of personalities and an ability to invest the simplest subject with warmth and humor. The scene is composed with admirable skill. Against the well-observed and carefully designed pattern of picturesque farm buildings, fences, and distant trees stand the bargaining figures. The patient stance of the saddled horse serves as a foil to the subtle interplay of wits between the two whittling men, the younger and more aggressive trying to break down the older man's quiet stubbornness. The weathered shingles, split and rotting wood, and straw-covered ground are described with the same affection and understanding as the baggy garments of the men and the sleek shining coat of the horse. Equally well-observed is the outdoor light—clear, cool, with sharp-edged shadows in which luminous reflected lights cast a golden warmth into even the darkest tones. While a host of lesser men around New York tried to imitate Mount's easy narrative style, none of them equaled him either as a draftsman or as an interpreter of folkways.

John Quidor and David Gilmor Blythe

Not all the painted anecdotes glorifying folkways were as restrained as those of Woodville and Mount. John Quidor (1801-1881) and David Gilmor Blythe (1815-1865) both painted with an enviable zest and energy. One might expect their humor and skepticism to have made them immensely popular, for Americans at this time had already displayed a distaste for grand sentiments and pretentious philosophies, but both men lived in obscurity.

John Quidor spent most of his life in New York City. He appears to have been an eccentric dreamer and to have derived his livelihood from painting fire buckets, fire engines, insignia, and banners. The subject matter for his imaginative and often fantastic paintings was taken largely from the whimsical stories of Washington Irving. The only artistic recognition he received during his life was an exhibition at the National Academy of Design of a series of paintings which illustrated Irving's legends of early New York. Sadly enough, these paintings never found a purchaser and Quidor gradually faded into obscurity. The vivid and fantastic grotesquerie of Quidor's imagination is well illustrated in *The Return of Rip Van Winkle* (11-15). The technique employed is a

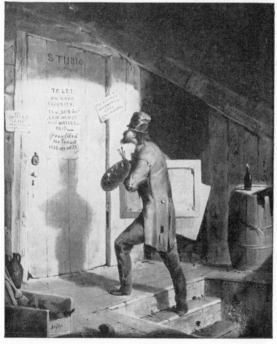

11-15 (*above*). John Quidor, *The Return of Rip Van Winkle*, 1829. National Gallery of Art, Washington, D.C., Mellon Collection.   11-16 (*left*). David Gilmor Blythe, *Art versus Law*, n.d. Brooklyn Museum, Brooklyn, N. Y.

painterly one, not the dry and precise style of the engraver or the popular illustrator of the day. Developed by underpainting and glazing, the forms swell up out of a luminous, golden, all-enveloping chiaroscuro. The paint, applied freely and zestfully, infuses the spaces and forms with a baroque animation. The figures move with a diabolic energy far beyond the gentle legends that inspired them.

David Gilmor Blythe was born on the Ohio frontier and was active in and around Pittsburgh, Pennsylvania. He was both self-taught as an artist and self-reliant. Trained as a wood carver, he painted, did carpentering, and wrote verses to make a living. Blythe painted Pittsburgh's traders, coal miners, and solid citizens with the energy and zest of a born caricaturist, and he was not above laughing at himself, as in *Art versus Law* (11-16). In this trenchant commentary on his own life as an artist we see the essence of his style. He had an innate feeling for the expressive gesture as well as the ability to make a character or situation come alive through a few broad strokes of the brush. The architectural setting for his witty commentaries is as vital as the figures which move within them. Since Blythe appears unconcerned with subtle painterly qualities, one is apt to overlook the crisp certainty of his brushwork, the forceful and clearly organized range of values, and the solid and reassuring impasto by which he built up his lights in contrast to his transparent and limpid shadows.

Still Life

The still-life painter is the genre painter of the inanimate. While the genre painter portrays the everyday life of people, the still-life painter concerns himself with the life of everyday things. The mid-century romantic was not only concerned with the exotic, the wild, the remote, and the unfamiliar—he was also sensitive to the poetry of the familiar and was able to weave a spell of sentiment about the most commonplace materials.

A catalogue of the Columbianum Exhibition of 1795 lists a number of still-life paintings, including still lifes by Copely, William Birch, and James Peale (see Chapter 10). James (1749-1831), the brother of Charles Willson Peale, did much to establish a school of still-life painting in Philadelphia early in the century patterned after traditional seventeenth-century Dutch and Flemish models.

The *Poor Artist's Cupboard* (11-17) is a charming still life of an original nature. The artist, Charles Bird King (1785-1862), is best known

11-17. Charles Bird King, *Poor Artist's Cupboard*, 1812. Corcoran Gallery of Art, Washington, D.C.

as a minor portrait painter. In the *Poor Artist's Cupboard* he foreshadows the *trompe l'oeil* of the latter half of the century. The unique charm of this still life results from the many avenues through which it appeals to our senses and our sentiments. First and foremost, one is aware of an intense and magical illusion of reality. The various surface textures are rendered so that they can almost be felt; the smooth glass, shiny seashell, old leather, and crusty bread are all painted to appeal to our tactile sense. Also contributing to the effectiveness of this painting is the animated pattern created by the various shapes, colors, and textures—the light paper shining out against dark book bindings, the sheen of glass, shell, and metal against the dull worn surface of red leather, the brightly illuminated lower left-hand corner contrasting with the shadowy and mysterious upper recesses of the cupboard. Though the pattern is complicated, the composition moves with gusto. The forms build up in vigorous diagonals, through the various books, the shell, a roll of paper and a curled print, to the sheriff's notice of sale that terminates the composition. The total effect is one of unusual vivacity. Still another source of interest is the story inherent in the subject matter. King's ironic humor is evident in the sequence of book titles; the *Lives of Painters*, the *Pleasures of Hope*, the *Advantages of Poverty*, and lastly, the sheriff's sale sign tell their bitter-sweet story without any other props, though the theme is reiterated by the glass of water and the loaf of dry bread. All these commonplace objects also have the seeming magic of discarded and long-forgotten things which convey a sense of the past and the passing of time. The *Poor Artist's Cupboard* and a very similar composition, *The Vanity of an Artist's Dream,* in the Fogg Art Museum, are among the great still-life paintings of the nineteenth century.

Still life has always been popular with the folk artist for the still life involves fewer challenges than other subjects. Every home, no matter how humble, can provide models and there are few of the problems that beset the landscape and portrait painter.

In this period when the folk arts flourished, painters from all walks of life painted still lifes—the sign or house painter with visions beyond the routine of his job, young ladies in seminaries, the housewife desirous of beautifying her home, and countless others. In answer to their need, sets of stencils of fruit and flower forms were manufactured to aid and guide the young or untrained painter. These stencil, or "theorem," paintings, in the hands of a person of taste, often yielded charming decorations that show a fine sense of color and a sensitive use of media.

THE FRONTIER

The frontier was ever present in the consciousness of nineteenth-century America. It was inevitable that the taste for genre would stimulate painters to depict the life of the frontier since no more colorful material could be found. A number of artists left the settled East to record the drama of the new settlements but most of them painted the West in terms of picturesque anecdote. It remained for a son of the frontier, George Caleb Bingham, to portray it with the dignity of a way of life.

George Caleb Bingham

George Caleb Bingham (1811-1879) was born in Virginia, but his family moved to the frontier of Missouri when he was eight. He was introduced to painting one year later when, quite by chance, he met Chester Harding who was traveling through Missouri in the hope of painting Daniel Boone's portrait. Contact with the artist stimulated young Bingham's ambition and he began to sketch and paint with whatever materials he could contrive in the frontier situation. During a second meeting with Harding some years later, he learned enough of the technique of portrait painting to enable him to start his career.

When he was twenty-six years old, Bingham realized the need for more training and set out for a period of study at the Pennsylvania Academy of Fine Arts in Philadelphia. Here he had a chance to observe the works of the American masters, West, Allston, and Sully, as well as paintings by some of the great Europeans. He profited greatly from this opportunity and his subsequent achievements indicate that he had an

11-18. George Caleb Bingham, *Fur Traders Descending the Missouri, c.* 1845.
Courtesy Metropolitan Museum of Art, Morris K. Jesup Fund, 1933.

astonishing capacity to absorb a knowledge of drawing and composition.
In addition, he learned to control his taste for bright colors, interweaving
and orchestrating the various hues so they build through subtle tints to
exciting accents that emphasize a gesture or single out an important character in the manner of the great Venetian masters. One of the wonders
of Bingham's painting is how, with only the most fragmentary exposure to
the great art of the past, he absorbed so much of its lesson.

After Philadelphia, Bingham spent a few years in Washington, D.C.,
as a portrait painter. Around 1844 he returned to Missouri, and in the
dozen following years he painted his masterpieces. In 1856 he went to
Düsseldorf for a period of study but on his return his political activities
absorbed his energies to the exclusion of painting.

The first painting Bingham produced after his initial return to Missouri is probably his best-known work, *Fur Traders Descending the Missouri* (11-18). Here he showed his ability to select a subject both singular

and typical, a subject as commonplace in his day as the activities of a garage mechanic are in ours. *Fur Traders Descending the Missouri* conveys the tone of life on the frontier even though it depicts that life in one of its quiet contemplative moments rather than in one of its moments of obvious action.

The composition is remarkably direct and effective. The brilliant forms of the rowing trader, the relaxed, smiling boy and the tame fox stand out with sparkling clarity against the quiet horizontals of the water and the spacious background of misty trees and the sunny, moisture-laden sky. The reflections in the water, by providing a transitional value, relate the bright colors and bold contrasts of the figures in the boat to the airy tints of the background. The exotic accent of the seated fox and its reflection in the water provides a dramatic and isolated vertical that acts as a foil for the dominant horizontals and also helps to carry the eye left to convey the quiet downstream movement of the boat.

The color is equally noteworthy. The brilliant turquoise and vermilion of the men's clothes and the inky darkness of the fox sing out against a tawny sky and the green-gold tone of the water. The drawing of the figures is incisive and sure, the paint is applied easily yet unobtrusively, and the forms are solid yet not ponderous. This ability to infuse the observed and described fact with sentiment and to invent an artistic structure to communicate the poetry of the commonplace situation constitutes the particular strength of Bingham. Nowhere is this power more apparent than in his *Fur Traders Descending the Missouri.*

Shooting for the Beef (11-19) reveals Bingham's mastery of another type of genre. Here the late afternoon light sheds its glow over the distant sky, illuminates the foreground figures with a warm light, and throws across the earth great transparent shadows that define the sequence of planes which move back into the canvas and provide the framework for the action. The low point of sight, skillfully reinforced by the bright shapes of the watching dogs, causes the frontiersmen to loom up manly and strong, and the pyramidal grouping of the secondary figures inevitably focuses attention on the principal actor, the man taking aim at distant target. The verticals of the figures and trees playing against the horizontal lines of the shadows, the vigorously sculptured forms, the convincing attitudes of men and animals all work together to translate the tense mood of the moment preceding the decisive shot into monumental terms.

Bingham was an ardent believer in the democratic processes and he understood the conflict and excitement, the elation and despair of election

11-19 (*above*). George Caleb Bingham, *Shooting for the Beef*, 1850. Brooklyn Museum, Brooklyn, N. Y.   11-20 (*below*). George Caleb Bingham, *The Verdict of the People*, 1855. Courtesy The Boatmen's National Bank of St. Louis, St. Louis, Mo.

time as one who had himself participated in the strenuous campaigns of Whigs versus Democrats. *Verdict of the People* (11-20) is one of the two great compositions he devoted to the election theme, a significant theme since the moments of political assembly were the moments when the drama of American democracy was translated into a visual spectacle. In these two paintings more than in any of his other works, we see Bingham's power as a master of dramatic narration. The astonishing facility with which he grouped great numbers of gesticulating, highly individualized figures into a lucidly organized composition which has both monumentality and action, both grandeur and narrative fluency, is doubly impressive in view of the relative isolation in which he developed his remarkable powers. In *The Verdict of the People*, one's eye moves into the painting via the dejected figure of the loser in the foreground. The eye mounts through a series of skillfully articulated diagonal lines that builds into a grand pyramidal grouping of figures. On the left the eye follows the line of the barrow, back into the picture through the body of the Negro, up through a group of secondary figures to the triumphant orator who, framed by the majestic columns and recessed portico, forms the apex of the pyramid. From the same foreground figure the other side of the pyramid mounts through the centrally located seated man, carries through the charming and wry note of the long-nosed cast shadow, to the same dominant figure of the speaker. On the far right, a balancing cluster of men takes the eye aloft and then turns one's attention back toward the center through the upraised arm of the smiling celebrant. The movement into the depth of the canvas is controlled with equal facility. There is not an ambiguous space nor an unrealized figure to confuse one in the entire picture. The vigorous color and the brilliant alternations of tone contribute to the vigor of the total effect. The painting is the positive and energetic statement of a healthy extrovert who delights in describing the vigorous processes of democracy and who wholeheartedly believes in *The Verdict of the People.* More than any other single individual, Bingham gave artistic form to the spirit of the western frontier.

George Catlin

George Catlin (1796-1872) went beyond the frontier for his inspiration. Catlin saw his first Indians when a delegation of Indian chiefs visited Philadelphia en route to Washington. The dignity of their bearing made a deep impression on the young man, and in his own mind he determined his future. ". . . The history and customs of such a people," he

11-21 (*above*). George Catlin, *A Bird's-eye View of the Mandan Village*, 1832. Smithsonian Institution, Washington, D.C.   11-22 (*below*). Alfred J. Miller, *Laramie's Fort*, 1858-1860, based on sketch made in 1837. Copyright 1951 by the University of Oklahoma Press.

wrote, "preserved by pictorial illustrations, are themes worthy of the life-time of one man, and nothing short of the loss of my life, shall prevent me from visiting their country, and of becoming their historian."

Catlin moved west and in 1832 he set out from St. Louis to spend eight years living among the Indians of the great plains. During this period in hundreds of drawings and paintings he recorded the customs and habits of the various tribes. A Bird's-eye View of the Mandan Village (11-21) is a fine study of Indian life, painted 1800 miles above St. Louis in the area of the present state of North Dakota. Catlin also sketched numberless portraits of Indian chiefs and other individuals who impressed him. An amusing record of his life among the Indians pictures him seated among a throng of onlookers, painting the portrait of a chieftain.

Catlin worked rapidly and his style is sketchy and free, tending to be graphic rather than painterly. The paint is applied directly in a thin wash; the color is bright, descriptive, but without subtlety. His particular ability lay in his capacity to establish a vivid sense of character, situation, or a complicated tribal maneuver without oppressing the onlooker with a tedious and labored mass of detail. Catlin was not a technically sophisticated artist, but he portrayed a fascinating and significant facet of American life. Much of what we know of Indian life we owe to Catlin.

Another artist who explored the Far West and painted and drew the first outposts of the frontier was Alfred Jacob Miller (1810-1874). Miller was born in Baltimore and studied with Sully. While painting portraits in New Orleans, he was persuaded to join an expedition being organized to explore the Rockies. During this expedition Miller produced his most notable works. These included both straight landscapes and studies of the life of the Indians and the early white settlers. Perhaps his most interesting works are the sketches which picture the conquest of the wilderness. His water color of the early outpost at Fort Laramie surrounded by an Indian encampment (11-22) reveals his fresh and lively style. The vivid and picturesque character of frontier life is pictured without the melodramatic tone that marred much late-nineteenth-century painting of the Far West.

John James Audubon

Not all the artists who traveled into the wilderness were looking for the melodrama of Indian warfare, the color of frontier life, or the vast sweep of the western landscape. Another aspect of American life that proved exciting to a small group of artists was the infinite number of

11-23. John J. Audubon, *Carolina Parroquet*, 1827-1838. Courtesy of New York Historical Society, New York.

birds, animals, and plants that inhabited the new and bounteous country.

John James Audubon (1785-1851) is by far the best known and most important of these artist-naturalists. Born in Haiti, Audubon had been educated in France where he received some instruction in drawing from David. After his arrival in America and subsequent marriage, he settled on the Kentucky frontier to make a living as a merchant. However, his love of the wilderness proved to be too much for his business career, and he finally forsook business to follow his great passion, which was to study and draw America's birds. After completing an initial series of water colors, Audubon conceived of the idea of publishing a comprehensive portfolio of his studies of American birds. He found little support for his idea in Philadelphia, the chief publishing center in America. Convinced of the merit of his idea, he set sail for England where his enthusiasm and perseverance bore fruit, and within ten years he achieved the astonishing feat of bringing this great project to completion. The labors involved were endless but *The Birds of America, from Original Drawings, With 435 Plates Showing 1,065 Figures* was brought out in four double-elephant folio volumes between 1827 and 1838, and the five volumes of accompanying text, the *Ornithological Biography* was completed in 1839. The original studies for the work had been executed in water color, and the engravings by Robert Havell, Jr., from which the plates were printed

11-24 (*below*). *Crucifixion*, 1800. Courtesy Metropolitan Museum of Art, Gift of Mrs. Robert W. de Forest, 1933. 11-25 (*right*). *Virgin Mary with Holy Ghost*, c. 1840. New Mexico State Tourist Bureau.

retained the decorative vigor and the informative clarity of the originals to a remarkable degree. *The Birds of America* is one of the great scientific and artistic achievements of the century.

Almost every plate in *The Birds of America* has its particular charm, and it is difficult to single out any one plate for discussion. *Carolina Parroquet* (11-23) is one of the many which displays his unusual talents —a rare decorative sense combined with an ability to provide a full cataloguing of the birds' identifying characteristics. In all of the plates the birds were pictured in their natural habitat, and the birds, branches, leaves, and flowers, grasses, rocks, and waves, were patterned over the pages with an infallible decorative sense. These forms were kept sufficiently flat so that they carry as simple patterns, yet within these flat patterns the details of forms and textures were developed through clearly defined lines and sharp-edged patterns. The subtle yet lively colors were distributed with an unerring eye for the total ensemble; still, they retain their factual validity. By not developing the forms to their full volume and by minimizing the envelope of air, Audubon avoided any possible ambiguity as to shape or marking and at the same time emphasized the decorative aspects of his charming subjects.

Audubon's oils are less well known than his illustrations, but their full-bodied realism makes it apparent that in the plates for his great book Audubon accepted the challenge of scientific illustration and from its limitations conceived and developed an original and decorative illustrative style.

RELIGIOUS FOLK PAINTINGS

The nineteenth century witnessed a revival of religious enthusiasm and this renewal of belief is particularly evident in the religious paintings of folk artists. Three examples of religious folk painting will introduce us to these direct and moving expressions of faith. A water color, dated around 1800, representing the Crucifixion (11-24) is from one of the Pennsylvania-German communities. The drawing is highly formalized. Christ on the cross, the two thieves, and the Roman soldiers are part of a design which includes conventionalized flowers, geometric patterns, and Biblical texts executed in fractur, the art of illuminated writing elaborated with pen-drawn decorations. The formalized and calligraphic nature of this Crucifixion in no way negates its expressive power. Despite its formal nature, to a degree because of it, it remains a moving testimonial to the sincere faith of the simple and pious country folk.

A second example of religious folk art is a retablo from New Mexico. The retablos were religious images painted, printed, or even carved on a flat surface by the Indians of New Mexico for use in a home shrine or in church. A retablo depicting the Virgin Mary with the Holy Ghost (11-25) is based on the traditions of Latin-American religious painting, but it achieves additional interest through its provincial Indian flavor. The forms are represented as flat patterns without perspective or foreshortening. The vigorous rhythmic lines and direct simple shapes create an image of dignity and grace. The compassionate Virgin, seated on a throne and radiating light, is depicted with the unquestioning assurance one finds in the works of primitive people and children, who allow no problems of representation to stop the direct flow of images.

A third example of popular religious painting, *The Peaceable Kingdom* (11-26), by Edward Hicks (1780-1849), provides a charming note on which to end this discussion of painting in America between the Revolutionary War and the Civil War. The life span of this naive sign painter from Bucks County, Pennsylvania, extended over most of the period under discussion. Hicks was a Quaker, and his paintings were an

11-26. Edward Hicks, *The Peaceable Kingdom, c.* 1848. Brooklyn Museum, Brooklyn, N. Y.

expression of his Quaker convictions, his deep faith, love of peace, and literal belief in the word of the Bible. His most popular subject was drawn from the prophecy in Isaiah of a day "when the wolf shall dwell with the lamb and the leopard shall lie down with the kid," and he painted this subject more than a hundred times, usually depicting an assembly of animals, carnivorous and herbivorous, resting together with children and cherubim in an idyllic landscape setting. Hicks frequently depicted in the background a secondary group of figures which reinforces the basic theme. William Penn signing his peace treaty with the Indians was his favorite secondary motif, since it represented both an American and Quaker contribution toward the happy state prophesied in Isaiah. He gave his paintings as gifts to his neighbors, acquaintances, and relatives to indoctrinate his fellow men in the ways of peace.

Hicks painted in the manner of most untrained folk artists. The forms are kept flat and the contours are clearly defined. The animal forms represent a charming combination of ideas and visual impressions. The glittering eyes of the cat family, the gay spots of the leopard, the placid ruminating oxen, the enfolded sleeping lamb are all translated into simple but vivid patterns, which, in turn, are embellished with lettered Biblical texts.

In his own day Hicks was not thought of as an artist. It is unlikely that he or any of the humble neighbors whose homes were graced by his pictures would have described his painting activities by so pretentious a term. Could he or any members of the rural community in which he lived have known that in a hundred years his paintings would be the prized possessions of museums and connoisseurs, they would with true modesty have probably attributed the success of his pictures to the source of his inspiration, the Holy Bible, rather than to the artistry of Hicks. For he was undoubtedly unconscious of his artistry. Like thousands of other Americans who painted from conviction rather than for profit, he felt impelled by some inner need to give form to his beliefs and convictions. He did this like the conscientious sign painter that he was—carefully, with craftsmanlike precision, using soberly defined forms and neatly applied pigments. Part of this simple and uncritical attitude stemmed from his childlike ability to draw on a deep reserve of images, images of remembered Biblical illustrations and of folk patterns. From these he created his direct statements of faith.

Today, having come through a long and arduous education designed to develop sophistication of technique and taste, we realize the power of the naive image born of conviction. Having almost lost the ability to symbolize our beliefs without self-consciousness, we have come to value direct self-expression more than technical virtuosity, sincerity more than facility, taste more than formula. And these are the qualities that we find and value in the statements of faith which Hicks and the other folk artists of America embodied in unique pictorial form during the nineteenth century.

Sculpture, Prints,

and Art Patronage

AN AMERICAN SCHOOL OF SCULPTORS, AS DISTINCT FROM the native school of folk carvers, came into existence in the interval between the Revolutionary War and the Civil War. This was largely an outgrowth of the surge of patriotic sentiment that resulted from the successful War of Independence. A desire for commemorative portraits made itself felt almost immediately after the Revolution. Sculptors at every level of competence and sophistication reacted to this demand, as can be seen from three sculptural versions of George Washington.

The first, *Washington on Horseback* (12-1), is an example of folk art. The artist is unknown, but since the figure comes from New Bedford, once the whaling capital of the world, it has been suggested that it was probably carved by a seaman on a long whaling voyage. The figure, 18 inches high, is painted in black, white, and gold with touches of other colors. Washington's enormous prestige moved all manner of people to express, as best they could, the esteem and veneration in which they held

325

12-1. *Washington on Horseback,* poly-
chromed wood, mid-19th century.
New York State Historical Association,
Cooperstown, N. Y.

him. The artless charm of this figure provides a touching testimonial to
the strong feeling the image of Washington held for the man who
carved it.

Victory Crowning Washington (12-2) provides an effective contrast to the folk tradition embodied in *Washington on Horseback.* The
unknown artist who created this almost life-sized wood carving employed
the symbols and forms of the classically oriented sculptors of the first half
of the century. The dignity of Washington's position is symbolized in a
conventional and proper way. Though formal, it is neither cold nor
rhetorical.

The third figure, a vigorous life-sized portrait of Washington (12-3)
by William Rush, seems to hark back to the great tradition of Renaissance
sculpture despite the fact that Rush had little formal training. Monumental in both form and concept, it stands as one of the first great pieces
of American sculpture, and it seems fitting that it should have been inspired by the person of Washington. These three figures of Washington
represent the three types of sculpture practiced in America during the
Federal period—first, folk sculpture; secondly, allegory and portraiture in
the classic revival style; and thirdly, monumental realistic sculpture.

12-2 (*left*). *Victory Crowning Washington*, 1850-1860. The Henry Francis du Pont Winterthur Museum, Winterthur, Del. 12-3 (*right*). William Rush, *George Washington*, 1814. Pennsylvania Academy of the Fine Arts, Philadelphia.

The successful conclusion of the War of 1812, coinciding as it did with the completion of a number of public buildings, created an unprecedented demand for figures, portraits, and commemorative groups to adorn the new public buildings. In 1812 no native sculptor was considered worthy of executing the statue of George Washington desired by North Carolina for its new capitol. At the suggestion of Thomas Jefferson, Antonio Canova, the brilliant Italian eclectic sculptor, was entrusted with the commission. Canova's famous figure of Washington was lost in a fire only a few years after it was completed.

Less than twenty years later, three American sculptors, Horatio Greenough, Thomas Crawford, and Hiram Powers, were well established in Italy and were executing large and lucrative commissions, so rapidly had a few American sculptors achieved fame and prestige. In the eighteen-fifties, dozens of American sculptors were studying in Florence and Rome and were sending back to America a steady flood of portraits and idealized allegorical and mythological figures patterned after those of Canova and the other classical revival sculptors. The same fever for the culture of ancient Greece that had produced a rash of white, porticoed buildings in every American city also demanded white marble figures, since that was considered the form in which the artistic genius of Greece had received its fullest expression. Italy was full of ambitious young American sculptors intent on satisfying this demand.

The astonishing florescence of American sculpture in the two decades between 1830 and 1850 had no parallel in painting, and during those years painting stood less high in the esteem of the public. The most concrete evidence of the value in which sculpture was held in this period are the prices the sculptors received for their work. Canova received over eleven thousand dollars for his North Carolina statue of Washington, an impressive sum when one realizes that the annual expenditure of the state was then about ninety thousand dollars. Hiram Powers, the most successful of the Yankee sculptors working in Italy, sold six replicas of the sensational *Greek Slave* (12-14) for prices averaging about four thousand dollars each.

The successful sculptors preferred to live in Italy only partly because of the inspiring treasures and the opportunity for study that existed there. Wealthy Americans were more available and were more in the mood to purchase works of art and commission portraits in the art-laden climate of Italy. Even more important, skilled Italian marble workers were available at a fraction of the cost of a workman at home, and these men could translate a crude clay sketch into a shiny finished product with a perfection of surface finish which glossed over weaknesses of structure or conception. The substantial monetary award available to sculptors was undoubtedly the chief reason that so many energetic and ambitious American boys chose sculpture, rather than painting, as a career. It may also explain why the sculpture produced in this period is so much less interesting than the painting. Much of the painting was born of a compulsion toward self-expression, irrespective of fame and fortune. Most of the sculpture was brought into being solely by the desire to make money.

FOLK CARVING

We have already seen a few examples of the wood carving produced during colonial times. This tradition flowered in the rich body of folk carving that developed during the early years of the republic. With the expansion of American shipbuilding after the Revolution there came an

12-4. Simeon Skillin, Jr., *Apollo*, poly-chromed wood, *c.* 1800. New York State Historical Association, Coopers-town, N. Y.

increased demand for the products of the skilled workers in wood. The wood carver tended to think of himself as a workman and so was content to remain anonymous. In this respect he was unlike the ambitious sculptor of the day who thought of himself as an artist and demanded both fame and fortune. Time has reversed the judgment. Today we seek the names of the men who made the charming and unpretentious carvings that graced the ships, shops, and homes of the early days of our republic while we try to forget the uncreative fabricators of the fashionable nymphs and goddesses. Fortunately the fame of a few of the master carvers was sufficiently widespread so that they have been remembered beyond the confines of the immediate locality where they worked.

We have already seen a Mercury attributed to the older Simeon Skillin. Three of his sons continued to practice his craft and from their shop in Boston they sent forth countless fine carvings to decorate Boston's ships, homes, gardens and public buildings. For the figureheads they carved they drew on varied sources, mythological and historical as well as purely fanciful. They carved gods, goddesses, and shepherds for man-tels and gardens, Corinthian capitals and yards of classic moldings for the new public buildings. Simeon Skillin the younger (1756-1806), fol-lowing in the footsteps of his father, was one of the ablest wood carvers of his day. His head of Apollo (12-4) is one of a pair of matched poly-chrome wood figures. The carving is boldly executed; all of the forms are fully developed and clearly articulated. While Skillin shared the current enthusiasm for classic subjects and the classic manner, he was not overwhelmed by it. Ancient precedent did not obliterate all traces of personality from the head, which has enough individuality of feature and expression to suggest that it might have been done from a sitter. The draperies, costume, hair, and acanthus headdress have the vigorous rhythm that enlivened the figureheads for which Skillin was famed. The polychrome color, the particular feature that distinguishes folk carving from "fine arts" sculpture, is also clear and lively.

Figureheads and Signs

Since shipping was one of the first industries to develop after the Revolution, it is not surprising that the carving of figureheads was one of our major crafts. Placed at the front of the ship under the bowsprit, the figurehead was the symbol of the vessel. It served no practical purpose, but was regarded with almost superstitious reverence by crew and owner alike, symbolizing pride in the beauty and sturdy strength of the ship. The most characteristic figureheads were full-length figures, often female. The subjects, usually related to the name of the ship, included historical figures, mythological and allegorical beings, portraits of the owners, and characters from legend, literature, and romance. Animals, sea serpents, dolphins, and mermaids were also used. The early figureheads stood almost erect, since the rounded hulls of the earlier vessels seemed to demand vertical figures. As the ships became sleeker and narrower, the figureheads leaned forward until on the clippers they were almost horizontal. Figureheads were usually carved from white pine, frequently from one solid block of wood, and were painted and gilded. Most of the men who carved figureheads had no training beyond that which they received as apprentices to a master carver. At the end of the nineteenth century the use of the figurehead disappeared. As steam replaced sail, the colorful carved forms of the earlier days gave way to more discreet symbols.

Isaac Fowle (1818-1853) carved some of the finest figureheads to come out of Boston, where he and his son were active for over sixty years. The boldly sculptured figurehead of a woman with billowy skirts (12-5) served as the sign which identified his shop. The body of the woman is solidly realized beneath the sweeping draperies. The vigorous rhythm which gives this figurehead its striking movement is established by re-

12-5. Isaac Fowle, ship figurehead, ivory-painted wood, *c.* 1830. Index of American Design, National Gallery of Art, Washington, D.C.

peating the bold sweep of the bow of the boat in the two massive folds of skirt and in the upward lift of the head. This figure has none of the sharp-edged stiffness that marred the products of inferior shops of the day; the sculptural form is realized with richness in both the voluminous forms of the figure and in the costume.

Another outlet for the talents of the wood carver was the wooden figures which were placed at the doors of shops to identify the establishment and attract attention. These gaily colored and often amusing figures constitute a charming part of our visual folklore. *Captain Jinks* (12-6) stood in front of a cigar store in Newark, New Jersey, for more than fifty years. The remarkable feeling of movement in the stationary figure is the achievement of a very capable and observant artist. A rhythmic line sweeps up from the beautifully simplified legs through the rigid body and folded arms to the erect head and creates an attitude in which movement and repose are skillfully related. The exaggerations of anatomical form—the long thin legs, puffed-out chest, columnlike neck, and egg-shaped head with aquiline nose and sweeping mustaches—express a light and ironic attitude toward military formality refreshing in an age that tended to be cloying in its propriety and sentimentality.

The most frequent figure to identify the tobacconist's shop was the

12-6 (*left*). *Captain Jinks,* polychromed wood, mid-19th century. Newark Museum, Newark, N. J.   12-7 (*right*). Cigar-store Indian, polychromed wood, n.d. Index of American Design, National Gallery, Washington, D.C.

wooden Indian, for tobacco was the best-known gift of the red man to our civilization. Though isolated figures of Indians appeared before 1800, wooden Indians only became popular with the advent of cigar smoking after 1840. By mid-century two to three hundred of these figures were manufactured yearly by firms in New York, Chicago, and elsewhere. The figures were usually hewn from white pine and were patterned after old prints and colored lithographs or were modeled from live Indians. The Indian chief (12-7) was the most popular figure although squaws and other types were occasionally produced.

The Little Navigator (12-8) probably marked a ship chandler's supply shop in New Bedford, Massachusetts, around 1835. The vigor of such a piece of sculpture results from the balance between the humorous aspects of the figure and the innate sculptural sense revealed by the consistent relationships of the chunky forms.

12-8. *The Little Navigator,* polychromed wood, before 1820. Whaling Museum and Old Dartmouth Historical Society, New Bedford, Mass.

Religious Carving, New Mexico

America produced little religious sculpture. The Protestant temper which dominated American religious life in most parts of the country considered religious sculpture to be identical with idolatrous images. Even the Catholic community through most of the country reflected this attitude, importing from Europe most of the little sculpture it employed. However, the Spanish-speaking Southwest did not share this aversion to the carved and painted image. Here, where Catholic ritual and Indian traditions had worked together to produce the mission church, the two traditions combined also to create a unique body of folk sculpture. The ritual of church services and processionals played a significant part in the lives of the Indian converts, who, still not far removed from pagan idolatry, needed images to symbolize their faith. Under the guidance of Spanish priests, the Indians were trained to copy the models set before them, to carve with metal tools, and to finish the carved wood figures with gesso, gilt, and paint. As time passed, the Indian carvers evolved their own simplified but expressive repertory of symbolic forms. The carved figures

12-9 (*left*). *Father Jesus,* polychromed wood, n.d. Taylor Museum of the Colorado Springs Fine Arts Center, Colorado Springs, Colo. 12-10 (*right*). *Our Lady of Guadalupe,* polychromed wood, *c.* 1820-1840. Museum of New Mexico, Santa Fe, N. M. New Mexico State Tourist Bureau photograph.

produced by the villagers of New Mexico were called *bultos,* signifying a three-dimensional image. The particular power of these images lies in the directness with which they communicate the deep religious beliefs of the simple men who produced them.

Father Jesus (12-9) reveals both the ancestry of the *bultos* and the direct impact they make upon our senses. The influence of the traditional polychromed sculpture of the counter-reformation is very evident—the figure is colored, clothed, and has real hair. But the astonishing illusionism of the European models has given way to bold simplifications of form and pattern that communicate only the essence of a situation. One is only conscious of the great sad eyes, the emaciated cheeks, and the streaming blood. Such a figure provides a symbol of Christ's torments and suffering reduced to their most elemental and readily comprehensible terms. Our Lady of Guadalupe, the patron saint of Mexico, was a frequent subject for the wood carvers of early New Mexico. Here (12-10) she is portrayed as the Virgin of the Immaculate Conception, standing in a crescent moon supported by flights of angels, crowned with a lily, radiating light. The iconography is traditional; the adoration bestowed on the subject appears doubly touching because of the humble naïveté with which the forms are developed. No display of technical virtuosity distracts us from feeling the childlike simplicity that prompted the creation of this symbol of purity. *Our Lady of Guadalupe* was produced between 1820 and 1840, a period that has been referred to as the "classic period" of the New Mexican folk arts because of the superb quality of the paintings and carving then produced.

THE NATIVE SCHOOL OF SCULPTURE

William Rush

It is difficult to draw a line of distinction between the folk carver and the sculptor. Certainly the sculptor seems to be more aware of the formal qualities of composition and the monumental aspects of form that have characterized the great sculptural tradition. William Rush (1756-1833), more than any other individual, provides a stepping stone from the folk carver who practiced his craft without self-consciousness to the artist concerned with the formal problems of sculpture. William Rush has frequently been called America's first sculptor. Perhaps it would be more accurate to say that he was the first man in America to whom the practice of sculpture was a major professional concern. Born in Philadelphia, the son of a shipcarver, Rush grew up with the wood carver's tools in his hands and wood was the material of much of his life's work. His output falls into three categories: ship carvings, allegorical figures, and portraits, which are usually bust but include a few full-length figures, notably the famous portrait of George Washington. The ship carvings by Rush were, in the opinion of his day, the finest produced in America, if not in the world. This was a genuine tribute in an age when ship carving was a living art with a highly critical audience.

Rush's life-sized figure of Washington (12-3), seen here in the form of a bronze cast, revealed both his skill as a wood carver and his power as a monumental sculptor. Rush had always been concerned with the

12-11. William Rush, *Marquis de Lafayette*, 1824. Pennsylvania Academy of the Fine Arts, Philadelphia.

inadequacies of wood as a permanent sculptor's material. In order to minimize the tendency of wood to shrink, check, and split, Rush states that he made it "hollow, so that air circulates through the inside . . . for it is not more than three inches on an average in thickness, is perfectly seasoned and saturated with oil." The figure is posed so that a vigorous S-curve unifies the entire figure, reaching its fullfilment in the beautifully poised, lifted head. The opposing movement established by the hand resting on the hip and continued through the extended right thigh and leg provides a strong counterbalancing stress. Rush was admirably ingenious in the way he reconciled the taste for classical attire in sculpture with his own penchant for realism. Washington is dressed in the costume of his day, amplified by sweeping draperies that fall across the hips and thighs. This device unifies the lower part of the figure by making one massive form of the separate legs while the draperies also add a note of official dignity to the figure.

Though wood was Rush's favored material, he handled other media with success. His terra-cotta portrait bust of the Marquis de Lafayette (12-11) is sharply observed and forcefully realized. No sentimental idealizations of form blunt the sculptor's clear vision. The firm jaw and strong mouth, the quizzical and inquiring expression of the lifted eyebrows and the half-closed lids create living portraiture without any dependence on the clichés of classic formula. Rush combined the requisites of a great

12-12. John Frazee, *Thomas H. Perkins*, 1834. Boston Athenaeum, Boston.

sculptor in his sense of formal and monumental qualities, in his feeling for the sculptor's materials, his ability to handle details of pattern and texture with grace, and his sensitivity to human values of character and personality. That some of his great potential remained unrealized was the inevitable result of the limitations of his milieu.

John Frazee (1790-1852), another native-born sculptor, bridged the gap from artisan to artist by commencing his career with the popular frontier pastime of whittling. When he was twenty he apprenticed himself as a stone cutter and subsequently acquired his initial training carving tombstones. When the successful conclusion of the War of 1812 brought a spell of prosperity, he established a business to produce a variety of ornamental items, including sculpture and cast or carved stone, metal and wood decorations. His sources for learning were meager, consisting of a few plaster casts and even fewer carved stone figures by the Italian stone cutters who had been imported to adorn the new public buildings. Frazee revealed an unusual capacity to learn, and in 1825 he executed the first marble bust to be made in America by a native-born sculptor—a monument of John Wells for St. Paul's Chapel in New York City. The successful completion of this project brought him a commission to execute seven portrait busts for the Boston Athenaeum. This was an important commission for that time, and the fact that it was awarded to a person of Frazee's limited background indicates the respect in which his achievements were held. The cloying influence of the classic ideal which was to infect his late work had not as yet impaired the talent for trenchant realism revealed in his portrait of Colonel Thomas H. Perkins (12-12), one of the most forceful of this group of seven heads.

Another American who created vigorous three-dimensional portraits early in the century was John Browere (1792-1834). Much controversy existed in Browere's day as to whether or not the portrait busts he made from casts taken from the living subjects were works of art or merely mechanical records of the appearances of his sitters. Browere's aim was to create a gallery of the busts of American heroes. He traveled from city to city to record the faces of heroes of the Revolution and the War of 1812, of presidents, vice presidents, and other notables. Between the years of 1825 and 1834 he assembled an impressive number of portraits of America's great. Browere's portraits, well-posed and finished, contributed to the country's evolving tradition of realism.

The Italian School: Greenough, Powers, Crawford

Local sculptors were not sufficiently recognized during the first years of the century to be considered for the sculptural decorations which were needed to complete the new capitols. Though Latrobe greatly admired the figureheads by Rush, declaring that no one in Europe could equal them and that they "seemed rather to draw the ship after them than to be impelled by the vessel," he did not direct any of the available sculptural commissions to Rush. Jefferson was determined to have well-trained men from Europe decorate the new government buildings. In 1806 Giuseppe Franzoni and Giovanni Andrei were brought from Italy to work on the House of Representatives, the first of a succession of competent, if uninspired, Italian sculptors to work first in Washington and then in the other cities of America. It was their influence, the fame of Canova, and the Italian museums that made Italy the mecca for the aspiring young sculptors of the next few decades.

No nineteenth-century sculptor has received more posthumous praise than Horatio Greenough (1805-1852), but it is as an esthetic philosopher rather than as an artist that he has received his recognition in modern times. Greenough was born in Boston and was encouraged to become a sculptor by Washington Allston. As a youth he made copies of the casts in the Boston Athenaeum, later attended Harvard, and at the age of nine-

12-13. Horatio Greenough, *George Washington*, 1832-1841. Smithsonian Institution, Washington, D.C.

teen set out for Italy. His first years in Rome were years of intense study and growth. He returned home in a few years because of illness and soon after executed his first important portrait, a bust of President Adams. Greenough's first portrait commissions were sufficiently successful so that in 1832, only one year after the disastrous fire in Raleigh had destroyed Canova's great figure of Washington, he was commissioned to do a monumental Washington for the rotunda of the United States Capitol. This was the first major sculptural commission to be awarded an American sculptor.

Greenough returned to Italy to carry out his assignment and labored on the great figure for nine years. His *George Washington* (12-13) was conceived in Olympian terms, like a Zeus seated erect on a marble throne —a drapery thrown over one raised arm and covering the lower half of his figure, the other arm grasping a spearlike scepter. The head was modeled after the famous portrait of Washington by Houdon. In 1841 the great marble mass, 10½ feet high and weighing twenty tons, was shipped across the Atlantic on a Navy sloop and with much expense was installed in the rotunda. Innumerable difficulties attended the installation —the underpinnings were inadequate, the lighting poor. Greenough protested, and Congress moved the figure to the east front of the Capitol where it stood under a makeshift and temporary shelter, for the most part unprotected, until half a century later when it was moved to its present inadequate quarters in the Smithsonian Institute. The public reaction to

12-14 (*left*). Hiram Powers, *The Greek Slave*, 1847. Newark Museum, Newark, N. J.   12-15 (*below*). Thomas Crawford, *Babes in the Wood*, 1851. Courtesy Metropolitan Museum of Art, Gift of Hamilton Fish, 1894.

the great statue was little better. The nude torso shocked the conventional, while the capital wits poked fun at the partially robed figure, one remarking that "Washington was too prudent, and careful of his health, to expose himself thus in a climate as uncertain as ours. . . ." Today we are conscious of the scale of Greenough's vision. No American of his time had conceived of a national symbol of such heroic proportions nor had thought in such monumental terms. The stately gesture and commanding pose represented a sculptural conception which in power and dignity went far beyond the topical and illustrational effects typical of the period.

Despite the importance of Greenough's *Washington,* his total achievement as a sculptor is less impressive than his contribution to American esthetic thought. Greenough commented significantly on the art of his day. He protested against the repressive influence of the antique and encouraged originality of conception and expression. Fifty years ahead of his time, he defined a theory of functionalism. Observing the beauty of a ship at sea he remarked, "What Academy of Design, what research of connoisseurship, what imitation of the Greeks produced this marvel of construction? . . . God's world has a distinct formula for every function

... we shall seek in vain to borrow shape; we must make the shapes. . . ."
A final summation of his philosophy appeared in his "Stonecutter's Creed."

> Three proofs do I find in man that he was made only a little lower than the
> angels—Beauty—Action—Character.
> > By Beauty I mean the promise of function.
> > By Action I mean the presence of function.
> > By Character I mean the record of function.

While Greenough typifies the artist-philosopher exploring the world
of ideas, Hiram Powers (1807-1873) represents the ultimate in the practice of sculpture as a business. Energetic, practical, ambitious, shrewd,
and ingenious, Powers constitutes a paradox, the Yankee businessman-
artist. Born in Woodstock, Vermont, Powers moved to Ohio as a youth.
He started his career modeling figures in a wax museum in Cincinnati
and at the age of thirty set out for Italy via Washington, D. C.; there he
executed a portrait of Andrew Jackson which remained one of the finest
achievements of his career. In 1837 Powers arrived in Florence, where
he spent most of his subsequent years. One of the first sculptors of his
day to settle in Italy, his career there represented the ultimate triumph
for an ambitious young sculptor. Born and brought up in humble circumstances, he achieved eminence among the aristocrats of lineage and
finance. Skeptical of all that was not immediately useful, he had little
interest in the deep philosophic concerns of a man like Greenough. The
ultimate mysteries of life and creation were not mysteries to him—one
lived to be successful; one created to sell. The typical patrons of his day,
the business tycoons, understood him and felt comfortable in his presence. He charmed them and asked enormous prices for his work. They
admired a forceful salesman, accepted his own evaluation of his worth,
and willingly paid him the impressive prices he demanded. Powers spent
most of his life in Europe, preferring it to America largely because he
could hire an efficient staff of workmen for a fraction of what they would
cost at home.

Powers' most famous single work was *The Greek Slave* (12-14). The
success of this work was a tribute to his shrewd awareness of his age and
its tastes. Based on the reputed traffic in Greek girls captured by the
Turks in the Greco-Turkish war, the appeal of the statue was overwhelming since it played on so many facets of public sensibility. The Greco-
Turkish war, still vivid in people's minds, stood as a symbol of Christi-
anity versus the world of disbelief and darkness—this in an age in which
a revived religious fervor was challenged by an increasing worldliness

and by the advance of science. In addition, the entire problem of slavery was a political and moral issue of the greatest timeliness. The classical attributes of *The Greek Slave* also insured its popularity, for it was patterned after the goddesses of Greece and Rome, the Aphrodites and Venuses whose antiquity permitted them to be admired as symbols of virtue rather than as pagan goddesses of love.

Powers exploited the nudity of the figure to the maximum. Aware that the fascination of the nude human body could be reconciled with the prudery of the age by clothing it in morality, he declared that his Greek slave girl stood exposed, not in body but in spirit, and that he had portrayed "what trust there could still be in a Divine Providence for a future state of existence, with utter despair for the present. . . ." Powers had the wisdom to have the statue approved by a body of clergymen, and when the statue was singled out for honors at the Great Crystal Palace Exhibition in London in 1851, his triumph was complete. Hailed as a rival of the Venus de Milo, a half dozen full-size replicas of the statue were sold, as well as hundreds of miniature copies, while an exhibition of the figure in New York netted over twenty-five thousand dollars in admissions. A number of admirers of the statue claimed that Powers surpassed the ancients, since his *Greek Slave* had all the attributes of the ancient goddesses plus a Christian soul that rendered her nudity chaste.

Another favored American was Thomas Crawford (1813-1857). Crawford was born in New York City and at the age of fourteen was apprenticed to a wood carver. A few years later he went to work for Frazee, cutting tombstones, and here he learned the rudiments of stone carving. In 1835 he departed for a period of study in Rome.

Crawford was the first American sculptor to settle in Rome and he was the leader of the American artistic group there, much as Powers was in Florence. During his lifetime he received the most flattering adulation. This was owed partly to his own modest charm; partly to his ambitious wife's activities, but mostly because the time seemed ripe for a national genius in sculpture. America felt sufficiently mature to dispense with the imported talents of the Canovas and the Houdons, and Crawford was hailed as the artist who "would enable America to be rescued from dependence on European artists, and to rejoice in a Phidias of her own." Crawford's recognition was more than verbal. He received many commissions for portraits and figure pieces, and the height of success came when he was commissioned to execute a monumental figure to crown the dome of the Capitol in Washington. For this lofty site he designed a great *Freedom,* which was installed with much fanfare in 1863. Certainly no statue in the United States enjoys a more elaborate pedestal nor a more important location, but the fact remains that the statue with all its elaborate detail remains almost invisible on its lofty perch.

Neither the extravagant eulogies nor the grand commissions which Crawford received during his lifetime represent an accurate estimate of his talents. His modest abilities appear to best advantage in such of his less pretentious works as *Babes in the Woods* (12-15). Here his love of anecdote, his delight in sentimental idealizations of form, and his skillful working of stone to simulate the texture of skin, hair, and fabric can be enjoyed thoroughly, since the group was made as a conversation piece to be viewed at close range and subjected to minute inspection. Crawford moved more effectively in the world of fairy-tale sentiment than in the realm of national symbols, despite the contemporary legend to the contrary.

The Greek revival movement in sculpture died with the Civil War. After the war the white marble goddesses and symbols of virtue gave way to bronze monuments and genre studies. Even Crawford himself declared that "The darkness of allegory must give way to common sense." Powers and Crawford had hardly closed their eyes when the taste for these chaste echoes of the past was outmoded. One of the critics of the day put it well when he remarked with tongue in cheek, "Purity has had her day; it's time she retired, and made room for nightmares and nastiness."

William Rimmer

Though clients and sculptural commissions were plentiful in the first half of the nineteenth century, not all of the sculptors enjoyed success and affluence. Unless the sculptor created statues that fitted into the conventions of his day, he attracted no attention. While recognition of William Rimmer (1816-1879) has grown through the years, during his lifetime no affluent commissions came his way and his great talents remained unrecognized except by an intimate circle of friends. Born in Liverpool, England, he was brought to Boston as a child. His talent for drawing, painting, and modeling appeared at an early age, but poverty and the need to make a living kept him from practicing the arts professionally. He engaged in various occupations to finance his studies as a physician and later practiced medicine in the poor village of Brockton near Boston. There a community of stoneworkers reawakened his youth-

12-16. William Rimmer, *Despair, c.*
1830. Museum of Fine Arts, Boston.

ful desire to become a sculptor. In 1855, he began to work in granite, and he gradually became more and more involved in the arts. He taught anatomy at the Lowell Institute in Boston and became famous for the virtuosity he displayed in illustrating his lectures. He could sketch the human figure hurtling through space, twisting, and falling, with the greatest freedom, foreshortening the anatomical forms with astonishing virtuosity. During these years he continued his activities as a sculptor though his output remained small.

His long years of struggle against poverty and indifference provided the dominant mood for Rimmer's work. His sculptures and drawings seem to be wrested from some deep inner pessimism. Even a work of his youth, *Despair* (12-16), foreshadows the tragic tone of his mature production. In *Despair* a dry-eyed, grim figure sits tense, constricted, and self-contained, contemplating the infinite frustrations of existence. The compact unity of the figure represents an essentially sculptural approach to expressive form seldom seen in an age when gesticulating figures and broken contours were the usual devices employed for conveying emotion. Within the simple basic form, the parts of the figure move with force and certainty, conveying a feeling of quiet intensity and psychological constraint. The detailed handling of the anatomy, the sense of bones, tendons, veins, and muscles evokes a quality of reality completely absent

12-17. William Rimmer, *Falling Gladiator*, 1860. Courtesy Metropolitan Museum of Art, Rimmer Memorial Society Committee and Rogers Fund, 1907.

from the slippery idealized popular forms of the period. It is not surprising that the prim Bostonians, looking in their sculpture for sentimental echoes of the past, found the harsh immediacy of *Despair* as disquieting as the strange, intense, shy man who created it. It is the direct expression of powerful and disturbing emotions that made Rimmer's work appear so foreign and out of tune in a day when sugary platitudes were considered sculptural masterpieces.

The *Falling Gladiator* (12-17), a life-sized bronze of Rimmer's mature years, was exhibited in Paris, where its startling realism brought forth the accusation that it had been cast from life. Here again Rimmer's knowledge of anatomy reinforced the powerful movements of the main masses of the form to establish an authenticity and dramatic force far removed from meretricious and niggardly realism of surface detail. The agitated surface of the bronze foreshadows the impressionism of Rodin and the late-nineteenth-century sculptors. The startling and anguished gesture of the figure reflects the pain of Rimmer's own unrealized yearnings, the tragedy of the unrecognized artist who, knowing the merit of his own work, saw recognition and financial success heaped upon men whose only strength was a petty talent combined with a shrewd ability to estimate public taste. Rimmer's deeply felt, disturbing, and personal vision contributed a singular element of sincerity to the sculptural expression of the age.

PRINTS AND PHOTOGRAPHY

The story of the artistic life of a nation is more than the recounting of the lives and works of individual artists. An important part of the story is concerned with the degree of interest with which the public at large regards the arts. Certainly the number of practicing artists in all fields had grown tremendously in the years before the Civil War. The general interest in the arts as evidenced by patronage, both public and private, had been most encouraging, the growth of institutions devoted to promulgating the arts was reassuring, and technological developments in printing, engraving, and photography contributed to the expanding intellectual and artistic atmosphere of America.

Probably the most far-reaching single influence on nineteenth-century culture was the general increase in literacy. With the development of a vast reading public came the daily newspaper, the increase in periodical literature, and the popularity of the novel, both in book and serial form. Pictorial illustrations contributed tremendously to the pleasure of the reading public, and the graphic arts were rapidly transformed by the demands for inexpensive and easily duplicated pictures. Wood engraving became immensely popular, lithography almost replaced the beautiful but difficult aquatint and mezzotint processes of an earlier era, and both steel and copper engravings flourished. As the passion for pictures increased, so did the variety—the illustrated journals demanded romantic illustrations, satiric and topical sketches as well as cartoons and caricatures. After the Civil War, satiric sketches with a social or political orientation had an increasingly important influence on American tastes and political trends.

Engraved and lithographic reproductions of the work of the principal painters achieved a wide circulation and served to familiarize the public at large with the popular painters of the day. Thomas Cole's allegories were engraved and widely circulated, and many people became acquainted with them in this form, who would never have otherwise heard of them. Vanderlyn's *Ariadne* and Trumbull's *Declaration of Independence* acquired nation-wide fame in the same way, while engraved "Views of American Cities" and "Scenic Wonders of America" contributed much to popularizing landscape painting.

12-18 (*above*). Thomas Worth, *Fashionable "Turn-outs" in Central Park*, Currier and Ives lithograph, 1868. J. Clarence Davies Collection, Museum of the City of New York, New York. 12-19 (*below*). George Fuller, *Steamboat Race on the Mississippi*, Knoedler lithograph, 1859. Library of Congress.

Currier and Ives

The mass production of prints designed to suit popular tastes was the particular achievement of the famous firm of Currier and Ives. In 1835 Nathaniel Currier and Merritt Ives embarked upon a career of publishing lithographic prints suitable for framing. Their catalogue eventually covered every imaginable kind of subject—portraits of notables; religious scenes; sketches of farm life, sports events, such famous catastrophes as fires and shipwrecks; straight landscapes; and genre studies. Currier and Ives prints provide a fascinating reflection of popular levels of taste in the nineteenth century and also form a valuable record of the period. *Fashionable "Turn-outs" in Central Park* (12-18), a colored lithograph, is an excellent example of the lively and topical nature of the prints. Produced for a literal-minded public, every detail of carriage and costume is depicted with precision. This single print almost provides a catalogue of the fashionable carriages of the day.

Currier and Ives were not the only company to publish lithographic prints of popular subjects. A *Steamboat Race on the Mississippi* (12-19) was distributed by M. Knoedler of New York, the New York branch of the famous Parisian art concern, Goupil and Co. The newly developed steamboats were the subject of great public interest and a print which pictured two of these pleasure palaces, the *Baltic* and the *Diana*, engaged in a race had wide popular appeal. The accurate and informative picture of the boats racing stern to stern, of the cloudy sky and quivering water, of the precarious raft in the foreground, all exquisitely rendered in meticulous lithographic technique, make this a most typical example of the popular tastes of mid-century.

Mathew Brady

The birth of photography also occurred at this time and augmented the public's very real interest in pictures. Daguerre perfected his process for recording an image on a silvered copper plate in 1837. Americans were producing sun pictures of their own almost as soon as the information concerning the process reached these shores. Studios for making portraits by the new photographic processes appeared in American cities in the early forties. Mathew Brady (1823?-1896) set up a gallery in New York and embarked upon the ambitious project of recording the image of every

12-20. Mathew Brady, *Ruins of Richmond, Va.*, photograph, 1865. Collection Museum of Modern Art, New York.

important person in his time when the Civil War intervened and provided him with a new and challenging theme. The genius of Brady immediately sensed the particular capacities of the new medium; his documentary studies of the Civil War place Brady in the front rank of camera artists. Brady possessed a true artist's sense of composition and this intuitive feeling for pictorial arrangement was augmented by the study of painting with William Page. His unerring sense of pictorial composition is well displayed in the powerful *Ruins of Richmond, Virginia* (12-20). In this print he reveals his skill by using a low eye-level to create a somber and monumental mood. The blacks, grays, and whites have been unerringly recorded as they move into the full depth of the picture from the ghostly nearby skeletons of broken walls to suggest the tragic wastes of the abandoned city. Brady revealed his genius through his ability to select the most effective point of view from which to photograph his subject and through his utilization of the full resources of the camera to capture the moment, rather than trying to simulate the textural effect of painting. Brady's portraits constitute a gallery of the notables of his time. Here, too, he displayed a capacity to record the surface forms so as to reveal the underlying character of the sitter.

INSTITUTIONS DEVOTED TO THE ARTS

A number of institutions devoted to the arts were established before the middle of the century. Boston had the Athenaeum, New York the American Academy of Fine Arts, and Philadelphia the Pennsylvania Academy of Fine Arts. Each institution held exhibitions, exhibited and sold works of art, and established models of propriety and taste in the form of casts of famous statues and copies of the works of great painters. Other cities soon followed the example set by the big three. Hartford, Connecticut, acquired the Wadsworth Atheneum, Albany, New York, the Albany Gallery of Fine Arts, and New Haven, Connecticut, the Trumbull Gallery at Yale College. The first art galleries of the country appeared around mid-century. In 1846, Goupil and Co., a well-known Parisian firm selling prints and engravings, sent Michel Knoedler to open a New York branch of the company. The Düsseldorf Gallery and the Belgian Gallery followed, and before long there were a number of salesrooms in New York prepared to capitalize on the growing picture market in America.

One of the novel and typically American organizations to appear at this time was the American Art Union, New York. First a private organization called the Apollo Association, it was reorganized as the Art Union in 1842. The Art Union was open to all for an annual membership fee. Once each year a drawing was held for a number of prizes, the prizes being original works of art. In addition to being eligible for the prizes, each member of the organization received a yearly engraving made from some well-known painting by an American master. Thomas Cole and Caleb Bingham were among the artists whose works were selected for reproduction, Cole's *Voyage of Life* being distributed to over sixteen thousand members. The American Art Union served a unique and useful role since it familiarized the entire country with the work of leading artists. In the course of its existence it distributed thousands of paintings and engravings by over a hundred and fifty American artists and was so successful that a number of cities started local Art Unions of a similar nature. The untimely end of the Art Union was brought about by a small group of artists who, envious of its success and feeling that they were being discriminated against, brought against the Union court action which resulted in its being declared illegal and outlawed as a lottery.

As mass interest in culture developed, there appeared a body of critical literature which focused on the arts. The writings of Hawthorne, Cooper, Emerson, and Greenough reveal a lively concern with the state of the fine arts in America. In 1834 the painter and dramatist William Dunlap published the first history of the arts in America, *The History of the Rise and Progress of the Arts of Design in the United States.* The first monthly magazine devoted to the fine arts appeared in New York in 1855 when W. J. Stillman, a painter-journalist, and John Durand, a son of the painter, founded *The Crayon.* America's first art magazine lasted less than a decade, but during its short life it wielded considerable influence.

At mid-century America gave promise of a new maturity in the arts. Sculpture, painting, in particular, and to a lesser degree, architecture, the crafts, and the newly evolving industrial arts seemed ready to burst into a new and splendid flowering. The tragedy of civil war intervened and the physical and spiritual strain revealed unexpected weaknesses in the cultural life of the country. Almost another half-century of growth and maturation was necessary before the promise of these early years was realized.

SELECTED REFERENCES

for PART III The Young Republic: 1776-1865

General References

Cahill, Holger and Barr, Alfred H., Jr., *Art in America, a Complete Survey*. New York, Reynal and Hitchcock, 1935.

La Follette, Suzanne, *Art in America*. New York, Harper & Brothers, 1929.

Larkin, Oliver, *Art and Life in America*. New York, Rinehart & Company, Inc., 1949.

Architecture

Andrews, Wayne, *Architecture, Ambition and Americans*. New York, Harper & Brothers, 1955.

Fitch, James Marston, *American Building*. Boston, Houghton Mifflin Company, 1948.

Hamlin, Talbot, *The American Spirit in Architecture*, Pageant of America Series, Vol. 13. New Haven, Yale University Press, 1926.

Hamlin, Talbot, *Greek Revival Architecture in America*. New York, Oxford University Press, Inc., 1944.

Sanford, Elwood Trent, *The Architecture of the Southwest*. New York, W. W. Norton & Company, Inc., 1950.

Tallmadge, Thomas, *The Story of Architecture in America*. New York, W. W. Norton & Company, Inc., 1927.

Painting and Sculpture

Barker, Virgil, *American Painting*. New York, The Macmillan Company, 1950.

Bauer, John H., *American Painting in the Nineteenth Century*. New York, Frederick A. Praeger, Inc., 1953.

Burroughs, Alan, *A History of American Landscape Painting*. New York, Whitney Museum of American Art, 1942.

Christ-Janer, Albert, *George Caleb Bingham of Missouri*. New York, Dodd, Mead & Company, 1940.

Eliot, Alexander, *Three Hundred Years of American Painting*. New York, Time, Inc., 1957.

Flexner, James Thomas, *The Light of Distant Skies, 1760-1835*. New York, Harcourt, Brace & Company, 1954.

Flexner, James Thomas, *Gilbert Stuart*. New York, Alfred A. Knopf, Inc., 1955.

Gardner, Albert TenEyck, *Yankee Stonecutters*. New York, Columbia University Press, 1945.

Isham, Samuel and Cortissoz, Royal, *The History of American Painting*. New York, The Macmillan Company, 1927.

Lipman, Jean and Winchester, Alice, *Primitive Painting in America, 1750-1950*. New York, Dodd, Mead & Company, 1950.

Neuhaus, Eugene, *The History and Ideals of American Art*. Stanford, Calif., Stanford University Press, 1931.

Richardson, E. P., *American Romantic Painting*. New York, E. Weyhe, 1944.

Richardson, E. P., *Painting in America*. New York, Thomas E. Crowell Company, 1956.

Richardson, E. P., *Washington Allston*. Chicago, University of Chicago Press, 1948.

Sellers, Charles Coleman, *Charles Willson Peale*. Philadelphia, American Philosophical Society, 1947.

Soby, James Thrall and Miller, Dorothy C., *Romantic Painting in America*. New York, The Museum of Modern Art, 1943.

Sweet, Frederick, *The Hudson River School and the Early American Landscape Tradition*. Chicago, Art Institute of Chicago, 1945.

Interiors, Furniture, and Crafts

Aronson, Joseph, *The Encyclopedia of Furniture*. New York, Crown Publishers, Inc., 1938.

Christensen, Irwin O., *The Index of American Design*. New York, The Macmillan Company, 1950.

Editors of *Life*, *America's Arts and Skills*. New York, E. P. Dutton & Company, Inc., 1957.

Ormsby, Thomas H., *Early American Furniture Makers*. New York, Archer House, Inc., 1957.

Phillips, John Marshall, *American Silver*. New York, Chanticleer Press, Inc., 1949.

Ramsey, John, *American Potters and Pottery*. Clinton, Mass., Colonial Press, Inc., 1939.

Rogers, Meyric R., *American Interior Design*. New York, W. W. Norton & Company, Inc., 1947.

Winchester, Alice, *The Antiques Book*. New York, A. A. Wynn, Inc., 1950.

PART IV

Between Two Wars:
1865-1915

13

Architecture:
The Birth of
the Skyscraper

THE CIVIL WAR, FOUGHT TO FREE THE SLAVES AND PRE-
serve the Union, placed the financial interests of the North in a position of
power which changed the economic and social character of the entire country. In a few decades following the Civil War the great commercial empires
of wheat and beef, iron and copper, railways and steamships, real estate
and banking were established. The geographic frontiers of America had
been settled during the first half of the century and now equally vast
economic frontiers were created by the rapid expansion of the Middle
and Far West and by the astonishing growth of the new metropolitan
areas. By exploring and exploiting the economic opportunities in this
expanding economy the great fortunes of late-nineteenth-century America
were established, and it was in the years immediately following the Civil
War that the millionaire became a symbol of America. By 1915 the characteristics of modern America had become firmly established.

Bigness characterized the age. The vast expanse of land from coast to coast was covered with railway lines, roads, and cities. The passion for bigness expressed itself in new industrial empires, in vast speculative activities, and in the rapid amassing of great fortunes. It also characterized the architecture of the period. The new industrial empires necessitated factories which covered acres of ground. Speculative builders covered miles of new metropolitan areas with row houses, apartments, and suburban villas. The new millionaires built mansions which boasted hundreds of rooms and cost millions of dollars. In the metropolitan centers, skyrocketing land values created fortunes and necessitated the construction of great multistoried business buildings to provide revenues proportionate to the cost of the land.

Technological advances whetted the taste for bigness. The invention of the elevator made the multistoried building economically feasible and permitted an endless number of equally accessible stories. The rapid expansion of iron production and the perfection of the Bessemer process for steel manufacture made mass-produced low-cost steel and iron available for building purposes. The production of glass also was industrialized, thus permitting the fabrication of the great plate-glass windows of the Victorian age. The telephone, incandescent light, modern plumbing, central heating, and a host of other inventions made possible the construction and operation of many kinds of buildings that were both larger and infinitely more complex in their interrelationship of parts than the buildings of preceding ages. They permitted an infinite number of men, machines, and materials to work together, independent of proximity. This, then, was an age of technological and social change, and its great monuments were tributes to those changes.

Three structures of this era, though not considered fine architecture by the connoisseurs of the day, revealed the new conquest of space made possible by technological advances. Only one of these was in America— the Brooklyn Bridge (13-1). In 1869, John Roebling (1806-1869), a German-born engineer, designed a suspension bridge to span the great East River between Manhattan and Brooklyn. Employing the principles of tension structure, he supported the roadbed of the bridge with cables woven of steel wire hung from two great towers. Completed in 1883, Brooklyn Bridge has never been surpassed in breathtaking clarity and directness of design. This was one of the first great engineering triumphs of the nineteenth century to abandon traditional masonry construction and employ steel to span a great void. Although it has been admired by the populace at large and copied by generations of engineers, the architects of the nineteenth century were slow to learn its lesson. For them the

13-1. John Roebling, Brooklyn Bridge (Currier and Ives lithograph), 1869-1883. New York City. Library of Congress photograph.

load-bearing masonry wall remained the symbol of the art of architecture and the litheness of steel seemed the antithesis of architectural dignity.

Two other metal structures pointed the way to the future of architecture for those who had eyes to see. In 1851 Sir Joseph Paxton, an Englishman, had completed the famous Crystal Palace of London to house an exposition of industrial progress. The Crystal Palace was one of the marvels of the age—probably the largest building the world had witnessed to date—a great glass and cast-iron shell, prefabricated, bolted together, and demountable, in which almost a million square feet of glass covered over 17 acres of floor space.

The impact of Paxton's Crystal Palace on American building practice was tremendous although its immediate influence on the architectural profession, like that of the Brooklyn Bridge, was nil. In 1853 New York constructed its own Crystal Palace (13-2) to house an exposition of industry. The New York Crystal Palace resembled its British prototype in its use of a brittle shell of iron ribs and glass panels arched to enclose extensive unobstructed spaces. Both buildings depended for support on the precise relationship of the various parts; thus the principle of strength through precision replaced the ancient one of strength through mass. Effective as public persuaders, the Crystal Palaces stimulated existing interest in iron as a building material, and cast iron used with glass was

13-2. Crystal Palace (Currier lithograph), 1883. New York City. J. Clarence
Davies Collection, Museum of the City of New York, New York.

readily adopted by practical builders searching for efficient materials.
An example in the Gothic vernacular has already been seen—the spectacular interior of the State House (8-5) at Baton Rouge, Louisiana,
where iron-ribbed columns and a glass and iron shell house the stairwell.

The third great structural feat of the period was the Eiffel Tower in
Paris. This structure, too, was executed in metal, for metal construction
alone could, to quote Alexandre Eiffel, "be planned with such accuracy
as to sanction the boldness which results from full knowledge." Eiffel's
use of wrought-iron bars in the underground concrete mats which supported the 1000-foot soaring tower anticipated the use of modern reinforced concrete, and his iron girders foreshadowed the steel members
used in modern construction both in profile and general shape. Architects
thought the Eiffel Tower an eyesore—Garnier, a leading French architect, circulated a petition that the Government demolish it—but builders
saw the advantages of many of the innovations introduced by Eiffel and
readily adapted them to the needs of the multistoried buildings they were
constructing.

Out of this ferment of invention, newly acquired wealth, sudden
growth, and rapid industrialization, the architecture of the post-Civil War

period was born. At the same time there occurred in architectural practice a rift separating architect from engineer and frequently separating both architect and engineer from builder. The professional architect, an artist trained in the beaux-arts tradition of France, designed buildings according to the conventions and ideals of earlier ages. The engineer was concerned with evolving a science of construction suited to the needs of the expanding society and utilizing the new industrial materials and processes. The builder was a composite figure combining the businessman who engaged in construction as a money-making activity and the carpenter-contractor who directed the actual construction of an edifice. Architectural practice was split three ways, and a discussion of building in the last half of the century can best be understood by viewing the activities of these three groups separately. First, we will look at the vigorous products of the unschooled builders educated largely in the carpenter-handbook tradition. Next, we will observe the dignified and handsome works of the architects trained in the beaux-arts academies. Third, we must trace the new forms developed by more imaginative designers to house the activities of a changing society.

THE BUILDERS

A tremendous increase in population, due to the influx of immigrants occurred in America in the seventies, eighties, and nineties. Cities doubled and tripled in size within a few decades; vast new territories were settled in the Middle and Far West; business buildings, factories, schools, homes, and a multitude of other buildings were constructed across the land, in most cases designed and built without the benefit of either architect or engineer. Professional advice often was not available, nor was the need felt for such services. As in earlier times, the carpenter-handbooks supplied builders with plans and exterior designs, and the average builder, true to the Yankee tradition of self-reliant tinkering, invented designs and structural devices when he could find no ready-made answer to his needs.

The most important single invention of the self-reliant builder was balloon framing. Balloon framing was first used in Chicago in 1833—in fact, for many years it was termed "Chicago construction." In balloon frame construction, thin two-by-four vertical studs and plates ran the entire height of the building and were held together by nails, providing a light and sturdy frame which was later sheathed with wooden siding or some other suitable material. Balloon framing, a child of the industrial

13-3. Wright House, 1870. Dayton, O. Henry Ford Museum, Dearborn, Mich.

age, was made possible by the development of machinery for manufacturing nails which, after the Civil War, cost only a few cents a pound. Even before the Civil War, however, use of this rapid, light construction had become widespread, and it has since remained standard in America. The rapid creation of entire new cities and of great residential tracts was greatly facilitated by this revolutionary mode of construction; in fact, it may well have contributed more to the rapid development of the west than did any one other factor. One observer remarked that "If it had not been for the knowledge of the balloon frame, Chicago and San Francisco could never have arisen as they did, from little villages to great cities in a single year."

Popular Housing

Three residences from the late nineteenth century supply a picture of the builders' tastes as they appeared in the typical homes of the period. The first is the Wright brothers' house (13-3), originally built in 1870 in Dayton, Ohio, and now in Dearborn, Michigan. Similar two-story frame structures were built all over America, filling endless acres in the rapidly growing cities, making up the quiet streets of small towns, and providing comfortable farmhouses. Unlike the majority of earlier houses, this was designed into the depth of the lot rather than facing the street, a type of plan adapted to the narrow lots by means of which subdividers squeezed a few extra dollars out of each city block. From a spreading porch decorated with machine-turned spindles, one entered a small vestibule which either opened into a hall or led directly to a parlor, dining room, and kitchen. A pantry, back porch, stairway to the basement, and downstairs bedroom completed the ground story. A staircase in the front vestibule led to the second floor, where bedrooms and, toward the end of the century, a bath, opened off a central hallway. The rooms tended to be small with no intercommunication other than doors, so that the house consisted of small isolated cubicles with windows opening to the outdoors and doors opening into halls.

A house in San Francisco (13-4) represents a more elaborate venture on the part of some builder who was probably in the lucrative practice of building speculative houses for the more prosperous members of the growing city. Such a house had three full stories and a basement, with back parlors and upstairs parlors, maids' rooms and nurseries, laundries and libraries providing for the various activities of large and busy families. The exterior illustrates what happened to the Gothic style when it was subjected to the enthusiasms of the uninformed builder assisted by the newly developed woodworking machines. Turrets, towers, porches, bays, gables, and projections divide and subdivide the basic forms of the building. Pointed arches, Tudor arches, barge boards, pendants, brackets, pinnacles, panels, and moldings break up the forms still more. And over it all the jig-saw cut-outs add patterns and textures until there is not one

13-4. House, late 19th century. San Francisco, Calif. Berton Crandall photograph.

13-5. Flood Mansion, 1875-1878. Menlo Park, Calif. Edward Farmer photograph.

spot on the entire tortured surface where the eye can rest. It is a triumph of energy and invention over taste, of enthusiasm over knowledge, of pretense over discipline.

Not all the energy and enthusiasm were misplaced on elaborations of the Gothic style. In the late eighteen-seventies, Senator James Flood built a country home in Menlo Park, California, in a carpentered version of the French baroque manner (13-5) then being revived in France. In the seventies and eighties, American enthusiasm for the mansard-roofed baroque style almost equaled that shown for the Gothic. In an age when wealth meant size and display, even a country house became an architectural extravaganza if the owner could afford it. In the Flood House the curious wooden translations of Garnier's baroque ornament rose tier above tier, like a gigantic wedding cake, to culminate in a cupola and tower with a mansard roof.

Fortunately the craze for elaboration was only part of the story of building in America during these years. One of the distinguishing characteristics of American building, in contrast to that of Europe, was a taste for unadorned surfaces and flexibility of plan. Many of the nineteenth-century handbooks on house design, which influenced the average builder much more than did the stylish writings, advocated abandoning all pretense and frippery, and planning for convenience. Lewis F. Allen, who

13-6. Kitchen work area. Catherine Beecher and Harriet Beecher Stowe, *The American Woman's Home* (1869).

wrote *Rural Architecture,* in 1852 advocated making plans which were based on the life that would be carried on in the house. He held fitness for purpose and harmony between parts as his ideal. In 1869 Harriet Beecher Stowe and her sister, Catherine Beecher, wrote a volume dedicated to the creation of a house "contrived for the express purpose of enabling every member of the family to labor with the hands for the common good, and by modes at once healthful, economical, and tasteful." The house they recommended was revolutionary in plan, with a central kitchen area (13-6), a family all-purpose room with movable screens, and other features which characterize advanced house plans today. The octagon house represented another deviation from traditional modes of domestic building.

The development of simple functional designs was not confined to houses. Barns, factories, warehouses, storage silos, New England meeting houses, and Shaker buildings testified that a taste for simplicity was a deep-rooted part of our native building tradition. The American sense of propriety, essentially an inheritance from our puritan background, provided a valuable countercheck to the nineteenth-century childish delight in the capacity of machines to produce endless streams of decoration.

BEAUX-ARTS ARCHITECTURE

While carpenters, contractors, builders, and real estate speculators were covering America with buildings which ranged from gingerbread

Gothic to bare box, trained architects were being sought with increasing frequency by discriminating clients. With wealth came travel and sophistication, and America's millionaires and civic leaders began to realize that, in addition to size and elaborateness, the handsome structures of Europe had a distinction that could only be duplicated by trained architects. As a consequence, an increasing number of mansions and civic structures in the eighties and nineties came from the drawing boards of trained men. The dominant mood remained romantic, and the Gothic style retained its popularity although the Venetian Gothic, introduced by the English critic, John Ruskin, vied with the French and English Gothic styles for popularity. Equally attractive to the world of fashion were the various baroque and Renaissance fashions being revived in Paris. Each style had its vigorous adherents and loquacious defenders and seemed particularly appropriate for certain types of buildings. Two impressive structures of the eighties—the great McCormick residence (13-7) in Chicago and the Museum of Fine Arts (13-8) in Boston—provide us with examples, one of French baroque and one of Venetian Gothic, as interpreted by the successful architects of that day.

Cyrus Hall McCormick acquired a great fortune from his invention of the reaper, and hired Cudell and Blumenthal, one of Chicago's most successful firms, to design his palatial home. Its heavy grandeur reflects the influence of Garnier's Paris mansions, in which the baroque designs of the great eighteenth-century French architect Mansard were modified to suit nineteenth-century tastes. In the hands of less skillful designers the heavy splendor of the McCormick House might have either degenerated into extravaganza like the Flood House or into such an oppressive and graceless brownstone front as lined the streets of upper middle-class residential areas through these years.

Gothic remained the popular choice for institutional architecture. Churches, schools, libraries, municipal and state buildings acquired an air of sanctity and authority from the dress of the Middle Ages. In 1851, Ruskin published *Stones of Venice* and his enthusiasm for the ornamental subtleties of the Venetian Gothic style gave the Gothic revival a new direction. Since the Venetian Gothic was based on decorative mannerisms rather than on a structural system, it was well suited to the plans of the late nineteenth-century architect. It was easy to adapt the unbroken Venetian façades to the straight streets and rectangular blocks of a modern city. The long arcades of pointed arches so characteristic of the style provided a handsome framework for the endless rows of windows necessitated by the nineteenth-century taste for light and air. It was possible

13-7 (*right*). Cudell and Blumenthal, C. H. McCormick House, 1879. Chicago. Wayne Andrews photograph. 13-8 (*below*). Sturgis and Brigham, Museum of Fine Arts, 1871-1876. Boston. University of Illinois photograph.

to translate the colored marble mosaics of Venice into such standard building materials as multicolored bricks, stones, and tiles. Sturgis and Brigham, a reliable if not inspired firm, designed the old Boston Museum of Fine Arts in the current version of the Venetian Gothic. This dignified building, clothed in a nineteenth-century version of fourteenth-century dress, provided for the needs of a public museum and maintained a borrowed air of authority but, like most of the architecture of its day, it fails to achieve the synthesis of all its parts that characterizes great architecture.

The Age of Elegance

The last two decades of the century have been termed "the Age of Elegance." A new level of disciplined taste and sophistication characterized the designs of McKim, Mead, and White in the metropolitan eastern centers, while the great mansions created by Richard Morris Hunt for millionaire socialites symbolize the opulence of the day.

McKim, Mead, and White opened their office in New York in 1879. All three men were talented and well-trained, and each had capacities that complemented those of the other two partners. Charles Follen McKim was a graduate of Harvard and had attended the *École des Beaux Arts* in Paris. William Rutherford Mead was graduated from Amherst, worked in an architect's office, and then traveled to Italy to study the great monuments of the past. Stanford White, immensely talented, had been trained, like McKim, in the studio of Henry Hobson Richardson, the most important American architect of his day, whose work will be discussed later. It was not long before the ability and taste of the three men brought them many important commissions. In 1887 they designed the Public Library in Boston (13-9); it was carefully patterned after the beautiful Bibliothèque Ste. Geneviève in Paris. McKim, Mead, and White absorbed the disciplined formality and restraint of the French original and produced one of America's handsomest public buildings. Though the Boston Public Library, like its counterpart in Paris, lacks the surging vitality of the greatest architecture, it is a distinguished and skillful design in which no false note or element of gaucherie mars the perfection of the performance. As during the Renaissance, the foremost artists of the day were engaged to decorate this great structure. Augustus Saint-Gaudens carved the seals above the entrance, and John Singer Sargent, Edwin Austin Abbey, and Pierre Puvis de Chavannes decorated the walls of the interior.

13-9 (*above*). McKim, Mead, and White, Public Library, 1887. Boston. University Prints photograph.   13-10 (*below*). McKim, Mead, and White, Villard group, 1882-1885. New York City. Wayne Andrews photograph.

Like all practitioners trained in the beaux-arts tradition, these three architects could design in a wide variety of styles with equal skill. One of their most subtle achievements was the great complex of five town houses (13-10) which they designed for the railroad promoter Henry Villard and four of his friends. Stylistically this handsome mansion draws on the Italian High Renaissance, but while the details of windows, stonework, and arcades may recall Bramante, the plan and the details have been worked out with originality and freedom. The Villard group is undoubtedly the finest Italian Renaissance design in America and probably is New York City's finest mansion.

When necessity dictated, McKim, Mead, and White could go back to antiquity for inspiration. Among their most stupendous assignments in the Roman manner was the Pennsylvania Railroad Station built in 1903. The great waiting room was inspired by the Baths of Caracalla. Though technically dependent on steel and though its role as a railway station made it a symbol of the new industrial age, nothing in the architectural details of the Pennsylvania Railway Station spoke of the twentieth century. McKim, Mead, and White were among the most persuasive architects of their age but they spoke the language of the past.

In the last decade of the century, New York fortunes leaped boldly up into the hundreds of millions. Expenditures followed accordingly, and hostesses vied with one another in their extravagances, gold plate, for instance, replacing silver. In this atmosphere Richard Morris Hunt (1827-1895) moved with assurance, providing the magnificent settings for this world of ostentatious luxury.

The son of a congressman, Hunt grew up in the best Washington society. Later he lived in Paris, traveled, and enrolled in the *École des Beaux Arts*. On his return to America he married a society woman and proceeded to develop a clientele among the wealthiest and most distinguished families.

Hunt wanted to bring the elegance and refinement of French architecture to America and in 1881 he introduced the chateau style in a mansion he designed for Mrs. W. K. Vanderbilt. Before long Hunt was famous for such palatial homes. His most stupendous creation in the French chateau style was Biltmore (13-11), the four-million-dollar country house which he designed for George Vanderbilt's 130,000-acre estate in the Great Smoky Mountains near Asheville, North Carolina. The staircase of Biltmore is reminiscent of Blois, and its roof line and windows of Chantilly, but it is Hunt's own creation. It took five years and hundreds of foreign artisans to complete Biltmore, which covers more than five

13-11. Richard Morris Hunt, Biltmore, 1895. Biltmore, N. C. Biltmore Estates photograph.

acres. It represented the ultimate attempt to clothe the present in the dress of the past, and as such it is a final monument to a way of life and a point of view doomed for client and architect alike. The millionaires had only a few more decades before new systems of taxation and anti-monopoly legislation began to restrict their activities and displays. For the architects the apparently inexhaustible well of tradition provided fewer and fewer answers to the questions presented by the burgeoning industrial democracy of twentieth-century America.

Henry Hobson Richardson

We must step back a few years to observe the work and influence of the only architect who seemed capable of drawing on the past for answers to the pressing problems of the emerging industrial age. The work of Henry Hobson Richardson (1838-1886) provided the bridge between beaux-arts architecture and the emerging Chicago school of the last two decades of the century. Richardson grew up on a plantation in Louisiana, attended Harvard, and then studied architecture at the *École des Beaux Arts* in Paris. When the Civil War blocked his remittances from home, he went to work under Labrouste, where he experienced the severe discipline that distinguished the work of the leading designers of France.

Richardson returned to Boston in 1865 and began his career by designing homes for the families of his friends. His most distinguished residence of those early years was the W. Watts Sherman House (13-12) in Newport, Rhode Island. In this handsome structure, with its bold geometric shapes and its rich textures of stone, brick, wood, plaster, and shingle, Richardson abandoned the pretentious splendor of the aristocratic modes of the day for the more modest and comfortable style initiated in England by William Morris, leader of the English "Arts and Crafts" movement. Seven years after his arrival in Boston, Richardson won a competition for the design of Trinity Church (13-13). This building remains his greatest achievement and is one of the most influential buildings in the history of American architecture. Like most American architects of the nineteenth century, Richardson had been deeply impressed with the power and richness of French architectural tradition, and like a true romantic, he found the styles of the Middle Ages particularly compelling. Aware of the irrelevance of academic revival styles to the surging forces of American life, his ideal was to draw on the rich inspiration of the past and from it to forge a style that would express the buoyant enthusiasm and youthful energy of America. For this purpose Richardson chose the French Romanesque for he found its strength, heavy vigor, and lack of standardization most compatible with his ideas of America. This choice was based on his own feelings—the prevailing taste was for the late Gothic, the Renaissance, and the baroque. The design he created for Trinity Church was not a copy of any existing structure but a conception of such originality and force that the building became the foremost church of its period in America. Working in the Romanesque manner, Richardson planned a structure of massive and dramatic masonry which moved in powerful rhythms from its wide portals and heavy transept and apse through its many turrets and pinnacles to the great central tower which dominates the composition by thrusting vertical masses. It was as complex, rich, and elaborate as any contemporary structure, but unlike less talented men, its creator was able to unite all the diverse parts into a unified and organic whole. The success of Trinity Church inaugurated the Romanesque revival in America, and Richardson remained its most successful practitioner.

The distinguishing characteristics of the style are well illustrated by Trinity Church although in later buildings the vocabulary of effects was enlarged. First, there is a romantic and picturesque mass, effective from any angle, made up of bulky forms, great rectangular towers, turrets, and soaring roofs. These masses are covered with a rich surface: heavy stone roughly hewn, brick, shingle, colored stucco. The surface materials

13-12 (*above*). Henry Hobson Richardson, W. Watts Sherman House, 1874-1876. Newport, R. I. Wayne Andrews photograph. 13-13 (*below*). Henry Hobson Richardson, Trinity Church, 1872-1877. Boston. Wayne Andrews photograph.

13-14. Henry Hobson Richardson, Crane Memorial Library, 1883. Quincy, Mass. Wayne Andrews photograph.

were often applied in a vigorous pattern. In Trinity, red sandstone was used to trim yellow-gray granite, and the two stones were combined in herringbone and checkerboard patterns. The dramatic masses and rich surfaces are enhanced by deep arched doorways, clustered columns, and windows grouped in arcaded series.

Richardson's standards were uncompromising. Craftsmanship and materials had to be the finest. He gathered the finest talents to design the stained glass windows and to decorate the great walls. Sir Edward Burne-Jones, John LaFarge, and William Morris Hunt helped create an interior worthy of his conception.

Trinity Church brought Richardson fame and commissions. In the ten years that intervened between the completion of Trinity and his death, he became America's most important architect. His ambitions encompassed the entire, bold, new adventure of America. "What I want most to design is a grain elevator and the interior of a Mississippi steamboat," he once said. It was in the coherent and simple solution he provided for some of the new kinds of buildings emerging in America that Richardson's impact on the future was most strongly felt. Libraries, schools, railway stations, court houses, jails, and lastly, the Marshall Field warehouse in Chicago all felt the impact of his vigorous and clear mind.

13-15. Henry Hobson Richardson, Marshall Field warehouse, 1885-1887. Chicago. Museum of Modern Art photograph.

One of his finest smaller designs is the Crane Memorial Library (13-14) in Quincy, Massachusetts. The familiar elements of Richardson's Romanesque style are apparent here—roughly hewn stone used in contrasting colors, the gables, towers, clustered columns and windows, and the heavy arched entranceway. What is most noteworthy is the clear statement of function both in the plan of the building and in the outward disposition of the parts. The entranceway, large reading room, stairs to the second story, extended area of the stacks provide the elements of this forceful design. There is no hesitation in the disposition of the masses, no niggling compromise in the statement of the plan. It radiates vitality— equally pleasing to the eye and mind.

No one building designed by Richardson reveals his ability to think and express himself in direct and fundamental terms more clearly than the great wholesale warehouse (13-15) he designed for Marshall Field of Chicago in 1885. The devastating fire of 1871 had left the city in ashes, and rebuilding the metropolis challenged some of the most inventive minds of the century. Richardson's appearance in Chicago had a most fortuitous effect on the subsequent development of building there. His direct and simple design for Marshall Field's warehouse—a seven-story embryonic skyscraper—proved his ability to grasp the essential problem and to provide a clear visual solution for it. Traditional in structure, the Marshall Field warehouse is constructed of stone, with its seven stories arranged around a central court. The uniqueness of the building lies in the directness with which the exterior design and plan express the nature of the building and acknowledge the systematic regularity and the cell-like divisions of its stories. The absence of the traditional emphasis on various focal points departs from the accepted compositional principles of that period; there is neither cornice nor column, pediment nor pinnacle. The main entrance is unaccented, the surface uncluttered, the profiles are unbroken. The succession of stories is saved from monotony by the subtle grouping of windows and the variation in size and shape of bays and window openings. The slight differences in the size and surface textures of the stone also contribute interest. Richardson saw the monopolistic nature of industrial organization and created an imposing monolithic structure as an expression of it. From this simple and fundamental statement a school of subsequent designers took their direction.

The Marshall Field building was Richardson's last achievement. Created at the moment the skyscraper was being born, it strongly influenced the new school of architecture. The sprawling, formless metropolis of Chicago was the focus of the agrarian and manufacturing empires of the Middle West. The growth of a multitude of neighboring cities and the rebuilding after the fire made it the center of the greatest construction boom in history. A number of imaginative and ambitious men moved from the East to this more challenging atmosphere.

Cast iron had been used as a building material since the forties, and in 1848 New York witnessed the construction of the first all cast-iron building, the James Bogardus factory. Bogardus pointed out that buildings of cast iron could be assembled at all times of the year by ignorant workmen without plumb, square, or level, as the parts needed only to be bolted together. In the eighteen-fifties, hundreds of cast-iron buildings were erected in Manhattan, and in 1857 the first practical passenger elevator was installed in the five-story cast-iron Haughwout Building (13-16). This meant that buildings could be erected to any desired height—cast-iron posts and beams made it possible to pile story upon story, and the elevator made all levels readily accessible. But the top

13-16. J. P. Gaynor, Haughwout Building, 1857. New York City. Wayne Andrews photograph.

eastern architects were not really concerned with the merits of iron as a building material for they were busy designing palaces for men of wealth. By the last decade of the century, Chicago had taken leadership as a creative center of architecture.

THE CHICAGO SCHOOL

It was in the ambitious and restless atmosphere of Chicago that the skyscraper was born. Following the fire, property values soared. The United States was leading the world in steel production. With steel to carry the load, with the inflated cost of land, and with the invention of the elevator, the multistoried building became inevitable. In 1883 William Le Barron Jenney (1832-1907) designed a ten-story building for the Home Insurance Company in Chicago. Using wrought and cast iron for the first six, and Bessemer steel beams for the next four stories, he proved that with metal construction buildings could be built to any reasonable height.

Two young men, William Holabird and Martin Roche, working in Jenney's office learned this lesson well and set up their own partnership. In 1886 they laid out the Tacoma Building (13-17). Twelve stories in height, it was the first structure to have a riveted skeleton containing steel, and cast and wrought iron. The Tacoma Building was not only revolutionary in construction but its exterior was equally unconventional. Designed in a succession of bays that ran the full height of the building, the surface was sheathed in glass and terra cotta, providing for each room

13-17 (*left*). Holabird and Roche, Tacoma Building, 1886. Chicago. Chicago Architectural Photographing Company. 13-18 (*right*). Burnham and Root, Monadnock Building, 1891. Chicago. Chicago Architectural Photographing Company.

a maximum exposure to light and air. There was no attempt to invest this light sheathing of glass with monumentality and weight. Here for the first time the exterior wall of a multistoried business building was treated as a thin protective skin, and the exterior design was a frank expression of the multicellular interior honeycomb.

Two other energetic and imaginative men, Daniel Hudson Burnham (1846-1912) and John Wellborn Root (1850-1891), also engaged in experimental building. Ambitious Burnham came to architecture from the business world. Root had been trained by some of the finest architects in the East. Together they helped rebuild Chicago. Of their many great buildings none created a more vivid impression than the Monadnock Building (13-18), completed in 1891. Root stated his convictions about business structures when he said: "The relation between dwellings and trade-palaces is the relation between an orchestra and a brass band.

Whatever is spoken in a commercial building must be strongly and directly said." The Monadnock Building had the directness and force of a trumpet blast. The massive regularity and bare vigor of this multi-storied, many-windowed building create an impression of grandeur far beyond that achieved by the devotees of traditional monumentality. Its sixteen stories thrust themselves into the air in one sweeping and unbroken movement without a single surface ornament or deviation of line to obstruct the movement. The soaring height is accentuated by the subtle chamfering of the corners which widen with the rise of the mass, and by the profile of the wall which dips in at the beginning of the second story and flares at the top like the pylon of an Egyptian temple. Despite its effectiveness, the Monadnock Building is less a forecast of the future than it is a bridge between the past and the future, for its effects were achieved by traditional building techniques. The sixteen stories are supported by masonry walls 17 feet thick at the base. Much of its grandeur results from the fact that the weight and volume of the walls are acknowledged visually. Built in a moment of transition, it foretold the future and echoed the past.

Louis Henry Sullivan

It was Louis Henry Sullivan (1856-1924) who gave final form to the architectural ferment of the Chicago area. He alone seemed able to combine the structural concepts found in such structures as the Tacoma Building with the architectural values that distinguished the Marshall Field warehouse and the Monadnock Building. Three cities formed Sullivan's genius—Boston, Paris, and Chicago. Boston, the city of his birth, provided him with his initial philosophic orientation. Paris gave him a sense of architecture and of artistic integrity. Chicago provided him with a theater for his immense talents.

Sullivan attended the Massachusetts Institute of Technology for a short time and then left school to acquire experience in an architect's office. He arrived in Chicago in 1873 when he was seventeen years old. For him the city was "magnificent and wild: a crude extravaganza, an intoxicating rawness, a sense of big things to be done. . . ." He went to work for William Le Baron Jenney, in an atmosphere where challenging problems were being met and solved. Later Sullivan went to Paris, but he remained skeptical of French academic architectural practice, which he suspected had lost the "primal inspiration" of the past. He returned to Chicago in 1879, was employed by Dankmar Adler, and two years later became a partner in the firm. Adler had an established practice and inventive ability, imagination, and taste. Sullivan had unlimited energy and ambition and an unusual capacity to think in basic terms. Together they left their mark through more than a hundred buildings. One of the first of their commissions was the immense Chicago Auditorium, containing a hall that would seat 4000 people, a 400-room hotel, and a great office building. The final design reveals the influence of Richardson's recently completed Marshall Field warehouse in its bold, simple plan using windows grouped within arches. But Sullivan did not merely imitate Richardson's surface details. Instead, he learned from the older man to think through the complexities of a project until a large synthesis was achieved, and then to develop a plan and façades that precisely expressed that synthesis.

Though the Chicago Auditorium was an impressive achievement, it did not contribute to skyscraper design as did the Wainwright Building (13-19), which Sullivan and Adler built in St. Louis in 1890. Here Sullivan, following his belief that form must follow function and express structure, gave significant form to the structural innovations that charac-

13-19. Sullivan and Adler, Wainwright Building, 1890. St. Louis, Mo. Museum of Modern Art photograph.

terized the Chicago skyscrapers. This concept was so clearly stated in the Wainwright Building that it established the prototype for skyscraper design for the next fifty years. The building is equally important as a timely solution of a critical problem and as a great work of art.

Significant as the Wainwright Building is in plan, it is in its visual impact that the building remains timeless. The role of the supporting steel structure is brilliantly emphasized by the vertical and horizontal pattern of the exterior. The impersonal quality of industrially produced architecture and the uniformity of the interior divisions is clearly stated by the regularity of the design. Mechanical monotony is avoided by varying the weight and shape of the windows of the two ground stories, by stressing the stringcourse that separates the second and third floors, and by introducing the handsomely textured panels that separate the windows. The vigor and gaiety of the frieze that animates the area under the cornice prevents a cold and mechanical aspect. In addition, the Wainwright Building dramatizes the most characteristic aspect of the skyscraper—the sense of height. Sullivan was stirred by the magnitude of a tall building and challenged by the possibilities of a "proud and soaring thing." The Wainwright Building soars.

Sullivan was not content with a single solution to the skyscraper problem. One of his most distinguished subsequent creations was the department store he designed for the Schlesinger-Mayer Company of Chicago, now the home of Carson-Pirie-Scott Company (13-20). Neither a vertical nor a horizontal emphasis represents an accurate statement of skyscraper construction, for structurally the steel supporting frame is a static cage. In the Schlesinger-Mayer Building this fact, and the need for maximum window area, dictated the design. Neither horizontal nor vertical elements were dominant—both piers and spandrels were reduced to an absolute minimum. In no building up to this time had the non-supporting role of exterior walls been stressed to such a degree. The extensive surface of glass appears to be only a protective curtain, and all pretense of the ground story supporting the structure above is abandoned. The Schlesinger-Mayer Building was particularly admired by the young architects of Europe. Many of its features, such as the bold juxtaposition of rectangular and curvilinear masses, the fluid continuity of surface, and the extensive areas of glass, became stylistic characteristics of twentieth-century architecture.

Nowhere did Sullivan's use of ornament receive a more refined expression than in the handsome cast-iron detail which decorates the two lowest stories of this building. This small-scaled pattern is a curious and

13-20 (*left*). Louis H. Sullivan, Carson-Pirie-Scott Building, 1904. Chicago. Chicago Architectural Photographing Company. 13-21 (*below*). Louis H. Sullivan, Transportation Building, Columbian Exposition, 1893. Chicago. Chicago Architectural Photographing Company.

personal combination of leaves, flowers, geometric motifs, classical ornament, and typical art-nouveau designs. Sullivan had declared that original and appropriate ornament "is a perfume," and his decorations for
this building add charm to the façade. The scope of Sullivan's capabilities
also included the practical aspects of store design. All the paraphernalia
of modern store-front design—awnings, ventilators, illumination, show
windows, and so on, have been used for over fifty years in the Carson-
Pirie-Scott Building without requiring any major alterations.

The Transportation Building (13-21), which Sullivan designed for
the World's Columbian Exposition of 1893 in Chicago, represented a
turning point in his career. The philosophic, social, and consequent architectural conservatism of the East was beginning to dominate the Chicago
area, and Sullivan found himself in conflict with the changing mood.
Daniel Hudson Burnham, in charge of planning the grounds and buildings, called in a number of such distinguished eastern architects as
Richard M. Hunt and Charles Follen McKim to help plan the Exposition.
To Sullivan's dismay, Burnham acquiesced to the plans of the eastern
designers, and a beaux-arts manner prevailed except for a very few buildings, among them Sullivan's Transportation Building.

Since this building was designed to display the newest Pullman cars
and railroad engines, Sullivan designed a long arcaded shed with a
boldly accented entranceway. Six huge concentric arches centered in a
bold, low rectangular block funneled the sightseers into the capacious
entrance which was painted brilliant colors. Even the gay, typically
Sullivan ornamentation that faces the arches and borders the building
was candidly a fluid and continuous molded stucco decoration that suggested poured plaster rather than carved stone. The rest of the fair was
housed in pseudo-classic architecture. The great white plaster façades
mirrored in the lagoons which filled the spacious courts made a deep
impression on the uncritical public. Sullivan was well aware of the
seductive power of this synthetic grandeur. "The damage wrought by
the World's Fair," he said, "will last a half century"—and his estimate was
correct. The Columbian Exposition's white classical architecture finished
the Romanesque revival and also terminated the Chicago school. Classic
revival became the style for institutional architecture for many decades.

Though Sullivan continued to produce distinguished structures well
into the twentieth century, commissions became less frequent and his
lecturing and writing became increasingly important. His *Autobiography
of an Idea,* in which he formulated his philosophy of architecture, and
his lectures to the Chicago Architectural Club, published as *Kindergarten
Talks,* spread throughout America and Europe the concept of form fol-

lowing function and his theories on design and ornamentation. Both by his work, writing, and lectures, and through a small group of young disciples, including Frank Lloyd Wright, Sullivan gave form to the major architectural trends of the twentieth century. A half century after he planted the seed, his concept of functional design took root and became the major working principle of twentieth-century design.

THE TWENTIETH CENTURY

Eclecticism

In the early years of the twentieth century the skyscraper became the symbol of American business enterprise and culture. American civilization was referred to as a "skyscraper civilization" with increasing frequency. The term was used in admiration to describe American energy, inventiveness, and wealth but also to decry the domination of business interests over the national life and the increasing tendency to value size and technical organization irrespective of the human consequence. The plan and structure of the skyscraper developed in Chicago was adopted universally, but the vigor and simplicity disappeared. As Sullivan had predicted, the influence of the Columbian Exposition was overwhelming. The entire repertory of historic architectural devices was resurrected to be stretched across towering façades in defiance of architectural logic. Cass Gilbert completed the Woolworth Tower (13-22) in 1913. The vertical sweep of the great mass is overwhelming from a distance where the frittery detail is lost in the thrust of fifty-six stories, but many occupants peer from their windows through a maze of terra-cotta gargoyles, buttresses, and pinnacles. The world was not yet prepared to be candid about its preoccupation with making money nor to accept the esthetic potential of the machine. Eclectic decorations, symbols of culture, served to obscure the predatory character of certain social patterns and to hide the industrial impersonality of modern technology.

Eclecticism completely dominated the design of public buildings during the early twentieth century. Architects from the *École des Beaux Arts* returned to America in increasing numbers, and schools of architecture patterned after the French academy were established in American universities. Increased travel and the publication of authoritative books on architecture created an informed public. As a consequence, impressive monuments in the various historic styles appeared all over America

13-22. Cass Gilbert, Woolworth Building, 1913. New York City.

between 1900 and 1915, a tribute to serious intention if not to creative vitality. America built efficiently and comfortably, even imaginatively, in terms of plans and technological developments during the years preceding World War I, but almost entirely in the manner of the past.

House design during these years reflected a continued attempt to reconcile comfort and efficiency with traditional concepts of beauty. Electricity, central heating, and plumbing contributed greatly to the livability of the American home, which remained more traditional in appearance than in fact. The early years of the century witnessed a revival of the Colonial Georgian manner as well as a rather thin and mechanical interpretation of Elizabethan half-timber. In California and Florida, stucco and tile were used in houses designed after the Mediterranean villas of Italy, France, and, particularly, Spain. Most of the more modest structures eliminated decorations except in a few strategic areas such as the entrance and the overmantel. Regional differences in house design nearly disappeared; by the second decade of the twentieth century the houses in all sections of the United States were almost alike except for a few from California and Florida. Industrial standardization made doors, window frames, shingles, siding, and a thousand other elements of house construction the same throughout the country. Goods and services and, consequently, living patterns were also becoming more uniform. The widespread standardization and leveling-off processes of modern life were beginning to be felt, and American building practices were character-ized by a monotonous uniformity when the influences of the craftsman movement and the genius of Louis Sullivan again made themselves felt.

The Craftsman Movement, Structuralism, and *Art Nouveau*

In 1900 one might have assumed that eclecticism had won the battle of styles and that the progressive architectural trends of the Chicago school had came to naught. But the followers of Sullivan and Richardson continued their search for a style suited to the new science of building. Parallel developments were occurring in Europe, and progressive de-signers on both sides of the Atlantic drew on the advances that were occurring across the ocean for inspiration and encouragement.

Three separate but closely related aspects of the progressive forces at the turn of the century can be identified. In England the influence of William Morris made itself felt in ever-widening circles through a revival of handicraft processes, simple carpentered construction, and the use of unpretentious building materials. This interest provided the basis for the craftsman movement. Secondly, a concern with the structural pos-sibilities of ferroconcrete, metal, and glass stimulated experiments in architectural design in Paris, Brussels, and Vienna; and this attempt to give logical architectural form to the evolving technology of the industrial age constituted a trend best described as structuralism. Thirdly, progres-sive designers were finding new sources of inspiration in the decorative arts of the Orient, in the arts of primitive peoples, in European peasant crafts, and in other unorthodox sources. The decorative style developed from these various ingredients received its most complete expression in the art-nouveau style.

In America, structuralism, the movement concerned with giving logi-cal architectural form to the evolving industrial technology, attained its clearest formulation in the work of Sullivan, which we have already described. The art-nouveau movement had a very limited impact on American design. The craftsman movement, on the other hand, received a forceful formulation in the hands of a number of American designers. In an age when pressed tin simulated ceramic tiles, cast iron pretended to be carved marble, and plaster was cast to copy stone, the artist of integrity

13-23. Purcell and Elmslie, Bradley House, 1912. Woods Hole, Mass. Wayne Andrews photograph.

valued honesty above all else. A respect for craft, for an unpretentious but skillful use of materials, and for an honest avowal of processes became a fundamental concern of many progressive designers in America in the years between 1900 and World War I and provided the basis for the craftsman movement. This movement extended beyond architecture to the allied fields of interior and furniture design.

The most forceful architect to lead the battle against sham in these crucial years was Frank Lloyd Wright (1869-1959). His contribution to the development of modern architecture in America through the formulation of his "prairie style" in the first decade of the century was as significant in its way as that of Sullivan had been in the preceding generation. Certainly no single individual did more to give direction to the evolving craftsman style. Wright's continued productivity through six decades of the twentieth century justifies delaying our study of his contribution to American architecture until the next section.

Only a few of the architects whose practice contributed to the distinction of the craftsman style in America have been recognized. William Purcell (1880-   ) and George Elmslie (1871-1952), like Wright, received their initial orientation working for Sullivan. One of their most effective designs is the Bradley residence (13-23), built in 1912 in Woods Hole, Massachusetts. Here two great geometric forms, the rectangular mass of the main section and the sweeping, circular bay, are composed to provide a magnificent view of the sea. The magnitude of the form is augmented by the simple texture of shingles which provide the surface sheathing. Unlike the many beach houses which merge with the landscape, the Bradley house dominates the promontory on which it stands by the bold counterpoint of its geometrical forms. Although the craftsman style was dramatic and monumental, it permitted a casual manner of living and increased enjoyment of nature. Interiors became more open and informal, and rooms were larger and fewer in number. House plans were carefully adapted to their site, rooms and views opened out into garden areas, and functional arrangements sought to provide for the easy disposition of the problems of family living.

The California School

Purcell's feeling for simple materials and informal house plans came not only from his experience in Sullivan's office but also from a stay in California. California was receptive to experiments; the mild climate, the spacious terrain, and the comfortable, rambling Mediterranean-style buildings of the Spanish settlers contributed to a taste for informal architecture. Since most of the cities in the state were not established until the end of the nineteenth century, there was little eclectic architecture to set a precedent. California designers were particularly concerned with sensible house design. The bungalow, the one-story cottage with no pretensions of elegance but with a predisposition toward comfort, almost became a symbol of California. The state's proximity to the Orient fed the current interest in the Japanese house. Reinforcing these trends came

13-24. Greene and Greene, D. R. Gamble House, 1909. Pasadena, Calif. Wayne Andrews photograph.

the craftsman concern with direct carpentering and straightforward use of simple materials, particularly wood, and in California, specifically redwood.

Charles Sumner Greene (1868-1957) and his brother, Henry Mather Greene (1870-1954), attended the Massachusetts Institute of Technology and about 1894 moved to southern California. In their hands progressive influences were integrated into a vigorous and unified style. The Greene brothers were masters of the extended one-story bungalow, the rambling, capacious, informal house that became almost part of the landscape, but they also have a number of handsome two-story designs to their credit. One of the most splendid of their larger houses is the Pasadena mansion (13-24) for one of the sons of Gamble of Procter and Gamble.

The Gamble residence, built in 1909, provides a distinguished example of the work of the Greene brothers and the craftsman style. The materials are redwood and shingle stained dark brown, combined with red brick in the chimneys. The wooden construction is candidly stressed —supporting posts carry extended beams and rafters to create a bold play of rectangular and diagonal patterns. The low-pitched roofs, broad gables, and open eaves contribute a delicate Japanese flavor further emphasized by the horizontal slats enclosing the porches and the open

13-25. Bernard Maybeck, First Church of Christ Scientist, 1912. Berkeley, Calif. Wayne Andrews photograph.

13-26. Louis Comfort Tiffany, Laurelton Hall, *c.* 1903. Oyster Bay, Long Island, N. Y. Wayne Andrews photograph.

trellises. The informal design is deceptive. The play of carpentered patterns, simple textures, and vigorous lights and shadows appears rambling and casual, but it has been carefully calculated to keep the massive house from appearing ponderous and pretentious.

Greene and Greene concentrated their activities in southern California but their influence was felt throughout the state. In San Francisco and the Bay area, Bernard Maybeck (1862-1957) combined the heterogeneous elements that were in the air to create his particular interpretation of the craftsman style. Most of his work reveals a concern with structural innovations and with the expressive and ingenious use of materials which relates it to other progressive designers of that period. Maybeck often expressed his inventive nature in the fantastic ornamental systems that contributed a strange and exotic mood to his work (13-25).

In the New York area the craftsman style received a unique and personal interpretation in the work of Louis Comfort Tiffany (1848-1933). Tiffany was more strongly influenced by the art-nouveau style of France than by the Chicago school or the English craftsman movement. This appears in his greater concern with decorative elements, which are frequently drawn from Islamic sources. While Tiffany was most active as a designer of interiors and *objets d'art*, his own home, Laurelton Hall (13-26), at Oyster Bay, Long Island, is an impressive example of domestic architecture in the new style, built around 1903. Though Laurelton Hall was a mansion, the design is straightforward and the materials simple. The various masses of the building and tower relate to the massed blocks of windows and the recessed entranceway to create a strong abstract pattern. True to the tenets of the craftsman tradition, the exterior design of the building reveals the interior plan without loss of clarity or dignity.

The conservative architectural tastes of the East prevented the craftsman style from enjoying the popularity which it had in California and in the Chicago area. Tiffany's influence on architectural practice was limited, and the east coast remained eclectic in its tastes until the middle of the twentieth century. An interior view of Laurelton Hall will be discussed in the next chapter.

In the years between the Civil War and World War I, America grew with fantastic rapidity. The pressure of expansion and growth stimulated an inventive approach to building, evidenced by the adoption of balloon framing, the development of steel construction in skyscraper design, and the advanced character of American house plans. The taste for size and elaboration characteristic of the seventies bore witness to the energy of the young nation. In the following decade Richardson combined American vigor and inventiveness with a creative rather than an academic use of tradition. Sullivan continued this creative approach to design when he transformed the steel-framed multistoried buildings of the Chicago area into powerful architectural forms.

Between 1900 and 1915 the rich promise inherent in the work of Sullivan and his followers appeared lost in a surge of unimaginative conventional building. But the concepts of the Chicago school and other progressive designers were too much an integral part of the evolving social and technological forces of America to be diverted. The inadequacy of the eclectic approach became increasingly evident, for the old architectural devices were not effective; nor could society pay for them. Though it was long delayed, in the years following World War II America witnessed a brilliant realization of the concepts of architectural design which had been initiated by Sullivan, his disciples, and the craftsman designers.

Interior Design,

Furniture, Industrial Design,

and the Crafts

ELEVEN YEARS AFTER THE CONCLUSION OF THE CIVIL WAR,
Philadelphia staged a great centennial exhibition to celebrate one hundred years of independence. Most of the nations of the world exhibited examples of their fine and industrial arts as well as of their household wares and machinery—exhibits notable for their size, elaboration, technical excellence, and novelty. The American wares were almost indistinguishable from the European except for the machines, in which a number of critics felt that American genius expressed itself most naturally. The most spectacular machine at the Centennial exhibition was the great Corliss engine (14-1).

The Corliss steam engine commanded the unqualified admiration both of the multitude and of the critics who visited the exposition. Towering 40 feet and weighing over 8000 tons, this great machine supplied the power to run all the mechanical devices on display. It was not only one of the largest and most powerful engines of its day and the

14-1. The Great Corliss Engine (chromolithograph), 1876. Philadelphia. Courtesy Metropolitan Museum of Art.

dominant feature of the Hall of Machines, but it made no concession to popular notions of beauty despite the fact that it was designed to play a conspicuous role in the exhibition. Not one extraneous ornamental device marred its surfaces. The public admired the silence and smoothness with which it ran and they also admired the turning wheels and the massive skeletal structure. Many laymen remembered the great Corliss engine long after the other exhibits had been forgotten, and a number of intellectuals understood the promise implicit in its forms. A French sculptor reported to his government that the engine had the beauty and almost the grace of the human form. A *London Times* correspondent stated that the Americans mechanized as the ancient Greeks had sculptured. The *Atlantic Monthly* philosophized, "Surely here, and not in literature, science, or art is the true evidence of man's creative power. . . ."

The Corliss steam engine, like the Brooklyn Bridge and the Tacoma Building, pointed the way to a new approach to design, one based on a candid statement of functional form. The purely utilitarian nature of the machine encouraged this direct approach since the need for the machine to operate at maximum efficiency was the primary force in determining the arrangement of the parts. The machines of the nineteenth century were in essence developments of earlier tools which had been marked by restraint, directness, and simplicity. American tools, in particular, had been distinguished by their lightness and efficiency. In such a tradition there was no room for the inefficient and the diffuse, nor were there resources to spare for ornamentation. This great machine, simply designed, making an unequivocal statement of utilitarian purpose, was awesome in its stark magnificence. Yet many years were to pass before its strength and beauty were to influence design by establishing the concept of unadorned functional form.

The distinction of the Corliss steam engine and its significance to the evolving concepts of design is most apparent when we compare it to typical cast-iron household wares of the day. Cast iron was one of the chief materials of industrial expansion in the late nineteenth century. There was little precedent for the design of many of the new cast-iron objects, and typical procedure was to evolve a functioning shape and then decorate it by strewing traditional ornamental borders, plaques, and architectural devices over the surface. An effective contrast to the Corliss engine is provided by a cast-iron sewing machine (14-2) from Connecticut. A classical column, rococo swirls, and a medley of other decorative motifs keep the machine from appearing plain and utilitarian. By such devices machines being manufactured for household purposes were reconciled with conventional tastes.

The Corliss engine was significant but not typical; it was in the interiors and household furnishing of the last half of the nineteenth century that the Victorian style assumed its most characteristic form.

14-2. Cast-iron sewing machine, c. 1857. Index of American Design, National Gallery of Art, Washington, D. C.

INTERIOR DESIGN AND FURNITURE

Four stages of development can be noted in the evolution of interior and furniture design between the Civil War and 1915.

(1) The tendency toward weight, elaboration, and complexity reached its height in the seventies. Diversity was valued above unity gusto above restraint. In the homes of the wealthy, heavily upholstered and elaborately carved pieces of furniture vied with patterned carpets, draperies, wallpapers, mirrors, pictures, and *objets d'art* to create ponderous Victorian interiors. French baroque and rococo decorative motifs provided the chief sources of inspiration but were interpreted to suit the current taste. Comparison of a rococo revival room of the fifties, the Milligan parlor (14-3) a fore-runner of the full-blown Victorian style, with the Stanford bedroom (14-4) of the late seventies reveals the shift toward elaboration that occurred during the decades following the Civil War.

(2) In the seventies and eighties a reaction against the pretentious character of fashionable styles was led by Charles Eastlake and others who turned from the French aristocratic styles and sought inspiration in the handicraft practices of the Middle Ages and the Renaissance (14-7). Fitness for purpose and honesty were valued above elaboration.

(3) Between the eighties and 1900, eclectic practices became more decorous under the guidance of the *École des Beaux Arts* and other academic sources. In very fashionable circles "authentic" period interiors replaced the earlier indiscriminate combining of styles.

(4) Between 1890 and 1915 the craftsman movement continued the reaction against eclecticism initiated by Eastlake (14-10). Emphasis in interior and furniture design was placed on practical considerations, on simple carpentered construction, and unpretentious materials treated to bring out their character. The simple and direct craftsman mode began to suggest an impersonal industrial style suited to mass production for a democratic society.

The Rococo Revival

French aristocratic styles remained popular through much of the last half of the nineteenth century. The Milligan parlor (14-3), Saratoga

14-3 (*left*). Milligan parlor, mid-19th century. Saratoga, N. Y. Brooklyn Museum, Brooklyn, N. Y.   14-4 (*below*). Bedroom, Stanford House, 1878. San Francisco, Calif. Stanford University Museum, Stanford, Calif.

Springs, New York, provides an unusually pure example of the Victorian rococo that came to its height in the fifties and sixties and enjoyed a particularly long period of popularity. In keeping with the spirit of the rococo, curvilinear rhythms dominated the room. Graceful, flowing lines appear in the rugs, draperies, ceiling, and fireplace as well as in the furniture, mirrors, pictures, and bric-a-brac. Reinforcing the curved lines to produce the desired effect of elegance was the sheen of smooth textures —satin, damask, gilt, varnished woods, polished marble, porcelain, and crystal. Patterned brocades and embroideries further enrich the shining surfaces. Though the Milligan parlor had plain walls, in many homes walls were covered with ornamental papers or rich damask fabrics.

Color was as omnipresent as pattern. An author of the day advised on the color scheme for a drawing room: "The color of a drawing room should be more gay than grave, hence the predominating colors should be rather light and delicate with a considerable proportion of gilding." In practice this turned into a preference for bright, even sharp, colors. Rose, blue, green, and gold competed with the rich colors of the highly finished woods, with cream, white, and multicolored marble, and with the gilt of mirror frames, picture frames, and bits of bric-a-brac. While rococo motifs dominate this room, most designers did not confine themselves to one style. Even here the molded stucco ceiling and the valances appear to be of baroque inspiration. Whatever the source of inspiration, the final effect is Victorian in essence—fussy and nervous rather than in the spirit of the original rococo. The eighteenth-century rococo interior had appeared spacious even when an effect of intimacy and informality was desired. The Victorian interior always appeared crowded, no matter what its size, because too many things and patterns were introduced into the room.

The Milligan parlor provides good examples of Victorian rococo furniture. In contrast to the eighteenth-century French rococo, which tended to be low and compact in contour, the Victorian furniture (particularly evident in the chairs) displayed the general tendency toward a high, narrow profile. The frames for upholstered pieces were thin, the legs long and narrow, and the backs of chairs heightened through the desire to create an impressive effect. The cabriole leg, the distinguishing mark of eighteenth-century rococo, here appears stringier and inadequate, lacking the variations in width that gave the originals a feeling of organic strength. Similarly, the excessive ornamental carvings seem applied rather than being an outgrowth of the sinuous movements of the forms on which they appear. Tables, chests, and dressers frequently were topped with gray or white marble. Mahogany continued to be popular, but rosewood, walnut, and oak began to share its popularity. The woods were finished with a high polish and shiny varnishes. Satins, damasks, and horsehair cloth were valued for their high sheen. An elaborately framed mirror like that over the mantel in the Milligan room usually provided the culminating note of splendor in an interior.

The most popular American cabinetmaker to work in the rococo revival manner was John Belter. Belter's workshop in New York provided furniture for the finest homes of the fifties and sixties and established the patterns for much later Victorian rococo furniture. A table from his workshop (14-5), like so much of Belter's furniture, is of superb craftsmanship, but careful examination reveals it to be a tour de force rather than a richly synthesized design. The legs appear almost too slender in profile since the open strapped effect, though admirable as an example of intricate craftsmanship, weakens the visual impact of the forms. The carved ornament is too large and tends to overwhelm the main lines of movement. Lastly, much of the ornamental detail of oak leaves, roses, and clusters of grapes is too naturalistic to become an organic part of the design.

A bedroom from the Stanford House (14-4) in San Francisco reveals the changes which characterized the seventies. The rococo lines began to give way to a more rectangular emphasis. The forms were more frequently drawn from baroque sources, as can be seen in the great canopied bed with its heavy rectangular footboard and crested headboard. Increased wealth demanded more ponderous and elaborate effects. Doors

14-5. John Belter, table, c. 1860. Museum of the City of New York, New York.

and windows were capped with crested panels, and panels framed with elaborate moldings were reintroduced on walls and ceilings. Patterned papers, embroidered draperies, lace curtains, painted ceilings, and great crystal chandeliers all contributed to the heavy magnificence so well suited to this aggressive and energetic age. The furniture in the room reveals three general characteristics. First, there was a tendency toward high and imposing profiles. Second, almost all pieces of furniture with any pretensions to elegance were marked by an excessive amount of ornamental detail. Third, other than in the pieces of rococo or neoclassic inspiration, the preference was for heaviness, frequently to the point of clumsiness.

The eighteenth and the early nineteenth century had been the age of the cabinetmaker—the last half of the nineteenth century was the age of the upholsterer. All through the century the French designers who dictated the fashions introduced increasingly elaborate forms of upholstered furniture. Divans, circular sofas, great poufs, love seats, including fancy S-shaped sofas that enabled couples to sit face to face, and all types of easy chairs became popular. The Stanford bedroom includes three of these massive, comfortable pieces. The large divan at the end of the room, like the two chairs, is a masterpiece of the upholsterer's art, with deep cushions, heavy springs, elaborate tufting, and long fringe creating the fashionable bulky silhouette.

While the mode was to cover completely the frame of upholstered furniture, other pieces of furniture featured elaborately carved frames which were further ornamented with inlay, gilding, and metal mounts. The tables in the foreground of the Stanford bedroom and the nightstands reveal the typical thin, mechanical carving, the gilt stripping, and the exaggerated shapes of finials and turnings. Designers drew on all periods of the past for ideas but current tastes determined the final effects more than the original source of inspiration. This is well illustrated by the bed with its Jacobean-flavored footboard surmounted by a French baroque canopy. Regardless of its source of inspiration, Victorian furniture, like architecture, remained Victorian.

Much furniture which was adaptable to machine production, and which exploited springs, hinges, and other metal devices, appeared in the eighties. A wicker platform rocker (14-6) from the end of the century, an excellent example of this "mechanical" style, reflects the inventive capacities of the age, its feeling for comfort, and its delight in heavy forms relieved by intricate and involved patterns. Because Victorian design

14-6. Platform rocker, *c.* 1880. Harry Mandoli, Lore Bloch photograph.

lacks many of the qualities of earlier periods, one is apt to overlook the vigor and gusto of such a design.

The Artistic Styles: Charles Eastlake

The most vigorous protest against the vulgar and pretentious character of Victorian design, particularly against the blind aping of aristocratic elegance, was launched by the English writer-architect Charles Eastlake. His *Hints on Household Taste,* published in Great Britain in 1866 and in America in 1872, was a formulation of principles which were applicable to the design of houses as well as interiors, furniture, and various household articles. He made an eloquent plea for honest craftsmanship—that materials be treated in a way to reveal their essential character and that design grow from function. The appearance of the book gave direction to the growing reform movement and encouraged propriety and restraint in the designing of interiors and household furnishings. A detail from the living room of the W. A. Clarke House (14-7) built in Butte, Montana, in 1885 reveals the changing tastes encouraged by the writing of Eastlake. Turning to the handicraft traditions of the late Middle Ages but also selecting stylistic details from sources as diverse as the Jacobean, Queen Anne, Japanese, and Near Eastern styles, Eastlake

14-7. Interior, W. A. Clarke House, 1885. Butte, Mont. Wayne Andrews photograph.

recommended rectangular, straightforward frame construction, rather flat paneling, the use of simple turnings, and shallow carved ornamentation employing naturalistic foliate and floral patterns. Oak, cherry, and other light-colored woods were finished to bring out their natural color and grain. Tile insets were considered practical and attractive, and the use of large, handicrafted hardware was encouraged. Many of the devices recommended by Eastlake appeared to be well adapted to machine techniques of production even though they were inspired by the handicraft processes of earlier times.

Some of Eastlake's suggestions for interior cabinetwork were more homespun than is suggested by the Clarke interior. Rectangular forms, carpentered construction using vertical supports, horizontal crosspieces, and diagonal braces were prescribed. Dowels, pegs, and chamfers were to be clearly evident, and the use of quite simple ornamental carving was recommended. Unfortunately, in the hands of designers without taste, these devices frequently led to clumsy heaviness.

Eastlake's theories on furniture design had considerable influence

14-8. Eastlake-style chair, 1880's. Matt Lehmann photograph.

on American manufacturers and accounted for some sensible and attractive furniture. A chair (14-8) of the eighties in the Eastlake manner provides a welcome relief from the extravagance of much of the fashionable furniture. The rectangular frame is sturdy but not too heavy and the joints are stressed to indicate structure. The back has a slight rake and this, together with the carving and the sturdy proportions, are concessions to a sensible level of comfort but certainly not to sybaritic indulgence in lounging. Such decorative elements as the channeled grooves, simple turnings, boldly articulated brackets, and flat, incised patterns represent an attempt to reconcile beauty with morality, or at least with common sense and practicality. Eastlake furniture was frequently executed in fruit woods or oak and was finished in a soft, natural manner rather than with a high-gloss varnish.

The Artistic Styles: Orientalism and the Craftsman Style

An interest in the Near and Far East had existed all through the century. In the eighties the vogue for wares from North Africa reached its height—in fact, a Turkish corner, a section of a room decorated with Oriental hangings, a table inset with colored tiles, lamps of damascened brass, and similar curios contributed a note of novelty to many interiors.

Not all of the Orientalism of the eighties, however, grew from a

14-9. Moorish room, John D. Rockefeller House, *c.* 1884. New York. Brooklyn Museum, Brooklyn, N. Y.

desire for novelty. A concern with problems of structure and the evolution of a fresh and dignified decorative style inspired a Moorish room (14-9) in the John D. Rockefeller House in New York in 1884. The more disciplined eclecticism that characterized the last decade of the century is revealed here by consistency of style. The rectangular framework of moldings and wood paneling provides a structural frame for the rich patterns which decorate all available surfaces. Geometric and conventionalized floral motifs of Islamic inspiration cover the walls, ceiling, and carpet, and the woodwork and furniture have been ornamented with borders and panels of the same Oriental-style motifs. All these rich and exotic patterns are held within definite borders and panels. A growing concern with structure is evident in the firm architectural framework which dominates the Rockefeller Moorish room. The Orient continued to provide inspiration, but the Near East soon gave way to Japan as a major stimulus to the craftsman designers.

The garish extravagances of the Victorian age tend to obscure the sensible advances that had occurred in house design in America, par-

14-10. Stairway and corner of living room. Gustav Stickley, *Craftsman Homes* (New York, 1909).

ticularly in the designing of upper-middle-class homes. A number of Richardson's houses from the seventies were spacious and uncluttered and reflected the growing influence of the English designer and theorizer, William Morris. Morris was the leader of a group of artists and craftsmen who tried to stem the debasing tendencies of nineteenth-century industrialization by reintroducing handicraft practices and standards into the production of textiles, wallpapers, furniture, metal wares, and related articles. In many of his great, comfortable shingle houses, Richardson allowed rooms to flow together, introduced great open bays with banks of windows, and finished the interiors with open beamed ceilings, unobtrusive rectangular paneling, simply plastered walls, and quiet wallpapers. A number of other architects continued to design country houses after the manner of Richardson, using informal plans and simple materials.

Louis Sullivan did not concern himself deeply with problems of house design, but his disciple, Frank Lloyd Wright, continued to explore and expand the concept of an organic house plan which would contribute to material comfort, efficiency, and spiritual serenity. His original and forceful formulations of the craftsman style will be discussed in relation to his subsequent work, for his unique importance lay in the manner in which he integrated the concepts of the craftsman movement with the

14-11. Craftsman-style chair. Marta K. Sironin. *History of American Furniture* (East Stroudsburg, Pa., 1936).

structural innovations and technological developments of the twentieth century.

The craftsman style, which appeared between 1900 and 1910, brought together the various reforms inherent in the simpler houses of Richardson and implicit in the evolving bungalows of the day. Its specific character, however, reflected the practice of William Morris and the English arts and crafts movement. The craftsman style received its most popular and explicit formulation here in the publications and designs of Gustav Stickley (1858-1942). Though the Greene brothers in California and Louis Comfort Tiffany in New York produced more distinguished versions of the style, Stickley was its most influential exponent. A design for the stairway and corner of a living room taken from his book *Craftsman Homes,* published in 1909 (14-10), reveals his characteristic interpretation of the style. Straightforward carpentered construction was employed throughout, with unadorned vertical posts supporting heavy horizontal crossbeams which, in turn, carried smaller ceiling beams. Walls were usually paneled to door height, and plain plaster or patterned paper filled the area between the top molding and the ceiling. Moldings were broad and flat; simple board and batten construction constituted the most frequent type of paneling. Windows were frequently small and arranged in groups and were glazed with small square panes of glass, and bookcases and interior doors were often treated similarly. Built-in corner seats, fireplace nooks, and other cozy devices were popular. Wood was stained or waxed, and dark colors were preferred.

The heavy beam construction permitted the elimination of many enclosing walls and encouraged an open plan. Living rooms frequently opened into dining rooms, libraries, or sun porches. Open stairs and wide double-sliding doors also contributed to a sense of continuity between the parts of the house. Broad verandas, large sun porches, and open dining rooms encouraged the easy movement between indoors and outdoors that has become such a vital part of contemporary living. At its best the craftsman house was comfortable, unpretentious, and charming—easy to care for and well adapted to middle-class family living.

The general principles of the craftsman movement also called into being a simple, sensible kind of furniture which rapidly became known as Mission-style furniture. Stickley was a leader in its manufacture. An occasional chair (14-11) reveals the characteristics of the Mission style. The structure is rigidly rectangular inasmuch as original Mission furniture was supposedly hewn from rough timber and joined together with mortise, tenon, and dowel, no nails or glue being used. Lines were severely straight and simple, the only concession to decoration being in the occasional use of small brackets to support arms or other extending parts. Upholstery consisted of lightweight leather cushions; frequently there were springs beneath the cushions for added resiliency. Oak became the standard wood used in such pieces, and it was finished in various weathered colors or in a light, dull-finished golden brown called fumed oak. The first Mission furniture introduced to the market was of heavy proportions but later pieces were lighter, more graceful, and almost slender in proportion.

The craftsman style as formulated by Stickley was most popular among the educated middle classes who valued its common-sense emphasis on comfort, practicality, and honesty.

A blending of influences is evident in the work of Louis Comfort Tiffany (1848-1933), son of the famous New York jeweler. The interiors he designed are elegant and stylish rather than practical, in accordance with the tastes of the fashionable circles in which he moved. Tiffany, like other advanced designers of his day, was in revolt against a shoddy industrialization, but under the influence of the French art-nouveau designers he turned to the Orient and certain peasant crafts for inspiration rather than to the English Middle Ages. A first glance at the court of Laurelton

14-12. Louis Comfort Tiffany, court, Laurelton Hall, *c.* 1903. Oyster Bay, Long Island, N. Y. Taylor and Dull photograph; courtesy Parke-Bernet Galleries, Inc.

Hall (14-12), the mansion which Tiffany built for himself at Oyster Bay, Long Island, about 1903, reveals only the exotic and decorative aspects of his style. Thoughtful examination, however, shows that Tiffany shared many common concerns with the craftsman designers. The clear articulation of all the structural supports on the ground floor as well as in the balcony, the conscious repetition of vertical and horizontal lines in the placement of the stenciled decorations which enrich the surfaces, the direct, clear framing of the entranceway and the accompanying sidelight all indicate that Tiffany sought to achieve serenity and order through a forceful emphasis on the architectonic elements of the design. The sense of carefully ordered space and the all-pervasive and unifying role of air and light, also in accordance with craftsman precepts, foreshadow the character of architectural design later in the century. The few pieces of furniture and the art objects in the room are arranged with the greatest formality, and their symmetrical groupings augment the sense of structure and order. The sensuous patterns and rich ornamental elements that grace this severe arrangement derive, like much art-nouveau ornament, from Oriental sources. The sensuous charm and exoticism of Laurelton Hall are uniquely Tiffany; the spacious orderliness relates the room to the progressive tendencies of the day. Tiffany is best known for his glass, ceramic, and metal wares, and this phase of his work will be discussed later in the chapter.

INDUSTRIAL DESIGN

A penchant for inventing ingenious mechanisms that would contribute to increased comfort and efficiency was evident all through the last half of the nineteenth century. Folding beds, adjustable chairs, combination sofa-bedsteads, and collapsible tables were among the many useful inventions of the age; they gave evidence of busy minds at work harnessing the productivity of the machine and utilizing the new mechanical sciences. The façade of surface ornament that characterized most household wares seldom provided a clue to the forward-looking character of the internal mechanisms.

Objects designed for outdoor use often revealed the simple, unceremonious adaptability of form to purpose which was to become increasingly characteristic of American industrial wares in the twentieth century. Boats, bicycles, rifles, and carriages (12-18) frequently had a lithe beauty, free of excessive ornament and imitative splendor, that foreshadowed the oncoming industrial style. In the eighteen-eighties, reapers and mowing machines employed the cantilever principle by carrying a shaped seat on a column of spring steel, a forerunner of the metal chairs of the twentieth century. In the seventies, molded plywood provided for mass seating in ferry boats and railway stations, and a model for a bent plywood chair (14-13), patented in 1874, reveals the advanced thinking that was directed toward utilizing the new industrial processes and materials to satisfy living needs.

Though the parlor echoed the past and changes were concealed beneath carving, upholstery, and fringe, the kitchen and bathroom gave direct evidence of the revolution that was taking place in living patterns. Harriet Beecher Stowe and her sister, Catherine Beecher, had already designed a kitchen (13-6) with built-in storage units and movable screens, antedating the modern concepts of flexible space and modular units of design. Plumbing provided running water in the home, and this convenience changed cooking procedures and initiated a host of new utensils. The indoor bathroom provided designers with another challenge. The development of the dynamo in the sixties resulted in incandescent

14-13. American bent plywood chair, 1874. Collection Museum of Modern Art, New York.

lighting in the seventies. The next two decades introduced a flood of new machines, tools, and services into the household.

A changing philosophy prevailed in relation to these new wares. They were regarded as tools designed to make life easier and were made to be sold, used, discarded, and replaced. Little thought was paid to shaping objects so they would be permanently satisfying to the eye or touch. Use and beauty were considered separate and unrelated qualities, the machine creating the new and useful things while the craftsman made what was useless and beautiful. Though there was a rich ferment beneath the surface, American industrial design in the years before 1915 did not live up to the promise inherent in the Corliss Engine. Another quarter century would have to pass before there would be an awareness of the esthetic possibilities of machine production.

CRAFTS

Mechanical inventions and growth provided a veneer of metropolitan sophistication to much of American life but the older patterns prevailed in many areas well into the twentieth century. Large-scale wooden animals and fanciful figures for carrousels and circus wagons retained the vigor of earlier shop figures. In the mountains of Tennessee and Kentucky women wove bedspreads and embroidered samplers which followed the patterns of long ago. As the older craft traditions disappeared from the building industry, cast iron began to replace the stone, wood, and wrought-iron decorations of the preceding age. Small foundries and blacksmith shops produced ingenious and amusing cast-iron hitching posts, lightning deflectors, garden sculptures, weather vanes, and other architectural ornaments. Glass and ceramic crafts fared less well. The large-scale production of glass became almost universal, and handthrown redware and stoneware almost disappeared.

On isolated farms and during long sea voyages lonely men still whittled on long evenings or in spells of bad weather. One of the most famous wood carvers in the last half of the nineteenth century was Wilhelm Schimmel, an itinerant farm worker and wood carver who frequented the Shenandoah Valley in Pennsylvania. He is most noted for his eagles (14-14), but he carved a variety of birds and animals in a spontaneous and vigorous manner. The animated silhouettes are enlivened by vigorous conventionalized patterns of fur and feathers and by the bold marks of knife and chisel.

One of the most astonishing house decorations from the last century is a 9-foot locomotive weather vane (14-15) from Michigan. This weather vane, made in the round, is a virtual replica of a locomotive. Cast-iron weather vanes were usually made by casting the metal in two thin sheets which were then soldered together to form a relatively light hollow object. Copper, brass, and zinc details were often included to provide variety of color. The detailed versimilitude of the locomotive is a tribute to the love of the people for the machines which were transforming society and providing new symbols of American pride. Though the parlor might belong to the past, the housetop proclaimed the glory of the present and the future.

In the decades following the Civil War, commercial pottery shaped in molds became almost universal, the most popular types were heavily decorated with naturalistic fruit and flowers, either in relief or painted on the surface. However, the influence of the English arts and crafts movement began to be felt in the eighteen-seventies, and the exhibitions of ceramics at the Centennial Exposition of 1876 stimulated potters with art training to produce wares which represented a distinct departure from those of the commercial manufacturers. The new "art pottery," as it was termed, represented a conscious effort to recapture the simple forms and the rich surface textures and glazes found in the hand-made potteries of earlier periods and cultures. The most consistent manufacturers of fine art pottery in the early twentieth century were the Rookwood potters of Cincinnati, Ohio. Rookwood pottery was produced

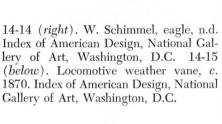

14-14 (*right*). W. Schimmel, eagle, n.d. Index of American Design, National Gallery of Art, Washington, D.C. 14-15 (*below*). Locomotive weather vane, *c.* 1870. Index of American Design, National Gallery of Art, Washington, D.C.

in subtle, dull colors and mat glazes, and the forms and decorations reflected art-nouveau influences.

Sharing the revival of the ceramic arts was an increased interest in ceramic tiles. A demand for architectural ceramics, stimulated by Eastlake, had been reinforced by the popularity of the Oriental styles. The Low Art Tile Company, Chelsea, Massachusetts, was the first firm to manufacture decorative and plain ceramic tiles for architectural use. With the expanding popularity of the craftsman styles, a number of companies in New Jersey, Ohio, and California started production of commercial building tiles, and the use of ceramic tiles in bathrooms and kitchens soon became standard practice.

Louis Comfort Tiffany

At the end of the nineteenth century, when the machine appeared to be ousting the artisan from industry, an increasing number of young

14-16. Tiffany stained-glass window, Heckscher House, *c.* 1910. New York. Collection Mr. and Mrs. Hugh F. McKean.

artists began to concern themselves with the production of fine household wares. The leader in this movement in America was Louis Comfort Tiffany, who invested the products of his studios with the same sophistication and elegance that characterized his own home. At the age of eighteen, Louis Tiffany decided to become a painter rather than enter the family business. He first studied with Inness, then went to Paris, and subsequently traveled in the Orient. On his return to America Tiffany became involved in a number of decorating and manufacturing projects, one of the most important being the production of stained glass for architectural use. His finest stained-glass designs, produced between 1890 and 1910, reflect the character of current French painting and art-nouveau design. A window from the Heckscher House (14-16) in New York reveals the typical use of naturalistic patterns combined with geometric and structural lines. Here both translucent and opaque colored glass were used in an intertwined grape and gourd motif to frame areas of clear glass.

14-17. Tiffany Studios, Favrile glass vases, *c.* 1910. Ward Mount Collection.

The handblown bowls and vases (14-17), named Favrile glass by Tiffany, were probably the best-known products of the Tiffany Glass and Decorating Company which the artist set up for producing his designs commercially. The graceful, elongated shapes were executed in iridescent colored glass and decorated with the swirling lines, veinings, spirals, and floating forms so natural to the process of blowing glass, for one of the chief tenets of the art-nouveau movement was that decoration should be a natural outgrowth of a medium and the process of manufacture. Patterns based on plant and flower forms were also popular, and Favrile glass was frequently designed in lily or leaf shapes.

Tiffany also sponsored a variety of fine metal crafts and produced bronze lamps, candlesticks, and lighting fixtures in a fascinating variety of sizes and shapes. The three bronze candlesticks illustrated (14-18) have the graceful elongation of form favored by art-nouveau designers as well as the somewhat whimsical details that suggest roots, stems, buds, and flowers.

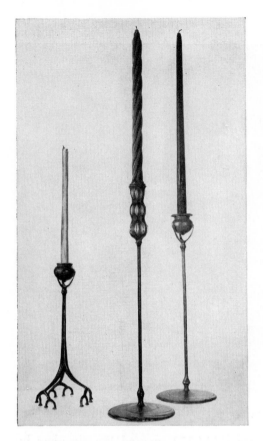

14-18. Tiffany Studios, metal candlesticks, *c.* 1910. Joseph Hill Collection.

The period between the Civil War and World War I was a time of great diversity and complexity. Despite the mediocrity of most architecture, furniture, industrial wares, and crafts, a new style—the style of the industrial age—was in gestation, A number of men helped to shape the esthetic concepts of the burgeoning industrial age. Early in the century Horatio Greenough had given literary expression to a credo which made honesty in the use of materials and suitability of design to function prerequisites to significant form in the arts. The example of Shaker architecture and furniture, of straightforward, almost styleless carpentered houses, and of a great popular vernacular of tools and household objects was ever-present throughout America. Close to our consciousness were the theories of the English esthetic philosophers—Charles Eastlake, William Morris, and even John Ruskin—encouraging escape from the pretentiousness of the Victorian pseudo-aristocratic styles. Richardson and others were designing the great shingle and half-timbered summer homes which reintroduced Americans to such elements of their colonial heritage as candid carpentered construction and the use of stained wood, brick, tile, and other unpretentious materials. In commercial architecture, the Chicago school, particularly in the work and writings of Louis Sullivan, gave forceful expression to an honest concept of functional design that grew out of American tastes, needs, and building procedures. Between 1900 and 1910 all these influences were synthesized in the work of Frank Lloyd Wright, Gustav Stickley, and other craftsman designers. Their houses exhibit a unified relationship between exteriors, interiors, and furnishings that was unique for that age and foreshadowed the future. Only today, in mid-twentieth century, is the promise inherent in their work beginning to be realized.

15

Painting:

Portraiture and Landscape

THE CIVIL WAR HAD LITTLE INFLUENCE ON THE COURSE
of nineteenth-century American painting except as a brief interruption.
The two decades following the war were particularly benign ones for
artists. Current styles of decorating demanded a liberal display of pictures; consequently paintings sold readily and commanded good prices.
There was a coincidence between the aims of the artists and the taste of
the public. The artists worked in an easily comprehended style which
required no particular sophistication of taste, and the uncritical public
responded with enthusiasm to the skilled naturalism that was current.

In the years immediately following the Civil War the intense romanticism of the early years gave way before an increasingly pragmatic outlook, and the taste for sententious historical canvases disappeared. Though
the Civil War stirred up intense sentiments and loyalties, painters were
not moved to record its great events upon canvas or on the walls of public
buildings. Winslow Homer painted and drew scenes from the Civil War,

416

15-1. Erasmus Field, *Historical Monument of the American Republic, c.* 1876. Springfield Museum, Springfield, Mass.

and a Chicago businessman commissioned a French painter to portray the battle of Gettysburg on a vast cyclorama, but otherwise there was little interest in exploring the heroic vein.

One of the last large historical canvases painted in America stands as a strange swan song to the patriotic painting that was so important in the early years of the republic. This was the 13-foot *Historical Monument of the American Republic* (15-1) by Erasmus Salisbury Field (1805-1900). Field, almost totally without training, prepared this vast canvas at the age of seventy as his contribution to the centennial celebration of American freedom. From a massive architectural base situated in a pleasant park peopled with strolling sightseers rise eight great towers which diminish in circumference as they raise their circular or polygonal towers into the air. Elevated bridges connect the towers at the top. These towers are encrusted with statues, columns, arcades, and fantastic bas-reliefs depicting episodes of our national history, ranging from the Bill of Rights to the discovery of the steamboat. Only a simple-hearted folk artist would attempt such an elaborate expression of patriotic fervor after the tragic episode of the Civil War and the subsequent economic conflicts.

15-2. William Page, *Portrait of Mrs. Page, c.* 1860. Detroit Institute of Arts, Detroit, Mich.

PORTRAIT AND FIGURE PAINTING

The Traditionalists

A bright and lively competence rather than a deep concern with style had characterized the successful portrait painters of the first half of the century. One of the first artists whose portraits and figure paintings represented a sharp departure from the bright objective style of the first half of the century was William Page (1811-1885). Page shared Washington Allston's enthusiasm for Venetian painting, and an extended period of study in Italy intensified his feeling for the grand tradition of the Renaissance. His portrait of his wife (15-2) is in his mature style. Large simple masses are arranged in monumental verticals and quiet horizontals. Both the limited tonal range, dominated by middle-value grays, and the rich and subdued color contribute to the general tone of restraint and dignity. The glowing, somber mood of his canvases stood in striking contrast to the bright clear effects of most of the painting of his day. Also, the simplified somewhat flat pattern evident in the portrait of Mrs.

15-3. William M. Hunt, *Self-portrait*, 1866. Museum of Fine Arts, Boston.

Page was in conflict with the current taste for fully developed three-dimensional form. Page had few followers—his style was too grave and serious to attract a popular following.

One of the most influential of the group of American painters who turned to France in their attempt to introduce a loftier vein into American painting was William Morris Hunt (1824-1879), the brother of the famous architect. Unsympathetic to the picturesque naturalism of the Düsseldorf school, Hunt moved to Paris where he became interested in the advanced movements in French painting as practiced in the studio of Millet. His *Self-portrait* (15-3), a grave and sensitive piece of painting, reveals the characteristics he acquired there—a taste for the direct use of a heavily loaded brush, simple, broad compositional concepts, warm but subdued color, and a somewhat generalized conception of form. Hunt's approach to portraiture was essentially that of the figure painter, and his paintings helped to educate the discriminating public away from the popular concepts of portrait painting. Though Hunt was best in small easel painting, he felt the great wall paintings of the Renaissance to be the most significant form of the painter's art and did much to awaken an interest in mural painting.

Hunt's high position in Boston society, the influence he wielded through his brother, and his own vivid personality all enabled him to interest an important sector of American society in French art, particularly that of the Barbizon painters.

Another painter of the late nineteenth century who brought French

15-4. John La Farge, *Athens*, 1893-1894. Bowdoin College Museum of Fine Arts, Brunswick, Me.

tastes and ideas back to America was John La Farge (1835-1910). La Farge was sent to France for his education, became interested in painting, and on his return to America he decided on a professional art career. His easel painting is characterized by an easy naturalism, direct free painting, and luminous rich color. Like Hunt, La Farge was concerned with the revival of mural painting and he executed a number of murals in which he turned to the Venetians for his compositional concepts and

15-5. Abbott H. Thayer, *Young Woman*, n.d. Courtesy Metropolitan Museum of Art, Gift of George A. Hearn, 1906.

15-6. Thomas Eakins, *Walt Whit-man*, 1887. Pennsylvania Academy of the Fine Arts, Philadelphia.

for his glowing color (15-4). Richardson used his paintings, as did McKim, Mead, and White; and Hunt also employed him to decorate some of his most splendid structures. The completion of his interior designs for Trinity Church initiated a wave of mural painting in America. La Farge did not restrict his activities as a decorator to one field. In his stained-glass windows he eliminated as many of the leads which traditionally separate the areas of color as possible, thereby transforming the entire window into one glowing color composition.

The spell of the past and Europe cast its magic over other American figure painters during these years. Abbott H. Thayer (1849-1921) and George de Forest Brush (1855-1941) both studied in Paris and acquired a disciplined technical skill as well as a taste for idealizing the human form to create symbols of nobility and morality. Abbott Thayer's *Young Woman* (15-5) is the typical tall, handsome, almost sexless, female for which he was famous. His idealized young woman in flowing robes appealed to the sentimental and moralizing tendencies of the age as did the scenes of family life by Brush.

The paintings of Page, Hunt, La Farge, Thayer, and Brush all have qualities in common—disciplined techniques, refined tastes, and painting concepts based largely on the Renaissance. Like the beaux-arts architects,

15-7. Thomas Eakins, *Pathetic Song,* 1881. Corcoran Gallery of Art, Washington, D.C.

these men submerged themselves in the great traditions of earlier times hoping thereby to create a rich and valid culture for their own day. Their importance as artists has lessened with the passing of time. Other men with more urgent modes of expression more closely attuned to the emerging forces of the day took the lead.

Thomas Eakins

One of these men was Thomas Eakins (1844-1915). Eakins was born in Philadelphia and spent his life there except for a period in Paris in the sixties. He was one whose appreciation of the vitality of American life was not vitiated by his contact with European culture. He studied with Gérôme, and from him acquired his disciplined knowledge, love for the human figure, and taste for factual statement. Study abroad turned the eyes of many American painters away from the realities of America but it enabled Eakins to see the life about him more clearly. He returned to Philadelphia and for the remainder of his years devoted all his energies to painting the life he knew—the sports, recreations, home life, and above all else, the people of his native city.

"I never knew of but one artist, and that's Tom Eakins, who could resist the temptation to see what they thought ought to be rather than what is," said the poet Walt Whitman in relation to his portrait (15-6) by Eakins. It was this clarity and honesty of perception that distinguished Eakins and constitutes his chief significance. In an age when manner, sentiment, and an over-concern with style were dulling the force of the artist's perceptions and when the arts were becoming separated from the life of their day, Eakins performed the significant service of rediscovering the rich source of stimulation existing in the immediate environment. His objectivity was of signal importance in that age of sentimentality and evasive symbolism, but his particular strength lay in his ability to cast his objective perceptions in firmly structured artistic form and endow them with the warmth of feeling and the compassionate understanding with which he regarded his environment and the friends who peopled it. Walt Whitman looks out of his portrait—expansive, optimistic, disheveled —loving the world yet not quite able to face its uncompromising realities. Eakins saw and painted the tender poet underneath the blustering exterior.

Most of Eakins's sitters were drawn from his circle of acquaintances: college professors, scientists, and his own immediate family. He preferred to depict his sitters in contemplative moods, turned in upon themselves. A flood of clear light throws the forms into bold relief against the simple background of home, laboratory, or study. The color is warm and dark, the brushwork controlled; there is no bravura of handling or theatricality of composition to throw a false aura of glamour over the familiar personages or scenes. Nowhere is Eakins's uncompromising honesty, power of analysis, and strength of feeling more apparent than in the handsome genre portrait *Pathetic Song* (15-7). Eakins painted a number of canvases depicting performing musicians but none surpass this in its power to evoke the magic moment when performers and audience alike fall under the spell of the music.

Loving the brilliant out-of-door light, and thereby antedating the impressionists of the next generation, Eakins painted scenes of typical sports of the day—men fishing, rowing, sailing, and swimming. *Max Schmitt in a Single Scull* (15-8) is based upon painstaking studies, but its sharp clarity and brilliant exactitude of form is misleading for the literal surface hides a firmly structured composition. Long, flat diagonal and horizontal lines frame the seated figure which is stabilized by the arch above his head. The deep space is bathed in sunlight but the sunlight

15-8. Thomas Eakins, *Max Schmitt in a Single Scull,* 1871. Courtesy Metropolitan Museum of Art, Alfred N. Punnett Fund and gift of George D. Pratt, 1934.

does not destroy the substantiality of the forms. Instead it becomes the primary means by which a sense of vital energy is communicated to the quiet scene.

Eakins's activity as a teacher was of great importance. He introduced living models into the Pennsylvania Academy of Fine Arts and taught his students to "draw with the brush" rather than to think of painting as a colored drawing. Most important, he turned his students to their surroundings for subject matter. His contribution to the American tradition was probably as great as that of any painter of his day for his work formed a bridge between Copley, Peale, and other early American realists and the twentieth century.

The Munich School: Frank Duveneck

While Paris was the leading center for European study, Munich was a close second, particularly in the seventies. Frank Duveneck (1848-1919), the precocious and talented son of German immigrants, went to Munich around 1870. Here he developed the style of painting that came to be called the "Munich Style"; it is characterized by vigorous brushwork and the dexterous manipulation of pigments with flashing lights painted as directly as possible into warm dark backgrounds. Picturesque persons and things drawn from everyday life provided the subject matter. The uniqueness of each subject was stressed, in contrast to the tendency of academic painters to idealize and generalize. It was essentially a painterly style by which unpretentious subjects were dramatized and given significance through the brilliant manipulation of the paint.

In 1875 Duveneck showed a group of his canvases in Boston. The bold brushwork, the rich color, and the forceful presentation of personality that characterized the portraits created a sensation. *Portrait of a Man* (15-9) displays the vigor of his style and the brilliant bravura of his brushwork. The character of the sitter is established by stressing the uniqueness of feature and the accidents of light and shadow. The absence of artifice, idealization, and elegance in Duveneck's painting provided a valuable antidote to the sentimental sweetness of the academic art of the day. Though he spent much of his life in Europe, his influence on his contemporaries was great, first on William Chase and his followers and, later, on the Ash Can school.

The Cosmopolites: Whistler and Sargent

From 1870 on, many American painters spent most of their life abroad and Paris became the center for these expatriate artists. The Parisian ateliers, true to the spirit of French art, stressed elegance and distinction of execution. The two great American painters, products of the Parisian ateliers, who epitomize the cosmopolitanism of these years are James Abbott McNeill Whistler and John Singer Sargent.

James McNeill Whistler (1834-1903) was the son of an American army engineer. He grew up in Russia where his father was engaged professionally, and except for a brief interval at West Point he spent his life abroad, knowing America only from a world of expatriates and travelers. In 1855 Whistler entered the atelier of Courbet in Paris. Courbet encouraged his students to go directly to nature for their subject matter but Whistler, poetic and esthetic by temperament, came under the influence of Manet and the impressionists. Like many of the impressionists, he also reflected the contemporary enthusiasm for Japanese prints and the elegant tonalism of Velasquez. In the sixties Whistler moved to London where he became a leading figure in the English art world. His position in England rested partly on the distinction of his own brand of tonal impressionism and partly on his disputatious and exhibitionist personality.

15-9. Frank Duveneck, *Portrait of a Man*, n.d. Brooklyn Museum, Brooklyn, N. Y.

English painting in the last half of the nineteenth century did not share the progressive characteristics of the French and German schools. For the most part, the English were out of sympathy with the sophisticated tastes of Whistler. He therefore became the champion of "art for art's sake" in England, the very vocal proponent of painting as an organization of colors and shapes which had the power to provide visual pleasure irrespective of any resemblance to the outer world. Whistler's dramatic defense of his views did much to familiarize American audiences with the aims of the advanced painters of his day.

Whistler's *Portrait of Théodore Duret* (15-10) is less radical than the views he espoused. In this elegant tonal study, the simplified and somewhat flat patterns suggest the influence of Manet and Degas. The portrait, signed with the butterfly symbol which Whistler adopted from the Japanese prints, combines a characterful face and pose with the carefully arranged pattern that distinguished Whistler's paintings.

Whistler was a prolific etcher and many of his etchings reveal a vigorous love for the flavor of picturesque everyday subjects that is far removed from the contrived elegance of his paintings (17-3). In many ways Whistler seems more a draftsman than a painter, and his etchings utilize his sense of line and tone most effectively.

America's other famous cosmopolite was John Singer Sargent (1850-1925). Sargent was born in Florence, of a wealthy Philadelphia family

15-10. J. A. McN. Whistler, *Portrait of Théodore Duret* (*Arrangement in Flesh and Black*), 1883. Courtesy Metropolitan Museum of Art, Wolfe Fund, 1913.

who had retired to Italy. Born into the expatriate world of cultivated leisure, Sargent seemed particularly fitted to become the foremost painter of the fashionable international set of his day. At eighteen he entered the studio of Carolus-Duran, a man who understood the importance of a broad massing of tone, a fluid continuity of line, and a direct and skillful manipulation of paint. Sargent proved to be a precocious pupil. He rapidly absorbed his master's precepts and settled down to painting portraits and occasional genre scenes for the brilliant society in which he moved. A portrait from his very early years, *Madame X* (15-11), reveals the seductive facility that made him the most popular and expensive portrait painter of his day. The simplicity of the conception is the most striking feature of *Madame X*. The single figure stands with fluid, controlled, but compelling grace; no distracting countermovements confuse the eye. The

15-11. John Singer Sargent, *Madame X*, 1884. Courtesy Metropolitan Museum of Art, Arthur H. Hearn Fund, 1916.

sweep of the vertical lines is reinforced by the subtle beauty of the tonal pattern in which brilliant light flesh tones contrast with luminous grays and blacks. The effortless execution contributes greatly to the distinction and grace of the painting as, of course, does the striking poise of the subject. Madame Gautreau stands as a symbol of fashionable elegance—beautiful and slightly disdainful. It was this ability to create a handsome symbol of social position that attracted his wealthy sitters and enabled Sargent to charge many thousands of dollars for his portraits.

Sargent's very strengths contributed to his weaknesses as an artist. His very facility mitigated against his knowing the sitter as a three-dimensional personality. He could so easily catch the external characteristics that he ceased to explore beyond the momentary impression. One knows the sitters only to the degree that is socially admissible—as one might see them at a fashionable gathering. Many portraits from his later

15-12. John Singer Sargent, *Daughters of Edward Boit,* 1882. Museum of Fine Arts, Boston.

years, distinguished only by vivacious execution, seem to be mere records of beautiful clothes and elegant postures which bore us despite their brilliance. His immense talents matured early and the most effective examples of his unparalleled virtuosity come from his early years.

A visit to Spain in 1879-1880 introduced Sargent to the great masterpieces of Velasquez and influenced much of his subsequent painting. The Spanish master's amazing ability to translate the visual image into planes of tone and color was particularly suited to Sargent's gifts. The airy spaciousness of Velasquez's great compositions, the effortless precision of his drawing, the luminosity of his surfaces as they receive or reflect the

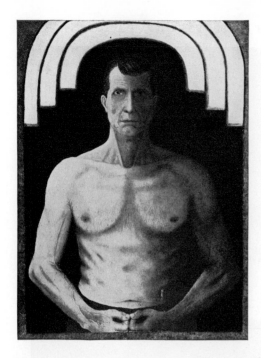

15-13. John Kane, *Self-portrait*, 1929. Collection Museum of Modern Art, New York.

light, all gave direction to Sargent's rich endowment. These qualities are most apparent in the *Daughters of Edward Boit* (15-12).

The four children seem to have been captured in the midst of play. The scattered and irregular placement of the figures and the spontaneity of the poses appear completely unpremeditated until one observes the unifying relationships that are established between the figures by the careful counterbalancing and repetition of line movements. The great shadowy room provides the setting, and from the airy depths luminous reflections shine forth like deep reverberating sounds. A whole way of life is pictured with an effortless charm that is unsurpassed. The shy, well-brought-up children standing in their starched dresses move back into the spacious and quiet dark of the apartment with the certainty of a vivid memory—a memory of both Velasquez and the nineteenth-century way of life. Like a brilliant musician whose virtuosity leaves one breathless despite the familiarity of his themes, Sargent's performance here is memorable less because of what he has to say than because of the brilliance with which he says it. Even so, the performance should not be underestimated.

Sargent's activities as a mural painter and watercolorist should also be mentioned. His mural decorations for the Boston Public Library and for the Boston Museum of Fine Arts, probably the most effective murals painted in America in this period, reveal an impressive ability to discipline his talents to the needs of a large decorative project. When Sargent traveled he made rapid water-color sketches that still astonish us with their brilliant color and breadth of handling. Sargent's undeniable gifts may have been held in too high esteem when critics and public alike were blinded by his virtuosity. Today we tend to underestimate his very real gifts. Sargent may not have been a great artist if, by artist, we mean one who enlarges our vision of the world, but he was undoubtedly a very great painter.

By the time of World War I, the traditional portrait as such had almost disappeared from the art world. Only a few primitive painters could invest the human image with fresh power through the direct force and naïveté of their vision. John Kane (1860-1935) spent his life as a laborer in Pennsylvania. He worked in the mines and on the railroad, and in his spare hours he painted. In his self portrait (15-13) he looks out at the world with an earnest strength and directness of vision that had been lost to the more sophisticated and worldly. Building up through a symmetrically placed figure to a triple row of concentric arches, the composition achieves a monumental dignity as sober as the reverent self-examination that inspired the portrait. Except for a few such isolated images, the portrait ceased to play a vital role either as a social symbol or as a vehicle for artistic expression. In the twentieth century, man seemed most interested in his fellow man either as an element of the social scene or as a body of psychological impulses. The portrait as it had been painted for four centuries appeared incapable of deepening our understanding of either.

LANDSCAPE PAINTING

The popularity of landscape continued undiminished all through the century. The grandiose panoramas introduced by Thomas Cole before the Civil War continued to be in demand through the seventies and the eighties. The three most forceful painters to specialize in large paintings of spectacular scenery were Frederick Church, Albert Bierstadt, and Thomas Moran. Frederick Church (1826-1900) grew up in New Haven, Connecticut, and after studying locally he became a pupil and friend of Thomas Cole. He had a remarkable aptitude for landscape and even his very early works show an unusual ability to combine sharp detail with panoramic breadth and still retain a unity of effect. From the beginning he

15-14. Frederick Church, *The Parthenon*, 1871. Courtesy Metropolitan Museum of Art, Bequest of Maria DeWitt Jesup, 1915.

revealed a natural facility for handling outdoor light and color. Church matured during the period when artists and the educated public alike were enchanted with the visions of endless time and space being opened up by travel and the expanding worlds of geology, archeology, history, and the natural sciences. With facile brush, sensitive eye, and reverent spirit he recorded the wonders of the tropics, the Arctic, the Near East, and Europe as well as of his homeland. The grandeur of his paintings of remote and hitherto inaccessible parts of the world caused one critic to exclaim, "This is art's noblest, truest function; not to imitate nature but to rival it." Church's painting of the Parthenon (15-14) has the precision and sharp detail of an archeological record but it is also infused with the ardent enthusiasm of the nineteenth-century sightseer. Though the meticulous execution sometimes detracts from the mood of lyric exaltation, there is nothing obviously facile about these canvases. Church was always a serious artist—never a mere showman. Among his most beautiful works are the little oil sketches he made on paper while traveling—for in these all his knowledge and skill appear transmuted by the enthusiasm of the moment of discovery.

Albert Bierstadt (1830-1902) specialized in portraying the spectacular wonders of the Far West. Bierstadt, born of German parents, studied in Düsseldorf in the fifties; on his return to America he joined an expedi-

15-15 (*above*). Albert Bierstadt, *The Rocky Mountains*, 1863. Courtesy Metropolitan Museum of Art, Rogers Fund, 1907.   15-16 (*below*). Thomas Moran, *The Teton Range*, 1897. Courtesy Metropolitan Museum of Art, Bequest of Moses Tanenbaum, 1939.

tion sent to map an overland wagon route to the Pacific. Bierstadt spent the summer sketching in the Shoshone Mountains and along the Wind River. On his return to New York the series of paintings he made from these sketches brought him immediate recognition. During the following two decades Bierstadt enjoyed a spectacular success. His enormous canvases of scenes in the Rockies and California found an immediate market and brought unprecedented prices in an age when large canvases brought from ten to fifteen thousand dollars. Paintings such as *The Rocky Mountains* (15-15) enjoyed an unlimited popularity because of their impressive size and rich abundance of skillfully portrayed detail. Bierstadt, like all students of the Düsseldorf school, described surface textures with great skill, and his predilection for dramatic lighting effects and picturesque incidental figure groups was in direct accord with the popular tastes of these years.

Depicting the wonders of the Far West brought success to other artists in the seventies and eighties. Thomas Moran (1837-1926) painted the Grand Canyon, the Teton Range (15-16), and the Sierra Nevada. Thomas Hill (1829-1908), a follower of Bierstadt, and William Keith (1838-1911) both settled in California and specialized in the wonders of Yosemite and the great groves of redwoods.

The Luminists

While Church, Bierstadt, and their followers were catering to the taste for spectacular canvases, other artists, termed *luminists,* were continuing the tradition established by Durand, Kensett, and the Hudson River painters of mid-century. Choosing their subjects from the settled communities of the East, this group of men painted the woods, marshes, waterways, and farmlands of the nearby countryside. The turbulent romanticism of the earlier years of the century gave way to a tranquillity, distinguished by a sensitive and poetic vein, which found expression in depiction of familiar scenes transmuted by varying moods of weather. The particular concern of the luminists was the character of light, especially the luminous tonality of changing lights on sky and water. The three most original and sensitive of this group were Worthington Whittredge, Martin J. Heade, and George Inness.

Worthington Whittredge (1820-1910), born on the frontier of southern Ohio, spent much of his life in Cincinnati, where there was a vigorous artistic life. In his youth he went to Europe with Bierstadt, a firm friend despite the differences of temperament revealed by their work. *Camp*

15-17. Worthington Whittredge, *Camp Meeting*, 1874. Courtesy Metropolitan Museum of Art, Lazarus Fund, 1913.

Meeting (15-17), like many of Whittredge's paintings, verges on the genre but the landscape dominates the scene. The solemn dignity and delicate grace of the trees, the quiet stream, the tremulous light in the clearing, and the airy distances are the real subjects of the painting. The people animate the scene, establish an effective sense of scale, and provide multicolored surfaces on which the light can vibrate. The composition is a characteristic one—long horizontal lines and stabilizing verticals dominate the picture and establish a sense of deep tranquillity. Though the artist's attitude is reverent, it is not ponderous or didactic. The fine scale of the detail, the delicacy of touch, and the discretion with which the literal treatment is controlled all contribute to the deep poetry that characterizes Whittredge at his best.

Martin J. Heade (1819-1904) was born in Pennsylvania and spent much of his time painting in New Jersey, although he traveled extensively. His particular sensitivity was for the dreamlike strangeness of the familiar scene when viewed under the unfamiliar light of early morning, late day, or, particularly, during a storm. His *Storm Approaching Narragansett Bay* (15-18) achieves its startling intensity by the brilliant contrasts of tone, the strangely rich and curious color, and the hallucinatory clarity of detail. His landscapes which depict the pearly mists of early morning floating over the meadows of New Jersey have an iridescence and a subtlety of tone that place Heade in the vanguard of American landscape painters. Works which differ decidedly from his landscapes are his flower paintings, many of which depict tropical orchids painted against the background of the exotic jungle. Because his precise edges, clear and detailed treatment of forms, and thin, even texture of paint did not con-

15-18. Martin J. Heade, *Storm Approaching Narragansett Bay*, 1868. Ernest Rosenfeld Collection. Museum of Modern Art photograph.

form to current tastes, Heade was virtually forgotten until the middle of the twentieth century.

George Inness (1825-1894) began his career painting in a precise, detailed, naturalistic style. Inness was born in Newark, New Jersey, and since, as a youth, he seemed an impractical dreamer, his merchant father set him up in business. His heart, however, was not in commerce, so he was sent abroad where he saw the work of the great English landscape painters as well as that of Corot, Rousseau, and the French Barbizon group. On his return home he embarked upon a painting career and though success came slowly he was able to make a living by painting.

"The true artistic impulse is divine," said Inness, and this lyric and visionary note characterized his life. He was indifferent to success and money, and he valued recognition only because it enabled him to support his family. His all-consuming passion was to translate the beauty of low rolling hills, stretches of quiet meadow, or the poetry of the woods into a richly brushed harmony of tone and color. *June* (15-19) provides an excellent example of the style of his middle age when the sharp deline-ation of details that characterized his early work gave way to a simplified, broadly brushed handling. The colors are cool and grayed: blues, blue greens, and soft ocherous greens that fade into rosy browns. The forms move back into space through easy, undulating planes. Though the draw-

15-19 (*above*). George Inness, *June*, 1882. Brooklyn Museum, Brooklyn, N. Y.
15-20 (*below*). George Inness, *Home of the Heron*, 1893. The Art Institute of Chicago, Chicago, Edward B. Butler Collection.

ing is firm and knowledgeable, it remains subordinate to an over-all harmony of tone and color. The style of painting recalls both Constable and the French Barbizon painters, but there is nothing exotic in the open fields, meandering creeks, and scattered trees. They form the typical landscapes that surrounded Inness's homes in Brooklyn, New Jersey, and Massachusetts.

In his last years, strong religious and mystical tendencies provided the predominant mood for his work. The out-of-door landscape continued to provide the subject but assumed less importance, while a mood of reverie drawn from the inner recesses of his mind predominated (15-20). The close values, strangely grayed colors, flickers of light, and quavering shadows create an unsubstantial world that expresses deep feelings of awe. For Inness, that was enough. "The aim of art," he said, "is not to instruct, not to edify, but to awaken an emotion."

The nineteenth century was the great age of landscape painting. The landscape provided a vehicle for expressing a number of the enthusiasms of the day—romantic sentiments, religious feelings, scientific interests, and patriotism, as well as antagonism toward the growing industrialization and urbanism. By the end of the century the possibilities of the landscape as subject matter for the artist had been explored as thoroughly as the continent itself. Painters moved on to new areas of concern, the inner world of subjective moods, the domain of personal style, the color and flavor of the city, and the complexities of social discord and psychological depth.

Painting:

From the Mystics

to the Armory Show

LANDSCAPE PAINTING

Mystic Painters

Ever since Allston had introduced a note of reverie in his later land-scapes a group of painters had continued his subjective vein and explored their inner moods of wonder and solitude. It was probably inevitable that this brooding note would receive its most intense expression when the extroverted expressions of American energy were at their height. In the years following the Civil War, when expansion, success, money, and progress were the predominant aspects of American life, many spoke for another way of life. For every man of action there was a dreamer; for every success, many failures; and for every Bierstadt, there were artistic and temperamental opposites. Three painters who explored this subjective mood of reverie were Elihu Vedder, Ralph Blakelock, and Albert Ryder.

Elihu Vedder (1836-1923) was descended from early Dutch settlers. After study abroad, he returned to New York but later spent much of his life in Italy. Vedder used the landscape as a setting for the unexpected and haunting images of his mind. He loved to wander among the mountains and through the remote villages of Europe and some of his most sensitive paintings are the warm, quiet little sketches he made on such trips. *The Philosopher* (16-1) reveals the mood of isolation and contemplation that so often prevails in his paintings. Vedder's landscape forms are vigorously drawn and the dark and light patterns are forceful, but despite the energetic and positive aspects of his manner, the predominant mood is passive and contemplative.

Ralph Blakelock (1847-1919) is one of the most tragic figures in the history of American painting. Like so many American painters, he started his career on a trip west. The awesome wilderness impressed him deeply and his memory of the great woodland areas flooded with moonlight or seen through the glowing mists of twilight supplied the images for his haunting landscapes. His moonlight scenes (16-2) appealed to only a limited market, and his failure and inability to cope with the business world and support his large family by painting finally drove him insane. He spent most of his mature years in an asylum from which he was released only a few months before his death.

Albert Pinkham Ryder (1847-1917) was the last and greatest of the mystic painters. He grew up in New Bedford, Massachusetts, with the sea as a constant companion. When he was twenty-one, his family moved to New York and he accompanied them and for a brief period of time studied painting. However, he was essentially a self-taught painter—both the design of his paintings and his method of applying the paint are highly personal and unrelated to the studio practices of his day. Ryder lived alone, a solitary in the midst of the crowded city. His one-room studio, almost without furniture, was a confused litter of papers, dishes, and rubbish. Here he painted pictures composed from the depths of his imagination augmented by memories of his youth and observations made during his lonely walks late at night. His simple wants were cared for by the occasional sale of a picture.

Most of Ryder's paintings were inspired by the ocean at night. Ryder was obsessed by a sense of the mystery and power of the sea, and to convey the intensity of his feelings he developed a personal style that was less related to visual perceptions than to his feeling for the elements of design. Ryder probed deeply within himself for the images that would express his feelings with eloquence; clouds, waves, boats, and occasional

16-1 (*above*). Elihu Vedder, *The Philosopher*, 1867. Newark Museum, Newark, N. J.   16-2 (*below*). Ralph Blakelock, *Moonlight*, 1882. Brooklyn Museum, Brooklyn, N. Y.

16-3. Albert Pinkham Ryder, *Siegfried and the Rhine Maidens*, 1875-1891.
National Gallery of Art, Washington, D. C., Mellon Collection.

headland were simplified in shape and organized into broad slow-moving
rhythms. Moonlight eliminates the details and bathes the forms in its
strange cold color. Ryder was almost never satisfied with his paintings.
Long after they were completed and sold, he continued to work over
them, glazing the surfaces with layer upon layer of transparent color
until the translucent masses glowed like jewels. Technically many of the
procedures he employed in producing his paintings are inadmissible—the
paintings have cracked and discolored badly, but cracking and discolora-
tion cannot destroy their magic.

Not all of Ryder's paintings were based on the sea. A number of them,
such as his *Siegfried and the Rhine Maidens* (16-3) drew on literary
sources for their subject matter. These tend to be more complex in design

than his sea and boat paintings but share the other general characteristics of his style. Though based on subjects drawn from Shakespeare, the Bible, and various other literary sources, they are less illustrations than symbolizations of subtle, poetic moods. Ryder expressed the nature of his strange explorations very well when he said, "Have you ever seen an inch worm crawl up a leaf or twig, and then clinging to the very end, revolve in the air, feeling for something to reach something? That's like me. I am trying to find something out there beyond the place where I have a footing."

The Impressionists

In the last decade of the century a number of the younger painters born in mid-century were attracted to the experiments of Monet, Pissarro, and other of the French impressionists.

16-4. Theodore Robinson, *Willows*, c. 1891. Brooklyn Museum, Brooklyn, N. Y.

Theodore Robinson (1852-1896) discovered impressionism in the eighties and adopted the new technique of using highly keyed, broken color to convey the shimmer of light and the cool tones of shadows. *Willows* (16-4) is typical of impressionist landscape painting in its breadth of handling, its bright color, and its informal, flat, patterned composition.

In 1895 a group of American painters, strongly influenced by the tenets of impressionism, exhibited together under the name of "Ten American Painters." Among the more important painters in the group were John Twachtman (1852-1902) and Childe Hassam (1859-1935). Both Twachtman's *Three Trees* (16-5) and Hassam's *Street Scene in Winter* (16-6) reflect the aims of American impressionism. Familiar scenes provide the motifs from which the artists created subtle webs of color and pattern. The visual world was relieved of its weight and volume and transposed into exquisite arrangements which reveal the surprising shapes embedded in the everyday milieu. Despite its light and fragile tone, impressionism grew from a serious effort to eliminate the trite and conventional elements from painting without having recourse to the exotic and remote. Impressionism represented, in essence, a turn-of-the-century combination of visual realism and esthetic sensitivity.

The Primitives

While painters on all levels of competence were depicting America with varying degrees of sophistication, the folk artists continued to paint their naive versions of the American scene for their own pleasure. We have already discussed John Kane's powerful self-portrait. His landscapes are equally forceful. Joseph Pickett (1848-1918) was a carpenter shipbuilder from Pennsylvania who painted as a hobby. His *Manchester Valley* (16-7) has been rendered with the exactitude of memory unblurred by sunshine, shadow or distance. The fresh patterns of Pennsylvania towns were presented with a sharp definition of form and texture, a refreshing antidote to the tendencies prevailing in sophisticated artistic circles to lose all detail in a mist of atmosphere, taste, or sentiment. In the mid-twentieth century when painting tended to become farther and farther removed from the common denominator of popular visual experiences, the works of the naive folk painters continued to provide valuable and refreshing reminders of the magic power of direct unsophisticated expression.

16-5 (*below*). John Twachtman, *Three Trees*, n. d. Brooklyn Museum.   16-6 (*right*). Childe Hassam, *Street Scene in Winter*, 1901. Courtesy Metropolitan Museum of Art, Bequest of G. D. Pratt, 1935.

GENRE PAINTING

Genre painting continued to be popular between 1865 and 1915, and three general types predominated. First, there were the paintings of life in the Far West. Secondly, there were the story-telling paintings. Lastly, there were the scenes of everyday life which depict people carrying on their daily activities.

Painters of the Far West

The painters of the frontiers of the Far West specialized in picturesque characters and violent action. Much of this painting was illustrational, and obvious in its appeal. Charles Christian Nahl (1818-1897), born in Germany, first painted in New York and after the Gold Rush settled in San Francisco. *Sunday Morning in the Mines* (16-8) is one of his most ambitious and successful canvases. The different vignettes of life in a mining community have been skillfully integrated into a unified composition. The generally warm and sentimental portrayal of incidents is enriched with much freshly observed detail such as the scattered mining instruments in the foreground, the hand-hewn shingles and boards of the cabin, and the distant ranges of receding hills. Nahl's paint is applied

16-7. Joseph Pickett, *Manchester Valley*, 1914-1918. Museum of Modern Art, New York.

with a smooth enamel-like finish and his hot, bright color seems well suited to the vivacity of his style.

The best-known painter of the Far West was Frederic Remington (1861-1909), whose records of the life of the cowboys, the Plains Indians, and of the open range reveal an exact and conscientious knowledge of his subjects. Remington came from a comfortable up-state New York family, and studied art at Yale. At nineteen he headed for the Far West, where he worked as a cowboy and ranch cook. Fascinated by the panorama of western life, he began to record it with pencil and brush before its rough vigor disappeared forever. He found a ready market for his sketches and paintings in the publishing world. From then on he created thousands of paintings and illustrations as well as a small number of bronzes depicting the tense drama of frontier existence. *Cavalry Charge on the Western Plains* (16-9) reveals his direct, animated style. With an unerring eye and a few sharply accented strokes, he could capture a movement, a gesture, or establish a vivid character. His dashing skill left no room for grandeur of feeling or monumentality of effect.

16-8 (*above*). Charles Nahl, *Sunday Morning in the Mines,* 1872. E. B. Crocker Art Gallery, Sacramento, Calif.   16-19 (*below*). Frederic Remington, *Cavalry Charge on the Western Plains,* 1907. Courtesy Metropolitan Museum of Art, Gift of Several Gentlemen, 1911.

16-10. Horace Bonham, *Nearing the Issue at the Cock Pit*, 1870. Corcoran Gallery of Art, Washington, D. C.

Anecdotal Painting

Story-telling genre pictures were popular until the end of the nineteenth century with certain painters excelling in special subjects. J. G. Brown (1831-1913), who painted in New York, was noted for his pictures, of ragged newsboys; William Beard (1824-1900) painted moral and sentimental stories in which animals personified human types. Some artists produced a few remarkable paintings and then fell into oblivion. Such a one was Horace Bonham (1835-1892). His *Nearing the Issue at the Cock Pit* (16-10) is a masterly genre painting. The drawing is skillful, strong, and sensitive, and the composition reveals an unusual ability to inject action and tension into a solidly structured group of figures. The centrally placed old man establishes a pyramidal form from which radiates an interwoven pattern of diagonal lines. Bonham's characters are sensitively observed and unhackneyed, and while colorful details of dress are observed with a loving eye he is not unduly dependent on the characteristic props of nineteenth-century anecdotal painters. The limited color and the lack of varied paint textures suggest inadequate training.

16-11 (*above*). Eastman Johnson, *The Nantucket School of Philosophy*, 1887. Walters Art Gallery, Baltimore.   16-12 (*below*). Eastman Johnson, *The Hatch Family*, 1871. Courtesy Metropolitan Museum of Art, Gift of Frederick H. Hatch, 1926.

Domestic Genre

The delights of domesticity and rural scenes continued to supply the genre painter with popular material. One of the most forceful American painters to specialize in such subjects was Eastman Johnson (1824-1906). Johnson was born in Maine, studied with a lithographer in Boston, and at eighteen was professionally sketching crayon portraits with great success. He subsequently painted in Düsseldorf, then traveled around Europe and spent an extended period in Holland studying the seventeenth-century Dutch painters. His admiration for the "Little Dutchmen" influenced his mature style toward a taste for warm brown and tan color harmonies, subdued tonalities; he preferred the dignified compositional effects of the Dutch masters to the more brilliant arrangements of the Düsseldorf school. Johnson returned home in the mid-fifties and settled in New York. *The Nantucket School of Philosophy* (16-11) illustrates the popular style of his genre themes. The color and flavor of daily life is depicted with warm affection and gentle humor. Johnson establishes the personalities of his sitters by a quiet insistence on a few telling gestures. The sense of air and space in the shadowy interior, the warm glowing color, and the varied surface textures are rendered with an easy facility that contributes to the relaxed tone of the performance.

Johnson's famous portrait of the Hatch family (16-12), painted in 1871, is in the most polished style of his later years. The predominant color note in the high-ceilinged interior is a warm shadowy red, almost a red-gold. The draperies, tables, and upholstery repeat the color. In the diffused glow of tempered light, amidst the gleam of figurines and the sheen of rosewood and mahogany, are the fifteen members of the Hatch family. The easy disposition of the large family group is achieved without any loss of individual personalities, yet Johnson has no recourse to theatrical characterizations or gestures. The individual figures stand defined and united by the all pervasive blond-red light and the sense of interacting personalities. *The Hatch Family* is one of the few great family portraits from nineteenth-century America, and it provides an unexcelled record of the way of life that characterized those years.

Mary Cassatt (1845-1926), America's greatest impressionist, was basically a genre painter who explored the mother and child motif to its fullest. Daughter of a wealthy Philadelphia family, she settled in Paris where she became one of the few artists to work under Degas. From Degas and the impressionist group she absorbed her precise, clear-eyed,

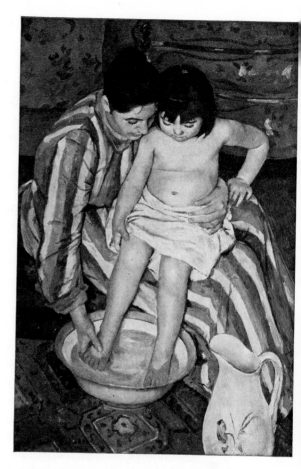

16-13. Mary Cassatt, *La Toilette, c.* 1891. The Art Institute of Chicago, Chicago, Robert Alexander Waller Memorial Collection.

and distinguished style, but her subject matter remained that of an American girl interested in running a house and raising children.

La Toilette (16-13) depicts one of her typical mothers caring for a child. This was the motif she chose to paint most frequently although she occasionally did other aspects of domestic life or the theater. With a warm heart and a sharp eye, Mary Cassatt caught every gesture and shape with unerring exactitude, and from these accurately observed forms she arranged her ingenious and surprising compositions. She employed typical impressionist compositional devices, frequently painting her figure groups from above so that the curious bird's-eye view throws familiar objects into unexpected shapes. Objects fill the canvas and run out of the edges of the composition, creating an effect of casual intimacy similar to those revealed by the developing art of photography. Patterns are sharp and clear-cut, and the painter is not dependent upon shadowy and ambiguous atmospheric moods. Instead the character of a situation is established by the exact realization of the nature of the objects described. Her color is fresh, light, and clear, sometimes almost sharp. She painted with a trenchant realism, a visual objectivity closely related in mood to the laboratory methods that were being developed for scientific research. This objectivity was endowed with esthetic significance by Mary Cassatt's scrupulous taste and the serene affection with which she regarded her subjects.

The impressionists were great admirers of the Japanese prints as is evident in Cassatt's charming *Young Woman Trying on a Dress* (17-4) a color aquatint combined with dry point distinguished by scattered patterns of stripes and flowers. The sharp clarity of vision that distinguished Mary Cassatt did not make for popularity at the turn of the century; indeed she was better known in France than in America.

STILL-LIFE PAINTING

The most distinguished still-life painter of the last half of the century was William Michael Harnett (1848-1892). Harnett was born in Ireland but grew up in Philadelphia. At seventeen he became apprenticed to an engraver and subsequently supported himself by engraving silver while he attended art school and learned to paint. Even his early still lifes, carefully rendered, tight little compositions, are personal and unique in their selection of subject matter, for he preferred worn and picturesque household objects—pipes, newspapers, a beer mug, old books, a quill pen, and frayed bills of worthless money—to the more conventional fruits, flowers, and table wares. These still lifes sold well enough to enable him to study abroad. He spent most of four years in the early eighties in Munich where he enlarged both his sense of composition and the size of his paintings and developed a richer and more painterly use of his medium.

After the Hunt (16-14) provides a striking illustration of Harnett's fully developed powers. Like much of his work it is a *trompe l'oeil* ("deceive the eye") composition in which a still life with narrative implications is depicted with striking illusionism and a bold decorative sense. The picture is large, almost 4 by 6 feet. It is beautifully organized with the vertical lines of the rabbit, the birds and the boards and the horizontals of the great hinges stabilizing the bold criss-cross of diagonals which lead with ever-increasing complexity to the circular forms of the hat and the hunting, powder, and deer horns. The organization of the

16-14. William Harnett, *After the Hunt*, 1885. Legion of Honor, San Francisco, Calif.

volumes parallels that of the line movements. The greatest depth in space is established by the hat, at which point there is also the most interesting assembly of shapes. As one's eye travels from this point back to the edge of the canvas, the depths diminish, as do the dark and light contrasts, the variety of forms, and the complexity of the line movements. To keep this carefully structured composition from being obvious, a few of the most fascinating elements of the design have been placed on the outer perimeter of the canvas—the handsome spiraling hinges and the intriguing key and keyhole. In addition many delightful *trompe l'oeil* elements have been exploited with zest—the spots of rust, the cracked and streaked paint, and the tricky iridescence of mother-of-pearl. Even while playing his most fascinating pranks on the eye, Harnett remained sensitive to the subleties of painting as an art and a craft. The colors are richly, even somberly, orchestrated, and the textures of the paint please even while they deceive.

While Harnett's paintings were popular, his example did not inspire an extensive following. His contemporary William Merritt Chase (1849-

16-15. William Merritt Chase, *A Friendly Call*, 1895. National Gallery of Art, Washington, D. C., Gift of Chester Dale.

1916) was both popular and influential. Chase was one of the most skillful still-life painters of his day, and his genre scenes frequently have the flavor of still-life painting about them. In *A Friendly Call* (16-15) the seated figures are single elements in a large ensemble designed to display the painter's facility in depicting all the various textures of an interior. Chase was an extraordinarily stimulating teacher and he communicated to his students his own composite talents—the fresh luminous paint of Munich and the sweeping brushwork of Sargent combined with the lighter colors and the clever arrangements of the impressionists.

THE INDEPENDENTS

Winslow Homer

While cosmopolitanism and sophistication were becoming the order of the day and the American painting tradition was reflecting a rich profusion of ideas from Europe, a small group of American painters, first Winslow Homer and later the Eight, performed the signal service of integrating these conflicting tendencies with the older indigenous tradition of American painting.

16-16. Winslow Homer, *The Lookout—"All's Well,"* 1896. Museum of Fine Arts, Boston.

Many diverse and seemingly contradictory tendencies come together in the work of Winslow Homer. The life of the frontier and the backwood is portrayed, not melodramatically but with the color and flavor of everyday life. The bold directness of his brushwork equals that of the Munich school, the simple breadth of his compositions rivals that of the Barbizon painters, and his clarity of visual analysis matches that of the impressionists. Homer chose his American experiences as his point of departure, and his masculine taste removed him from the fashionable world with its undue concern with trivial refinements of style and taste. All of these qualities give a stature to his canvases that lifts them far above the general level of his day.

Winslow Homer (1836-1910), born in Boston, came from a seventeenth-century American family. His father was a merchant, but since Homer preferred a career in art, he was apprenticed to a lithographer at nineteen and eventually became a free-lance illustrator. He worked for seventeen years as an illustrator, largely for *Harper's Weekly,* and this invaluable experience in disciplined observation intensified his natural enjoyment and understanding of people and of the workaday world. This earlier period of his life received its most powerful expression in the drawings and paintings he made of the Civil War. They are distinguished by their freshness of observation, their direct vigor of line, and their forceful but simple relationships of tone. Since these studies were done as illustrations, they had to be sufficiently simple to be translated into wood engravings for reproduction. *The Sharpshooter* (17-1) reveals the direct energy, sweeping line, and vigorous tonality of these sketches.

In the last half of his life, Homer abandoned the lively narrative style of his early years for a more simple and monumental one. In 1881 he gave up his career as an illustrator. After a two-year interval in England, he settled at Prout's Neck on the coast of Maine where he produced the large oil paintings which mark his mature style. These paintings are concerned with the sea—gray, granite-bound, powerful, and mysterious—and the fisherfolk of New England. The endless conflict between man and the forces of nature provided the drama which Homer treated with understanding and diginity. *The Lookout—"All's Well"* (16-16) reveals his ability to take the fisherman's life, as commonplace and routine for that day as that of a truck driver today, and from that familiar material to create a monumental symbol characterized by plastic power, vigor, and authenticity of atmosphere. As in all Homer's paintings, the basic design is simple. The rather large forms move across the canvas in simple diagonal movements that suggest the rolling and unstable motion of a boat. The forms are modeled simply and broadly, as though the misty and diffused sea light eliminated the details that might distract the eye from the grandeur of form. The world of ropes and heavy clothing and the harsh struggle with the sea is neither romanticized nor idealized, though Homer remains very aware of the lyric grace of the bell and the curl of the strap that hangs free from the oilskin hat. The direct, almost brusque quality of the brushwork contributes to the vigor of the surface and reveals the painter's feeling for his medium. The color, carefully observed and harmonized not by formula but by feeling, provides a full-bodied accompaniment to the forms.

Throughout his years in Maine, Homer took long trips for a change of scene. The Caribbean islands, the Adirondacks, and the Canadian woods were favorite spots. On these trips he made the vigorous water-color sketches that established water color as a major medium for American landscape painters. The *Sloop, Bermuda* (16-17) has the breadth of handling and the strength and simplicity of design that distinguish his oils. While water color had been used for sketching purposes by many painters before Homer, few had handled it with his certainty and masculine vigor.

16-17 (*above*). Winslow Homer, *Sloop, Bermuda*, 1899. Courtesy Metropolitan Museum of Art, Lazarus Fund, 1910. 16-18 (*below*). Winslow Homer, *Huntsman and Dogs*, 1891. Philadelphia Museum of Art, Philadelphia.

Homer's hunting and fishing episodes provided the basis for some of the great oils of his last years. His *Huntsman and Dogs* (16-18) transforms a familiar facet of the American adventure into an austere and powerful canvas. Against a luminous cloudy sky, the dull mass of the mountain raises its long, unbroken silhouette. The line of the diagonal cloud, the mountainside, the tree root, and the dogs repeat the same movement with an almost monotonous rhythm. The vertical of the great stump, the boy's body, and the deerskin stand in somber, dignified contrast. It is the harsh, brooding, and graceless world of the hunter that is depicted, and the authenticity of tone adds to the drama implicit in the theme. This quality of harsh strength disturbed the critics and public of his day, but they could not deny the power of the canvases. Henry James, that most perceptive of critics, found them "almost barbarously simple," but he granted that Homer had managed to treat the least pictorial features of our civilization as though they were "every inch as good as Capri or Tangiers." In the final analysis, the significance of Homer's paintings grew from his ability to participate imaginatively in the familiar experiences of American life and in so doing to create timeless symbols of man's work and play. The power of these symbols results from their dual authenticity—their authenticity as powerfully wrought works of art and as sympathetic and informed observations of a way of life.

The Eight

The significant artists whom we have seen painting in America at the end of the nineteenth century were not the individuals who constituted the official world of the arts. Ryder, Homer, and Eakins were hard at work, but none except for Eakins, who was teaching in Philadelphia, had any following. The official world of exhibitions, art schools, and critical approval was dominated by the mood of genteel refinement initiated by the Ten American Painters when they first exhibited in Boston in 1895. The dominant schools of painting featured a combination of watered-down impressionism and suave brushwork. Familiar subjects were arranged in pleasing patterns. Colors were discreet and harmonious. It was an art created for a few people insulated from the raw vigor of much of American life by the amenities of well-ordered living, money, social position, and conventional education. But American life and culture were too turbulent and vigorous for such anemic fare, and in the first decade of the twentieth century a new group of painters challenged the discreet taste of the official art world. This group called itself the

16-19. Robert Henri, *Mary Gallagher*, c. 1924. Newark Museum of Art, Newark, N. J.

Eight, but the critics and public who were disturbed by the rough vigor and challenge of their work called them "the Ash Can school."

The leader of the Eight was Robert Henri (1865-1929). Henri was born in Cincinnati. He studied under Anshutz, who continued the tradition of Eakins at the Pennsylvania Academy of Fine Arts. Later Henri studied in Paris and then returned to teach in Philadelphia. A magnetic teacher, he gradually established a coterie of followers. In 1900 he commenced teaching in New York where he became the very articulate spokesman of a philosophy of painting which stressed the importance of "life" in art rather than style. Henri urged his followers to immerse themselves in the vigorous metropolitan atmosphere, to enjoy the rich flavor of its great masses of humanity, and to paint this world with vigor and spontaneity. His philosophy of art was put forth in a collection of his lectures and criticisms called *The Art Spirit*. Robert Henri's own paintings are direct, boldly brushed portraits and figure studies. He selected his colorful sitters from the poorer sections of New York City—immigrants from Europe and Asia, the very old, and the very young. *Mary Gallagher* (16-19) displays the dramatic dash and fire of execution by which he captured the vigor of his sitter's personality.

In 1907 the jury of the National Academy of Design rejected a number of paintings by Henri's friends and followers. The intolerance of the jury nettled Henri, and he withdrew his own entry in protest. The fol-

16-20. John Sloan, *The Picnic Grounds,* 1906-1907. Whitney Museum of American Art, New York.

lowing year the Macbeth Galleries in New York, the first gallery to specialize in American painters, sponsored an exhibition of the rejected artists and some sympathetic fellow painters. There were eight all told: Henri and four of his followers—Glackens, Luks, Sloan, and Shinn—and three painters who were affiliated with Henri's group more through temperament than style—Prendergast, Davies, and Lawson. The impact of the Eight was enormous. They achieved for American artists what Dreiser, Lewis, Anderson, and a subsequent generation of writers achieved for the literary world—they turned the eyes away from the niceties of the genteel tradition toward a more vigorous and all-inclusive picture of the country and its people.

John Sloan (1871-1950) remains the most original and powerful painter of the original Eight. Before coming under Henri's influence Sloan had been a newspaper artist, and the illustrative emphasis provided an important element of his style in later years. He moved to New York from Philadelphia in 1904; there the vigorous life of the city provided him with his principal motif. True to the teachings of Henri, he immersed himself in the life of the city—the crowded streets, parks, homes, and places of entertainment—and his spontaneous records reflect the zest with which his keen eye and lively mind reported on his experiences.

The Picnic Grounds (16-20), painted around 1907, reflects the enthu-

16-21. John Sloan, *Backyards, Greenwich Village*, 1914. Whitney Museum of American Art, New York.

siasm of his early years in New York. Like most of Sloan's early works, it is conceived in broad masses of dark and light so that a postery vigor characterizes the work. The breadth of gesture and the almost vulgar vitality of the scene illustrate the aptness of the statement by Lloyd Goodrich that ". . . His art had that quality of being a direct product of common life, absolutely authentic and unsweetened, that has marked the finest genre of all time." It was not surprising that the advocates of quiet arrangements, pleasing subjects, and gentle color harmonies dubbed the Eight the Ash Can school.

In *Backyards, Greenwich Village* (16-21) we again see Sloan's ability to invest a drab city scene with his own zest for life, to perceive the lusty pursuit of human activities behind the façade of the city slums. The grubby buildings, broken fences, telephone poles, and clothes lines provide the background for the busy children and animals. Though the setting might appear grim according to the conventional and proper standards, Sloan saw it as glowing in color and infused the scene with his

16-22. George Luks, *Mrs. Gamley*, 1930. Whitney Museum of American Art, New York.

own love of life. After 1930 Sloan became interested in certain colorist innovations of the post-impressionists and abandoned his vigorous reporting of the American scene for studio painting.

Sloan contributed considerably to the revival of interest in prints which occurred among artists and collectors early in the twentieth century. His background as a newspaper illustrator provided him with unusual graphic facility and his etchings are delightful commentaries on the human foibles and fancies revealed by the metropolitan milieu (17-7).

George Luks (1867-1933) recorded the same world as Sloan, but Luks was concerned more exclusively with the human component. His was a colorful personality with a flair for depicting the colorful personalities of others. *Mrs. Gamley* (16-22) is typical in subject matter and handling. Luks, admiring Frans Hals beyond all other painters, subordinated his sense of color to his taste for dramatic dark tonalities. He applied his paint in broad, flat masses, and there is a suggestion of Manet in the simplicity of his planes and the way in which form is suggested by the subtle modeling of the edge of a plane.

Time has altered our judgment concerning the importance of some of the Eight although the importance of the movement cannot be over-

16-23 (*above*). Maurice Prendergast, *Early Summer*, 1916. Arizona State College, Collection of American Art, Tempe, Ariz.   16-24 (*below*). Arthur B. Davies, *The Dream*, n.d. Courtesy Metropolitan Museum of Art, Gift of George A. Hearn, 1909.

estimated. William Glackens (1870-1938), like Sloan and Luks, started his professional life as a newspaper illustrator and then became a painter. Under the influence of Renoir, his mature style lost the exuberance of his early work and became distinguished by large simple forms, rhythmic lines, and rich color.

Everett Shinn (1876-1953), the youngest of the group, loved the world of fashion, restaurants, and the theater and painted gay illustrational street scenes and vignettes of theatrical life.

Ernest Lawson was primarily a landscape painter.

While, as a group, the Eight were opposed to the anemic academic impressionism being produced in America, they were, in spirit, close to the French impressionists. Manet, Degas, and others of the French group, like the Eight, had painted the colorful life of the city about them without stressing symbolic or moralistic values. The French impressionists also were admirers of Hals, Velasquez, and Goya as masters of vigorous brushwork and dramatic tone. But though the Eight were influenced by the spirit of French impressionism, they avoided the more obvious aspects of their manner. This is most evident in the paintings of Maurice Prendergast (1859-1924). Unlike the other members of the group, Prendergast, a Bostonian, traveled and painted abroad, and only lived in New York for the last ten years of his life. *Early Summer* (16-23) displays the highly personal style of his oils—a mosaic of flat planes which build up into a tapestrylike surface of rich color. Prendergast's color was based on that of the impressionist landscape painters, with yellow and orange tones dominating the sunlit areas while blue and violet shadows replaced the browns and blacks of the more conventionally oriented colorists. His favorite subjects were crowds of people on the beach, walking along the streets or quays of foreign villages, or groups of nursemaids and children playing in the park. These are composed in dominantly vertical and horizontal relationships with awkward simplifications of form contributing a certain gaucherie. For Prendergast the world appeared as a rich visual fabric in which the human element was only part of a vast encompassing glitter.

Stylistically Arthur B. Davies (1862-1928) was quite unrelated to the group but he was one of the leaders in the fight against academic timidity and it was largely because of his efforts that the Eight held their initial showing. A painter of poetic memories and idyllic reveries, his canvases are composed of handsome nude figures in quiet landscape settings. Rhythmic line movements and muted colors contribute to the sensuous charm of his dream world (16-24).

16-25. George Bellows, *Dempsey and Firpo*, 1924. Whitney Museum of American Art, New York.

George Bellows

The trenchant realism of Henri, Sloan, and Luks formed a bridge between the nineteenth-century realists and the later painters of the American scene. George Bellows (1882-1925) was a vigorous painter who followed the lead of the Eight. He selected much of his subject matter from the swarming city streets, but his compositions have more subtlety and complexity than those of his predecessors, and his power as a draftsman contributes an added force to his paintings. *Dempsey and Firpo* (16-25), a subject drawn from the common stuff of American life, immortalizes the moment when the Argentine pugilist, Firpo, knocked the heavyweight Jack Dempsey completely out of the ring. The picture is composed with great slashing diagonals which move across the canvas to create the dynamic and tense mood of a boxing match. The contrast of brilliantly lighted figures against the dark background and the direct and forceful brushwork also contribute to the vivid effectiveness of the painting.

16-26. George Bellows, *Mr. and Mrs. Phillip Wase*, 1924. Courtesy estate of Mrs. George Bellows.

Bellows's subtlety as a draftsman and power as a psychologist are most evident in his portraits. In *Mr. and Mrs. Phillip Wase* (16-26) he created a remarkably sensitive group portrait that probes deeply into the roots of America. The aged couple are seated in the lace-curtained Victorian parlor. Mr. Wase dominates the picture in action. His active and aggressive body sits restlessly on the horsehair sofa; unaccustomed to posing, he stares stubbornly and awkwardly forward. Mrs. Wase sits quietly, looking straight ahead. Her worn face, strong arms, and sensitive hands tell of a lifetime of housework and care—her thoughtful spirit has guided the household through the long years. The forms and spaces of the composition establish the relationships between the two people—the man's larger body occupying the greater space while the woman's verticality and accented pattern provide the focus. The textures have been richly developed and the paint is handled with assurance but without display.

Bellows contributed materially to the revival of the print processes that occurred in the early years of the twentieth century; his lithographs reveal a vein of irony that is seldom suggested by his paintings (17-6).

In 1913 a number of America's most progressive artists, including most of the members of the Eight, arranged to bring the famous Armory Show to New York. This extensive exhibition was designed to acquaint the public at large with the new movements in painting at home and abroad. At the Armory Show an astonished American public was introduced to the vanguard of French and Continental painting and sculpture —cubism, expressionism, and the violent fauvism—as well as to the trenchant realism and the highly personalized styles of the younger Americans. Though scorned by most critics and laughed at by the public at large, the impact of the show could not be erased; the Armory Show signaled the eclipse of academic impressionists and of devotees of the "genteel tradition." From here on American painters, like European, were involved in a number of new approaches to painting which, for lack of a better name, we know as "modern" painting. This complex and multifaceted body of work will be our concern in a subsequent chapter.

The Graphic Arts,

Sculpture, and

Art Patronage

THE GRAPHIC ARTS

Illustration

Producing illustrations for an ever-increasing flood of books and periodicals provided a livelihood for many artists after the Civil War. While some important painters, like Winslow Homer, served their artistic apprenticeship in this capacity (17-1), only a few of the professional illustrators were sufficiently forceful and original to achieve distinction. Most notable among them was Thomas Nast (1840-1902). Nast, from a family of liberal German refugees, spent his professional life fighting for social reform as a staff artist for *Harper's Weekly*. In this capacity he developed a forceful style of caricature with which to conduct his endless warfare against the corruption and evil which were eating into the full realization of America's promise. His vitriolic attacks upon the corrupt

17-1 (*below*). Winslow Homer, *The Sharpshooter*, 1862. International Business Machines Collection.
17-2 (*right*). Thomas Nast, *A Group of Vultures Waiting for the Storm to "Blow Over"—"Let Us Prey,"* 1871. New York Public Library.

and powerful Tweed Ring which dominated New York City in the latter half of the nineteenth century were probably the most effective editorial cartoons ever produced in America. Nast helped to unseat the Tweed Ring and in so doing created political symbols that have remained a part of our national imagery—the Tammany tiger, the Republican elephant, and the Democratic donkey. Justifiably, one of his most frequently reproduced cartoons is *A Group of Vultures Waiting for the Storm to "Blow Over"—"Let Us Prey"* (17-2). Most evident here is his remarkable ability to translate personalities, events, and social forces into vivid and readily understood symbols. Nast made his original drawings in pencil with clear, incisive lines which could be easily translated into the linear style of wood engraving. This linear, hard-textured style has an aggressive, masculine vigor well-adapted to the combative role of his work. Nast, more than any other individual, established the cartoon as an important political force in America.

Prints

The late nineteenth century witnessed an increase in the popularity of the various print processes. In the expanding middle-class American society there was no established body of art patrons; consequently the inexpensive print played a particularly important role since it enabled individuals of modest means to collect works of art and thereby share and contribute to the artistic life of the country. With the increased use of lithography and wood engraving for commercial and journalistic purposes, the various types of etching again became popular as fine arts media.

Prints frequently reveal a style halfway between the artist's most serious work and the popular taste of the day. Many of Whistler's finest etchings have a strong pictorial and illustrational emphasis that he would have considered too obvious for his full-sized paintings. *Black Lion Wharf* (17-3) combines a free sketchy charm and an accurate delineation of the sagging old wharves with a solidly wrought composition. Such scenes of the London waterfront reveal a graphic facility and vigor lacking in many of Whistler's paintings and so round out our sense of his artistic potential.

Mary Cassatt explored and rediscovered the possibilities of color etching, aquatint, and other print media usually neglected in favor of

17-3. J. A. McN. Whistler, *Black Lion Wharf*, 1859. International Business Machines Collection.

17-4. Mary Cassatt, *Young Woman Trying on a Dress*, n.d. Courtesy Metropolitan Museum of Art, Gift of Paul J. Sacks, 1916.

more commercially feasible processes. Japanese prints contributed to her feeling for flat decorative effects. In *Young Woman Trying on a Dress* (17-4) the subtly modulated color, pale and crisp, is as feminine and sensitive as the scattered patterns. Here again, one finds the characteristically impressionist translation of the familiar into the exotic.

Both John Sloan and George Bellows made prints on social and political themes which have a satiric thrust absent from most of their paintings. Sloan's *Fifth Avenue Critics* (17-5) achieves its aim as an amusing social commentary without weakening its impact as a richly designed, vigorously toned etching. Bellows's *Dance in a Madhouse* (17-6) has a power far beyond the journalistic zest that characterized most popular printmaking in these years. The tragic scene is depicted with compassion and irony. The spirit with which the dancers cavort in the gloomy ballroom surrounded by the depressed and isolated onlookers creates a paradox with overtones of both humor and horror. Velvety blacks, luminous grays, and sharp whites contribute to the dramatic effectiveness of the scene.

The etchings of architectural subjects, particularly cathedrals (17-7), by John Taylor Arms (1887-   ) reveal an incredible technical pro-

17-5 (*above*). John Sloan, *Fifth Avenue Critics*, 1905. Whitney Museum of American Art. New York.   17-6 (*below*). George Bellows. *Dance in a Madhouse*, 1917. Whitney Museum of American Art, New York.

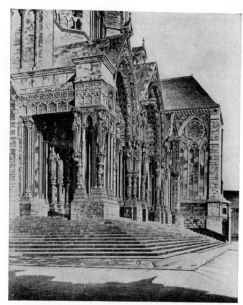

17-7. John Taylor Arms, *In Memoriam*, 1939. International Business Machines Collection.

ficiency, comparable to the works of medieval miniaturists in the skill with which microscopic details are depicted.

Joseph Pennell (1860-1926) illustrated books and magazines in a crisp pen-and-ink style which reproduced with clarity and effectiveness. His etchings reveal his skill with line and masses of line which build into broad tones. Pennell discovered the power of American industrial architecture, and some of his etchings of skyscrapers under construction or of steel mills belching smoke were most original in their perception of the visual grandeur of our great industrial centers (17-8).

Photography

The relationship between photography and art continued to be a subject of controversy well into the twentieth century. A number of technical advances in the nineties made obsolete the instruments with which Mathew Brady had made his records of the Civil War. Camera clubs flourished in the major American cities and a body of theoretical literature on the art of photography appeared. *Camera Work*, a quarterly, the most influential journal devoted to the new art of photography, appeared in 1900. Published under the leadership of Alfred Stieglitz (1864-1946), it encouraged a conscious esthetic emphasis on the part of the photographers. Stieglitz believed photography could become a major art form

17-8. Joseph Pennell, *Things That Tower*, n.d. Courtesy Metropolitan Museum of Art, Gift of David Keppel, 1917.

only by a sharp appraisal of the potentialities and limitations of the camera, and he recognized that the unique aspect of photography lay in the capacity of the camera to record the exact character of a situation. His esthetic sensibility was equaled by his sense of the socially significant moment and his deep human sympathies (17-9). Not all of his photographs, of course, were as direct and forceful as *Steerage*. Like many of his contemporaries, he frequently sentimentalized or dramatized the camera's objective records, manipulating the photographic image while exposing the film, developing the negatives, and making the prints.

Stieglitz, Edward Steichen, and a host of others explored the possibilities of creating photographic effects of a pictorial and painterly nature as in *Lady in Black with Statuette* (17-10) by Clarence White, published in *Camera Work* in 1908. The continuous movement of the light from the hand at the lower right to the statuette at the upper left reveals a conscious concern with compositional principles. The all-encompassing harmony of tone and the rich textures have been calculated with care. There was a continuous effort in the first decades of the century to

17-9. Alfred Stieglitz, *Steerage,* 1907. Philadelphia Museum of Art, Philadelphia.

17-10. Clarence White, *Lady in Black with Statuette,* 1908. George Eastman House, Rochester, N. Y.

17-11. Jacob A. Riis, *Bandits' Roost,* c. 1888. Jacob A. Riis Collection, Museum of the City of New York, New York.

discover new ways whereby the photographer might rival the painter in producing "artistic" effects. Painterly subjects were carefully arranged, and unusual textures were produced by making prints on heavily grained or very light papers. Etching needles and painter's brushes were used to enrich the negatives, and tissue paper was placed in front of the lens to create the much-admired diffused textures.

Not all of the photographers at the turn of the century were experimenting with painterly effects. A host of energetic minds and eyes used the camera to record the faces and figures of our leading personalities as well as the multifaceted variety and fascination of metropolitan life. Much of this photography had a humanitarian and democratic orientation and was directed against the inhumanity of the city slums and the squalid horror of poverty and evil. *Bandits' Roost* (17-11), by a Danish immigrant, Jacob Riis (1849-1914), is one of the earliest examples of documentary photography. Riis became a police reporter and, shocked by the sordid conditions of immigrant life which he knew from first-hand experience, photographed the ominous squalor of Mulberry Street with the directness and force born of indignation.

SCULPTURE

By the conclusion of the Civil War the passion for white marble sculpture and classic idealization of form had disappeared. An increasing number of sculptors decried the need to study abroad, stayed home, and

17-12. John Rogers, *Checkers Up at the Farm*, 1875. New York Historical Society, New York.

prided themselves on the fact that both their subject matter and their style were typically American. The foremost example of a sculptor whose success was based on his homespun tastes was John Rogers (1829-1904).

Rogers enjoyed a phenomenal success as the producer of small sculptural groups which depicted genre subjects, amusing anecdotes, and current events of historic and topical interest. When Rogers discovered the wide appeal of his figure groups he developed a flexible mold that would permit the manufacture of plaster copies of the originals. He set up a factory in New York, employed as many as sixty workmen, and mailed out printed circulars listing the various items and their dimensions and prices. *Checkers Up at the Farm* (17-12), one of his most popular groups, displays the characteristic combination of a vivacious narrative, convincing details, warmth, and humor. The forms, though not monumental, are vigorous, full-bodied, and well observed. Rogers shows an enviable facility in composing his groups to tell their story clearly and forcefully. The direction of gestures and glances moves in lively interplay with the main masses of form to create an animated relationship of all the parts. It is far from great sculpture, but it is honest, unhackneyed, and closely attuned to the life of the country. The verisimilitude of surface details, of textures of cloth, hair, basket, and barrel, the convincing facial expressions and character types are sculptural equivalents of the qualities that distinguished the genre paintings of Mount or Woodville.

17-13. John Q. A. Ward, *Indian Hunter*, 1866. New York Department of Parks photograph.

John Quincy Adams Ward (1830-1910) shared Rogers' skill in creating small figure groups but he did not restrict his activities to small-scale sculpture. Ward was one of the first of the mid-nineteenth-century sculptors to develop what was then considered an "American" style of handling life-size figures, which meant a somewhat dry and detailed realism. Ward was born in Ohio and in his youth showed an interest in modeling. At nineteen he went into the studio of Henry Kirke Brown where he served a short apprenticeship, while Brown was working on a great equestrian statue of George Washington for the city of New York. Ward had no formal training except for his contact with Brown.

After leaving Brown's studio, Ward spent a few years traveling on the western frontier and living among the Indians. The *Indian Hunter* (17-13), which now stands in New York's Central Park, was inspired by his observations of Indian life. The lithe, heavily muscled figures of the scowling Indian and his dog move in tense unity. Though the details of muscles, hair, and fur are sharply articulated, the powerful sense of movement and form carries the detail along with it. *Indian Hunter* was the first of a long line of sculptures depicting Indian life; in fact, a number of later sculptors such as Cyrus Dallin established their reputations as masters of the American style by specializing in Indian subjects.

After Ward's return to the East he was commissioned to do a number of life-size bronze figures of which his portrait of *Henry Ward Beecher*

17-14. John Q. A. Ward, *Henry Ward Beecher*, c. 1891. Courtesy Metropolitan Museum of Art, Rogers Fund, 1917.

(17-14) is the acknowledged masterpiece. The heavy, characterful crusader stands firm, relaxed, and unafraid, ready to carry on his fight for the freedom of the slaves. Ward appears to have been untouched by the corrosive devices of neo-classicism—the togas, rhetorical gestures, and idealizations of form. Instead, he created a monumental symbol in his figure of the courageous minister through his sympathetic understanding of the confident and dedicated personality. Without the obvious trappings of leadership, Ward's Beecher stands resolute, a leader of men. The vigor of this work leaves no question as to Ward's natural endowment as a sculptor.

Sculptors of the Far West

Indian lore and the life of the frontier provided some indigenous themes for the sculptors who preferred vivid local color. Frederic Remington, best known as a painter and illustrator, created some animated bronzes of cowboys and horses which are sculptural equivalents of his paintings. *Bronco Buster* (17-15), with its vigorous action and vivid character, re-

17-15. (*left*). Frederic Remington, *The Bronco Buster*, modeled *c.* 1890, this cast made *c.* 1901. Courtesy Metropolitan Museum of Art, Bequest of Jacob Ruppert, 1939. 17-16 (*below*). Gutzon Borglum, *Mares of Diomedes*, 1904. Newark Museum, Newark, N. J.

17-17. Augustus Saint-Gaudens, Farragut monument, 1881. Art Commission, New York, photograph.

veals his analytical eye as well as his thorough knowledge of the life of the cowboy. Remington's sculpture, like his paintings, shows little interest in academic concepts of design. Instead the tense and nervous forms and the broken surface textures express his direct reaction to the rigors of frontier existence.

The Borglum brothers also portrayed typical western subjects. Solon Borglum (1868-1922) created vivid small bronzes of bucking broncos and stampeding horses. Gutzon Borglum (1871-1941), the better known of the two brothers, is most famed for the two great sculptural projects in which he shaped the sides of mountains into the images of some of America's heroes. His portraits of Robert E. Lee in Georgia and of Washington, Jefferson, Lincoln, and Theodore Roosevelt on the face of Mount Rushmore in South Dakota are among the largest sculptural projects ever attempted. Tributes to the energy and engineering skill of the artist, their very size precludes the possibility of subtle sculptural values. Borglum's *Mares of Diomedes* (17-16) was the first piece of sculpture by an American to be purchased by the Metropolitan Museum of Art. The plunging mass of stampeding mares has been translated into sweeping lines, broken textures, and catapulting planes without violating the unity of the group or the character of bronze. Though many American sculptors prided themselves on constituting an American school of sculpture, there was a constant interplay between American and foreign, particularly French, influence. Even Borglum, an enthusiastic patriot, studied abroad and the *Mares of Diomedes* owes much of its sketchlike intensity to the example of Rodin.

Augustus Saint-Gaudens

The dominant figure in American sculpture from 1880 until his death in 1907 was undoubtedly Augustus Saint-Gaudens (1848-1907). Saint-Gaudens was born in Ireland of an Irish mother and a French father who immigrated to America while Saint-Gaudens was an infant. He commenced his study of art in New York, after a short time continued it in Paris, and followed this with a trip to Rome where he had an opportunity to observe the great sculptural monuments of the Renaissance. On his re-

17-18. Augustus Saint-Gaudens, Adams Memorial, 1893. Rock Creek Cemetery, Washington, D. C.

turn to America his sincerity and talent were readily recognized and by 1880 he was established as America's leading sculptor. Saint-Gaudens brought a grandeur of conception and subtlety of design to American sculpture that had hitherto been lacking. His sober realism and emotional restraint are typical American traits and his subject matter was drawn largely from American history. Saint-Gaudens' work falls into three general categories: large public monuments which represent his most ambitious undertakings and which added to the dignity of many American cities, full-length symbolic figures, and numerous sensitive portraits executed either in the round or as bas-relief plaques.

Saint-Gaudens introduced a number of innovations in designing public monuments. In collaboration with the architect Stanford White, he evolved a new type of base for a monumental figure in which the pedestal for the figure rises from a handsome high-backed bench decorated in bas-relief motifs related to the main figure. One of the early and very successful designs of this type is the Farragut monument (17-17) in New York City. Another innovation which Saint-Gaudens introduced was the use of ornamental lettering of great distinction as an element in the total decorative ensemble. The thoughtful interrelating of all parts of a monumental sculptural group—the base, figures, lettering, and ornamental detail—created new standards of excellence for commemorative monuments.

One of the handsomest memorials created by Saint-Gaudens was the tomb designed for Mrs. Henry Adams (17-18) at the request of her husband. The tomb is simple and austere in its main concept. A seated bronze figure, wrapped in voluminous draperies, leans against a great unbroken block of granite. The forms are broad and generalized and the disposition of light and shadow is masterly. The flowing contours of the draperies envelop the brooding head in a wavering, triangular arch, and from the evocative shadow, the face projects its grave poetry. The strength with which this figure projects its mood of inner quietude makes it a landmark in an age when sculptured memorials tended to be obvious in their elaboration and trite in their symbolism. The quiet figure lost in reverie has been variously interpreted as a symbol of grief, death, or divine peace. Though its specific meaning is obscure, the mysterious and solemn spirit that emanates from the figure creates a rare mood of spiritual intensity.

Saint-Gaudens created a number of portraits of great Americans in which the nobility of character is interpreted with both reticence and frankness. His portraits of Lincoln have become national symbols, and

17-19 (*left*). Daniel Chester French, *Alma Mater*, 1903. Columbia University, New York.   17-20 (*right*). Daniel Chester French, *Mourning Victory*, 1915. Courtesy Metropolitan Museum of Art, Gift of James C. Melvin, 1912.

they, in particular, reveal the sculptor's ability to endow the outward forms with a rare inner grace that appears almost at variance with the unidealized naturalism of external appearance. Saint-Gaudens even translated the awkward clothing of his era into bronze without any loss of realism or sculptural distinction by combining the broad simplifications of form necessary to achieve monumental grandeur with delicately articulated detail.

Daniel Chester French

Daniel Chester French (1850-1931) shared the major commissions of the late nineteenth century with Saint-Gaudens. Though French was not so powerful nor so sensitive as Saint-Gaudens, his ability to translate American types of men and women into idealized sculptural symbols insured his continued popularity well into the twentieth century, when he remained the chief practitioner of commemorative sculpture in the beaux-arts vein. French was born in New Hampshire, studied with Ward for a very short time, attended Rimmer's exciting lectures in anatomy, and with this sketchy preparation proceeded to execute a number of monuments. His early commissions were carried out in a somewhat dry and detailed manner. Later he spent a year in Italy, and in the eighties he studied in France. While abroad, he acquired the freer and more sensitive modeling and the nobler forms which distinguished the work of his later years. After his return from France, French executed a great number of sculptural monuments which, along with those of Saint-Gaudens, dominated the character of American sculpture until after World War I, when the more abstract and stylized manner replaced the traditional beaux-arts treatment of form.

The *Alma Mater* (17-19) at Columbia University reveals both the strength and the weakness of French's symbolic figures. The general massing of the form is broad and handsome and the figure has a quiet dignity well suited to its role. However, the idealized head, the broad gestures, and obvious symbolism appear conventional and trite, and the figure is without tension and a sense of inner life. Though conscientious and skilled, it lacks conviction and urgency.

French appeared at his best working with the semi-nude figure. His easy disposition of a decorative flow of lines can be seen most effectively in such monuments as his *Mourning Victory* (17-20). This memorial to three brothers who lost their lives in the Civil War is impressive because of its simplicity and the effective manner in which the handsome symbolic figure emerges from the stone stele. The full-bodied, almost sexless figure is enveloped in an easy flow of draperies which move with the elongated rhythms of the art-nouveau designers. The almost too facile perfection of the figure is accented by the subtle play of textures, of smooth skin against rough draperies which contrast, in turn, with the slightly horizontal pattern of chisel marks on the main mass of the stele. The rhythms of the figure are paralleled and complemented by the movements of the draperies; as the forms rise, the rhythmic movements of the draperies quicken and the space relationships deepen and become more complex. Though *Mourning Victory* is conventional in sentiment, the intelligence, taste, and skill of the artist almost obscure the lack of intense feeling.

French is probably best known for his seated Lincoln, in the Lincoln Memorial in Washington, D.C. The effectiveness of the figure results from the scale, the setting, and the dramatic lighting, for French is least effective in the monumental portrait. His was an art of sentimental idealism and technical proficiency which achieved a borrowed elegance by adopting the academic skills and tastes of late-nineteenth-century France.

17-21. Lorado Taft, Fountain of Time, detail, 1920. Art Institute of Chicago photograph.

Taft, Barnard, and Others

At the turn of the century Lorado Taft and George Gray Barnard were the leaders of a younger group of Paris-inspired men who reflected the powerful influence of Auguste Rodin. While the *École des Beaux Arts* inspired suavity of handling and elegance of effect, Rodin encouraged his disciples to work for intensity of feeling. Particularly persuasive were Rodin's vigorous, roughly modeled surfaces and his practice of allowing the partially completed figure to emerge like a nascent form from the surrounding envelope of material. Lorado Taft (1860-1936) was born in Illinois, attended the University of Illinois, then spent three years at the *École des Beaux Arts* in Paris. Taft's major commissions were large fountains such as the Fountain of Time (17-21) in Chicago. His early sculptures espoused the Renaissance ideal; his later works reveal the influence of Rodin—the detailed forms fuse with and emerge from the enveloping matrix. In the Fountain of Time the great panorama of civilization is symbolized by a sequence of figures representing crucial periods and episodes in history. This ambitious project, too pictorial to carry as a sculptural whole, has some fascinating and powerful details, but a tendency toward sentimentality and obvious idealizations frequently detracts from the effectiveness of the conception. In addition to his great fountains, Taft produced a number of portraits and memorial figures, taught and lectured at the Art Institute of Chicago, and wrote the first history of American sculpture.

17-22. George Gray Barnard, *Two Natures of Man*, marble, 1893, from plaster model, 1887. Courtesy Metropolitan Museum of Art, Gift of Alfred Corning Clark, 1896.

George Gray Barnard (1863-1938), born in Pennsylvania, spent most of his youth in the West. Driving ambition and an ability to endure great privation enabled him to spend twelve years living and working in Paris where he studied the great masterpieces in the Louvre and profited by the example of Rodin and the other late-nineteenth-century French sculptors. Barnard was an ardent disciple of Michelangelo and, like him, chose the nude as the vehicle for expressing powerful emotions and symbolizing moral values. A work of his youth, *Struggle between the Two Natures of Man* (17-22) provides an effective embodiment of his talents. In this work Barnard symbolized man's conflicted nature—his base and noble potentialities—through a pair of powerful figures bound together in a handsome baroque swirl of movement. The massive figures, inspired by Michelangelo's *Bound Slaves* and carved directly from a great block of marble, reveal his driving energy and philosophic temperament. Though the stone surface has been carefully finished and some of the anatomical detail elaborately developed, the total effect is unlabored and free since many areas have been left undeveloped and sweeping movements carry through all parts of the composition. The *Struggle between the Two Natures of Man* remains Barnard's best-known work. Its success rests not only on its visual effectiveness but also on the universality of its theme.

Frederick W. MacMonnies (1863-1937) introduced a gayer and more sensuous note. MacMonnies was born in Brooklyn and was a student of

17-23. Frederick W. MacMonnies, *Bacchante, c.* 1894. Brooklyn Museum, Brooklyn, N. Y.

Saint-Gaudens from his sixteenth to his twenty-first year. Temperamentally he had little in common with Saint-Gaudens although he acquired an admirable technical training from the American master. His style was strongly influenced by his later years in Paris where he acquired a vivid pictorial manner characterized by animated surface modeling. MacMonnies executed a number of elaborate public monuments in which his large compositions, whether in bas-relief or the round, reveal an extraordinary skill in organizing large numbers of forms into a unified composition that is picturesque and vivid in its pictorial elements. A marble replica of his *Bacchante* (17-23), originally done in bronze, reveals his taste for a vivacious, charming subject. Like most of MacMonnies' work, it has no hidden symbolism or earnest message—it exists as an end in itself. The introduction of this Gallic note of candid delight in sensuous beauty particularly distinguished MacMonnies from the other sculptors of his day.

In the first decade of the twentieth century certain innovations which were to flower in the period following World War I began to be evident. Sculptors abandoned the practice of first modeling forms in plaster and began to work directly in permanent materials. The more progressive sculptors turned to the arts of the Orient, to archaic cultures, and to primitive peoples for fresh inspiration and variety. Most significantly, monumental realism, the goal of sculptors since Renaissance times, and the use of allegory and symbolism gave way to a greater concern with the purely visual elements of sculptural design.

INSTITUTIONS AND ART PATRONAGE

Private collections of distinction became increasingly frequent in the years following the Civil War. In 1864 James Jackson Jarves, whose own collection was to form part of the nucleus of the Yale University Gallery of Fine Arts, noted: "It has become the mode to have a taste . . . private galleries in New York are becoming almost as common as private stables." Just as the Jarves acquisitions laid the foundation for the Yale collection, the Walters collection provided the start for the Walters Gallery in Baltimore, while the Corcoran did the same for Washington, and the Crocker for Sacramento. Not only were private collections of significant proportions being formed, but by 1870 the National Museum in Washington was receiving federal support and a number of state museums had been established. Within the next few years two of the most important museums in the United States were instituted—the Metropolitan Museum of Art in New York and the Museum of Fine Arts in Boston. Both of these were chartered with boards of trustees to direct their affairs, and they received municipal financial support. Through their organization these institutions established the pattern for American museums, the majority of which were founded between 1870 and 1915. While at first the museums of art concentrated upon the acquisition of paintings and sculpture, in 1906 the Metropolitan Museum acquired an extensive collection of decorative arts and established a department of European Decorative Arts. Soon such departments became a part of most of the major museum collections.

James Jackson Jarves not only affected American taste through his distinguished collection, but he also pointed to the need for schools which would provide a more solid foundation of skill in the arts. By the time of his death in the 1880's, the Pennsylvania Academy of Fine Arts, Philadelphia, and Cooper Union and the Art Students League, both of New York, were well established, and such mature painters as Hunt, Eakins, Chase, and Duveneck were teaching on their staffs.

American universities also reflected the growing interest in the arts. Charles Eliot Norton of Harvard instituted a series of lectures on art history. Bernard Berenson, the great critic of Renaissance art, and Mrs. Jack Gardner, one of Boston's most ambitious collectors, both came under Norton's sympathetic tutelage. Under the stimulus of Norton's example at Harvard, other universities instituted courses in art history. As a liberal philosophy of education began to permeate the American schools, courses in painting, drawing, and design became part of the university curriculum.

Instruction in art in the public schools began in Massachusetts in 1872, when Walter Smith was brought from England to become the State Director of Art Education. He served as the first principal of the Massachusetts Normal Art School, where he drafted a curriculum to train qualified teachers of art for the public schools. Within a relatively short time, art instruction was introduced in the upper grades and in the secondary schools in many parts of the country. Simultaneously, a wide variety of art activities was included in the growing kindergarten movement, for one of its chief tenets was to avoid undue emphasis upon verbalization and to stimulate small children to work freely with various materials to develop their creative powers.

Concurrent with the growth of museum facilities and art education, there was an increase in the publication of periodicals and books devoted to the arts. By 1914 America had achieved an impressive level of maturity in the arts. In architecture, painting, sculpture, industrial design, and crafts as well as in institutional organizations and patronage, America was prepared to take her place beside the older cultures of Europe when another great cataclysm, World War I, broke the continuity of development.

SELECTED REFERENCES

for PART IV Between Two Wars: 1865-1915

General References

Cahill, Holger and Barr, Alfred H., Jr., *Art in America, a Complete Survey.* New York, Reynal and Hitchcock, 1935.

La Follette, Suzanne, *Art in America.* New York, Harper & Brothers, 1935.

Larkin, Oliver, *Art and Life in America.* New York, Rinehart & Company, 1949.

Mumford, Lewis, *The Brown Decades.* New York, Harcourt, Brace & Company, 1931.

Architecture

Andrews, Wayne, *Architecture, Ambition and Americans.* New York, Harper & Brothers, 1955.

Fitch, James Marston, *American Building.* Boston, Houghton Mifflin Company, 1948.

Hamlin, Talbot, *The American Spirit in Architecture,* Pageant of America Series, Vol. 13, 1926. New Haven, Conn., Yale University Press.

Hitchcock, H. R., Jr., *The Architecture of H. H. Richardson and His Times.* New York, Museum of Modern Art, 1936.

Morrison, Hugh, *Louis Sullivan, Prophet of Modern Architecture.* New York, W. W. Norton & Company, 1935.

Mumford, Lewis, *Sticks and Stones.* New York, Boni, 1924.

Tallmadge, Thomas, *The Story of Architecture in America.* New York, W. W. Norton & Company, 1927.

Painting and Sculpture

Barker, Virgil, *American Painting.* New York, The Macmillan Company, 1950.

Bauer, John H., *American Painting in the Nineteenth Century.* New York, Frederick A. Praeger, Inc., 1953.

Burroughs, Alan, *A History of American Landscape Painting.* New York, Whitney Museum of American Art, 1942.

Boswell, Peyton, *George Bellows.* New York, Crown Publishers, Inc., 1942.

Eliot, Alexander, *Three Hundred Years of American Painting.* New York, Time, Inc., 1957.

Frankenstein, Alfred, *After the Hunt: William Harnett and Other American Still Life Painters*. Berkeley, Calif., University of California Press, 1953.

Goodrich, Lloyd, *Thomas Eakins, His Life and Work*. New York, Whitney Museum of American Art, 1933.

Goodrich, Lloyd, *Winslow Homer*. New York, The Macmillan Company, 1944.

Goodrich, Lloyd, *Albert P. Ryder*. New York, Whitney Museum of American Art, 1947.

Goodrich, Lloyd, *John Sloan*. New York, Whitney Museum of American Art, 1952.

Isham, Samuel and Cortissoz, Royal, *The History of American Painting*. New York, The Macmillan Company, 1927.

Larkin, Oliver W., *Samuel F. B. Morse and American Democratic Art*. Boston, Little Brown & Company, 1954.

Lipman, Jean and Winchester, Alice, *Primitive Painting in America 1750-1950*. New York, Dodd, Mead & Company, 1950.

McCausland, Elizabeth, *George Inness*. New York, American Artists Group, 1946.

Neuhaus, Eugene, *The History and Ideals of American Art*. Stanford, Calif., Stanford University Press, 1931.

Richardson, E. P., *Painting in America*. New York, Thomas Y. Crowell Company, 1956.

Sweet, Frederick, *Sargent, Whistler and Mary Cassatt*. Chicago, Art Institute of Chicago, 1954.

Taft, Lorado, *History of American Sculpture*. New York, The Macmillan Company, 1930.

Interiors, Furniture, Crafts, and Industrial Design

Aronson, Joseph, *The Encyclopedia of Furniture*. New York, Crown Publishers, Inc., 1938.

Christensen, Irwin O., *The Index of American Design*. New York, The Macmillan Company, 1950.

Kouwenhoven, John A., *Made in America*. Garden City, N. Y., Doubleday & Company, 1949.

Editors of Life, *America's Arts & Skills*, New York, E. P. Dutton & Company, 1957.

Lynes, Russell, *The Tastemakers*. New York, Harper & Brothers, 1954.

Rogers, Meyric R., *American Interior Design*. New York, W. W. Norton & Company, 1947.

PART V

Today: 1915-1960

Contemporary

Architecture

TRAVEL, THE UNIVERSALITY OF LITERATURE AND PICTORIAL materials, museum collections, and scientific thought have made contemporary culture international. Each year architecture, painting, sculpture, and the household and industrial arts grow more alike all over the world. One can logically think of the modern style as world-wide, subject to national and regional variations.

Change has probably been the outstanding characteristic of the years following World War I and nowhere is the changed character of modern life more evident than in the United States. Age-old traditions and handicraft practices are disappearing all over the world before industrialization and the attendant standardized production of goods, and these processes have been greatly accelerated here.

A brief outline of the steps through which building styles have evolved in the United States since 1915 may help clarify this complex period.

(1) In the years between 1915 and 1925 the brilliant innovations of Sullivan, Wright, and the craftsmen designers were in eclipse. Most of the building in these years was sensible, practical but uninspired, with the many technological advances receiving little stylistic acknowledgment.

(2) From 1925 to 1940, the mechanized, geometrically precise mode of building that grew so naturally from modern standardized and industrialized building practices received a brilliant expression in skyscraper design (18-2).

During these same years Frank Lloyd Wright assumed the position of leadership implicit in his early work. Wright "humanized" the architecture of the industrial age, introducing a fresh feeling for materials and site as well as for dramatic and emotional values into contemporary practice (18-9).

(3) The influence of many European designers, forced to flee to America in the early thirties, became increasingly apparent in the late thirties. These men practiced a logical, refined, and esthetically conscious interpretation of precise mechanized architecture. Termed the International Style it became firmly integrated into American building practices in the years following World War II (18-16).

(4) Since 1945 new technology for building with metal, glass, and concrete as well as for handling more traditional materials such as wood, stone, and brick has stimulated fresh and imaginative designs for houses, stores, parking garages, and a wide variety of other types of building (18-23).

A number of contemporary designers are enriching current practices by reintroducing such traditional elements as heavy timber construction, ornamental tiles, mosaics, and other structural devices and decorative materials. There is promise that increasing diversity will characterize building practices in the future (18-31).

THE SKYSCRAPER

By 1915 it appeared that the vigorous and direct expression of form through function that had characterized skyscraper design in the Chicago area at the end of the nineteenth century was destined to disappear. In the battle between the progressive architects and the academicians, the conservative forces won, as they had in many other areas of American life during these years. The business districts of our major cities grew at a startling pace, particularly during the twenties, and buildings soared ever

18-1. Eliel Saarinen, Second-prize design for Chicago Daily Tribune competition, 1922. Chicago Tribune photograph.

higher in a continuous effort to increase revenue. As though to hide the purely commercial nature of these edifices, the street façades were loaded with attached columns, pilasters, arches, rows of attached arcades, string-courses, and classical moldings. The whole composition was inevitably capped by a heavy projecting cornice, the final and decisive gesture for making a twentieth-century commercial building academically respecta-ble. Revealing a fundamental esthetic dishonesty was the custom of decorating only the street façade, leaving the remaining walls ugly sur-faces of brick or concrete punctured with windows.

As the buildings towered higher, the narrow streets became shadowy canyons, congested and cut off from light and air. During the hours when the great buildings disgorged their workers, the streets became virtually impassable. In order to control the growth of these chasms, New York City passed a 1916 zoning ordinance which limited the height to which buildings could rise directly from the sidewalks. This forced builders to design very high buildings or buildings facing narrow streets with a series of setbacks, creating a sequence of receding building blocks placed one above another. These receding steps not only permitted light and air to enter the street below but also provided more variety of form in the buildings. Soon other American cities followed the example of New York and passed ordinances limiting both the total height of buildings and the height to which they could rise directly above the curb.

In 1922 the Chicago Daily Tribune held an international design competition for a great skyscraper to house their main offices and provide rental space. More than two hundred and fifty designs were submitted. The prize-winning design by John Howells and Raymond Hood combined certain characteristics of the evolving stepped-back skyscraper with such Gothic details as flying buttresses, pinnacles, and stone tracery. Though more suave than the Woolworth Building and bolder in its vertical thrust, it made no significant contribution to skyscraper design. The second-prize design (18-1), by a Finnish architect, Eliel Saarinen, appeared at a most propitious moment. Architects were striving to find a form for the piles of building blocks created by the new zoning laws, and Saarinen suggested an original solution. Saarinen's design for the Tribune tower is made up of a series of great vertical rectangular masses which build into a central tower. The expression of upward growth against a composition of rectangular masses is continuous and rhythmic. All cornices and horizontal accents are eliminated so that the vertical piers between the windows and at the corners of the building continue upward until they appear to pierce the skyline. Instead of conceiving of the skyscraper as a pictorial composition of flat façades, Saarinen approached it as a problem in three-dimensional composition. Seen from the perspective of time, Saarinen's conception seems tentative and fussy in detail, but its importance lay in the timely direction it gave to skyscraper design. Its influence was tremendous and immediate. A vertical emphasis, the play of rectangular masses of form against one another, and a stylistically effective simplicity became characteristic of the new school of skyscraper design.

Raymond Hood

Raymond Hood (1881-1934), one of the creators of the Chicago Tribune Tower, designed a number of brilliant and original skyscrapers between 1925 and 1935, a decade which produced some of America's largest and most impressive buildings. In the Daily News Building (18-2), New York City, the skyscraper concept was reduced to its essentials. Here

18-2 (*left*). Raymond Hood, Daily News Building, 1929. New York City. New York Daily news photograph. 18-3 (*right*). Raymond Hood, McGraw-Hill Building, 1931. New York City. McGraw-Hill Company photograph.

the tendency toward simplification which grew from the underlying pressure for economy as well as from the impersonal character of modern industrial processes became a deliberate stylistic and esthetic device. In the Daily News Building regularity and impersonality are translated into continuous, cold polished surfaces, soaring lines, and the precise geometry of sharp-edged forms. By being tied into continuous vertical stripes through the insertion of dark-colored surfacing between them, even the windows cease to relate the scale of the building to man, thereby increasing the impersonal and abstract character of the structure. No sculptural ornaments relieve the flat planes of the surfaces, no moldings or cornices encumber the sheer, clifflike walls. The Daily News Building owes its

18-4. Raymond Hood and associates, Rockefeller Center, 1931-1935. New York City. Ewing Galloway photograph.

effectiveness to the brilliance with which it states the skyscraper concept without any concessions to popular tastes.

Raymond Hood was not content to repeat the formula that was used so successfully in the Daily News Building. In 1930 he designed the McGraw-Hill Building (18-3), which provides an equally brilliant statement of another aspect of the skyscraper. The McGraw-Hill Building dramatizes the role of the wall as a protective sheathing rather than as a weighty support. The continuous bands of window glass encircle the structure, story above story, revealing the light, nonsupportive character of the exterior sheathing. As in the Daily News Building, all of the traditional devices which suggest weight and sculptural richness have been eliminated, and the only decorative elements are the geometric stripes created by the bands of windows. The great monumental bulk of the building soars above its surrounding, a powerful tribute to the technology of the industrial age and to the industrial empires of America. Rockefeller Center (18-4), on which Raymond Hood cooperated, presents the most extensive assemblage of skyscrapers to be erected in a related scheme.

The size of the entire project as well as of the individual buildings is awesome—the RCA Building lifts its seventy-story tower in one sheer upward thrust. The fifteen buildings which make up Rockefeller Center, often called a "city within a city," achieve their effectiveness by size, by the dramatic relationships between towers, lower buildings, and surrounding empty spaces, and by the brilliant elimination of trite ornamental devices. The entire project represents the ultimate development of the multistoried business building as it had been conceived of in the period before World War II.

The skyscraper was the most obvious symbol of American society in the early twentieth century. A direct outgrowth of the wealth, power, and technological efficiency of our industrial order as well as of the mercantile orientation of our culture, it expressed both the scale of our industrial empires and the cold impersonality that characterized many aspects of our industrial society. Though the most spectacular symbol of American building, it represented only one of the many architectural forms that developed during these productive years. Hundreds of special types of buildings evolved in answer to the increased complexity and specialization of American life. Motion-picture theaters, department stores, schools, and hospitals reveal the endless adaptability, ingenuity, and inventiveness of the American designer. The great factories (18-5) provided a particularly forceful expression of the dynamic vigor and size

18-5. Ford factory, Dearborn, Mich.
Ford Motor Company photograph.

of American industry. The stark power of the industrial world stands in undisguised nakedness. The formidable cubes, spheres, and interlacing runways and scaffoldings, sheathed in iron, glass, concrete, and brick are not softened by any sensuous enhancements but express the complex processes and interrelationships of our industrial organization with a brutal but magnificent strength. The skyscraper provided the façade for the American industrial system; the factory, the workshop.

Frank Lloyd Wright

It is significant that the foremost American architect of the twentieth century, Frank Lloyd Wright (1869-1959), never concerned himself seriously with the problem of skyscraper design. Instead, Wright stood as the opponent of skyscraper culture and spent his life in a continuous battle against size for its own sake, against mechanization irrespective of human values, and against the antisocial aspects of metropolitan life. In his work, Wright, more than any other individual, achieved a synthesis of all the varied and conflicting tendencies which characterized twentieth-century architecture. Particularly significant was his ability to accept and utilize the machine and industrialization without sacrificing dramatic and emotional values. To appreciate fully the significance of his contribution to the history of American architecture, it is necessary to move back to the nineteenth century, for Wright was a creative force for more than sixty years.

Frank Lloyd Wright was born in Michigan. His father had come from the East to teach music but became a Unitarian minister instead, and Wright grew up in an atmosphere of poverty, music, morality, and Welsh sentiment. Early in life he adjudged the Middle West as the home of the "real American spirit capable of judging an issue for itself upon its merits." At eighteen he quit the School of Engineering at the University of Wisconsin. Within a year he was working in the office of Adler and Sullivan. With his forthright egotism, he claimed to be "the best paid draftsman in the city of Chicago." The six years that he worked for Adler and Sullivan constituted his education in architecture. When Daniel H. Burnham tried to lure him into his office by offering to pay all his living expenses for a protracted period in France and Italy, Wright declined on the basis that Sullivan had spoiled the *Beaux Arts* for him, and him for the *Beaux Arts*. In 1893, he opened his own office. From the beginning Wright practiced his profession according to his convictions. He designed what he termed "organic" architecture, in which the form was determined

18-6. Frank Lloyd Wright, Robie House, 1909. Chicago, Museum of Modern Art photograph.

by the function and the construction—architecture which grew from the "inside out," as he put it. He sought inspiration in the great periods of organic architecture of the past. He admired the architecture of the Middle Ages, although he never imitated its surface mannerisms, and paid tribute to the Japanese, who, he declared, "have never outraged wood in their art or in their craft."

Feeling that the democratic spirit needed something better than the box in which to develop, he proceeded to ignore the cell-like partitioning of houses into separate rooms and used walls as screens to direct the flow of space and increase the mobility of the living patterns within the home. A number of his early houses designed for the Great Plains area represented an astonishing revolution in domestic architecture.

One of the greatest of his early designs is the Robie House (18-6), built in Chicago in 1909, in which he achieved a most distinguished statement of the "prairie style." The keynote is the forceful emphasis on horizontal lines created by the extended floor plan, the spreading terraces, horizontally grouped rows of windows, low roofs, and broadened and lengthened eaves. The horizontal emphasis relates the house to the terrain; the house seems to emerge slowly from the prairie and gradually to build to a massive chimney. The long, low line of the eaves also repeats the distant horizon and thereby relates the building to the spaciousness of the western plains. The extending eaves temper the hot summer sun and the harsh glare of winter's snow, permitting extensive use of window areas which relate the interior to the outdoors.

In the Robie House, Wright also demonstrated his ability to combine weight and monumentality with exhilarating movement. This is achieved by the bold repetition of dominant lines counterbalanced by strategically placed oppositional lines. The air-borne quality of the winglike spread of roof strikes an almost prophetic note. Here too one perceives his feeling for the decorative effect of great unbroken surfaces and of geometric forms which are a foil for the surrounding natural forms and patterns of light and shadow. Noteworthy, too, is the simplicity of the materials. At a time of artificiality and pretentious elaboration, the dramatic simplicity and integrity of the Robie House were revolutionary.

The interiors of the prairie houses (19-1) followed Wright's credo as conscientiously as did the exteriors and were as far removed from the modes of the day. In the interests of serenity and repose, they contained as few rooms as intelligent living permitted. Doors and windows were part of the structural and visual patterns, not mere holes punched in walls. Decorative effects were produced by the imaginative use of such structural necessities as exposed beams and carpentered joints. Appliances, fixtures, and furniture were assimilated into the design of the whole, thereby creating a unified and harmonious entity. Wright's contribution to interior design is discussed more thoroughly in Chapter 19.

Wright created a number of notable houses in the Middle West, but not all of his genius was expended on domestic architecture. One of his early designs for industry was the Administration Building for the Larkin Company of Buffalo, New York, which set a precedent for dignity and orderliness in a business structure. In 1905 he established a milestone for ecclesiastical design in Unity Church of Oak Park, Illinois, through his use of concrete, a material which had been considered lacking in any esthetic potential. He poured the concrete in great masses, relieved only by the slightest surface textures, so that the monumental forms have the dignity of an Egyptian temple without the irrelevance of an anachronism.

In the years between World War I and the nineteen-thirties, Wright seemed particularly concerned with the structural possibilities of the new materials being made available by modern industry and with devising more effective floor plans for a variety of buildings ranging from simple cottages to large hotels. Though he utilized steel, glass, concrete, and other modern synthetics, he remained devoted to such traditional materials as wood, stone, brick, and tile. In exploiting glass and steel and open space, he never lost his mastery of weight and monumentality. Though keenly aware of the esthetic potential of the machine and modern mass-production techniques, Wright retained a high regard for ornamentation

18-7 (*above*). Frank Lloyd Wright, S. C. Johnson & Son Research Center and Administration Building, 1930-1951. Racine, Wis. Corning Glass Works photograph. 18-8 (*right*). Frank Lloyd Wright, S. C. Johnson & Son Administration Building, interior. S. C. Johnson & Son, Inc., photograph.

18-9. Frank Lloyd Wright, Falling Water, 1936. Bear Run, Pa. Wayne Andrews photograph.

and the craftsman who creates it. Like Sullivan, he continued to employ ornament as a lyric modulation of the surface, a delicate "perfume" which adds another dimension of beauty to architecture.

The work of Wright's later years reveals his inventive approach to structural problems and his rich feeling for form and materials. One, the Research Center and Administration Building (18-7) for S. C. Johnson and Son in Racine, Wisconsin, is composed of two related buildings, one constructed in the thirties, the other in 1951. The interior of the Administration Building is distinguished by its great "lily pad" columns (18-8). These columns represent a structural device of great visual beauty and efficiency. They spring from a narrow base, expanding at the capitals to support a most unusual ceiling of pyrex glass tubing which admits a beautifully diffused light. The later Research Center has been described as a "web of glass spun around a hollow reinforced concrete stem." The smooth bulk of the towering mass reconciles conflicting architectural ideals by appearing both monumental and without weight.

One of Wright's great houses from the thirties helps to round out our picture of the scope of his imagination. Falling Water (18-9), a house built at Bear Run, Pennsylvania, for Edgar J. Kaufmann, has been termed "a matchless fusion of fantasy and engineering." The great projecting cantilevered levels of the house which hang over a turbulent mountain stream have been anchored into the surrounding stony walls of the mountain. The house is built largely of rough stone, although photographs

18-10. Frank Lloyd Wright, Taliesin West, 1938. Phoenix, Ariz. Wayne Andrews photograph.

emphasize the bold projecting white concrete porches. The three main elements of the structure—the handsome stone masonry masses, the concrete cantilevered horizontal porch forms, and the great expanses of glass —create a beautiful abstract crystalline structure which is at the same time an admirable country home. Bear Run combines the smooth continuity of line and the light spaciousness of the contemporary style with a romanticist's love of natural materials and feeling for nature.

This fusion of today and yesterday also distinguishes the two dramatic and highly original houses Wright built for himself. In speaking of Taliesin North, his summer home in Wisconsin, Wright said, ". . . no house should ever be on any hill. . . . It should be of the hill, belonging to it." Taliesin North stands as a tribute to his belief that the character of a building must be inextricably related to its site. Taliesin West (18-10) was Wright's winter home near Phoenix, Arizona. Built of red desert stone, canvas, and weathered timbers, Taliesin West spreads its bold angularities of form and startling contrasts of color and tone into the brilliant glare of the desert light with an assured sense of the drama of the southwestern landscape. This conception, of sufficient power to hold its own amidst the vast spaces and powerful forms of the desert, is a tribute to Wright's ability to invent the forms demanded by the landscape. Though living in a period when mechanization seemed about to exclude all earthy, warm, and human touches from building, Wright proved able to accept the machine and utilize it, but remain free of its domination. In an age increasingly urban in outlook, Wright remained committed to what is rural.

Human nature, the rich heritage of world culture, the landscape, and a wealth of simple building materials remained his sources of inspiration. The machine remained his servant.

EUROPEAN INFLUENCES

Except for Wright there was little progressive architecture in the second and third decades of the century. America was content to build bigger and more comfortably, if not better and more beautifully, and the center of progressive architectural design shifted to Europe. France witnessed experiments in architectural design as daring as those which were revolutionizing French painting and sculpture. The Scandinavians, in a period of social enlightenment and economic expansion, undertook extensive building programs. Germany, Austria, Czechoslovakia, and Holland, recovering from World War I, were in the throes of reconstructing their demolished cities and of reorganizing their dislocated economies. The older architectural concepts which stressed a weighty, monumental, ornamented mass were completely unsuited to the exigencies of the new day. The urgent need was to rebuild and expand the cities of central Europe so as to provide business and manufacturing facilities, and housing for the middle and working classes. Under great economic pressures, the progressive European architects of the postwar years shifted from a building tradition based on ancient handicraft practices to a modern mass production basis. At the same time they faced the problem of evolving a modern style which would provide a refined and powerful esthetic expression to the technological resources and the social forces of the twentieth century. The architectural style of the twentieth century, the International Style, was one answer. The term International Style became widely accepted because the technology and social organization that provided the basis for the style overrode national boundaries, and the style developed almost entirely independently of the older local and national architectural traditions. The center for the formulation of the International Style was the Bauhaus school of design in Dessau, Germany.

Two social catastrophes reunited the architectural developments in Europe and America. In Germany in the early thirties the advent of fascism forced a large number of the most progressive designers to flee for refuge to America. Here, a great economic recession, followed by World War II and the subsequent building boom, revealed the need for a fresh evaluation of American building practices. Among the distinguished architects who sought asylum in America were Walter Gropius

(1883-   ), Ludwig Miës van der Rohe (1886-   ), Eric Mendelsohn (1887-1953), Richard Neutra (1892-   ), and Marcel Breuer (1902-   ). These men established themselves as teachers and designers during the thirties, and in the period of expansion that followed World War II had a significant influence on American building practice.

Walter Gropius

Walter Gropius led the Bauhaus from its inception because of his clear perception of the role of the arts in an industrial age. Founder of the Bauhaus and its first director, he designed the buildings for the school when it moved to Dessau, and in so doing provided one of the purest formulations of the new style. Gropius believed that modern designers had to be trained in the resources of industry and machine production to provide an all-embracing esthetic philosophy governing architecture, the applied arts, painting, and sculpture. In America, Gropius has continued to direct contemporary thinking as the head of the School of Architecture at Harvard. In addition, he has remained active as an architect through The Architects Collaborative, where he works with Marcel Breuer and others. One design emerging from this fruitful interplay of talents is the Junior High School (18-11) in Attleboro, Massachusetts,

18-11. Walter Gropius, Attleboro Junior High School, 1948. Attleboro, Mass. Ezra Stoller photograph.

which takes advantage of an uneven site to avoid the monotony that so often characterizes a public school. The classrooms form the main two-story block of a group of interdependent connected buildings. The gymnasium and the auditorium establish their individual entities through differences in height and specialized forms. The view of a wing of classrooms and an inner court from a glazed corridor reveals the serenity that results from a regular rhythm of forms integrated into a lucid functional arrangement.

Ludwig Miës van der Rohe

One of the prophetic individuals in formulating the principles of the International Style was Ludwig Miës van der Rohe. As a result of the distinction of his brilliant designs in the early twenties, Miës was appointed director of the Werkbund exhibition in Stuttgart in 1927, which presented a summing up of the advanced current practices in architectural design. His first major commission executed in the United States was his design for the Illinois Institute of Technology. This great project, extending over several city blocks, includes classrooms, laboratory buildings, a chapel, faculty living quarters, and a boiler house (18-12). Miës related and unified this great complex of specialized buildings by developing his plan in 25-foot units applied like a grid over the entire site. The individual buildings have been conceived primarily as problems in structure. The steel supporting frames, clearly articulated, supply both the structural

18-12. Ludwig Miës van der Rohe, Illinois Institute of Technology, boiler plant, 1950. Chicago. Hedrich-Blessing photograph.

18-13. Ludwig Miës van der Rohe, Farnsworth House, 1950. Plano, Ill. Bill Hedrich, Hedrich-Blessing photograph.

framework and the element of visual regularity so essential to the anonymous dignity that distinguishes the buildings. Panels of brick and glass provide the enclosing walls. The austerity of the project comes as a surprise after the elegance of Miës's distinguished European buildings until one recognizes that the same high standards of craftsmanship and the same clear statement of structure are dominant elements both here and in his earlier designs, and that the visual differences are a logical outgrowth of the differing functions of the buildings and of the building materials.

The Farnsworth House (18-13), built in 1950 by Miës van der Rohe, revealed a number of the elements traditionally associated with his name —the extensive areas of glass, the dominantly horizontal emphasis, the transparent openness, the graceful light supports and thin floating horizontal planes, and the machined elegance that results from exquisite craftsmanship. The house consists of a floor and roof plane supported by eight steel columns. A broad, low platform, also supported by steel posts, is set to one side of the main slab and provides a terrace for outdoor activities. A wood-paneled enclosed area at one side of the interior contains heating, bathroom, kitchen, and storage facilities. The glass exterior walls are draped. The concept of architecture embodied in such a structure is a crystallization in contemporary building techniques of a concept of living as radical as the architectural style. A number of the characteristics of the International Style which have received an unusually pure and brilliant expression in this building and in the boiler room of the Institute of Technology might well be summarized here.

The use of steel and concrete for structural purposes eliminated the load-bearing function of the wall and permitted the enclosure of extensive interior spaces with glass and other lightweight surfacing materials. Walls, freed from their load-bearing role, served as baffles or boundaries to define the movements of space and light, and the continuous flow of light and air became as important in the modern style as weight had been in earlier times.

The International Style depended on the factory and the industrial technology of our age, on standardization, mechanization, and the pre-fabrication of interchangeable parts. Instead of striving for the picturesque and unique effects savored by the nineteenth-century romantics, the esthetic possibilities of regularity, of repetition, of mechanical perfection, and of a certain abstract impersonality were utilized. Making a virtue of necessity, the varied forms demanded by the specialized nature of much modern building were emphasized with bold forthrightness to create stark and expressive shapes of great diversity. Extensive expanses of bare wall, long continuous bands of window glass, the geometric patterns of structural steel and open beams became positive stylistic factors. Applied decoration was rigidly eliminated, making color and surface texture increasingly important esthetic elements. The exterior sheathing provided a smooth, all-encompassing skin, stretched tight over the surfaces like a protective membrane.

In general, the International Style was technological rather than geographical in its orientation. This explains one of the major differences between the thinking of a man like Miës van der Rohe and of Frank Lloyd Wright. The International Style remained much the same whether practiced in New York, Los Angeles, Rio, or Berlin.

The style demanded a fresh evaluation of contemporary living patterns to provide plans commensurate with current social needs and practices. Sheathing the entire exterior of the Farnsworth house with glass, like the current practice of providing parking space for automobiles on the roofs of department stores, involved a sympathetic acknowledgment of the changes that were revolutionizing modern life.

Mendelsohn and Neutra

A number of the influential architects who came from Central Europe during these years were not directly associated with the Bauhaus.

18-14. Eric Mendelsohn, Maimonides Hospital, 1950. San Francisco, Calif. Wayne Andrews photograph.

Eric Mendelsohn's most striking early work in Germany had been more related to expressionism than to the mechanistic style of the Bauhaus group. He designed Maimonides Hospital (18-14) in San Francisco in the idiom of the International Style, but the rhythmic semicircular extensions of the balconies recall his earlier taste for a sculptural treatment of architectural form. A one-story entrance pavilion leads to a landscaped inner court and then to the fourteen-story main building. The continuous glass façade, the ramp, the doorway, and the protective overhang of the entrance pavilion have been treated with the impersonality of a geometric theorem. No dramatic or decorative interruptions soften its severe regularity. On the garden façade rise the successive balconied stories, cantilevered out from the supporting columns and framed by projecting end walls. The semicircular balconies enclosed by light iron railings, both useful and visually diverting, create a buoyant composition of geometric forms. The building provides a pure, lucid, and impersonal solution of

18-15. Richard Neutra, Warren Tremaine House, 1949. Montecito, Calif. Julius Shulman photograph.

the specialized problems of a convalescent hospital, using modern building techniques without sacrificing vivacity or variety.

Richard Neutra settled in Los Angeles in the late twenties and contributed greatly to the development of modern residential architecture in California by using regular 3-foot modules to insure efficiency and visual consistency. Neutra was one of the first to use light steel posts and to standardize details for framing doors, windows, roofs, and built-in furniture. The handsome houses of his later years are more expensive and luxurious than his early work. In his house for Warren Tremaine (18-15), built in Montecito in 1949, weightier supporting posts, ceiling beams, and stone walls act as a counterpoint to the broad expanses of glass and the flowing open spaces. The living-dining areas provide a center for the four extended wings which house bedrooms, a swimming pavilion, and various services. The roof is a thin slab of concrete supported by beams and posts of reinforced concrete. The house is well adapted to the handsome site and to the warm climate and informal social life of southern California.

In the late thirties the paralyzing grip of the depression began to lift, and America was about to resume building, but World War II stopped all normal activity. By the end of the war there was an acute need for housing, industrial architecture, and commercial building. Costs soared and there were few experienced craftsmen. The inadequacy of the older eclectic revival modes of building was apparent to even the most conservative designers. The International Style as practiced here by the distinguished émigré designers provided an answer to many of America's building problems. In the years since World War II, a new incisive kind of thinking accompanied by intensive technological developments has resulted in much exciting architecture.

TECHNOLOGICAL FRONTIERS

Metal and Glass

Three skyscrapers from the postwar period reveal the impact of the International Style and of the changing contemporary technology on American architectural practice. One of the most effective designers of large-scale commercial structures is the firm of Skidmore, Owings & Merrill. The refined and precise elegance of their designs recalls the manner of Miës van der Rohe. Lever House (18-16), on Park Avenue, New York, built in 1952 to house the executive offices of the great soap manufacturing company, demonstrates an effective use of the curtain wall in skyscraper design. Since the multistoried tower of the building covers only part of the ground area, it stands free, surrounded by space, light, and air, and its beauty is visible from a number of vantage points. The shimmering surface of the tower, sheathed in glass and stainless steel, is divided into handsomely proportioned rectangles which reflect the surrounding buildings and the patterns of the sky in the geometric mosaic of its surface. True to the tenets of the style, little sense of weight or bulk is conveyed by this enormous structure. Its crystalline surface and soaring forms appear to float above the thin piers and open sections of the ground floor.

A cantilevered two-story ground floor covering the full block provides a spacious entrance and contains the lobby of the building (18-17). The lobby achieves a particularly effective relationship between the outer world and the space within the building through the ever-present transparent and reflecting glass. The planters and shrubs also continue the movement between indoors and out. The shadowy serenity of the sheltered, open ground floor comes as a happy contrast to the confusing press of activity on the street.

One of the most original interpretations of the curtain wall is the Alcoa Building (18-18), Pittsburgh, designed by Harrison & Abramovitz. The wall is composed of light, 6-by-12-foot panels of aluminum only ⅛-inch thick. These permit the very rapid sheathing of the exterior. Stamped in a pattern of triangular facets for greater rigidity and attached to the supporting framework, the panels were then sprayed with a 4-inch layer of perlite and sand for insulation. The almost square reversible windows are literally holes punched in the center of the panels, equipped with a single pivoting unit of green-tinted heat-resisting glass. As seen

18-16 (*left*). Skidmore, Owings & Merrill, Lever House, 1952. New York City. Skidmore, Owings & Merrill photograph. 18-17 (*below*). Skidmore, Owings & Merrill, Lever House lobby. Skidmore, Owings & Merrill photograph.

from the street level, the triangular facets of the panels break the light into shifting geometric patterns while the round-cornered windows contribute interest through their contrasting shapes. The use of aluminum for surface sheathing reveals changing building techniques resulting from technological advances.

The United Nations Secretariat building (18-19) was the joint achievement of architects from many countries working with Wallace K. Harrison. Here the concept of the office building as a glass-surfaced slab received its ultimate expression. The thin, shimmering rectangle rises directly from the ground for thirty-nine stories and is terminated by an aluminum grill which conceals the elevator equipment and other services. The main façade is divided into three bands by two floors faced with aluminum grills that cover additional servicing equipment. The façade is sheathed with green-tinted glass—the end walls with grayish white marble. Slender and lyrical, the Secretariat is in essence a soaring vertical shaft—a multifaceted mirror in a white marble frame which houses three

18-18. Harrison & Abramovitz, Alcoa Building, 1952. Pittsburgh, Pa. Samuel Musgrave photograph.

thousand four hundred workers. Acting as a horizontal foil to the Secretariat is the low conference area and the General Assembly Hall, with a smooth, almost unbroken, curved façade.

A second Skidmore, Owings & Merrill structure distinguished by a particularly pure and elegant interpretation of the contemporary functional style is the Fifth Avenue office of the Manufacturers Trust Company of New York (18-20), opened in 1954. As the entrance is on the cross street, the façade of the building presents a great glass wall unbroken by doorways, permitting the passerby a full view of the interior. A beautiful geometric pattern is created by the intersection of the interior forms with the elegantly proportioned windows of the façade. The slender metal supports of the windows, graceful flutings of draperies, and subtle details of landscaping combine with the reflections and cast-shadows to create a quality of sensuous refinement that contrasts effectively with the clumsy and seemingly crude surfaces of the neighboring buildings. The interior (19-3) has the same smooth polished elegance as the exterior.

Eero Saarinen, the son of Eliel Saarinen, in conjunction with a Detroit firm of architectural designers, designed for General Motors a great Technical Research Center (18-21) containing twenty-five buildings arranged about a great rectangular pool. Almost all the buildings are composed in 10-foot modules, and the long expanses of regularly spaced vertical struc-

18-19 (*above*). Wallace Harrison and associates, United Nations Headquarters, 1952. New York City. United Nations photograph.   18-20 (*below*). Skidmore, Owings & Merrill, Manufacturers Trust Company, Fifth Avenue office, 1954. New York City. Ezra Stoller photograph.

18-21 (*above*). Eero Saarinen and associates, General Motors Technical Research Center, 1951. Detroit, Mich. Ezra Stoller photograph. 18-22 (*right*). Eero Saarinen and associates, General Motors Styling Auditorium, 1951. Detroit, Mich. Ezra Stoller photograph.

tural elements suggest, most appropriately, an architecture of industrial origin, turned out endlessly in standardized units. Here aluminum provides both the structural elements and the surface sheathing. Walls of prefabricated aluminum frames are covered with glass or aluminum panels. The smooth dome of the Styling Auditorium (18-22) provides a foil to omnipresent rectangularity and horizontality. To avoid monotony, solid-color panels of bright blue and burnt-orange glazed bricks are interspersed between the glass and aluminum surfaces and sheath the end walls. These rectangles of brilliant color contribute visual accents without violating the mood of serene impersonality that dominates this great research center.

Concrete

The kaleidoscopic variety of contemporary building practices have encouraged many exciting departures from traditional forms and struc-

18-23. Matthew Nowicki and William Deitrick, Livestock Judging Pavilion, 1953. Raleigh, N. C. Wayne Andrews photograph.

tural concepts. The most impressive development has occurred in the structural uses of concrete. In its early years, concrete had been poured into the rectangular or heavy arched forms of its masonry precursors, and the later use of concrete in conjunction with skeletal steel construction also predisposed the designers toward rectangular forms. After the thirties, concrete was stripped of its masonry connotations and was used in sinuous flowing lines with increasing frequency, particularly in highway and bridge construction. Thus, the increased structural efficiency of concrete poured into curved or bent shapes was discovered. The newer methods of using concrete permit a great variety of architectural forms,

18-24. Yamasaki, Leinweber, & Associates, Parke-Davis & Company warehouse, 1958. Menlo Park, Calif. Parke-Davis & Company photograph.

18-25. Victor Gruen Associates, Millirons Department Store, 1949. Los Angeles, Calif. Julius Shulman photograph.

a lithe fluidity of line as well as a light elegance. These qualities are apparent in the handsome pavilion (18-23) for judging livestock in Raleigh, North Carolina. Conceived by Matthew Nowicki, the project was completed by William Dietrich. Two great concrete and steel arches which interlock near the ends are supported by thin steel box columns. The roof is carried on free cables which pass between the two arches, creating an interior of uninterrupted space bounded by graceful flowing forms. Here is a structural conception derived from bridge design, as contemporary in its esthetic appeal as in its engineering and technical aspects. Steel, concrete, and glass create a rhythmic series of forms that appear to be enclosed in a translucent curtain of light.

An even freer disposition of architectural forms has been achieved by the use of ferroconcrete construction which exploits the structural efficiency of the thin bent slab or beam, as well as the curved concrete shell or stressed skin. A thin, curved concrete surface, like the shell of an egg, can enclose vast spaces by means of a continuous self-supporting form.

An imaginative use of this structural device is seen in a warehouse (18-24) designed for Parke-Davis in Menlo Park, California, by Yamasaki, Leinweber & Associates. Thirty thousand square feet of interior space have been roofed by sixty-four steel-edged, precast concrete quarter-sections which are carried on a reinforced concrete structural skeleton. The rhythmic pattern created by these light arched concrete vaults is becoming a familiar element in the American scene. A pleasantly landscaped sheltered patio links the employees' lunchroom and the administration offices in front with the warehouse behind.

Providing parking space for today's automobiles taxes the ingenuity of modern designers, and some lively architectural shapes are appearing in response to this problem. Victor Gruen Associates have dramatized the ramps which lead to the parking area atop a Los Angeles department store (18-25) by using ribbonlike planes that flow through space like

18-26. Weed, Johnson Associates, parking garage, 1949. Miami, Fla. Weed, Johnson Associates photograph.

the space-modulators of the constructivist sculptors. This free disposition of forms is made possible by the use of the thin bent concrete shell used in conjunction with reinforced concrete and steel supports. A parking garage (18-26) in Miami, Florida, designed by Weed, Johnson Associates, derives its form directly from its structure and purpose, with the least possible elaboration of unnecessary features. The curtain has been stripped from the curtain wall, creating the maximum illusion of extended horizontal planes floating on vertical supports. Again the resemblance to certain abstract sculptures is vivid.

Another imaginative construction utilizing the light concrete shell to cover an extended area can be seen in the Ida Cason Callaway Gardens (18-27) at Robin Lake, Georgia. Here Aeck Associates have

18-27. Aeck Associates, Ida Cason Gallaway Gardens, 1958. Robin Lake, Ga. Rodney McCay Morgan photograph.

18-28. Charles Eames, Case Study House, 1949. Santa Monica, Calif. Charles Eames photograph.

erected twenty-one giant concrete and steel mushrooms to create a breeze-swept dining pavilion seating a thousand persons. The kitchens and other service areas are in two circular enclosed buildings. The fanciful and gay design creates a festive atmosphere while the great overhead umbrellas permit the free circulation of air so necessary for comfort in the humid South.

The increased use of structural steel in conjunction with broad expanses of glass has initiated some interesting experiments in house design. Charles Eames built his Case Study House (18-28) in Santa Monica, California, for his own use and as part of a research program for the magazine *Arts and Architecture*. Essentially a two-story cage, the house was built with standard factory-produced elements, utilizing readily available steel frame windows, sliding doors, and structural beams. Though Eames considered the enclosure of the maximum amount of space at the minimum expense his major problem, he achieved a house of singular distinction. Occasional opaque stucco walls and transparent and translucent glass areas of different sizes vary the patterns of steel frame to extract an unexpected Japanese flavor from the industrial techniques. The view through the open door reveals the pervasive sense of space, air, and light. Partitionlike sections of wall separate the areas within so as to provide for various living activities. While the fore part of the living room is two stories high, the farther section has an open balcony and sleeping space above the dining and kitchen space. The glass doors and windows leave one continuously aware of the verdant surroundings. The reflections of the trees and the sky in the numerous glass surfaces and the pattern of sunlight and shadows play against the subtle textures and planes of the house to create a powerful esthetic unity. The lightly framed walls and windows minimize the sense of separation between the indoors and the outdoors. While the walls actually function as a shield against the weather and the intrusion of the outdoor world, visually they bring inside and outside together, serving as space and light modulators by defining the planes of the various surfaces as they transmit or reflect images. Modern science and technology work together here to create a house that can be constructed rapidly, at moderate expense, and at the same time reintegrates man with nature.

REINTEGRATION: PAST AND PRESENT

Change appears to be a keyword in twentieth-century life. New living habits resulting from increased mobility and other mutations of social practices, as well as the technological advances we have just been discussing, are revolutionizing contemporary architecture. But the past is not forgotten. Heavy-beam construction, part of our colonial heritage, has been reintroduced into current practice to enclose extensive areas when neither concrete nor steel is desirable. Brick, stone, and wood retain their place beside glass, steel, and modern synthetic building materials. Much of the value of the historical approach to the study of art comes from perceiving the continuity of a tradition in which familiar elements are fused with new developments. A brief glance at a few contemporary structures which combine yesterday and today will close our discussion of twentieth-century architecture.

William Wurster began his career designing buildings which appear deceptively casual, for close examination reveals an unusual degree of elegance in his interpretation of the California carpentered-redwood tradition. Wurster's early success encouraged him to organize the firm of

18-29 (*above*). Wurster, Bernardi and Emmons, Center for the Advanced Study of the Behaviorial Sciences, 1954. Stanford, Calif. Morley Baer photograph.   18-30 (*below*). John Yeon, Visitors Information Center, 1949. Portland, Ore. Roger Sturtevant photograph.

Wurster, Bernardi and Emmons; this talented team has explored a number of fresh and original ways of reconciling the past with the contemporary idiom. The Center for the Advanced Study of the Behavioral Sciences, at Stanford, California, was designed to provide work space in a rural setting for fifty scholars, permitting the maximum of privacy and yet providing ample opportunities for informal discussions and larger group conferences. A series of secluded offices connected by sheltered walks crowns the crest of the hill on which the Center is located. The windows of these private offices face out on the quiet landscape, creating an atmosphere conducive to work and devoid of pressure. A central group of offices and conference rooms (18-29) houses the administrative agencies and provides for group discussions. The pitched roofs, extended across the walks on simple redwood posts and beams, create the sheltered galleries that constitute such an attractive part of California's architectural heritage. Extensive windows and glazed walls contribute light, air, and charming vistas of rolling hills. Broad eaves permit the maximum pleasure and the minimum discomfort from the bright sunshine. Carefully calculated proportions and fine craftsmanship add refinement and sophistication to the simple materials and direct construction. The various needs of an unusual institution have been met with great effectiveness in this complex of buildings designed in the airy, light, spacious contemporary manner while retaining many elements of traditional California architecture.

The Visitors Information Center (18-30) in Portland, Oregon, by John Yeon, makes effective use of an open trellis to connect four rectangular buildings of varying height which contain staff offices, exhibition areas, rest rooms, and outdoor recreation facilities. The lively rectangular patterns overhead and the slender posts repeat the delicate scale of the enclosed structures and intensify the weightless effect created by the thin plywood walls and the extended areas of glass. Many devices have been explored to establish continuity between the outdoors and the indoors, but none seems to accomplish this in a more effortless fashion than the time-honored open trellis. Color again plays an important role here. The exterior walls are dark blue-green, the exposed framing of the buildings is blue-black, the trim in pale green, the doors red.

Since the curtain wall replaced the monumental masonry façade, modern architects have been loath to burden the light surfaces with enrichments, for decoration inevitably increases the suggestion of volume and weight. Unlike Sullivan, who had extolled the lyric role of ornament, and Frank Lloyd Wright, who never succumbed to the chill beauty of the

18-31. Edward Stone, Stanford Medical Center, 1959. Stanford, Calif. Stanford University photograph.

bare wall, most contemporary architects chose to exploit the drama of sheer surfaces and weightless volumes, thereby avoiding trite effects and decorative clichés. The aseptic clean style which resulted was refreshing at first, but with the passing of time, the bare walls, sharp forms, and cold surfaces began to appear sterile and mechanical, lacking in lyricism and exuberance.

One of the leaders in the movement to reintroduce surface enrichment into modern architecture is Edward Stone. The device most readily associated with his name is the use of walls and screens of concrete tiles cast in open pierced patterns. Such walls create decorative baffles which permit the eye, as well as light and air, to move freely through masses and spaces. In his designs for the new Stanford Medical Center (18-31), walls of pierced concrete tiles permit the ready perception of the interrelated outdoor courts and enclosed areas. In addition, the solid concrete wall has been cast in patterned blocks, and these recessed geometric reliefs, assisted by the great aerial planters, augment the imposing scale of the three-story columns that support the broad extended eaves. The patterns not only add visual interest but contribute a reassuring sense of weight. There is promise here of a new architecture characterized by the rich plastic values that have distinguished the great periods of the past.

Through the ages, man has shaped the great conformations of the landscape to provide a place for assembly. No more majestic site can be imagined than the rock-framed sloping valley near Morrison, Colorado, where Burnham Hoyt placed what may well be the most monumental

18-32. Burnham Hoyt, Red Rock Amphitheater, 1941. Morrison, Colo. Suter, Hedrich-Blessing photograph.

outdoor amphitheater in the world. Red Rock Amphitheater (18-32), designed for the city of Denver, is a great horseshoe-shaped embankment of seats which flows down a sloping valley between the cliffs of two converging buttes to focus on a simply curved proscenium framed by massive stone walls. The potentialities of this unusual site were realized with rare sensitivity by incorporating the towering buttes into the plan and hiding much of the man-made structure. This fortuitous shaping of

18-33. Lloyd Wright, Wayfarer's Chapel, 1951. Palos Verdes, Calif. Julius Shulman photograph.

18-34. Sherwood, Mills and Smith, architects; Constantino Nivola, sculptor, Mutual of Hartford Insurance Building sand-cast concrete bas-relief, 1958. Hartford. Sherwood, Mills and Smith photograph.

nature provides a dramatic example of the way in which modern technology can serve the needs of the ever-growing gregarious population without violating the landscape—the ultimate aim of all creative plans for site development.

An equally reverent utilization of a magnificent site has been achieved by Lloyd Wright, son of Frank Lloyd Wright, in the Wayfarer's Chapel (18-33) in Palos Verdes, California. Redwood frames support the glass walls, and the roof trusses are filled alternately with glass and pale blue tiles. One sees the sea and sky through continuous patterns of ascending linear triangles—shapes that seem particularly suited to the purpose of the building, for the aspiring triangles inevitably recall the forms of the Gothic cathedral. Eventually, giant redwoods will enclose the chapel in an arched pattern of sunlight and shadow.

The planned integration of the fine and decorative arts into modern architecture holds great promise for the future. Since 1950, an increasing number of architects have utilized stained glass (19-18), cast-concrete relief (18-34), monumental sculptures, tile, mosaic, and a wide variety of other art forms to enhance modern buildings. The Fifth Avenue office of the Manufacturers Trust Company of New York was one of the first

18-35. Harry Bertoia, sculptured metal screen, 1954. Manufacturers Trust Company, Fifth Avenue office, New York. Manufacturers Trust Company photograph.

to employ sculpture on the grand scale, both for practical and visual purposes. A sculptured metal screen 70 feet wide and 16 feet high, by Harry Bertoia, divides the main banking room of the second floor, separating the public lobby from the employees. A close-up detail (18-35) of the abstract sculptured screen reveals rich surface textures and a play of geometric forms in space which both characterize modern sculpture and make it particularly appropriate for use in a modern architectural setting. By enriching our brilliant contemporary style of building with the emotional warmth and spiritual exuberance of the fine arts, the modern architect again approaches the full satisfaction of man's emotional and esthetic needs.

Architecture is a communal art. Social organization and the current technology supply the means for shaping the environment to serve man's needs. A corps of designers, engineers, draftsmen, technical consultants, and businessmen work in close collaboration to produce the magnificent steel, concrete, and glass buildings of today. Modern architecture, like much of the great architecture of the past, involves the talents of a large section of society. In addition to the designers and engineers who plan a modern building, an army of workers contribute their services—the men who mine and mill the raw materials, the factory workers who fashion these materials into prefabricated parts, the transport workers, as well as the host of technicians, who provide the various utilities and services necessary for the life of the building.

But architecture is more than technology. The ultimate values of a society determine its architectural forms. Whether man lives within the shadow of the skyscraper or in the open country, whether the most imposing structure in a community is the department store or the library depends upon the ultimate goals of the social order. The capacities of our technology to provide a benign environment and of our architects and designers to shape that environment have barely been touched. The handful of masterpieces that distinguish the current scene promise well for the future. The degree to which this promise will be realized depends on the ideals and social forces which shape our future, ideals and social forces which in the final analysis depend on each individual citizen.

19

Interiors, Furniture,

Crafts, and

Industrial Design

INTERIORS

Between 1900 and 1915 the modern interior received its initial formulation in the craftsman rooms, and no one contributed more toward the creation of a distinguished version of this style than Frank Lloyd Wright. From 1915 to 1930 there was a period of quiescence. Since 1930, the modern interior has developed its own striking character, in no way less impressive than the external aspect of modern architecture.

Frank Lloyd Wright struck deeply into the problem of interior design through his concern with the floor plans which shaped the original and striking exteriors of his houses. Following a tradition long extant in America, Wright sought to re-examine the living patterns of his day and to design interiors which would contribute to both a more efficient and a more dignified way of life. In his best houses, such as the Coonley House (19-1) of River Forest, Illinois, the conventional division of the interior

532

into cell-like cubicles gave way to a free movement from room to room which would further group living. Walls became screens which directed the flow of space without creating restrictive barriers. Long banks of windows and an increased number of doors provided communion with and access to the outdoors.

Many of the concepts which Wright employed were common to the craftsman houses of the day—the opening of rooms into one another to convey a sense of spaciousness, the easy access between indoors and outdoors, the use of heavy timbered framing combined with cantilevered construction, the candid statement of structure and the use of unpretentious materials. A view into the living room from the hall of the Coonley House reveals Wright's capacity to cast the craftsman mode into rich and original esthetic forms. There is an exciting and continuous flow of form and space augmented by the open beams (which recall the barns of the midwest) and the newel posts, which, acting as space modulators, contribute an airy contrast to the massive elements of the woodwork. The low-pitched ceiling, pierced by skylights patterned in Wright's typical multisized rectangles, provides an engaging play of angles. As in most of Wright's great designs, this interior combines space, movement, and monumentality with a feeling for informality and the dramatic use of familiar materials.

Wright's later interiors are distinguished by an increased boldness in the disposition of visual and structural materials. In Taliesin West (19-2) the unusual slant of walls and ceiling, the rough concrete, stone, and wood, and the bold scale of the beams create a sense of drama and excitement that makes the Coonley interior of thirty years earlier appear decorous and well-mannered. Through an imaginative and dynamic organization of stone and heavy timbers, timeless elements of our architectural heritage have been combined with the contemporary taste for light, air, and space. Taliesin West seems close to nature not only because one continually sees the out-of-doors but even more because the structural materials relate to the landscape in form, texture, and color.

The craftsman and the machine have been said to represent the antipodes of modern design. In Taliesin West, Wright created an eloquent modern design in the rustic craftsman vernacular. An interior from the Fifth Avenue office of the Manufacturers Trust Company of New York embodies the opposite pole of modern design with equal effectiveness. The lobby on the executive floor (19-3) achieves its effect of machined elegance through the contrast of its sweeping, unbroken surfaces with

19-1 (*above*). Frank Lloyd Wright, Coonley House, view into living room, 1908. River Forest, Ill. Chicago Architectural Photographing Company photograph. 19-2 (*below*). Frank Lloyd Wright, Taliesin West, interior, 1938. Phoenix, Ariz. Wayne Andrews photograph.

precise and delicate details of hardware, moldings, and light fixtures. The fine woods, marble, glass, and metal, the general polished character of the surface materials, the broad expanse of space, and the geometric severity of the furnishings all contribute to the atmosphere of urbanity and distinction. The patterns of wood grain and marble, the handsome sculptural group, and the painting provide a foil for the smooth surfaces and contribute a needed warmth without which machined elegance may turn into sterility.

An air of impersonal distinction, appropriate to executive offices in a building which is in essence a showroom, might well be overwhelming in a home. A view into the living room from the central patio of the Chesnut House (19-4) in Sausalito, California, reveals a combination of machine and craftsman modes. The architect John Hoops has created a suburban home in which the precise, smooth, and shining is balanced against the rough, picturesque, and earthy to provide for an orderly, gracious, but informal mode of living. The rooms are composed around a small patio which serves as an outdoor extension of the house. A compact utility core divides the house into areas for sleeping, work, and entertaining.

The structure of this house is as direct and sensible as the plan. The post-and-beam framework is inexpensive and efficient. A system of double posts holding the beams between them eliminates the use of expensive heavy timbers. A neat system of glass and plywood inserts completes the building with logic and grace. While the Chesnut House has the sharp, light rectangularity derived from the esthetics of the machine, it remains part of the landscape—board patterns, wood grain, and brick provide a happy foil to the shining glass. Here, as in many modern houses, continuous interplay between indoors and outdoors provides one of the principal means for integrating the geometry of modern building with the forms of nature.

A few generalizations concerning the modern style can be drawn from the observation of these three domestic interiors. These generalizations can be made more meaningful by a quick glance back at the Stanford bedroom (14-4) or the Milligan parlor (14-3).

The open plan and the absence of cell-like enclosed rooms give an effect of airy spaciousness. Rooms are arranged to function efficiently and to be visually expressive of the life carried on in them. Furniture is grouped in relation to daily activities—eating, sleeping, conversation, listening to music, or watching television and also in relation to windows, fireplace, and other such architectural factors. Most designers today prefer

19-3 (*above*). Skidmore, Owings & Merrill, Manufacturers Trust Company, Fifth Avenue office, lobby of executive floor, 1954. New York City. Ezra Stoller photograph.   19-4 (*below*). John Hoops, Chesnut House, central patio, 1955. Sausalito, Calif. Morley Baer photograph.

a somewhat spacious, almost empty-looking room to a crowded or a cluttered one. In general, pattern is used sparingly. Draperies, upholstery fabrics, curtains, and carpets are usually solid-colored and provide a textural foil to the wood, plaster, concrete, and brick of the walls, floors, and ceilings. Furniture is low in contour, simple in shape, and usually without carving or applied ornament.

The architectural decorations of earlier times—moldings, wall paneling, and the framing of doors, windows, and mantel areas—have been eliminated. Ease of upkeep and a clean look are primary goals in planning contemporary rooms. Wall-to-wall carpeting, glass-topped tables, formica or plastic work surfaces, the general absence of heavy carving, and the elimination of elaborate objects and looped and festooned draperies, all provide for ease of maintenance. Smooth reflective surfaces and the absence of pretentious furbelows contribute to the air of polished understatement desired by today's interior designers.

Paintings, sculptures, and ceramics play a most important role in modern interiors, since the general absence of pattern and applied ornament focuses all attention upon the art object. Since much of the furnishings used in contemporary rooms is rather standardized, works of art provide for an expression of the more subtle and intimate qualities of personality. At its best, modern interior design is dedicated to a most austere and lofty ideal: to create a living environment which is both an expression of our highly organized technology and of the unique aspects of the individual personality, or to quote the Swiss architect Le Corbusier, to produce a practical, functioning "living machine," and at the same time an esthetically moving work of art.

FURNITURE

There was little progressive furniture design in the years immediately following World War I. Even the straightforward Mission style gave way before the anemic traditionalism which dominated furniture production during the twenties and early thirties. The older styles of furniture were scaled down in size, and the rich, carved ornament of earlier days was simplified in response to the exigencies of machine production and the general taste for less pretentious effects. Many of the simpler historic styles were revived during this period, early American and Shaker furniture, Windsor chairs, French provincial styles, and modified versions of Jacobean and William and Mary replaced the more extravagant baroque and rococo modes in popular taste.

19-5. Bentwood chair, 1935. Lore Bloch photograph.

A more vigorous and experimental spirit prevailed in Europe. In Germany and Austria a heavy geometric interpretation of the craftsman style appeared, characterized by weighty, unrelieved rectangular forms and smooth surfaces. The Scandinavians experimented in bentwood and molded plywood furniture, and the curvilinear elements introduced by

19-6. Paul McCobb, designer, and Calvin Furniture Company, Irwin Collection, 1951.

this method provided a welcome relief from the mechanical regularity of the prevailing modern styles.

During the mid-thirties a very limited amount of American furniture reflected these advances (19-5), but American designs for the most part remained traditional until after World War II. Since that time, furniture has responded to the changing technology, architectural styles, and tastes of our day.

A contemporary designer divided modern furniture into three basic types, furniture having the machine look (19-6), the handicraft look (19-10), or the biomorphic or sculptural look (19-7). While few pieces of furniture conform entirely to one of these categories, these classifications provide an excellent orientation to contemporary trends.

A collection of furniture designed by Paul McCobb and assembled for display purposes (19-6) is dominated by the machine look of modern architecture. The forms are consistently rectangular, supports are predominantly vertical, surfaces are smooth and continuous, and as in modern architecture, the general effect is light, airy, and open. Even the cushions and the padded areas of upholstered chairs have been kept thin so as to avoid bulk and to retain a feeling of rectangularity. The large coffee table topped with white glass is carried on an iron frame, and slender iron rods support the ottoman. The handsome cabinet in the back of the room provides both enclosed space for storage and open areas for display; the resulting alternations of recessed and built-out rectangles create an interesting play of forms and spaces. The opposition between the major horizontal divisions and drawers of the cabinet and the pre-

19-7. George Nelson, designer, and Herman Miller Furniture Company, plastic and metal chair, 1959.

dominantly vertical wood grain animates the surface by providing contrasts. Practicality, comfort, and a certain light grace have been achieved; and although the results are not distinguished, the total effect is pleasant.

While modern tables, cabinets, and storage units most frequently have an architectural machined look, an increasing number of chairs and related pieces are distinguished by molded and flowing forms of a biomorphic orientation. *Biomorphic* is a word coined by modern designers to describe forms related to living organisms, and the biomorphic approach to chair design considers anatomical forms and the problems of support and action involved in sitting. Biomorphic designs use molded plywood, plastics, rubber, and metal, and the biomorphic concept seems particularly congenial to the processes by which modern plastics are shaped (19-7). The chair by George Nelson for the Henry Miller collection has a fluid, enveloping, weightless shell that is as pleasant to look at as it is practical and comfortable. The rubber tipped, enameled, metal legs provide a light, slender, but solid base. Graceful and eminently useful, this chair is only conceivable in terms of contemporary materials and manufacturing processes.

Charles Eames has been one of the most inventive of the contemporary American furniture designers, particularly in adapting plywood, plastics, and metal to modern requirements. Eames designs parts that can be produced by mass production methods and assembled rapidly and easily. One of his earliest and most successful designs for a chair is made from molded plywood parts which are cut and shaped by machine and then assembled (19-8). The seat and back are designed to support the

19-8. Charles Eames, plywood chair, 1945.

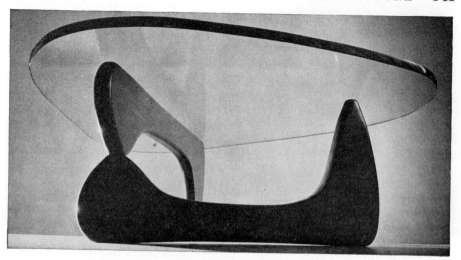

19-9. Isamu Noguchi, designer, and Herman Miller Furniture Company, coffee table, 1946.

body comfortably, and the graceful forms are as efficient as they are pleasing to the eye. The Eames chairs are assembled with metal and rubber mounts which provide a desirable flexibility since the chairs respond to changes in body position and so combine some of the support of rigid chairs with some of the comfort of upholstered furniture. Here Eames finally provided a gracious solution to the problem of the molded plywood chair initiated sixty years earlier (14-13).

Not all of the furniture with curvilinear and organic shapes has been concerned with body needs and actions. A handsome coffee table (19-9) by Isamu Noguchi draws its inspiration from modern abstract sculpture. The great, heavy piece of glass which forms the top rests on an ingenious wooden sculptural base made of two free forms, and part of the interest comes from knowing that the weight of the glass holds the supports in place. The beauty of this table results from the sensitive use of materials, the heavy transparency of the glass and the strong organic forms of the wooden supports. Despite the weighty parts, fluid lines, a transparent top, and open supports keep the table from appearing ponderous.

Much fine furniture being produced today relates closely to handicraft practices. An unstained birch breakfast table and chair (19-10) designed by George Nakashima suggest early American prototypes. The chair has a heavy, shaped plank seat with inset legs and spindles, which recall, as does the circular back rest, the traditional Windsor chairs. The

19-10 (*left*). George Nakashima, designer, and Knoll Associates, Inc., chair and table, *c*. 1948. 19-11 (*below*). T. H. Robsjohn-Gibbings, designer, and Widdicomb Furniture Company, chair and ottoman, designed 1936, shown 1948.

absence of turnings and the sleek, simply modulated forms are, however, more in character with the machine concept of design than with the sculptural forms of earlier times. The table also reflects Colonial and Shaker modes. The subtle shaping of the top and the tapered legs inject a note of style into an extremely simple piece of furniture.

An upholstered chair and stool (19-11) designed by T. H. Robsjohn-Gibbings is designed for more conventionally elegant interiors than the furniture we have been discussing. The separation of the wooden supporting frame from the cushions suggests contemporary Scandinavian practices. The frame has been treated as a delicately sculptured wooden support for the heavier cushions, and the wooden parts are subtly shaped so that their taperings and swellings carry the eye from part to part with an easy continuous movement. The suave contours and delicately molded surfaces of the frame involve certain traditional handicraft practices; consequently such furniture is more expensive than that conceived in the modern industrial idiom. Despite a constant concern with practicality, modern furniture at its best, whether custom-made or mass-produced, achieves a quality of grace and elegance that makes it comparable to the fine furniture of earlier days.

CONTEMPORARY CRAFTS

The flourishing state of contemporary crafts is one of the paradoxes of today. In the late nineteenth century, handicrafts seemed doomed. The machine appeared to have taken over except in isolated instances. Only a few reformers, William Morris in England, Sullivan and Wright in America, protested against the debauched standards of prevailing design and envisaged a day when men would live and work in a benign environment and produce beautiful, well-made objects for everyday use. Though they seemed lost voices, these few men did much to perpetuate and revive handicraft traditions and practices. Today a large number of craftsmen are working in ceramics, glass, metal, wood, and plastics and are weaving handsome textiles. The products of their hands supplement the abundant body of machine-made merchandise which for the most part satisfies the mass markets.

The areas of modern craft activity remain traditional. Silversmithing remains a popular craft, with the majority of craftsmen preferring to make jewelry rather than household silver. The increased popularity of iron, bronze, and lead as sculptural media has almost obliterated the distinction between artists and craftsmen among metalworkers. Metal sculpture will be discussed in Chapter 22. Ceramics is probably the most popular contemporary craft since the equipment and materials necessary are relatively simple. Though many excellent craftsmen are engaged in its commercial production, glass is seldom an area of amateur craft activity. A number of fine weavers are at work today, and it is almost impossible to draw the line between commercial and amateur weaving, for many hand weavers design fabrics for industrial production by machine-powered looms.

Silver and Metalwork

Most modern silverware is factory-made, and traditional patterns have remained popular. Even the traditional designs, however, reflect the tendency toward simplicity that characterizes the styles of today. In general, the commercially produced silverware of modern design follows the example set by the contemporary silversmiths. A five-piece table setting and serving spoon (19-12) designed by Arthur J. Pulos reveals the elegant simplicity preferred by many modern designers. The fundamental shapes of the parts are designed to combine maximum efficiency with chaste purity of form. The handles are thickened so that the individual pieces can be easily grasped and also to provide the feeling of weight and substance compatible with silver. Modern flatware is designed with shorter handles than traditional table silver, and this contributes toward ease of handling. Today, stainless steel, handsome in finish and

19-12. Arthur J. Pulos, silver place setting and service spoon, 1953. Detroit Institute of Arts, Detroit, Mich.

form, vies with fine table silver in popularity. Stainless steel does not tarnish and is extremely durable.

Ceramics

The ceramic arts constitute one of the most vital fields of contemporary craft activity. Modern potters continue to make traditional vase and bowl forms to be used for flower arrangements, as storage containers, and as table wares. They also make an increasing number of pieces that are handsome essays in the ceramic arts with no other purpose than to provide visual pleasure.

Contemporary ceramic artists have been primarily concerned with reviving the art of throwing pottery, that is, of using the potter's wheel to replace the molds and casting processes employed in commercial ceramic production. In doing this, they have rediscovered the character of clay, its weighty full-bodied plasticity, and they have also rediscovered the tremendous range of interesting surface textures that can be produced in the processes of throwing, firing, and glazing. Three pieces of pottery by Bois Wildenhain (19-13) illustrate the character of much contemporary ceramics production. The simple forms, classic vase and bowl shapes which serve as efficient containers and flower holders, sit solidly

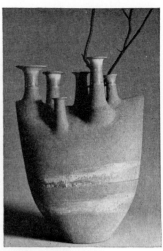

19-13 (*left*). Bois Wildenhain, pottery, *c.* 1955. M. H. de Young Memorial Museum, San Francisco, Calif. 19-14 (*right*). William Wyman, branch holder, *c.* 1955. Museum of Contemporary Crafts, New York.

and have a pleasant weighty feeling. Varied surface textures have been combined with the rich colors and soft sheen of the glazes to create handsome unpretentious examples of the potter's art.

Modern ceramic artists, like modern painters and sculptors, have found inspiration in the arts of primitive peoples and exotic cultures.

A partially glazed branch holder (19-14) by William Wyman is very much of today yet there is also something reminiscent of the past in its forms and surface textures. The simple purity of its contours as well as its gracefully shaped openings recall an early Greek amphora. The almost unglazed surface enriched only by the simple lines of the potter's tool and the swipe of glaze reminds us of the potteries of primitive peoples. The ingenious use of multiple openings makes this branch holder well-adapted to the modern fashion of arranging interesting natural materials for home decoration.

Peter Voulkos began his career making pots and bowls. Though he still considers himself a potter, much of his contemporary work is essentially abstract sculpture. An example of one of his bold ceramic forms (19-15) stands 42 inches high and, like much modern painting, shows the direct vigor with which the materials have been manipulated. The rather crude spherical masses that constitute the main form have been textured by such manipulations as hammering, scraping, and smearing. The result is as astonishing as an impertinence, and yet the weighty character of the forms contributes a sculptural dignity to the whole.

19-15. Peter Voulkos, *Tarantas*, ceramic, iron red slab cut and hammered, 1957. Oppi Untracht photograph.

The vigorous contemporary development of the potter's art has had a strong influence on commercially produced tablewares. Much of the output today reflects the taste for simple heavy forms and interesting colors and textures. Commercial pottery has made impressive inroads on the use of thin-walled fragile china that constituted the ideal of "good" tableware a generation ago.

Glass

Most contemporary table glass, whether blown, or pressed and shaped in molds, is simple and functional, and either exploits the tendency of molten glass to assume rich globular shapes or glorifies the elegance of thin crystalline forms. In decorative glass, there is a tendency to employ a minimum of applied pattern and a frequent use of heavy forms which distort the transmitted light into fluid rhythmic patterns. Some of America's finest glass combines the talents of the glass blower and the modern

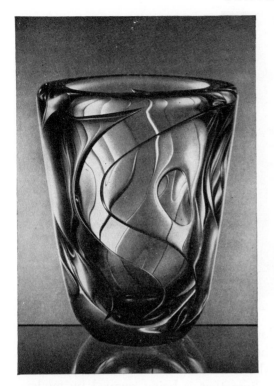 

19-16. (*left*). John Dreves, for Steuben Glass, "Air Trap," *c.* 1947. Courtesy Metropolitan Museum of Art, Purchase, 1950. Edward C. Moore Gift Fund. 19-17 (*right*). Bruce Moore, for Steuben Glass, Huckleberry Finn vase, 1956.

designer. "Air Trap" (19-16), a vase of colorless crystal by John A. Dreves, has been decorated by a manipulation of bubbles introduced between the inner and outer walls of the vessel during the blowing process. The special properties of glass and of the twisting actions involved in glass blowing have been brilliantly exploited here to create the rhythmic elongated spirals.

The smooth surface of glass is well adapted to the engraving process, and the old techniques of engraving glass are still practiced. The Huckleberry Finn vase (19-17) designed by Bruce Moore is one of a series of engraved vases by the Steuben Glass Company each of which features a unique design by a contemporary artist. This slender vase on a hollow base is engraved with the ragged figure of Huckleberry Finn leaning on his gun as he watches a river boat floating down the Mississippi. An emblem composed of crossed pipes interspersed between the letters of his

19-18. Robert Sowers, stained-glass chapel door, 1956. Stephens College, Columbia, Mo.

name accents the base. The shallow intaglio of the engraved design stands out in brilliant relief against the crystalline clarity of the beautifully polished blown crystal forms of the vase.

Stained glass is another medium that is being revived by modern craftsmen and being adapted to the requirements of modern architecture. Robert Sowers designed a stained-glass door (19-18) for the chapel of Stephens College at Columbia, Missouri. The bold translucent areas contrast with the heavy leaded divisions to form a striking contemporary architectural decoration.

Textiles

Never before in history have the textile arts displayed the variety of today. To satisfy our many needs, modern textiles are woven in every conceivable combination of natural and man-made fibers to create textured effects that range from silky-smooth to rough, and these fabrics in turn are decorated by an equal variety of printing, embroidering, weaving, and dyeing techniques. Both the textural character and the decoration of modern textiles have been strongly influenced by current artistic trends. As usual, handwoven textiles provide models for commercial production, and manufacturers tend to draw upon the avant-garde of handweavers for their ideas and inspiration. The designers of contemporary woven textiles strive to achieve surface interest through subtle

19-19. Dorothy Liebes, textile, *c.* 1946.

and varied surface textures, and handicraft weavers have led the way through their use of unconventional materials. A number of handweavers create striking fabrics by combining a variety of materials in a single textile to provide for a wide range of textural effects. A hand-woven fabric (19-19) by Dorothy Liebes combines wool, cotton chenille, raw silk, three types of metal strips, and silk cord; thus, crinkly, rough, smooth, sparkling, and dull sensations are communicated by a single fabric. As the handweavers expand the range of textural effects in their fabrics, the commercial weavers adapt the innovations to the mechanical looms, often with suprising success.

The renaissance of textile arts in our day has brought about a revival of such traditional arts as appliqué and tapestry weaving. Tapestries are essentially woven paintings designed as wall decorations. Their sumptuous colors and rich textures make them particularly effective in this capacity. *The Phoenix and the Golden Gate* (19-20), by Mark Adams of San Francisco, provides a brilliant example. This tapestry was designed to be an integral part of the reading room of a library. Robert Pinart designed for Congregation B'nai Israel of Bridgeport, Connecticut, an appliqué embroidered ark curtain (19-21) which achieves a rich variety through its combination of materials and embroidered stitches. Intriguing both as a decoration and in its religious symbolism, it provides an excellent example of the contemporary revival of liturgical arts.

Contemporary craftsmen make no attempt to compete with the machine. Instead, they supplement its somewhat standardized output by producing objects which are unusual and distinguished because they

19-20 (*above*). Mark Adams, designer, and Paul Avignon, *The Phoenix and the Golden Gate,* tapestry, 1957. Marina Branch, San Francisco Public Library, San Francisco, Calif.   19-21 (*below*). Robert Pinart, ark curtain, 1958. Congregation B'nai Israel, Bridgeport, Conn.

19-22. Henry Dreyfuss, designer, and Mosler Safe Company, vault door, 1951.

reflect the unique abilities and tastes of creative individuals who wish to explore beyond the common denominator of contemporary taste. While a limited number of contemporary craftsmen make a living through their craft activities, many are amateurs who enjoy the doing as much as the results. In this age when mechanization takes over an ever-increasing share of human activities, people derive great satisfactions from involving themselves in manipulative activities. But craft activities do more than involve the hand and eye. Distinguished achievement in the crafts, as in any other field of expression, is a matter of taste and creativity and draws on the full potential of the craftsman.

The activities of the contemporary amateur and professional craftsmen also have a vital relationship to the great body of machine-made merchandise being produced for the mass markets. The industrial designer of today, whose creations are sold by the thousands, is tied to the drawing board, the machines, and the complexities of large factories and routine sales channels. The artist-craftsman is much freer to experiment and explore. As a consequence, the craftsman may create new modes and discover new ideas which later enrich the more conventional avenues of production. The contemporary craftsman in his studio, by exploring new directions in design for commerce and industry, functions much as a research worker in a laboratory.

INDUSTRIAL DESIGN

The close relationship that exists between our contemporary industrial technology and the modern style can be made evident by observing

19-23 (*left*). Henry Dreyfuss, designer, and Deere & Company, farm tractor, 1956. 19-24 (*below*). Raymond Loewy Associates, designer, and Pennsylvania Railroad Company, locomotive, 1942.

the interactions between painting (21-1), sculpture (22-22), and the architecture of our industrial age (18-26) or by comparing a piece of modern sculpture (22-24) and a piece of furniture (19-7). The artist explores; the industrial designer applies. Both work within the framework of the age, shaping its spirit and its physical form. A systematic survey of the endless stream of objects influenced by the contemporary industrial designer is beyond the confines of these pages, but a few selected objects may indicate the variety, vigor, and refinement of modern industrial wares.

A handsome vault door (19-22) designed by Henry Dreyfuss shows a striking stylistic similarity to much of the architecture of our day although its highly specialized nature endows it with qualities of weight and bulk which we do not consider typical. A vault door is not only the most protective unit in a bank but is also a symbol of security and integrity. This design eliminates the traditional maze of bolts, pressure bars, and hinges which reduced the visual impact of earlier doors and also made them hard to clean. This great gleaming, massive door functions as a piece of architectural sculpture and creates the image of solidity so important to depositors. Despite its unique function, this door reveals the simple contours and smooth flowing surfaces characteristic of much contemporary design. In conformity to current tastes, details are made unobtrusive and are incorporated into the main mass to stress basic forms rather than to emphasize the separate parts.

Much of our industrial produce continues to display the simplified functional forms and the sparse grace that has always characterized American artifacts. In the pots, pans, and kitchen utensils, as well as in the tools, machines, and endless other pieces of equipment so essential to contemporary living, efficiency of form is often augmented by an unusual refinement of finish made possible by modern technology.

While the apprehensive opponents of industrialization in early times foresaw only sterility and uniformity for the products of the machine age, the vitality and variety of modern life is too great to permit the domination of any one simple formula. Though our busy and complex age seeks for restraint, simplicity, and discreet elegance and for a quiet integration of details into a simple structure, the world of men and muscle also demands functional organic designs for machines with an appearance that reflects their function. A farm tractor (19-23), also designed by Henry Dreyfuss, suggests work through all its energetic form from its great chevron-patterned tires, cambered front wheels, and ribbed radiator to its high-riding seat. No inappropriate concept of suavity has been allowed to interfere with this straightforward solution to a workaday problem.

There is often an appropriate implication of movement beneath the smooth-flowing contours of modern machines. In the locomotives designed by Raymond Loewy for the Pennsylvania Railroad Company (19-24), the forms of the great all-encompassing shell appear as the concrete embodiment of speed and power while the exposed mechanism of wheels, main-rods, and other moving parts reveals the dynamic elements of its complex of working parts. Raymond Loewy sought to combat the disconnected and clumsy look of earlier locomotives by simplifying and unifying the body shapes with a welded shell, which also eliminated the unsightly patchwork of riveted sections. In so doing, he lowered manufacturing costs by many thousands of dollars, simplified maintenance problems, and produced a design that was also more satisfying visually.

In contrast to the direct honesty of the farm tractor and the magnificent strength of the locomotive, many objects produced for popular consumption today are marred by excessive ornamentation or superficial styling designed to catch the untutored eye. The automobile, as often as any other object, reveals the general characteristics, strengths, and weaknesses of our contemporary industrial merchandise. Fundamentally, contemporary American automobiles are magnificently designed steel and glass objects—graceful, efficient, and expressing their function through their form. But they are too often marred by undue size and flashy exaggerated decorations which constitute the "styling" devices used to stimulate sales and create an artificial obsolescence. Automobile design today reflects a conflict between our scientific and technological organization and our irrational moneymaking goals.

The varied products of modern industry constitute a most significant facet of the arts of our age. Today's machines constitute the tools whereby contemporary man shapes his environment to serve his needs. To an increasing degree each year, the machine frees man from unending toil and produces the goods that enable him to live with greater dignity and self-realization. Much that is produced displays the sure sense of form and fitness to purpose that comes only with maturity.

Modern Painting,

1915-1945

WHILE PROGRESSIVE AMERICAN PAINTERS IN THE EARLY
twentieth century were familiar with advanced European painting, the
public at large was introduced to modern art by the Armory Show of
1913. This exhibition created a furor. Many people were astonished,
confused, and even indignant at work which violated their conventional
and limited concepts of art. The press, always aware of the news value
of the novel and sensational, made the most of the shock value of the
exhibition. Critics laughed derisively at paintings like Duchamp's *Nude
Descending the Stairs* and encouraged the public to attend the exhibition
in a carnival spirit. While most of the onlookers were amused or outraged,
the impact of the exhibition remained. A small group of painters, intellectuals, and collectors were deeply impressed, and the abstract and
stylized modes of painting and sculpture seen by many for the first time
have since become intrinsic elements of American painting. Although

555

there were vigorous schools of modern painting in Germany, England, and Italy, the influence of Paris dominated the Armory Show and subsequent American painting. The continuous swing since 1913 toward abstraction and stylization is, of course, not primarily the result of the Armory Show. Changing intellectual concepts and social tendencies have led man's inquiring eye in new directions. The impulse toward exploration and deeply felt expression has penetrated all phases of intellectual and artistic life both in Europe and America; the Armory Show served to crystallize these impulses.

In the years immediately following 1913, there was little painting, but the decade which followed World War I was one of gestation and change. It was a period when American artists realized both the cultural limitations and the identity of America. Artists and writers fled to Europe, particularly Paris, to escape American provincialism, and in so doing they came to realize how deeply America was a part of their being. After an extended period abroad, most of the artists and writers returned home, their tastes and attitudes immeasurably broadened by their travels. They were excited, dedicated to the new avenues of expression being explored in Europe, but they needed the sights and experiences of home as a stimulus toward productivity. Returning home, they found the familiar scene illuminated by new and more unconventional ways of seeing.

Because of the expatriate experience, much of the important painting in America during the twenties treated American subject matter in the manner of French painters, particularly of Cézanne and the group of early-twentieth-century French painters termed *Les Fauves*, "The Wild Beasts." To a lesser degree, the influence of the Central European expressionists and the Italian futurists was also evident. As a consequence, a taste for a more stylized way of painting than had been previously practiced in America seemed to have become a permanent part of our heritage. There was also a noticeable tendency to seek out geometric elements in the American landscape, so that a kind of realistic cubism appeared, depicting cityscapes, industrial architecture, and machinery. An interest in compositional values and pictorial structure also remained of immediate concern to many of the younger Americans who placed strong emphasis on rhythmic elements and employed broad simplifications of form to emphasize both the structural and dramatic aspects of their paintings. Equally important was an impulse toward direct uninhibited painting, a vehement and intense expressionism born of the urgencies and tensions of changing times.

STYLIZATION AND ABSTRACTION—AFTER THE ARMORY SHOW

John Marin

One of the first of the American painters to develop a personal vehicle of expression from the new movements abroad was John Marin (1872-1953). Marin drew on French contemporary sources for many of his stylistic and technical devices, but he received his source of inspiration at home, did most of his painting here, and retained many traditional American elements in his work. While there is much of Cézanne and the *Fauves* in Marin, there is also much of Winslow Homer in his direct fresh reaction to the coast of Maine and the out-of-doors. Marin went abroad between 1905 and 1910, but he seemed unaware of the more radical movements abroad until he returned home and became one of Alfred Stieglitz's protégés.

Stieglitz not only played a leading role in the development of modern photography in America; he also opened a New York gallery which was one of the first to sponsor modern painting. Stieglitz recognized Marin's ability and originality, exhibited his work and sold it to collectors, and introduced him to modern painters from abroad. In this catalytic atmosphere Marin developed his natural bent toward a spontaneous, uninhibited, bold and generalized style of painting. His earliest and best-known work was in water color. *Sunset* (20-1), painted in 1914, reveals the character of that early work. The compositional arrangement is simple. The main masses establish the spatial relationships between the foreground and the sparkling agitated water, sun-drenched distant islands, and radiant sky. The artist invented his own symbols to convey his elation at the splendor of the scene before him, and there is a perfect union between the direct, uninhibited manner in which he worked and the water-color medium. The fluid nuances of tone, the direct calligraphy of the brush work, the range of texture all convey the painter's excitement. The color is equally expressive, intense but neither arbitrary nor literal.

In *Deer Island, Maine: Stonington Waterfront*, 1924 (20-2), Marin employed a compositional device suggested by cubism but adapted and used by him in a very personal and original way. The paper is arbitrarily divided by great slashing lines which separate yet relate two views of the subject and at the same time create a sense of foreground, space, and

20-1 (*above*). John Marin, *Sunset*, 1914. Whitney Museum of American Art, New York. 20-2 (*below*). John Marin, *Deer Island, Maine: Stonington Waterfront, 1924.* Yale University Art Gallery.

distance. Equally arbitrary framing lines also provide a dynamic device for focusing attention on the various elements of the subject. Here again the direct brushwork and fresh textures not only describe the picturesque and shabby waterfront but communicate the painter's excitement and ardor. Marin was one of the first American moderns to attract buyers, and his success encouraged other artists to free themselves from tradition and explore new ways of working.

Feininger and Some Experimentalists

Lyonel Feininger (1871-1956), was a contemporary of Marin who also drew largely on cubism for his stylistic devices but adapted cubism to his own particular needs. Feininger left America for Germany when he was sixteen and much of his strongest work was done there. He did not return until he was sixty, but in the paintings done after his return here, such as *Tug* (20-3), he achieved a subtle distillation of a logical yet intensely poetic style. In *Tug* an almost architectural simplification of the great planes of water, sky, and floating smoke is infused with a vivid sense of the poetry of light, air, and space. The ink lines and fluid washes

20-3. Lyonel Feininger, *Tug*, 1941. Solomon R. Guggenheim Museum, New York.

20-4. Max Weber, *Chinese Restaurant*, 1915. Whitney Museum of American Art, New York.

combine in a personal way, and the delicacy of handling is so apparent that one is hardly aware of the strength of the organization.

Feininger and Marin represent opposite polarities of expression. Each projected a deep emotional reaction to visual experience, but where Marin was impulsive and direct, Feininger's expression was methodical, structured, and employed a most disciplined exercise of the painter's craft.

Some of the artists who helped to familiarize Americans with the conventions and innovations of modern painting failed to develop as personal a style as did Marin and Feininger. Maurice Sterne (1877-1957) used an adapted Cézannesque angularity to paint both exotic and American subjects, but the passing of time has revealed their mannerisms and lack of a personal quality of vision. Max Weber (1881-   ) spent three years in France in the first decade of the century and became acquainted with Picasso, Matisse, and other young radicals. His *Chinese Restaurant* (20-4), painted in 1915, remained closer in both spirit and methodology to the synthetic cubism being developed in Paris than did most American painting. Here a series of planes enriched with patterns suggested by a Chinese restaurant are arbitrarily juxtaposed in a series of kaleidoscopic movements to shift the eye in space, suggesting multiple perspectives and a variety of simultaneous impressions. As the years passed, Max Weber, like the cubists abroad, abandoned cubism for less formal modes of expression. His later themes, drawn from New York Jewish life, are treated with expressionistic exaggerations to create a fervent but affectionate kind of caricature, reminiscent of the work of Marc Chagall, a Russian-born expressionist. Walt Kuhn (1880-1949) also went abroad, became ac-

20-5. Walt Kuhn, *Young Clown,* 1945. Collection of American Art, Arizona State College, Tempe, Ariz.

quainted with the heady and vigorous experiments of the young Parisian painters, and returned home to paint acrobats and entertainers with the direct and broad simplifications of form that characterized much of the early work of the *Fauves. The Young Clown* (20-5) reveals the awkward simplicity and strength of feeling with which he portrayed his monumental figures from the world of vaudeville. Perhaps Walt Kuhn's greatest strength came from his singleness of purpose. He restricted himself to familiar subjects and to a single way of working and thereby avoided the tendency to lose himself in experimentation which vitiated so many of the painters of his day.

Arthur Dove (1880-1946) was one of the first artists almost completely to eliminate representational elements from his painting. He went to Paris in 1907, and when he returned home he naturally gravitated into the Stieglitz orbit. As his style matured, his inner moods and emotions became more important to him than external facts. *Distraction* (20-6), painted in 1929, forecasts the abstract expressionism of the fifties. The broadly painted symbols appear to have been put down without premeditation, according to the dictates of momentary feelings. While the patterns might be interpreted as flower and landscape forms treated with childlike naïveté the symbolism is less important than the mood and manner. Arthur Dove was also one of the first Americans to try collage— his portrait of his grandmother was made of a bit of her needlepoint, a

20-6. Arthur Dove, *Distraction*, 1929. Whitney Museum of American Art, New York.

page from her Bible, and a few ancient pressed flowers assembled on a weathered shingle background.

Hartley, Dickinson, Demuth, Stella, and O'Keeffe

Five major painters from this period, like Marin and Feininger, absorbed the new influences from abroad, related these influences to the older tradition of American painting, and achieved a mature realization of their own potentialities. These five artists are Marsden Hartley, Preston Dickinson, Charles Demuth, Joseph Stella, and Georgia O'Keeffe.

Marsden Hartley (1887-1943) was one of the first American painters to be more strongly affected by German expressionism than by Parisian painting. His painting is rugged, to the point of a seeming awkwardness, which is often the result of a conscious avoidance of slick forms and obvious clichés. The forms are generalized, composed with powerful angular rhythms and painted in a thick impasto with sharp lights and heavy darks. Like Winslow Homer and John Marin, he loved the landscape of Maine. *Log Jam, Penobscot Bay* (20-7) reveals the strength of his mature style. The forms of the landscape have been reduced to their fundamentals of

20-7. Marsden Hartley, *Log Jam, Penobscot Bay,* 1940-1941. Detroit Institute of Arts, Detroit, Mich.

pattern, tone, and color. By eliminating the literal and the trivial, Hartley communicates the truth of his insight and the strength of his feeling. No attempt is made to alleviate the ominous strength or lighten the brooding darkness of the Maine landscape. Though his idiom is of the twentieth century, Hartley's direct honesty and his concern with fundamentals relate him to Winslow Homer and the traditions of New England.

Preston Dickinson (1891-1930) developed a strong personal style out of French post-impressionism and cubism. Like many American painters of the twenties, Dickinson found that the city provided him with the play of angles, planes, geometric forms, and spatial thrusts that he loved. He did most of his paintings in Quebec and New York, working in turn with oils, water colors, and pastels, all of which he used with sensitivity and vigor. In *Bridge* (20-8) the foreground plane is firmly established with a few bold, clean forms. The bridge projects the eye forcefully into space while the horizontal lines of the distant shore close the space and resolve the movements initiated by the more dynamic forms in the foreground. Cubism revealed to Dickinson the fascination of precise geometric patterns, shifting planes of movement, and dynamic compositional ar-

20-8. Preston Dickinson, *Bridge*, n. d.
Newark Museum, Newark, N. J.

rangements; and Dickinson perceived these qualities in the cityscape. Unfortunately for American painting, he died before reaching the age of forty.

Like Dickinson, Charles Demuth (1883-1935) was fascinated with the cubist patterns he saw about him. Born in Lancaster, Pennsylvania, he studied at the Pennsylvania Academy of Fine Arts, visited Paris in 1904 and again between 1910 and 1914. Cubism heightened his sophisticated esthetic tastes and his sensitivity to simple shapes, clean lines, and geometric patterns. An aloof elegance distinguished his paintings, which ranged in subject from illustrations of vaudeville and café life through still life to his most fully realized works, extolling the indigenous architecture of America. In *Eggplant and Plums* (20-9) the crystalline clarity of the water color is matched by the precise elegance of the forms of fruit and vegetables, disembodied, weightless, and translated into a network of delicate planes, clear colors, and bold patterns. *My Egypt* (20-10)—its very title relates the past and present—is one of the first paintings to reveal the monumental nature of the industrial architecture of America. The cubist pattern which overlays the forms serves to emphasize the geo-

20-9 (*below*). Charles Demuth, *Eggplant and Plums*, n. d. Art Institute of Chicago, Chicago, Gift of Annie Swan Coburn in memory of Olivia Shaler Swan. 20-10 (*right*). Charles Demuth, *My Egypt*, 1925. Whitney Museum of American Art, New York.

metric components of our industrial architecture and evokes a sense of the timeless grandeur of these severe utilitarian structures. In an age of pallid, imitative architecture, Demuth was one of the first to recognize the dignity and distinction of the native vernacular. Demuth's color shares the cool clarity of his forms. In *My Egypt* the gray-white of the concrete grain elevators stands against the sharp turquoise of the sky. The sand and terra-cotta buildings at the bottom add a warm note which serves as a foil to the predominantly cool color harmony. It is a discreet and controlled color scheme, consistent with Demuth's reserved tastes.

Joseph Stella (1876-1946) found his inspiration in the American city but he was moved most by the tempo of the modern city rather than by the facts of appearance. Stella came to America when he was nineteen and began his career as an illustrator. A return trip to Europe brought him into contact with the French cubists and the futurists of his native Italy. The Italian futurists, particularly concerned with portraying the dynamics of the new industrial age, frequently painted machine forms and other objects in a sequence of positions suggesting motion. Like the cubists, they also portrayed their subjects as though seen simultaneously from a variety of points of view. Aware that these devices were well suited to his needs, Stella returned to America prepared to describe the exciting world about him. *Skyscrapers* (20-11) is one of five panels called "New

20-11. Joseph Stella, *Skyscrapers*, 1922. Newark Museum, Newark, N. J.

York Interpreted." The patterns of the buildings rise in soaring lines, the vibrating darks and lights and shifting planes creating an intense and very personal vision of the city. The colors have the bright, sharp quality of artificial illumination. Stella's paintings have the geometric precision of the forms of the new industrial age, but more important, they convey the dynamics of the American city, a sense of unlimited energy and movement.

During the twenties and early thirties, New York was unquestionably the center of modern art in America. The progressive galleries as well as the critics and periodicals were there. Greenwich Village was the heart of the New York art world; Fifty-seventh Street was just becoming the show window. Artists from all over America were drawn to the metropolis in search of recognition and stimulation. Georgia O'Keeffe (1887-   ) was one of the many to search for success in New York. An art teacher isolated in a small town, she could hardly believe that there existed an audience which would understand her almost abstract drawings and paintings. Stieglitz recognized her power and originality and

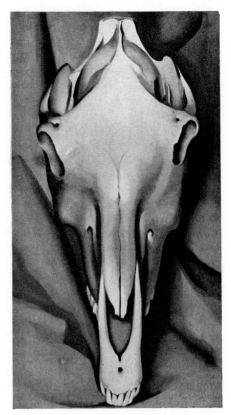

20-12. Georgia O'Keefe, *Horse's Skull on Blue*, 1930. Arizona State College, Collection of American Art, Tempe, Ariz.

gave her a show. Eight years later, he married her. Her early works were frequently pure abstractions; later her subjects were clearly recognizable. No artist has painted a greater range of subject matter than Georgia O'Keeffe—New York skyscrapers, Pennsylvania barns, the canyons and bleached bones of desert New Mexico, leaves and flowers examined closely and then enlarged to reveal their fascinating complexity and beauty. *Horse's Skull on Blue* (20-12) reveals her sensitivity to rhythmic line and bold pattern no matter what the source. Her paintings are typically feminine—intense and lyrical. Blue sky above, flowers in hand, clean white siding of a barn, or blanched skull in the sagebrush all stimulated her to transmute commonplace experiences into elegant clear patterns.

THE "AMERICAN SCENE"

The late twenties witnessed a change of mood. It was as though the artists, ever sensitive, felt a premonition of economic disaster and social chaos and wanted to return to a more familiar and secure world. Most of the expatriates came home more sophisticated and perhaps even wiser, accepting the creative artist's need for his native environment. They had learned much from the disciplines of cubism, expressionism, and abstraction. Even when they were painting with photographic fidelity to actual appearances, as Sheeler did, they thought in terms of formal and abstract elements, building their line movements, dark and light patterns, and color harmonies into formal compositional structures. Though carefully designed, their paintings were also strongly felt, and the sensitivity to formal values did not preoccupy the artists to the exclusion of simple human values. Three men, Charles Sheeler, Edward Hopper, and Charles Burchfield, stand out in retrospect as having done more than any others to fuse the experiments that followed the Armory Show with the older American scene tradition of Homer, Eakins, and the Eight.

Charles Sheeler

Charles Sheeler (1883-   ) has much in common with Demuth. Like Demuth, he was born in Pennsylvania, was introduced to cubism abroad, and discovered in American traditional architecture and contemporary industrial buildings, clear forms consonant with cubist tastes and ideals. Cubism sharpened his vision and photography, a means of earning a livelihood, revealed the cubist elements around him. From these two disciplines, he evolved his sharp, objective style of painting. Sheeler believed that "a picture could have incorporated in it the structural design implied in abstraction, and be presented in a wholly realistic manner" and that the greatest artists present an object "in all its three hundred and sixty degrees of reality rather than the hundred and eighty degrees which the physical eye takes in." *Upper Deck* (20-13) has been viewed with both the physical eye and the mind. Its clarity of form is supra-visual, a reflection of the discerning artist who sees in the utilitarian ventilators and motors fascinating complexities and beauties of form.

Sheeler made a number of paintings of the great industrial plants around Detroit between 1927 and 1930, and these paintings are permeated with an optimistic feeling of confidence in the industrial scene before him. Man was ordering nature along rational and productive patterns, and in his paintings the towering factories and storage silos stand with the same grandeur and dignity as the columned temples of ancient Greece. Where others a few years later would see the industrial scene as a source of exploitation, injustice, and conflict, Sheeler saw it as serene and orderly.

20-13 (*left*). Charles Sheeler, *Upper Deck*, 1929. Fogg Museum of Art, Harvard University, Cambridge, Mass. 20-14 (*right*). Charles Sheeler, *Incantation*, 1940. Brooklyn Museum, Brooklyn, N. Y.

Much of Sheeler's love of industry grew out of his love for geometric patterns, and many of the paintings of his later years are dominated by this love of pure geometric form. *Incantation* (20-14) approaches abstraction. Here the rational, even formal compositional arrangement, the striking simplifications, the disciplined techniques, and the austere but elegant taste implicit in the painting reveal the artist's essentially classic orientation. It is this unique and timely combination of the abstract painter, the realist, and the classicist that has made Sheeler a particularly significant figure in the art of our day.

Edward Hopper

Edward Hopper (1882-   ) also served his apprenticeship in Paris and experienced the discipline of modern experimental painting, but his deep need to create an art of intense reality out of the familiar world led him to abandon the rising tide of stylish international painting. Hopper stated his credo as, "Instead of subjectivity, a new objectivity; instead of abstraction, a reaffirmation of representation and specific subject matter; instead of internationalism, an art based on the American scene." The first of Hopper's paintings to attract the attention of critics and collectors were of New England—paintings of homes and lighthouses illuminated by

20-15. Edward Hopper, *Early Sunday Morning*, 1930. Whitney Museum of American Art, New York.

the cool light of the seashore. Even after Hopper found the subject matter of his mature years in the life of the city, particularly New York, this sensitivity to the quality of light, whether electric light, dawn, or dusk, remained one of the deeply emotive elements of his art.

Architecture, too, seems to play a fundamental role in Hopper's paintings by providing the setting for the drama, for his paintings always imply a drama, albeit a drama of routine human existence. Never melodramatic, always on the level of everyday living, the human factor, too, is ever present, suggesting the continuous flow of life. This suggestion distinguishes Hopper's paintings from those of most of his contemporaries and gives them an added importance. One is keenly aware of the quality of human life behind the façades he paints—life in all its loneliness, ugliness, affection, and nobility. Archetypes of commonplace existence, each Hopper painting sums up a myriad of familiar visual experiences and from them creates a powerfully wrought, deeply emotive work of art.

Early Sunday Morning (20-15), painted in 1930, is one of Hopper's greatest paintings. Here, as in all of his major works, the subject is drawn from the most familiar level of experience. A sense of drama is created by the absence of people, ordinarily an integral part of the scene, and by the warm low light of early morning. The rising sun catches the ripple

20-16. Edward Hopper, *New York Movie*, 1939. The Museum of Modern Art, New York.

of an awning and throws the long shadows which, like a stir of life, silently foretell the coming day. The somber harmony of red brick and green store fronts is relieved by a few sharp bright accents, the striped barber pole and yellow window shades. Color is never used for its sensuous charm alone, just as no forms are introduced only to satisfy an arbitrary concept of composition.

The play of rectangles in the second-story windows, like the alternate door and window shapes of the ground floor, are varied as slightly as the monotonous street, continuously the same and continuously different. This is not the sharp, exciting geometry of Sheeler's industrial world, but the pattern of everyday living—the shabby rectangularity of prosaic life with its chipped corners, its leaning verticals, its eventually sagging horizontals. There is nothing depressing in the vision, for Hopper is not cynical about life. The familiar world is accepted, seen in dignified, monumental terms, and enriched with feeling.

Most of Hopper's paintings are in oil, and he handles the medium in broad planes without a flourish. He neither makes a fetish of a painterly handling of oils nor loses sight of their rich heaviness. His water colors reveal an equal sensitivity to that medium, never lapsing into thin generalities or brushy virtuosity.

New York Movie (20-16) takes as its subject the gaudy, synthetic baroque movie palace of the city with its promise of life, warmth, and excitement. Its glowing lights and ornate furnishings, like the glamorous events on the luminous screen, seem designed to keep out the cold dark streets and shabbily furnished apartments from which the patrons seek escape. Hopper composed the various elements involved in this drama of space, light, form, and human experience with admirable power. The great vertical mass of the foyer wall provides a ponderous, immovable form that establishes both the actual scale and the pretense of the interior. On one side of the wall, the deep emotive space of auditorium carries one's eye to the luminous image on the far screen. In the shallow undistinguished aisle at the right, the usher stands in boredom as mesmerized by her thoughts as the patrons are by the shadows on the screen. The forms and spaces are solid realities, weighty, voluminous, tangible. The light provides the drama; the human dream, the mood. A myriad of such commonplace impressions register in our unanalytical consciousness each day and lie dormant, a potential reservoir of deep feeling. Hopper's unique capacity is his ability to cast these impressions into memorable monumental patterns.

Charles Burchfield

Charles Burchfield (1893-   ) also loved the face of America, but while Sheeler found beauty in the contemporary technology and Hopper in the big city, Burchfield is the interpreter of the American small town and rambling suburb. Burchfield grew up, and did his first paintings, in Salem, Ohio—a town with a railway line, a few factories, stores, quiet streets, and unpretentious houses set amidst farm lands, a link between

20-17. Charles Burchfield, *Ice Glare*, 1933. Whitney Museum of American Art, New York.

America's past and present. Later a position designing wallpaper took Burchfield to live in Buffalo, and he purchased a home in a small nearby town. Here he proceeded to develop as an artist. In his earliest work Burchfield employed decorative simplifications of line and pattern to communicate his strong sense of the rhythmic forces of nature. As he matured in his control of form, space, and color, he kept his tendency to simplify and dramatize. *Ice Glare* (20-17) is in his mature style. Burchfield works most effectively in water color, but his use of the medium is personal and unique, consisting of small brushstrokes of transparent color laid one over the other to build up solidly wrought forms and spaces. *Ice Glare* could be a winter's day in Buffalo or in the back streets of any middle-sized midwestern community. *Ice Glare* reveals a world of awkward angularities—porches, brick warehouses and treeless streets, unrelieved except for the harsh accents of telephone poles. The frame houses and brick buildings typify everything the expatriates hated about America, but Burchfield, like a host of writers from this period, knew these prosaic scenes with both love and hate and from his ambivalence could create powerful images. From this shabby and unprepossessing material the sharp sunlight

20-18. Charles Burchfield, *Sun and Rocks*, 1918-1950. Room of Contemporary Art Collection, Albright Art Gallery, Buffalo, N. Y.

and bold shadows create a world of energetic shapes; the artist is constantly aware of the vigor and sense of life created by these bold patterns. Burchfield, like Hopper, is a master of light, light as it reveals, conceals, and dramatizes, and by its use he creates patterns that we know and therefore have power to move us.

In his most recent work, Burchfield has returned to the awarenesses of his childhood, to the wonders of nature revealed as he wandered through the woods. The wind and the sun, the changing seasons, the forces of growth and decay now provide his subject matter (20-18). By means of stylized simplifications of form and sweeping rhythms of line suggesting the decorative style of his earliest works, he attempts to symbolize the mysterious forces of nature. Burchfield creates in big, bold patterns to convey his strong feelings. The rhythmic movements with which he designs his large compositions are as fundamental as his human convictions, and the strength, honesty, and simple humanity of his paintings provide a valuable counterbalance to the overwhelming sophistication of much contemporary expression.

The "New York" Scene

No painter chronicled the throbbing, intense life of the modern metropolis with more enthusiasm than Reginald Marsh (1898-1954). After graduation from Yale, Marsh studied with Sloan and Luks and served as an illustrator for magazines and the tabloid *Daily News.* This experience, his own temperament, and later study with Kenneth Hayes Miller turned him toward his eventual subject—the life of New York and its continuously fascinating human types and activities.

Marsh's characteristic paintings depict the energy and vitality of the city. His preference was for the crowded streets, the burlesque shows, the honky-tonks and teeming beaches. He painted Coney Island (20-19) endlessly because "a million near-naked bodies can be seen at once, a phenomenon unparalleled in history." The cavorting beach crowd provided him with a panorama of the thin, the fat, the old and young, struggling, making love, sleeping—without dignity or beauty, or for that matter ugliness, but living and exuding energy. It is this sense of overwhelming energy that provides the reaffirming note in Marsh's paintings. Marsh drew on the Renaissance and baroque tradition rather than the impressionist, postimpressionist, and modern. Hogarth and Rowlandson, Rubens, and the great Venetians suggested his mode of representing the human figure through a clearly articulated anatomical structure. The Renaissance

20-19. Reginald Marsh, *Coney Island Beach, Number 1*, 1943. Whitney Museum of American Art, New York.

masters also inspired his compositional arrangements, for it was by building up pyramidal structures from the masses of undignified writhing bodies that he endowed his beach scenes with monumentality of scale. Marsh painted in a variety of media. *Coney Island Beach, Number 1*, like many of his later paintings, is in water color and ink with only occasional additions of pale color animating the black, white, and gray. The pale airy tonality achieved by the limiting of color provides a note of esthetic restraint which keeps the exuberant action and complicated design from overwhelming the observer.

The Soyer brothers, Moses (1899-   ), Isaac (1907-   ), and Raphael, were also painting the New York scene in the thirties and forties. The theater, shop girls, public parks, and street scenes provided the subjects for their Degas-like vignettes. *Office Girls* (20-20), by Raphael Soyer (1899-   ), strikes a note that is both sentimental and reticent. Though the subject matter comes from the same city streets that Marsh painted, Soyer invested it with quiet dignity through simplifications of form, richly brushed paint textures, and closely harmonized colors. Alex-

20-20. (*left*). Raphael Soyer, *Office Girls*, 1936. Whitney Museum of American Art, New York.   20-21 (*right*). Isabel Bishop, *Two Girls*, n.d. Courtesy Metropolitan Museum of Art, Arthur H. Hearn Fund, 1936.

ander Brook (1898-   ), Louis Bouché (1896-   ), and Isabel Bishop also concentrated on the human aspects of the city. Isabel Bishop (1902-   ), like Marsh, prefers the full rounded forms and the stable compositional arrangements of the old masters. Her *Two Girls* (20-21), with its pale colors and richly textured surface, reveals sympathetic observation and sensitive and persuasive draftmanship.

THE SOCIAL COMMENTATORS

The affirmative note that distinguished the American scene paintings was not to be maintained for long. A new and more strident tone was forthcoming, for the American economy and way of life was to be challenged by a series of economic and social disasters. The crash of the stock market in 1929, the great depression of the thirties, the threat of fascism abroad, and the second great World War in the early forties introduced an urgent and at times combative note that was new to American painting.

The depression was to the artists of the thirties what the Armory Show had been to those of the twenties, providing the key to the chief departures from the dominant conventions of the preceding period. The painter of the twenties saw no need to concern himself as a painter with the general problems of our economic life and social organization, feeling that if he painted honestly and managed to support himself he was satisfying his social obligations.

The great depression of the thirties turned many eyes to the fundamental human problems of social and economic dependence. Artists, never too secure, found themselves in a particularly precarious situation. As private fortunes shrank, the artists' regular patrons disappeared. Isolated from the general public by a long tradition of mutual distrust and indifference, artists realized that even the tax-supported relief program instituted by the Federal government depended on public sympathy. Specialized and esoteric esthetic concerns on the part of the artists could alienate the public and endanger the little economic assistance available.

Not only personal need turned the artists' attention to economic problems and away from a too exclusive concern with matters of style. As the depression deepened, many became conscious of inequalities which threatened the democratic way of life. The tragic plight of the vast numbers of unemployed necessitated tax-supported public relief programs which made inroads on the comforts and privileges of the upper-middle and wealthy classes and intensified conflict between the haves and have-nots. Since the Renaissance, artists have participated in political and social struggles. Many American artists of the thirties jumped into the fray, and a vigorous school of social propagandists appeared.

Problems of style, naturally, remained fundamental, but style was disciplined to achieve social effectiveness. Some of the most belligerent of the painters adopted a journalistic manner in which broad, almost cari-

20-22. William Gropper, *Migration, c.* 1932. Arizona State College, Collection of American Art, Tempe, Ariz.

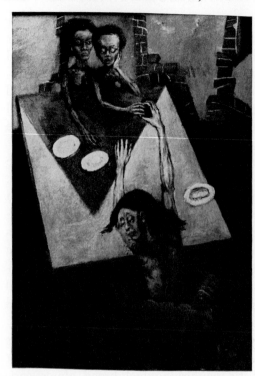

20-23. Philip Evergood, *Don't Cry, Mother*, 1938-1944. The Museum of Modern Art, New York.

catured simplifications were used to provide maximum impact. William Gropper (1897-   ) was one of the most vigorous propagandists. A professional caricaturist, in his paintings he employed the same broadly conceived, simplified symbols of workers, capitalists, politicians, and others that marked his journalistic production. *Migration* (20-22) dramatized the plight of dispossessed farmers of the Southwestern dust bowl, forced to leave their arid and barren farms and wander across the face of America in search of a livelihood. The gaunt forms, harsh tonalities, and simple compositional relationships were carried to the point where they ceased to provide moving symbols of this great and tragic drama and instead become visual clichés. Despite the obvious limitations of Gropper and his fellow propagandists, their passionate indignation helped make America aware of mounting social responsibilities.

Not all of the painting which focused on the social problems during the thirties and early forties drew on journalistic caricature for stylistic inspiration. Philip Evergood (1901-   ) clothed his angry protests against hunger, war, and injustice in an intense and vehement expressionism. *Don't Cry, Mother* (20-23) drew on deep levels of bitterness for its powerfully realized forms. The curious triangle on the table top drama-

20-24. Peter Blume, *Light of the World*, 1932. Whitney Museum of American Art, New York.

tizes the empty plates and reinforces the anguished gesture of the mother and the hopeless apathy of the starving children. Evergood's angry intensity was derived largely from the expressionists and the social realists of central Europe, and he employed typical expressionistic distortions of anatomical forms, exaggerations of details, and violations of perspective and naturalistic proportion.

Peter Blume (1906-   ), born in Russia, came to America as a child, lived on the Lower East Side of New York, and later moved to Brooklyn. Growing up in an atmosphere of skepticism concerning the established order, he included an element of social criticism, either directly stated or implicit, in his painting. His style reveals the impact of the meticulous, sharp-focus manner of the German social-realists of the twenties who combined awkward angularities and curious, almost caricaturelike distortions in precise clear images. *Light of the World* (20-24), like much of his painting, implies a generally critical attitude toward modern life rather than attacking a particular facet of the social order. A marvelously radiant symbol of electricity occupies the center of the canvas. It is surrounded by awe-struck gaping people who, though obviously bewildered, look to the radiant miracle of modern science and engineering for their salvation. The church, the "Light of the World" in past ages, stands in darkness.

The affinity between the social realists and the expressionists of Central Europe was strengthened by the arrival here of a number of refugee artists who left Germany after the advent of Hitler. Hitler declared war on all progressive artists, particularly the propagandists who had attacked reaction and fascism. George Grosz (1893-1959), probably the most influential German refugee artist to seek asylum in America, had been one of the vitriolic critics of the greedy parasitic groups who exploited disorganized Germany after World War I. After his arrival in America, Grosz continued painting in the brilliant, ironic, and bitter style that had brought him renown in Europe. Grosz was above all else master of the expressionistic water color. *Couple* (20-25) reveals his unique ability to expose the weaknesses and complacency of the soft, luxury-loving, self-satisfied urban dweller. The human animal is seen stripped of all nobility and virtue, the self-indulgent product of a decaying society. Grosz was particularly deft at describing a wide variety of surface textures with water color, using biting lines and shimmering luminosities to suggest crepey skins, boney protuberances, rouge, satin, fur. No artist has used water color with a greater sense of its fluid loveliness, but the sensuous charm of the medium never softens his bite.

20-25. George Grosz, *The Couple*, 1934. Whitney Museum of American Art, New York.

20-26 (*above*). Ben Shahn, *Scotts Run, West Virginia*, 1937. Whitney Museum of American Art, New York.　20-27 (*below*). Ben Shahn, *Handball*, 1939. The Museum of Modern Art, New York.

Shahn and Levine

Tragic events of an all-encompassing nature evoke reactions of corresponding intensity. Two artists of particular originality who reacted with power and maturity to the violence of fascism and World War II were Ben Shahn and Jack Levine.

Ben Shahn (1898-   ) was born in Lithuania and came to New York as a child. He grew up in a tough, realistic atmosphere where hatred of injustice and distrust of authority were both common, and he has used his art to give an impassioned expression to these attitudes. At the age of sixteen he went to work as an apprentice in a lithography house, where he developed his certainty of line and uncanny sense of telling detail. In the twenties he traveled and studied in Europe, then returned to America to resume his fight against the evils of a society that was daily sinking deeper into a slough of despondency and conflict. *Scotts Run, West Virginia* (20-26) is in the bitter and powerful style which first attracted attention to his painting. The men stand idly among the lean shabby houses and angular boxcars. Their sad eyes, hard bitter faces, and lax gestures are endowed with a biting intensity through Shahn's harsh delineations and expressive exaggerations. The intense compassion that lies behind this harrowing protest against the tragedy of dispossessed people and wasted lives is made all the more effective by Shahn's avoidance of the stylistic clichés of righteous indignation and moral fervor.

Equally telling in its evocation of atmosphere is *Handball* (20-27). Here Shahn shows himself to be a master of analytical observation. There is no moral fervor driving him; he is absorbed in describing the familiar environment with a passionate clarity of vision. Since World War II, the intensity of feeling in Shahn's paintings has been softened by more sophisticated esthetic values. Surface textures are complex and involved, and color harmonies are subtly modulated. There is little chance that Shahn will lose his sense of human values in the rising tide of contemporary sophistication, for he is reputed to have said, "Is there nothing to weep about in this world any more? Is all our pity and anger to be reduced to a few tastefully arranged straight lines or petulant squirts?"

Jack Levine (1915-   ) is the youngest and perhaps last of the great social satirists born of the troubled mid-century. Levine was born in Boston. He attended a settlement house art class and his talent came to the attention of a Harvard art professor who introduced him to the old masters, including Daumier. Like Daumier, Levine is at his most brilliant when he is attacking the corrupt, hypocritical, and self-indulgent elements

20-28. Jack Levine, *Welcome Home*, 1946. Brooklyn Museum, Brooklyn, N. Y.

of society. *Welcome Home* (20-28) reveals his distaste for success, authority, and the shrewd men and women who, he feels, dishonor power. Levine's devices for distorting and editorializing tend to be more traditional and painterly than those used by Ben Shahn. The heads are enlarged as in a medieval Flemish painting. The physiognomy is exaggerated to create vivid types and the shimmering luminous paint surfaces often recall Rubens. The moderns too have contributed to his style—Soutine, the anatomical distortions with psychological implications; *Les Fauves*, the color. Though Levine is very aware of the great masters of today and the past, there is nothing academic nor derivative about his art. His intensity of feeling and splendid indignation are unique. Light glints from the writhing surfaces of his forms which seem to swell and shrink under the pressure of subterranean emotional pressures. Somewhere Levine has stated that the artist's function is to bring "the great tradition and whatever is great about it up to date." His own work has contributed to this worthy ideal for he has related twentieth-century American painting to Hogarth, Goya, Daumier, and the other great social satirists of the past.

The socially conscious artists almost disappeared after World War II. Even Ben Shahn and Jack Levine tended to be less indignant and more beautiful. This general tendency to subordinate social themes to esthetics

20-29. Robert Gwathmey, *End of Day*, 1943. International Business Machines Collection.

is well exemplified in the paintings of Robert Gwathmey (1903-   ). The subject of *End of Day* (20-29) is one which might be charged with indignation or compassion, but this handsome organization of patterns, line movements and colors, transmutes the spectator's emotional reactions to an esthetic plane. The faded work clothes provide a muted harmony of grays, blues, rose-browns, and pale pinks; the play of verticals and horizontals creates a spirited abstract composition, and the stylizations elevate and abstract the play of sympathy and sentiment. The step toward abstraction in the arts has been all-pervasive in the years since 1945. Even the few artists who still appear to be motivated by social problems prefer to sacrifice immediacy to sensuous and formal qualities.

THE MURALISTS

The years of the depression and of social upheaval also witnessed a temporary stimulation of mural painting in America. During the twenties, America had become increasingly aware of a vigorous school of mural painting in Mexico. Mexico was experiencing a social revolution, and a large group of progressive painters, headed by Diego Rivera, José Clemente Orozco, and David Alfaro Siqueiros, initiated a program of mural painting as a means of furthering that revolution. Their wish was to create an art that was monumental, national, and heroic, one that would become part of the national consciousness. American artists watched the development of the Mexican school of mural painting with intense interest, and many felt that the Mexican artists gained in stature as they dedicated themselves to communal goals. Rivera and Orozco were invited to the United States in the late twenties and early thirties to execute mural projects, and their presence here stimulated a revival of mural painting.

Thomas Hart Benton (1889-   ) was best known of the American muralists, for he was productive, vocal, and disputatious. Benton was born in Missouri, and both family tradition and temperament were conducive to a strong affection for the customs and the landscape of the Middle West. As a youth he studied in New York and Paris, but the decorative and stylistic abstractions then in vogue did not appeal to his argumentative and chauvinistic nature. The success of the Mexican muralists suggested an outlet to Benton for his essentially popular point of view. He commenced painting murals in which a sequence of related

20-30. Thomas Hart Benton, *Arts of the West,* 1932. Art Museum of the New Britain Institute, New Britain, Conn.

20-31. Anton Refregier, *Fire: 1906*, 1947. Rincon Annex Post Office, San Francisco, Calif.

scenes overlap and interpenetrate one another to create a lively, almost journalistic style. *Arts of the West* (20-30) has seven or eight vignettes of western life related by this effective compositional device. The restless movements and brilliant tonal and color patterns are skillfully counterbalanced to create a painting that is dynamic rather than architectonic. Benton's view of America is essentially a picturesque one. His caricatured personalities and colorful versions of local customs were in accord with popular conceptions of the American scene, and in his subsequent writings and paintings he remained the champion of popular concepts, particularly of the vigorous West as against the effete and inbred East.

Among the relief programs set up to care for the unemployed during the depression were various projects to care for artists. A number of fine murals were painted for public buildings as part of these projects, and in 1935 a section of Fine Arts was formed by the Federal government under the auspices of the Treasury Department. This bureau was not designed primarily to provide economic assistance to artists but to enrich our public buildings with the talents of America's leading painters. *Fire: 1906* (20-31), by Anton Refregier (1905-   ), depicting an episode in the history of San Francisco, is part of a large mural decoration in the Rincon Annex Post Office in San Francisco, executed immediately after World War II. About this time the entire program was discontinued, partly as an economy move in government and partly because the murals too frequently provoked controversy. While many of the murals executed under this program hardly merited monumental proportions, a number of our most distinguished painters received their first important commissions under the program and many of our public buildings are handsomer because of it.

REGIONALISM

Regionalism developed during the thirties as a reaction against the cosmopolitanism of the previous two decades. Many artists returned home disillusioned with the expatriate world and the sterility of Bohemian life to find an America different from that they had left behind. Much of the complacency was gone, and the sense of national peril that accompanied the economic crisis of the depression brought about a general re-evaluation of American culture and its promise. The picturesque variety of American life and the significance of its traditions were discovered. Part of this rediscovery grew from the government-sponsored relief programs for needy artists. Local art centers and classes in the arts and crafts were set up in widely dispersed areas throughout the country, and people were encouraged to develop their abilities and continue the practice of local traditions in the arts. In addition, a great historic research project was initiated to record our native tradition in the arts and crafts. This resulted in the authoritative survey of American crafts known as "The

20-32. Grant Wood, *American Gothic*, 1930. Art Institute of Chicago, Chicago, Friends of American Art Gift.

20-33. Ivan Albright, *Fleeting Time, Thou Hast Left Me Old,* 1929-1930. Courtesy Metropolitan Museum of Art, George A. Hearn Fund, 1950.

Index of American Design" which provided many of the illustrations used in this volume.

These projects and the general temper of the times combined to produce a lively "back-to-the-soil" movement and redirected the artists' attention to their native haunts. The regionalist painters were supported by a group of such writers as William Faulkner, John Steinbeck, and James Farrell, who used their talents to describe the problems and ways of life of different localities. Even the folk music of the remote parts of America was rediscovered at this time. Thomas Benton, one of the chief spokesmen for the regionalism of the thirties, devoted much of his talent to a glorification of the folk ways of his native Missouri.

One of the most effective painters of the Middle West was Grant Wood (1892-1942). Grant Wood grew up in Cedar City, Iowa, where his ability received sufficient recognition and support to enable him to go abroad for a period of study. Paris introduced him to impressionism, and while his work in this style was competent, it was neither distinguished nor highly personal. During a second trip abroad, Wood became interested in the meticulously wrought paintings of the Middle Ages. He then realized that he was most moved by paintings of familiar and homely things seen and described with love and intensity. He returned home determined to paint his Iowa neighbors and environment with all the truthfulness and affection that had distinguished the medieval Flemish and German painters. *American Gothic* (20-32) is a tribute to the success with which he realized this ambition. The sober faces of his sister and dentist have been recorded with medieval sobriety and concentration. The clothes, pitchfork, and Gothic revival farmhouse in the background are unequivocally authentic. While such a painting might appear to be an expression of unselective realism, Wood has done his own very subtle editorializing. He has selected types of personalities that extoll the quiet, honest, hard-working life of the Middle West. The sober verticality of the main compositional masses and the pyramidal grouping of the figures in relation to the gable of the house establish a feeling of sober stability. Lastly, the implication of spirituality in the Gothic window and the title all bespeak a conscious rejection of urbanism and Bohemianism as well as of the sophistication of modern art.

The regionalism of the thirties was not only a rediscovery of America; it was also an attempt by artists to achieve a reintegration with the traditional pattern of American life and a reaffirmation of faith in that life. John Steuart Curry (1897-1946), Peter Hurd (1904-   ), Aaron Bohrod (1907-   ), and a host of others painted their familar environment with affection and pungent realism and did much to popularize the American scene and create a new clientele of middle-class patrons.

Ivan Le Lorraine Albright (1897-   ), a Chicagoan, shares almost nothing with the other mid-western painters except the accident of geography; indeed, the independence of his style is the antithesis of the grassroots popularity of much regional painting. Stylistically as independent of New York as he is of the regional idiom, Albright reveals the deep ferment and originality of middle-western culture. He first attracted notice when the Chicago group came to national attention. Albright is a painter of people and things, and his pinpoint vision is attuned to the corrosive, sad poetry of time. In *Fleeting Time, Thou Hast Left Me Old* (20-33) he developed the theme in his typical manner. The forms are bathed in a harsh raking light that reveals all the worn surfaces—the wrinkles, hairs, and veins with which age covers the human body, as well as the frayed, tattered, mildewed, and cracked surfaces which the passing of time brings to things. From such tawdry material, Albright created a strange, melancholy, and haunting vision of curious strength and originality. He works on each of his canvases for many years, slowly building up the intricate surface textures and involved forms to achieve his own particular intensity. The title of one of his latest canvases, on which he labored for over fifteen years, sums up his unique and pessimistic attitude toward life with peculiar fitness—*Poor Room—There is No Time, No End, No Today, No Yesterday, No Tomorrow, Only the Forever, and Forever, and Forever, Without End.*

Regionalism ceased to be a conscious artistic movement in the forties, but by then it had achieved certain ends. A number of local schools of painting had developed in the Middle West, the Far West, the South, and the Southwest, though New York still remained the center of the art world. America had rediscovered itself and its rich diversity of customs, peoples, and resources.

Modern Painting:

Since 1945

THE MOST OBVIOUS CHARACTERISTIC OF AMERICAN PAINT-
ing since 1945, the end of World War II, has been the overwhelming
trend toward abstraction and the attempt on the part of each artist to
develop a highly personal and unique style of painting.

During the years of war, the art world lay relatively quiescent, but
the end of the war witnessed a rebirth of painting in America. As in the
period following World War I, a host of new influences from Europe
were operative. Picasso, Miro, Tanguy, Dali, Klee, Hoffmann, Mondrian,
and many others were all discovered or rediscovered, and by their example
or presence (Tanguy, Dali, Hoffmann, and Mondrian had settled in America), they directed American painting into new paths of exploration.
Fantastic inventiveness (Picasso), brilliant wit (Miro), strangely haunting dreams (Tanguy and Dali), supersensitive whimsey and naïveté
(Klee), violent spontaneous expression (Hoffmann), geometric impersonality (Mondrian) were all re-established as legitimate goals.

591

Many factors contributed to the development of abstract and highly personal modes of expression. First, these tendencies had already been initiated here by Marin, Dove, O'Keeffe, Stella, and others in the twenties. Second, the representational vein had achieved a mature formulation in the work of the American scene painters; the overemphasis on picturesque aspects of the environment that characterized the regionalists already foreshadowed the demise of that tradition. The younger men in the army who saw the great collections of Europe felt an affiliation with the great arts of all times that superseded any local loyalties and made them cultural internationalists.

A more deep-seated concern also influenced a turn from the older tradition of realism. The horror, waste, and tragedy of war made it difficult to glorify man and his works. After World War I, Dada had expressed disillusion and disbelief in traditional institutions. Again after World War II, the artist felt impelled to find some eternal and timeless truths beyond the pitfalls of love, hate, patriotism, and nationalism—noble sentiments that repeatedly led to slaughter and violence. Abstract art held out this promise, for it was an art based on the pure, timeless, and universal art elements—line, form, space, color, texture, and the compositional verities. Artists sought to develop a new and universal language of plastic expression, fundamental to the great art of all the ages, and so to arrive at a universal language beyond the boundaries of nationalism and of any one period in history.

In addition to being abstract, American painting became increasingly personal after 1945. Even though an artist spoke a timeless language he spoke as an individual, a unique human being who neither thought nor felt identically with any other person. It was therefore necessary to forge a personal mode of expression from this universal language. Consequently, each artist worked to develop a unique and singular manner of speech by following the dictates of his own ideas, impulses, and feelings.

The amount of painting produced since the end of World War II is prodigious in quantity and variety. Its vigor and quality attest to the vitality of the modern movement. In order to get any systematic picture of the kaleidoscopic range in styles of the contemporary scene, some system of classification is necessary. Any such system involves rather arbitrary pigeonholing which distorts and simplifies the complexities of the artist's impulses. The two terms that most conveniently describe the extreme tendencies in contemporary painting, *abstraction* and *expressionism* are in themselves subject to a wide range of interpretations and represent overlapping categories. The attempt to classify styles as abstract or expressionist is complicated further by the fact that each of these general terms represents a tendency inherent in all art. The tendency to abstract is a tendency to formalize, simplify, and generalize. The tendency toward expressionism is a tendency to emphasize, exaggerate, and editorialize. All art involves both. Both seek essences—the abstract artist, the visual essence; the expressionist, the emotional essence. Since it is impossible to say where realism ends and abstraction or expressionism begins, no system is valid which does more than classify according to general tendencies and thereby provide a picture of the range and diversity of the contemporary scene. The following system of classification may help to provide such a picture.

The Abstract Painters
    (1) Geometric Abstraction
    (2) Symbolic Abstraction
    (3) Expressionistic Abstraction

The Expressionist Painters
    (1) Abstract Expressionism and Action Painting
    (2) Traditional Expressionism
    (3) Romantic Expressionism
    (4) Primitivism

The Traditional Painters
    (1) Surrealism
    (2) Precisionism

The following discussion is organized around the classifications described above with a few typical, well-known members of each group selected for discussion. We are too close to the period to profit from the perspective of time and state who among the contemporary artists will appear the most significant to later generations. That will depend upon the interests of those generations. Most of the artists to be discussed were born after 1900 and achieved their artistic maturity during the postwar years. Many were born abroad but have settled in America. Today, being an American artist is largely a matter of residence. The contemporary art world is cosmopolitan and international in flavor. Publications, reproductions, and traveling exhibitions make all artists familiar with and influenced by what is being done elsewhere. Therefore, foreign-born artists who have established their residence in America are included in this survey of contemporary American painting while Americans who live abroad are, for the most part, omitted.

21-1 (*left*). Piet Mondrian, *Composition in White, Black, and Red*, 1936. The Museum of Modern Art, New York. 21-2 (*right*). Josef Albers, *Homage to the Square: "Ascending,"* 1953. Whitney Museum of American Art, New York.

THE ABSTRACT PAINTERS

Geometric Abstraction

The most extreme painters of geometric abstractions restrict themselves to the use of geometric forms. The awkward term *neo-objective* has also been applied to this kind of painting. Piet Mondrian (1872-1944), who was born and started his career in Holland, has been a leader of the group. Mondrian, like many painters associated with the Bauhaus in Germany, the constructivists of Central Europe, and the Stijl group in Holland, employed painting to investigate the stylistic problems that grow from the mechanistic character of our contemporary industrial technology. Mondrian's early paintings veered off from cubism toward geometric abstraction but retained the vibrating surfaces and painterly handling of the cubists. The paintings in his final style, like *Composition in White, Black and Red* (21-1), are as clean, sharp-edged, and pure in their geometric formality as if they had been produced by precision tools. Using only lines and rectangles, Mondrian achieves a maximum of interest by his sensitive variations of size, shape, and color. The pleasure one derives from such a canvas is conveyed by the sense of order and "rightness" in the relationship of parts. Here, all of the sentimental, humanistic, and associative elements of painting have been removed, leaving only the formal and abstract elements. The result is a rarefied, impersonal kind of

21-3. Irene Rice Pereira, *Green Depth,* 1944. Courtesy Metropolitan Museum of Art, George A. Hearn Fund, 1944.

beauty that reminds one of the German art critic Winckelmann's famous dictum, "Pure beauty, like pure water, is tasteless." Mondrian's painting has had a tremendous impact on modern architectural and industrial design.

Josef Albers (1888-   ) came to America from Germany where he had been associated with the Bauhaus group. In *Homage to the Square: "Ascending"* (21-2), as in much of his painting, Albers restricts the forms to squares, going even farther than Modrian in eliminating variety of form in his search for simplicity and order. By restricting the variety of forms in his paintings Albers is able to explore the possibilities of color more completely. Each of his compositions represents a color experiment. Albers will surround a neutral gray with two brilliant colors which, upon prolonged observation, will modify the gray and cause a sensation of continuously changing color relationships. Albers, like Mondrian, approaches the art of painting as would a scientist or engineer, albeit a scientist or engineer with exquisite taste.

A number of painters in the early fifties were involved in extending the range of abstract painting without including representational ele-

21-4 (*left*). Bradley Tomlin, *No. 1, 1951*. Munson-William-Proctor Institute, Utica, N. Y., Gift of Edward Root. 21-5 (*below*). Jimmy Ernst, *Alone*, 1954. Solomon R. Guggenheim Museum, New York.

ments, and their thoughtful explorations of the varying phases of geometric abstraction have been continuously interesting. Irene Rice Pereira (1907-   ) employs a variety of forms and adds variations of surface texture and a strong movement in space to increase the interest and complexity of abstract painting. *Green Depth* (21-3) carries the eye back and forth in a series of regular but rhythmic movements that suggests a musical fugue in its involved and repetitious complexity. In some of her compositions Pereira has intensified the sense of movement in space without recourse to traditional perspective by attaching layers of transparent and translucent materials to the canvas. By employing plastics and synthetics she has suggested new avenues of technical exploration in transparency, translucence, refraction, and color modulation.

Two other paintings further indicate the range of geometric abstraction. *No. 1, 1951* (21-4), by Bradley Tomlin (1899-   ), is both geometric and painterly; that is, it candidly avows the character of oil paint and the brushing activity. Although it repeats a few basic motifs these motifs are developed with a rich variety. *Alone* (21-5), by Jimmy Ernst (1916-   ), employs a great variety of lines, tones, and textures and yet manages to establish an integrated relationship between its differing forms. Though he has used geometric elements, the artist seems more concerned

21-6. Stuart Davis, *Something on the 8 Ball*, 1953-1954. Philadelphia Museum of Art, Philadelphia.

with communicating human experience and relationships than with formal problems of composition. The title and the enigmatic huskiness of tone and color lend a sense of the essential isolation of all human beings. The mood of *Alone* is not too far removed from that of Hopper's *New York Movie*, but the means could hardly be more different. Ernst frequently employs symbolic rather than geometric elements in his composition.

Symbolic and Expressionistic Abstraction

Much abstract painting employs forms derived from the visual world around us, formalized to the point where we see them as symbols or interesting patterns rather than as representations of the visual world.

Stuart Davis (1894-   ), who belongs to an earlier generation than most of the painters now being discussed, is probably the American pioneer of this kind of stylized abstraction. Davis was schooled on the colorful later phase of cubism and from this stimulus he developed his bold, postery, witty style. Though an abstract painter, Davis is a painter of America; he loves jazz, loves its precision, rhythm, vigor, and inventiveness—qualities which are reflected in his paintings. He sees many things about him that make him want to paint—"the brilliant colors on gasoline stations, chain store fronts, and taxicabs—fast travel by train, auto, and airplane—electric signs." In texture, character, and tempo, his paintings suggest contemporary American life even though, like *Something on the*

21-7. Mark Tobey, *Threading Light*, 1942. The Museum of Modern Art, New York.

8 Ball (21-6), they do not describe the American scene literally. His amusing interpolations of lettering and street signs add an unexpected but typical contemporary element to his compositions. The art of Stuart Davis reflects a gay, hedonistic, contemporary mood. The handsome colors, ingenious patterns, dynamic rhythms, and frequent surprises reveal taste, wit, originality. It is a sophisticated art which has developed from our rich cosmopolitan culture.

Mark Tobey (1890-   ) also employs an amalgam of identifiable symbols and purely abstract elements in his subtle and elegant art. He is from Seattle, Washington, and, like many painters from the Far West, he has absorbed much from the Orient. His sensitive linear and calligraphic patterns and his taste for muted color harmonies both reveal his admiration for traditional Chinese painting and Oriental prints. *Threading Light* (21-7) seems to have been inspired by night photographs made of moving lights. The ever-moving white lines swirl, dip, sink into space, and encircle a number of enigmatic symbols. Careful observation reveals bird forms, wine glasses, a guitar player, a seated Buddha, musical instruments, and other objects. *Threading Light* might be about either an automobile trip or an intellectual journey, but in either case its relationship to actual experience is less important than its fascinating visual complexity.

THE EXPRESSIONIST PAINTERS

Abstract Expressionism and Action Painting

The latest arrivals in the field of abstract painting, the abstract expressionists provide a bridge between abstraction and expressionism. Freely painted, their abstractions frequently seem dictated by the natural movements of the hand, by the shapes of the brushes, and by the texture of the paints. "Action" painters stress direct execution, so that the observer can respond kinetically to the movements whereby the painting was created; consequently one of their primary aims is to preserve the line movements and forms that reveal the process of painting. The medium and the tools used in the painting act are of primary importance also since they facilitate, inhibit, and to a degree control the painting activity. Frequently the action painters start out with no guide or plan beyond an initial impulse. The painting develops from the painter's continued power to invent, improvise, and expand. When completed, the painting stands as a pure expression of the artist's creative impulses as they have been poured forth in a frenzied interaction between the developing mass of color, line, tone, and texture and the artist's physical, intellectual, and esthetic make-up.

21-8. Hans Hoffmann, *Construction,* 1948. Whitney Museum of American Art, New York.

The chief personality behind the development of abstract expressionism was Hans Hoffmann (1880-   ), who came to America from Germany, an expressionist who owed much to Kandinsky. Hoffmann introduced many American painters to expressionism, stressing the importance of the direct expression of kinesthetic elements, of the tension and "push and pull" inherent in all space and form relationships. In his early teaching here, the direct response of the hand to the movements of the eye was emphasized, and later the painting act became of primary importance.

In *Construction* (21-8) Hoffmann applied the usual artist's oil paint with the traditional brushes, and consequently the qualities of shape, texture, and line are of a familiar painterly nature. Freely painted lines, textures, and patterns are woven through a rectangular structure with the impact of an exclamation or a vehement gesture. Such abandon can be exciting. This is painting as an elemental act, exhilarating in its spontaneous unfolding.

The most publicized of the abstract expressionists was Jackson Pollock (1912-1956), who painted his huge canvases by laying them on the floor and pouring and splashing paint from buckets or dripping it from sticks. Pollock used commercial enamels for his paintings because the texture of the enamels was better suited to the pouring and dripping activity than the usual, heavy, artist's oils. The result was a fascinating labyrinth of interweaving lines which move in a vehement tangle through space and create exciting patterns. In *Autumn Rhythm* (21-9), Pollock achieved a certain finality by pushing the whirling linear movements resulting from the pouring and throwing action as far as Mondrian and Albers pushed geometric abstraction.

While Pollock used fine lines and spatters to create his whirling textured surfaces, Franz Kline (1910-   ) brushes thick masses of heavy oil into angry patterns which achieve power through their massive simplifications of shape and movement and the elimination of color (his characteristic palette is black and white). Part of the impact of Kline's painting is dependent on size. *Siegfried* (21-10) is over eight feet high, but even a small reproduction carries the vehemence of a grandiose gesture of heretical intensity. Kline achieves what appears to be a pure projection of violent emotion into painted form, but his canvases reveal little variety.

In *Wall Painting* (21-11), Robert Motherwell (1915-   ) stays closer to traditional concepts of compositional organization than Pollock and makes a more considered disposition of forms than Kline. In this painting, the astonishing shapes appear consistent with one another in their size and weight, and the dispositions of dark and light and of colors have been

21-9 (*above*). Jackson Pollock, *Autumn Rhythm*, 1950. Courtesy Metropolitan Museum of Art, George A. Hearn Fund, 1957.   21-10 (*below*). Franz Kline, *Siegfried*, 1958. Carnegie Institute, Pittsburgh, Pa.

21-11 (*above*). Robert Mother-well, *Wall Painting*, 1950. Samuel Kootz Gallery, New York.   21-12 (*left*). Willem de Kooning, *Woman I*, 1950-1952. The Museum of Modern Art, New York.

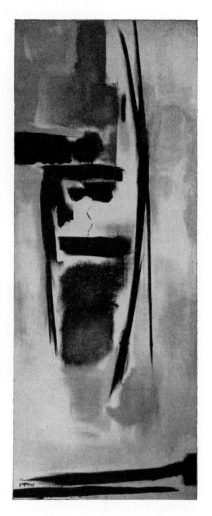

21-13 (*below*). William Baziotes, *Flame*, 1954. Solomon R. Guggenheim Museum, New York. 21-14 (*right*). Theodore Stamos, *Greek Orison*, 1952. Whitney Museum of American Art, New York.

calculated with an eye to a balance of weight and movements within the confines of the canvas. Much of the effectiveness of the painting comes from the element of surprise and paradox, the almost tender awkwardness, the curious dissonances of shape, the enclosing and bursting through. By violating the clichés of decorous arrangement, Motherwell achieves a new vigor.

Willem de Kooning (1904-   ) has been one of the leaders of the action painters. In his *Woman I* (21-12) he painted with a furious abandon equal to that of Hoffmann or Pollock, but from the tempest of slashing lines, rich smears, and runs, the form of a woman appears. A suggestion of volume, of the human form composed in space, and of a predatory, masklike face might be considered representational elements, but the

21-15. H. Bryan Wilson, *Ross Snow Geese*, 1958. Allen Gallery, New York.

essence of the painting seems expressed through its vehemence rather than its subject matter.

Not all of the abstract expressionists are action painters. William Baziotes (1912-   ) uses curious and cryptic symbols that appear to well up from the subconscious. Though the shapes may not be calculated, the execution appears deliberate and the compositional arrangements seem carefully considered. Baziotes, too, begins with as much spontaneity and as few preconceived and limiting ideas as possible. As the painting is completed, the subject reveals itself. *Flame* (21-13) is logically organized but logic does not explain the fascination of this mysterious but simply patterned canvas. There is a surrealist flavor about Baziotes, and his curious over-sized paintings recall the works of both Klee and Miro as well as the enigmatic symbols ancient people carved on rocks. Theodore Stamos (1922-   ) is an abstract expressionist whose paintings reveal an elegance far removed from the turbulent vehemence associated with the group. His paintings may be executed in a direct and unpremeditated manner, but he retains traditional compositional concepts in organizing his highly refined relationships of lines and tones and his subtle low-keyed colors. In *Greek Orison* (21-14), as in most of his canvases, the vivid calligraphy of the strong lines and accents constitutes the chief emotive element. These richly brushed lines, often thickened to the point where they constitute masses, are sensitively composed in relation to the long vertical shape of the panel and the logically disposed tonal pattern. Stamos uses quiet, closely harmonized colors, with grays, browns, dull greens, and creamy whites predominating.

The abstract expressionists, also known as the "New York School," constituted the most vociferous group of painters in the New York area in the late forties and early fifties. San Francisco also had a vigorous and highly vocal group of abstract expressionists. Richard Diebenkorn (1922-), a leader in the San Francisco group, has re-emphasized figurative elements and an expressive development of spatial and color elements since the mid-fifties. Bryan Wilson (1927-   ) has moved continuously toward a broader and more summary style of painting with the forms of the western landscape, its animals and birds in particular, providing the principal elements in his vehement and subtly colored canvases. *Ross Snow Geese* (21-15), a large casein in which grays, olive greens, blacks, and whites predominate, reveals his interest in simply but tensely assembled compositions.

21-16. Abraham Rattner, *The Emperor*, 1944. Whitney Museum of American Art, New York.

21-17. Rico Lebrun, *Crucifixion*, 1950. Collection of Syracuse University.

Traditional Expressionism

The traditional expressionists strive for the direct communication of strong feeling by the vigorous use of line, color, and tone, and the free distortion of form and space relationships, but the content of their paintings remains readily recognizable. Many of the social commentary painters like Shahn, Levine, and Evergood might be logically included in this group.

A tremendous number of distinguished painters might be discussed here, but limitations of space permit discussion of only a few. Abraham Rattner (1895-   ) was born and raised in the United States but spent most of the twenties and thirties living and painting in Paris, where he absorbed many of the ideas of Picasso, Braque, and Rouault. His mature paintings are rich and full-bodied in color, using jewel-like, intense colors in complexly orchestrated relationships. The paint is applied in a thick impasto so that it has a heavy glittering texture, and frequently the rich masses of color are outlined with black or strong darks to stress the formal aspects of the design. *The Emperor* (21-16) employs a number of expressionistic devices—the head seen in profile and then full face, the bold and arbitrary dislocations of anatomical forms and space relationships, and the vigorous angularities of pattern. *The Emperor*, like many of Rattner's paintings, uses an accepted symbol as the basis for a multifaceted state-

21-18. Stephen Greene, *The Deposition*, 1947. Whitney Museum of American Art, New York.

ment with broad philosophic implications. The emperor, a ruler of men, appears at the same time a questioning, uncertain, perhaps even a frightened man. Though he is a ruler who imposes his will on others, he too seems like a pawn in a chess game. It is an ambiguous statement, full of ironic implications, a stimulus to further thought and observations.

Rico Lebrun (1900-   ), like Rattner, uses a formalized expressionist style that reflects the influence of Picasso. In his *Crucifixion* (21-17) he employs traditional religious iconography to create a deeply disturbing and compelling modern version of his theme. Like Picasso's famous *Guernica*, Lebrun's *Crucifixion* is not a pictorial illustration even though the various episodes and elements of the Crucifixion can be identified. Instead, it is an epigrammatic distillation, through the use of formalized, abstracted and distorted naturalistic forms, of the mood of tragedy, suffering, and sacrifice.

The story of the Crucifixion also provided the theme for *The Deposition* (21-18), by Stephen Greene (1917-   ), which employs a sensitive, personal kind of expressionistic distortion. The slight modulations of tone by which the forms are modeled, the curious angularities of pattern, and the emphasis on gestures and facial expressions to evoke a tremulous atmosphere of bereavement recall certain mannerisms of the medieval painters. One cannot but be impressed by the range of expressionist painting, which encompasses both the tender sentiment of Greene's *Deposition* and the anguished intensity of Lebrun's *Crucifixion*.

Romantic Expressionism

A curious vein of sentimental or romantic expressionism also appeared in the forties, derived, to a considerable degree, from the French neoromanticism of an earlier decade. A number of American painters, Eugene Berman (1899-   ), Morris Graves (1910-   ), and Loren MacIver (1909-   ), became involved in a type of moody subjective painting which explored the world of dreams and meditative moods and drew upon a vast storehouse of subjective impressions for devices to communicate their mood.

21-19. Loren MacIver, *Hopscotch*, 1940. The Museum of Modern Art, New York.

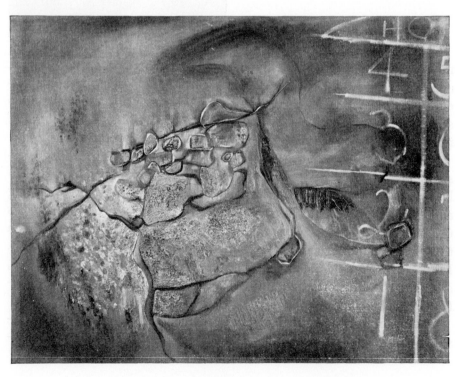

An air of quietude and dreamy subjectivity characterizes much of the work of Loren MacIver, who employs simplifications of form and various ingenious distortions to intensify the subtle poetry of her paintings. Sometimes, as in *Hopscotch* (21-19), she appears to do little more than record what she observes, but in the act of recording she creates unique and evocative compositions which disclose a telling selectivity and personal emphasis. In *Hopscotch* the scarred and oily sidewalk reveals its illusive and magical patterns. Painters of lyric subjectivity, like Loren MacIver, have frequently been classified as "magic realists," realists who see the strange and fantastic aspects of commonplace things. The magic realists, like many of the surrealists, use precise objective techniques to intensify the mood of fantasy which characterizes their vision of the world.

Primitivism

The arts of primitive cultures and of "primitive" (that is, untrained) artists have introduced a number of fresh approaches to painting. The world of children's art and the artistic expression of the insane have also provided intense and powerful symbols and expressive devices that come directly from subterranean sources within the human psyche. Many of the distortions of proportion and perspective used by the expressionists, like enlarging important parts of the body for emphasis or showing x-ray

21-20. Joseph Glasco, *Figures in Landscape*, 1954. Private collection.

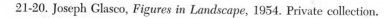

views into objects, have been suggested by children's art. Adolph Gottlieb (1903-   ), William Baziotes, and a number of the other previously mentioned painters frequently seem inspired by the enigmatic symbols with which primitive peoples adorn their dwellings, ceramics, and bodies. The evocative power of surfaces that appear enriched by fading and worn by time and ritual also is exploited.

Figures in Landscape (21-20), by Joseph Glasco (1925-   ), appears childlike on the surface but the precise compulsive linear patterns and the strange rigidity revealed by closer examination seem more related to the art of schizophrenics. Elements in Glasco's paintings also suggest the magic repetitions and formalizations so characteristic of the arts of primitive cultures. The curious patterns have a strange capacity to evoke a sense of the morbid complexities of emotional disturbances. It is as though one were suddenly enabled to see into the fearful world of the deranged.

THE TRADITIONAL PAINTERS

In one sense significant painting is almost never traditional since painters achieve significance by enlarging the domain of perception and going beyond existing traditions. There is, however, a continuing body of painting being produced in America that employs more traditional representational disciplines and painting techniques and still conveys a sensitive and personal point of view. In the thirties Eugene Speicher (1883-   ), Henry McFee (1886-1953), and others created solidly wrought compositions which in no sense repeated timeworn clichés. Since then the surrealists, the precisionists, the magic realists, and others have continued to create distinguished and perceptive paintings that convey contemporary perceptions but employ the more traditional language of painting.

Surrealism

Surrealism was never a vigorous movement in America though much contemporary American painting reveals overtones of fantasy and subjectivity derived from the surrealists. Yves Tanguy (1900-   ), born in France, settled in America in the thirties and helped to popularize surrealism here. *Fear* (21-21) is typical of his style. A deep vista of space is peopled with enigmatic shapes and glimmering, luminous streaks of light. The foreground is filled with curious, involved forms which at first glance suggest undersea life, but on closer examination appear to be

21-21. Yves Tanguy, *Fear*, 1949. Whitney Museum of American Art, New York.

fantastic, spreading growths of an organic, bonelike character. The color is gray and spectral. The painting is rendered in a detailed representational style, exact, precise and controlled so that, as is implied by the term "surrealism," an illusion of super-reality is created.

Pavel Tchelitchew (1898-1957) was born in Russia but developed his highly personal style in Paris in the twenties. He too came to America in the thirties. Here he contributed to the development of the fantastic and imaginative vein in American painting. *Hide and Seek* (21-22) illustrates a curious amalgam of characteristic elements. The forms appear visceral and embryonic, bathed in body lymph and veined with blood vessels. These organic forms drift in deep emotive spaces. The space effects are intensified by exaggerations of perspective and other expressionistic devices. Tchelitchew delights in "double images," forms that appear, disappear, and turn into other forms. All of this surrealist imagery is intensified by his incredibly skilled draftsmanship. His biologically oriented nightmares remind us that a close relationship exists between the unknown recesses of the body and the mind.

Surrealism was the one movement imported from Europe in the thirties that moved away from abstraction and stylization. Illustrational in essence, surrealism was more dependent upon subject matter and sym-

21-22. Pavel Tchelitchew, *Hide and Seek*, 1940-1942. The Museum of Modern Art, New York.

bolism than upon style. By drawing on subterranean fears, dreams, and morbid fantasies for forms and symbols and then rendering these symbols with a hallucinatory clarity and specificity, the surrealists frequently established an atmosphere more intense in mood than everyday reality. There have been few American surrealists but the impact of the movement has been great. Surrealism has encouraged artists working in a wide range of styles to draw on their inner selves for moods and symbols, and the taste for the strange, emotive image permeates much modern expression.

Precisionism

In the forties, a group of American painters, influenced by the surrealists, took up precisionism, painting curious aspects of commonplace

21-23 (*above*). Bernard Perlin, *The Shore*, 1953. Private collection.
21-24 (*below*). Walter Stuempfig, *Two Houses*, 1946. Corcoran Gallery
of Art, Washington, D. C.

experience with an almost hallucinatory sharpness of form and clarity of detail to achieve effects of magical strangeness. Bernard Perlin (1918-   ) painted *The Shore* (21-23) so that the boat and the rowing figure float in jeweled radiance. The marvel of the painter's skill augments the wonder of light, transparency, and nature's prodigal abundance. Other contemporaries, like Andrew Wyeth (21-26), achieve an admirable intensity through the use of this exact and precise manner of painting.

THE CONTINUING TRADITION

Many contemporary painters refuse to fit into any of the categories we contrived for purposes of classification, for human expression is too subtle and complex for cataloging. Walter Stuempfig (1914-   ), for instance, paints shabby towns and houses and communicates the wonder of age, space, and light. *Two Houses* (21-24) reveals a debt to the surrealist, for Stuempfig has employed the emotive device of sharp converging perspective by which certain surrealists intensified their dream images. By creating an almost ambiguous sense of nearness and distance between the single figure and the pair of houses, related verticals in a dominantly horizontal composition, Stuempfig communicates the lonely and nostalgic emptiness of the beach with the sweet intensity of a daydream. Ever since Raphael Peale painted *After the Bath* and Charles B. King immortalized the strangeness of familiar things in the *Poor Artist's Cupboard,* Ameri-

21-25. George Tooker, *The Subway*, 1950. Whitney Museum of American Art, New York.

can artists have been celebrating the wonder of commonplace objects observed with sympathy. Stuempfig finds his imagination stirred when some magical effect of light and color transmutes the shabby relics of earlier times into evocative symbols. He might well be called a romantic realist.

Geometric abstraction has influenced many representational painters to base their compositions on clearly defined planes of form and angular patterns. *The Subway* (21-25), by George Tooker (1920-   ), provides a forceful though depressing commentary on the deadly monotony of much modern urban living. The painting is also interesting as an illustration of the way in which the various schools of abstract painting contribute to contemporary traditional expression. In *The Subway*, Tooker stresses the geometric framework within which we spend so much of our lives today. The carefully composed repetitions of bars, railings, and girders and the almost endless perspectives of corridors, stairwells, and subway exits seem like some geometric abstraction translated into a grim three-dimensional nightmare. Even the shadows of the automatons who inhabit this mechanized world fall in geometric patterns. The use of deeply emotive perspectives and meticulously defined forms as well as the obsessive effect achieved by the repetition of identical elements, particularly the figures in the phone booths, are all devices from the surrealist vocabulary. *The Subway* illustrates the way in which all works of art are shaped by the interplay of three forces—the artist's personality, the physical world in which he lives, and the culture which molds his vision.

American painting was born on the Atlantic seaboard and it seems appropriate to end our discussion of contemporary painting with an artist who spends his summers in Maine and his winters in Pennsylvania. Andrew Wyeth (1917-   ) draws his subject matter from these strongholds of American life and paints with a point of view that is both rooted in our early traditions and infused with a contemporary vitality. Winslow Homer and Thomas Eakins were among the artists Wyeth admired most during his formative years, and their spirit has helped shape his vision. His father, N. C. Wyeth, was one of America's most brilliant illustrators at the turn of the century, and the younger man had the advantage of a thorough training in drawing as well as in the craft of painting. Like Homer and Eakins, Wyeth loves both nature and man with a gloomy intensity, and his sharp-focus precise technique is admirably adapted to communicate both the objectivity of his vision and the strength of his feelings. A citizen of our troubled contemporary world, he does not lose himself in a romantic or idealized past. Wyeth remains continuously aware of today and

21-26. Andrew Wyeth, *Christina's World*, 1948. The Museum of Modern Art, New York.

that the drama of life contains hardship and suffering as well as serenity and beauty. An almost surrealist mood of strangeness and oppression often hangs over the sunny world he depicts. This too is an element of our Puritan background, for our forefathers were continuously reminding us that all was vanity in this vale of tears. A true colonial sparseness characterizes Wyeth's paintings. Each composition that he paints is reduced to its essence; he has said, "When you lose the simplicity, you lose the drama." *Christina's World* (21-26) contains the elements that typify Wyeth's art. The barren and harsh New England landscape and the indomitable human spirit provide the drama. The pitiless glare of light reveals the forms with a clarity that is equaled by the meticulous draftsmanship and the brilliant technical facility of the artist. One senses a lucid intelligence and a compassionate nature in interplay, overwhelmed by the strange beauty of life as well as by the tragedy and hopefulness that appear to be the inevitable counterparts of man's existence.

No one school of painting represents contemporary America. The artist of today inherits a tradition of infinite complexity and variety. Sharp-focus naturalism with its almost obsessive detail represents one end of the range of contemporary painting while the geometric abstractionists and abstract expressionists represent the other. Such range and latitude of style means that there is room today for every form of artistic expression. Within a short span of years, John Marin, Marsden Hartley, and Andrew Wyeth reacted to the same New England landscape in three unique and individual ways—the first impulsive and ecstatic, the second tender and disturbed, the third incisive and brooding. Democracy derives its strength from this full range of human expression.

Viewed in moments of depression, the paintings of the last decade suggest only nihilism and chaos. In moments of optimism, one feels not only that the valid aspects of the old tradition are still with us but that we are witnessing the birth of a new tradition. Form, space, color, line, and texture are being developed as elements in a new symphonic kind of painting that is free from the role of naturalistic representation as music is free. Such an art can attack the senses directly and vehemently to transmit profound intimations of order. Moods of optimism and pessimism both have validity. Modern painting is as it is because of the multiplicity of our culture. We have a heritage of age-old conflicts which can lead the world to chaos, but we also have a heritage of knowledge, achievement, and change that holds a promise of orderly progress into the future.

The Graphic Arts
and Sculpture

THE GRAPHIC ARTS

Prints

Contemporary prints reflect the tendencies of the various modern schools of painting, and many painters in the twenties and early thirties used the print media for commenting on the contemporary scene. *Queer Fish* (22-1), a lithograph by Mabel Dwight (1870-   ), like many prints of the twenties, is characterized by carefully graded tonalities, rounded forms, and a gentle humor. *The Great God Pan* (22-2), by Adolph Dehn (1895-   ), foreshadows the changing temper of the times. The angular patterns, sharp textures, and bold contrasts of tone give a vehemence and bite to the Dehn lithograph that is absent from the prints of an earlier decade. Dehn's style, in which elements of caricature contribute expressive power, was strongly influenced by the German satirists, particularly George Grosz.

22-1 (*above*). Mabel Dwight, *Queer Fish*, 1936. International Business Machines Collection, New York.   22-2 (*below*). Adolph Dehn, *The Great God Pan*, 1940. International Business Machines Collection, New York.

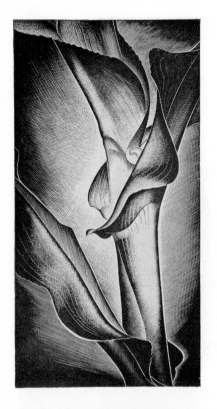

22-3. Paul Landacre, *Growing Corn*, 1940. International Business Machines Collection, New York.

22-4 (*left*). Mabel Farmer, *Salute*, 1937. **Dr.** Edward Robbins Collection. 22-5 (*below*). Frederico Castellon, *Of Land and Sea*, 1939. International Business Machines Collection, New York.

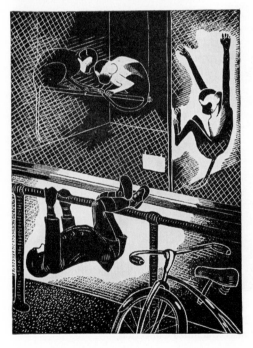

During the socially conscious thirties, topical prints of a sharp and critical tone were popular for treating the controversial issues of the day, since black and white had a pungency and force that made for dramatic effectiveness. William Gropper, Philip Evergood, and many other painters focused their graphic commentaries on areas of social discord. Most of the social commentators remained conservative in style, for their desire was to cultivate a broad audience rather than appeal to the established art patrons—preferring, as one artist stated, to have their work owned by large numbers of people because it was good rather than by a small number because it was rare. We tend to remember the satirical prints from this period because of their disputatious liveliness. Many print makers, however, stayed with conventional themes and emphasized traditional esthetic values.

In the late thirties print makers became less concerned with social themes and began to pursue various technical and esthetic explorations, for the complex graphic processes suggested new esthetic possibilities for each medium. *Growing Corn* (22-3), by Paul Landacre (1893-   ), is a brilliant achievement technically and at the same time reflects the growing interest in formal compositions and patterns. A small section of a corn plant is composed to provide an elegant arrangement of rhythmic line movements and bold tonalities. Landacre has taken full advantage of the orderly sequence of parallel and crosshatched lines by which the wood engraver achieves tonal variations, and the methodical and disciplined character of engraving is reflected in the controlled lucidity of the design.

Salute (22-4), by Mabel M. Farmer (1903-1956), explores another aspect of wood engraving. Here a simple but effective composition is created by a disciplined use of arbitrary areas of black and white. The bold dark and light pattern is further enriched with a web of fine lines. The abstract nature of the engraving process is used to communicate an affectionate and gentle humor.

Surrealism was illustrational by nature, and certain of the print media were well adapted to the meticulous detail by which surrealist themes were made convincing. One of the most brilliant of the surrealist print makers was a young Spanish-born American, Frederico Castellon (1914-   ). Though his lithograph *Of Land and Sea* (22-5) has none of the more obvious devices of the surrealists, its strange and haunting atmosphere of reverie and its almost compulsively refined technique place the print in the surrealist category.

Since the forties, print makers, like painters, have become more and

22-6. Guy Maccoy, *Melon and Apples,* n.d. Courtesy of the artist.

more involved in exploration, devising new combinations of media and inventing ways of handling traditional procedures to create unusual textures and patterns. Silk-screen printing, a new print media also called serigraphy, has become popular. *Melon and Apples* (22-6), by Guy Maccoy (1904-   ), illustrates the variety of linear and textural effects available to the silk-screen artist. Dotted, crosshatched, dry-brushed, and stippled textures, broken and irregular lines as well as heavily pigmented areas in rich intermingled colors have all been used here with great effectiveness.

Traditional print media have also been revived and imbued with a new vitality through vigorous designs and an imaginative use of line effects and textures. Such time-honored processes as wood engraving, copper engraving, and wood cutting have been adapted to contemporary tastes through direct and expressive cutting methods and an imaginative exploitation of new tools and techniques. Contemporary etchings, in particular, reveal a vast and unexpected variety, for the modern etcher no longer limits himself to the traditional tools and acid baths. Stipplings, roughly burred lines, mottled and blotched patterns, scratched and cross-hatched textures, all reinforced by dry point, mezzotint, aquatint, and other intaglio processes, facilitate a wide range of tonal, linear, and textural effects. The frequent use of color also makes contemporary etchings rich and complex in their visual appeal.

Photography

The modern camera, an instrument born of our scientific and mechanical age, has gained in importance as a means of artistic expression since World War I. Lenses, camera mechanisms, films, filters, printing processes, and materials have all undergone continuous development until today camera images can be recorded at speeds of a thousandth of a second. Telescopic lenses make it possible to photograph the surfaces of other planets, and microscopic lenses record the smallest fragments of matter. Color photography has opened up new vistas and greatly enlarged the esthetic potential of the photographic processes. All of these developments have made photographers increasingly independent of painting in developing their art.

Early in the century Stieglitz and a host of others debated the merits

22-7. Edward Weston, *Reclining Nude*, 1936. Collection the author.

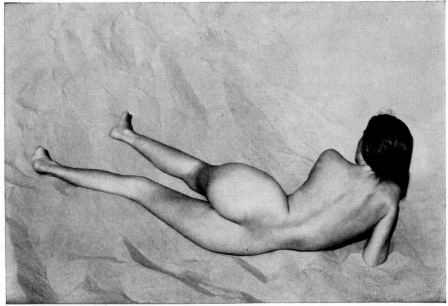

of the documentary photograph versus the "art" photograph. While paint-ers were becoming involved in arbitrary departures from visual reality, photographers moved in the opposite direction. The unique potentiality of the camera appeared to be its ability to record a wide variety of visual phenomena, ranging from everyday scenes to fleeting moments, infinitely complex textures, and subtleties beyond the grasp of normal eyesight. Thus a school of photography based on the specificity of the camera image came into being. While the role of the camera as a documentary instrument became ever more evident, it also became apparent that the power of photography lay in the eye and mind of the photographer rather than in the camera. In the hands of a man with a commonplace mind and conventional eye, the camera, no matter how fine an instrument, recorded commonplace and conventional images.

The signal achievement of the photographers during the period of national self-criticism in the thirties was to provide America with an incisive self-portrait. Paul Strand, Walker Evans, Berenice Abbott, Mar-garet Bourke-White, and Edward Weston made particularly significant contributions to this end. Most of these photographers were exponents of "pure" photography. In pure photography, the photographer selects a point of view so that the subject composes itself expressively, sets the camera exposure, and then develops the negative and the print without recourse to any further manipulations of the processes involved.

The undisputed master of pure photography through the thirties and forties was Edward Weston (1886-1958). Weston lived on the beautiful Monterey peninsula of Central California. His particular strength lay in his ability to perceive beauty of form and texture in unexpected subjects and places. His knowing eye encompassed landscapes, figures, architec-tural subjects, and still life, and he approached all of these categories with a fresh, poetic, and unconventional viewpoint. Weston discovered the beauty of driftwood, of the flotsam and jetsam of the sea, and of the incisive textures of the woodlands, but he was equally sensitive to the smooth magnificence of the forms of a bell pepper or the detail of a figure photographed at close range. His complete control and knowledge of the resources of the camera resulted in prints of unusual tonal brilliance and textural richness. *Reclining Nude* (22-7) reveals his capacity to re-vitalize even as trite a photographic subject as the nude by means of the intensely lyric and personal quality of his vision. A masterly print has been produced by emphasizing the contrast between the rounded lumi-nous forms of the body and the dull, more angular patterns in the sand. The contrast is strengthened by the exquisite sharpness of the contours of the figure. Most of Weston's compositional arrangements are simple; much of their visual effectiveness results from this simplicity. Here the graceful arc of the body has been fitted into the horizontal rectangle with the certainty that reveals the master.

SCULPTURE

The development of American sculpture since 1915 might be summarized as follows: In the decade following World War I, a vigorous nonacademic realism developed, largely inspired by Rodin and his followers. Concurrently, and becoming increasingly important during the late twenties and thirties, an interest in problems of sculptural composition and style was stimulated by French cubism, Italian futurism, and Central European constructivism. (Constructivism was concerned with the relationship between scientific thought, modern technology, and the fine and industrial arts.) The chief influence of these movements in America was in directing sculptors toward a simplified and stylized realism. Since 1940, American sculpture has become increasingly abstract. Many contemporary sculptors have forsaken traditional sculptural media for the materials of the foundry and the factory.

The Realists

In the exciting days following the Armory show, Rodin played much the same role in relation to the development of modern sculpture that Cézanne played in relation to painting. It was largely the example of Rodin and his European followers that stimulated American sculptors to abandon trite academic formulas and to initiate a vigorous though short-lived school of nonacademic realism. These younger men followed Rodin's preference for roughly modeled surfaces as well as for projections and hollows that reflect the light with vigor. One of the first of the young realists, Mahonri M. Young (1877-1957), left Salt Lake City to study at the Art Students League in New York. From New York he moved on to Paris where he saw how Rodin gave expression to his belief that sculpture was the art of "the active line of the plane found, the hollows and projections rendered." Young returned to America where he sketched and practiced a sculptural equivalent of the lively, almost journalistic painting of the Eight. Young's bronzes of ditchdiggers, prize fighters, and other

22-8. Mahonri Young, *Right to the Jaw*, 1926-1927. Brooklyn Museum, Brooklyn, N. Y.

genre subjects display a surging vitality. *Right to the Jaw* (22-8) is a characteristic bronze in which the freely modeled anatomical forms are composed in sweeping curves and large opposing diagonal movements. Mahonri Young revealed his feeling for metal by casting his bronze in lithe twisting forms rather than in the monumental patterns dictated by stone.

Jo Davidson (1883-1952) was a New York youth who first studied at home and then in Paris. He too derived from Rodin a feeling for the expressive force of a directly modeled surface. Davidson modeled the heads of many great personalities of our age. Throughout the course of his long professional career, he managed both to retain his integrity as a sculptor and to satisfy the demands of his clients for an incisive likeness. His portrait study *A New Englander* (22-9) achieves a subtle projection of a reticent introspective character by its combination of strong structure and free but sensitively modeled surface.

While Rodin was the dominant personality in late-nineteenth-century sculpture, not all of the emerging sculptors were temperamentally sympathetic to the vigorous modeling and the intense romantic emotionalism

 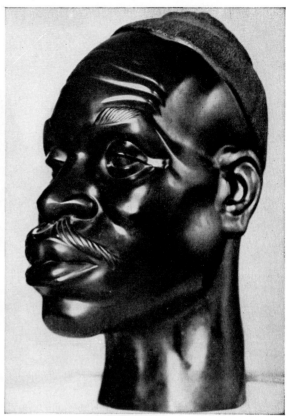

22-9 (*left*). Jo Davidson, *A New Englander*, 1935. Museum of Fine Arts, Boston.
22-10. (*right*). Malvina Hoffman, *Senegalese Soldier*, 1928. Brooklyn Museum,
Brooklyn, N. Y.

of his style. Malvina Hoffman (1887-   ) was born in New York and
after a period of study went to Paris and worked with Rodin. However,
Rodin's vibrating surfaces and psychological subtleties had little influence
on her style, which is characterized by large generalized forms and bold
simplifications of surface. Miss Hoffman's effectiveness can best be seen
by contrasting her black marble *Senegalese Soldier* (22-10) with Davidson's subtle characterization of a New Englander. Miss Hoffman's brilliantly polished surfaces and simplified forms create a mask which repels
any attempt to go below the surface—the form is clear but the personality
remains an enigma. Her most impressive achievement is a series of
bronzes representing the world's ethnic types, executed for the Field
Museum of Chicago.

Much early-twentieth-century sculpture revealed the impact of
archeological and anthropological study. In reaction against the fervid

22-11. Paul Manship, *Indian Hunter*, 1926. Courtesy Metropolitan Museum of Art, Gift of Thomas Cochran, 1929.

romanticism of Rodin, a number of artists were attracted to the formal qualities of design and the monumental simplifications of form that distinguished the great sculptures of primitive peoples, archaic cultures, and the Orient.

Paul Manship (1885-   ) was born in Minnesota and after a brief period of study in the East departed for the American Academy in Rome. Rome still dwelt in the shadow of eclecticism, but attention had turned to the earlier periods of Greek art and to the monumental styles of the ancient world. Manship found the formalizations of the archaic Greek sculptors and the rhythmic simplification of the Orient well suited to his own taste for disciplined elegance. His *Indian Hunter* (22-11) reveals the thoughtfully balanced rhythms of his compositions, wherein curves are carefully juxtaposed and act as a foil to the straight lines. The simplified patterns of hair and drapery masses reveal familiarity with ancient and exotic practices as do the careful formalizations of anatomy. Manship's obvious decorative appeal, his taste, and his high level of technical competence made him the recipient of many major commissions in the twenties and thirties, by which time his archaic and Oriental mannerisms had become acceptable in conventional and academic circles. While most sculptors turned to Rodin, the Orient, or Ancient Greece, a few sculptors found inspiration in the urgent carvings of the Middle Ages. Ivan Mestrovic (1883-   ) and Alfeo Faggi (1885-   ), though their style reflected Romanesque and Gothic mannerisms, sculped without undue formalism and frequently achieved an ardent intensity.

The Moderns

The greatest stimulus toward a new approach to sculpture came from the avant-garde movements in Europe during the first two decades of the century. One of the central figures in the vital experimental atmosphere of Paris during these years was Elie Nadelman (1885-1946). Like Manship, Nadelman was deeply imbued with the spirit of early classic art, but unlike Manship, he was less interested in the surface mannerisms of early art forms than in the fundamental problems of artistic structure. Nadelman was born in Poland and after a short period of study in Germany moved to Paris. Like many of progressive young sculptors around 1900, Nadelman was strongly influenced by Rodin's thinking but he rapidly moved into the orbit of the cubist and *Fauve* group. In this stimulating atmosphere he began a most fruitful series of drawings and experimental sculptures in which he constructed his forms by means of emphatic planes and curve-edged forms. Nadelman produced a number of heads, full figures, genre figures, and animal forms during the first two decades of the century; these vary in character from angular abstractions

22-12. Elie Nadelman, *La Mysterieuse*, n.d. Brooklyn Museum, Brooklyn, N.Y.

22-13 (*above, left*). Alexander Archipenko, *Woman Combing Her Hair*, 1915. The Museum of Modern Art, New York, 22-14 (*above, right*). Gaston Lachaise, *Standing Woman*, 1912-1917. Whitney Museum of American Art, New York. 22-15 (*left*). Jacques Lipchitz, *Sacrifice*, 1948-1952. Whitney Museum of American Art, New York.

of naturalistic forms to rhythmic curvilinear studies of classic derivation. At first glance the classic derivation of *La Mysterieuse* (22-12) seems to overpower the originality of the concept. Further study, however, reveals that the sculptor's concern has been with the purification and abstraction of the form and its relation to the material, since the polished white marble was a dominant factor in determining the degree of abstraction and generalization invoked by the artist. Nadelman, like most of the cubist sculptors, abandoned the practice of modeling the sculptural forms in clay and then casting them. By the direct cutting, carving, and polishing of the stone or wood, the sculptor became increasingly sensitive to the esthetic potential of his materials. Nadelman moved to America from France in 1914, established a studio near New York, and lived and worked in semiseclusion during his remaining years.

The Cubists

Cubist sculpture, like cubist painting, was short-lived, but the indirect influence of the movement was incalculable. Alexander Archipenko (1887-) was born in Russia and studied in Paris during the early years of cubism. During these years Picasso, Lipchitz, and Nadelman had carried out some interesting experiments in dissecting the structure of human form and breaking it down by a severe geometrical faceting of its important planes. Archipenko carried these experiments further, composing his *Woman Combing Her Hair* (22-13) with concave and convex forms and open and closed spaces. By means of this device Archipenko not only created a vigorous sense of abstract form but also suggested some of the dynamics of movement. The elegance of his polished surfaces also reflected the growing concern of sculptors with the nature of materials. Archipenko settled in the United States in the early twenties, and although his later work did not live up to the promise of his early years, he had a decisive influence on a host of younger men.

Lachaise and Lipchitz

Gaston Lachaise (1882-1935) came to America from France in 1906, a master craftsman in wood, metal, and stone, and became an assistant to Paul Manship and other American sculptors. While working for others he perfected his own very original and powerful style. Lachaise most frequently chose the nude female figure as his subject and the essence of his style is exemplified in his great bronze *Standing Woman* (22-14). The ample swelling forms spring from the arched feet and carry up

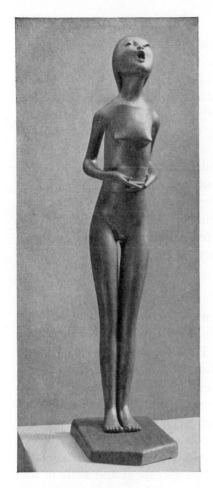

22-16. Hugo Robus, *Song*, 1934. Courtesy Metropolitan Museum of Art, Rogers Fund, 1947.

through the figure in a series of powerful rhythms to culminate in the poised head and gracefully gesturing hands. The magnificently realized, full forms are based on a sympathetic observation of human anatomy which was subsequently simplified and generalized to achieve a unique combination of monumentality and voluptuousness. In some of Lachaise's later works, the massive anatomical forms become almost abstract rhythmic elements in a composition employing voluminous ovoid masses. This tendency toward abstraction in his late work is further emphasized by the smooth perfection of his surfaces. In a period when experiment and theory were directing sculptors' attention away from the human content of their work, Lachaise combined a personal and intense lyrical reaction to his living experiences with an intuitive feeling for both structure and formal esthetic values.

One of the major figures in Paris in the exciting second decade of

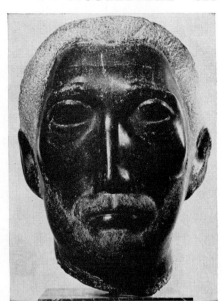

22-17. William Zorach, *Head of Christ*, 1940. The Museum of Modern Art, New York.

the century, when the principles of cubism were being formulated by painters and sculptors, was Jacques Lipchitz (1891-   ). Born in Poland, Lipchitz went to Paris to learn stonecutting, modeling, and casting at the Academy Julien. Around 1914 his style underwent a radical change under the impact of cubism. Much of his early work was along orthodox cubist lines, simplifying the surfaces of forms to indicate structure and breaking the forms into interpenetrating planes. Some of his most original sculptures during these early years employed the formalizations of Negro sculpture, reflecting the cubists' enthusiastic discovery of primitive art.

Lipchitz settled in the United States in 1941, and much of his sculpture since that time has been essentially expressionistic in character, employing rich, voluminous forms, and full, almost baroque, curvilinear rhythms. The themes are sometimes mythological, frequently liturgical. *Sacrifice* (22-15) exhibits the religious intensity and the violence that characterize much of his late work. The anthropomorphic, semiabstract forms, fearsome and ponderous, suggest myth in a way that is both mysterious and explicit. The priestly figure, whose enigmatic, concave facelessness at the same time reveals features, pierces the breast of the sacrificial cock with solemnity. The heavy forms, brutal in their awkward and primitive fearfulness, suggest that the sculptor abandoned the formal concerns of cubism to explore the depths of fear and awe that gave primitive religious art its power.

22-18. John Flannagan, *The Beginning*, n.d. Arizona State College, Collection of American Art, Tempe, Ariz.

Most of the younger sculptors who were practicing in the twenties and thirties, men born in the last two decades of the nineteenth century, had an initial try at cubism and then abandoned the cubist idiom for a stylized and monumental simplification of natural forms. An analytical attitude toward form and structure and a sense of the sculptor's materials, however, remained, along with a distaste for the trivial prettiness of academic practice. The exciting discoveries being made in the field of pre-Columbian art contributed to the taste for weighty generalizations and voluminous simplifications designed to reduce form to its sculptural essence.

For sculptors, even more than for painters, New York was the center of the American art world. The sculptor's craft involves expensive materials; the works are heavy and cumbersome, and many of the processes

22-19 (*below*). Ahron Ben-Shmuel, *Pugilist*, 1929. The Museum of Modern Art, New York. 22-20 (*right*). Chaim Gross, *Acrobatic Dancers*, 1942. Whitney Museum of American Art, New York.

involved, like casting, demand special technical facilities. Too, only in an art-minded metropolitan center can the sculptor find a clientele. Hugo Robus (1885-   ) was born in Cleveland, Ohio, but like most sculptors of his day, he gravitated to New York. Almost self-taught, he created sculptures characterized by the unusual combination of elegance, simplicity, and wit. *His Song* (22-16) is unpretentious and charming, its fluid lines and simplified anatomical forms well-suited to the gleaming brass in which it is cast.

William Zorach (1887-   ) came to New York from Lithuania.

Zorach began his career as a painter but soon turned his attention to sculpture. He found little interest in the sleek perfection of early cubist sculpture, and after an initial essay in abstraction projected his warm and reverent feeling for people as well as animals into recognizable form. He chose handsome and intractable materials; his *Head of Christ* (22-17) in black granite has the austere dignity of an ancient Egyptian portrait, and as in Egypt, the massive form was achieved by an endless struggle with the obdurate stone. Zorach's integrity extends far beyond a respect for materials and processes. His stylistic preferences have been determined by his deep feelings for all life and for the great historic sculptural tradition which harks back to the beginning of civilization.

John Flannagan (1895-1942) came to New York from his North Dakota birthplace via the Minneapolis Institute of Fine Arts. Flannagan first carved in wood. Later he turned to field stone, and he extended his preference for direct carving even to metal, working directly on unfinished bronze casts. Flannagan combined a lively emotional warmth with an original sense of form. Frequently, as in his bronze *The Beginning* (22-18), a playful note adds a dimension of humor to his directly formed, original conceptions.

The tradition of monumental simplicity continues in the work of some of the sculptors who were born after 1900 and are working today. In his *Pugilist* (22-19), Ahron Ben-Shmuel (1903-   ) exploits all the massive weightiness of stone to suggest the formidable heft of his subject. Chaim Gross (1904-   ) carved his bulging *Acrobatic Dancers* (22-20) to emphasize the grain and sheen of the ebony as well as the textures of the cutting tools. There is a sophisticated playing with exaggerated volumes, rhythmic curves, bulges and hollows, but sophistication and formal concerns have not overwhelmed the expressive note. Much of the ponderous seriousness of acrobatic dancers has been communicated, but at the same time there is a pleasant harking back to the gay tradition of folk carving and toy making. The abstract, the concrete, folk ways, and the grand tradition are all in interplay in this entertaining and very lively piece of sculpture.

Geometric and Nongeometric Abstraction, 1940-1960

Most of the sculptors to be discussed in the last section of this chapter achieved their mature artistic style in the years following World War II. The general tendencies which characterize painting since 1940 also apply to sculpture although in modern sculpture the formal aspects of abstraction predominate over the expressionistic elements. Abstract sculpture can be classified as geometric, symbolic, or expressionist according to the character of the forms employed. A predilection for strange, even ominous forms and surface finishes reveals the influence of surrealism and the neo-romantic movement. As with painting, the system of classification used to describe modern sculpture involves an oversimplification which is useful only in that it points up current trends.

Sculpture which is essentially geometric in its forms was first produced in Russia in the years immediately following World War I by a group who called themselves "constructivists." Accepting the premise of a scientific and technological society, these men developed a body of art which glorified mechanistic and technical forces. By utilizing the forms of industry and industrial materials, the early constructivists created new concepts of beauty and new art forms of great significance to the industrial age. Antoine Pevsner (1886-   ) and his brother Naum Gabo are two leading constructivists who continued producing their brilliant abstractions in various European centers after they left Russia. Naum Gabo (1890-   ) came to the United States in 1946, but his influence had preceded him. The pure forms in his *Construction* (22-21) appear to have been shaped by the mathematician and the machinist, and the beauty of these precise shapes is augmented by the lucid clarity of transparent and reflective materials. Using wire, plastics, and glass, polished metal and other unorthodox materials, Gabo and his followers carried on a series of experiments both in the relationships of materials to form and in the interpenetration of space by various transparent "space-modulating" agencies. The impact of these sculptural essays in geometric abstraction is evident in contemporary architecture.

Since World War II many sculptors have continued to explore the possibilities of geometric abstraction initiated by the constructivist sculptors. Three examples indicate the range of contemporary activity in this category. Sidney Gordin's (1918-   ) *Construction #5, 1951* (22-22) is a sculptural essay in tonality, geometric patterning, and space-modulating transparencies. The play of white and black, of in, out, up, down, and across, of solid and transparent, of line and mass is developed with vivacity and taste. Like so much contemporary sculpture, *Construction #5* is executed in steel, in this case painted. Richard Lippold (1903-   ) has conducted a more complex essay in the interpretations of space with

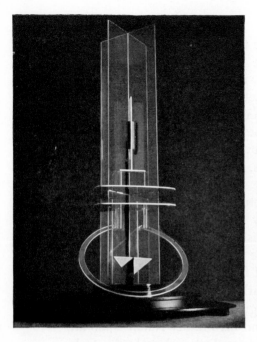

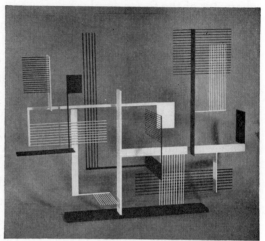

22-21 (*left*). Naum Gabo, *Construction, 1923.* The Museum of Modern Art, New York. 22-22 (*below*). Sidney Gordin, *Construction #5, 1951.* Newark Museum, Newark, N. J.

an intricate linear geometric pattern. His 10-foot-high *Variation No. 7: Full Moon* (22-23) is executed in nickel chromium wire, stainless steel wire, and brass rods. The exquisite delicacy of the light lines intersecting space and the radiance and shimmer with which the light is reflected by the clusters of fine lines represent a most sensitive and poetic development of geometric abstraction. The craftsmanship involved in the construction of such an elaborate structure contributes to its refinement. For the artist, these delicate constructions are more than sources of visual delight; they are philosophic statements about modern life. Of one of his sculptures, Lippold has said, "Once installed, nothing can disturb it except the most delicate of matter; dust, a piece of paper, an enthusiastic finger. Again we must remember that a slip of paper in the wrong place—someone's desk or a portfolio—can now destroy mankind. It is not the main tensions we must fear, it is the little delicate relationships we must control."

The curve holds as much delight for the geometric abstractionist as the straight line. A contemporary master of curvilinear formalism is Jose de Rivera (1904-   ). His *Yellow-Black, 1946* (22-24), in painted aluminum, appears to be a pure distillation of technological skills. Its flawless thin shell punctuated by perfect circles almost hypnotizes the eye with the effortless flow of its rhythms. De Rivera has constructed a number of shining stainless steel parabolas which rotate slowly in space, thereby adding another element, that of motion, to their shimmering loveliness.

22-23. Richard Lippold, *Variation No. 7: Full Moon*, 1949-1950. The Museum of Modern Art, New York.

22-24. Jose de Rivera, *Yellow-Black, 1946*. Whitney Museum of American Art, New York.

22-25. Alexander Calder, *Pome-granate*, 1949. Whitney Museum of American Art, New York.

Movement also adds an unorthodox dimension of interest to the sculpture of Alexander Calder (1898-   ), the son of a sculptor. Calder introduced his very original "mobiles" and "stabiles" in the early thirties, when their fragile and airy grace added a welcome note of lightness to the sculptural scene. At the same time their wit and whimsical charm provided an antidote to the generally sober and tendentious character of the art of the depression years. Though Calder's sculpture is essentially abstract, the shapes suggest symbols from the world of organic forms rather than geometry. *Pomegranate* (22-25) is executed in painted sheet aluminum and steel. As in most of Calder's mobiles, the gaiety and grace of the forms and the fanciful arabesques which they perform as they move through space can distract one from the sculpture's fundamental refinement and elegance. The flat sharp shapes Calder employs as well as the thin lines and wry bits of humor are reminiscent of the works of Miro. The technical perfection with which the metal parts are shaped, the ingenuity with which they are combined, and the amusing and thoughtful involvements and counterbalancings of movement also recall the long tradition of Yankee tinkerers.

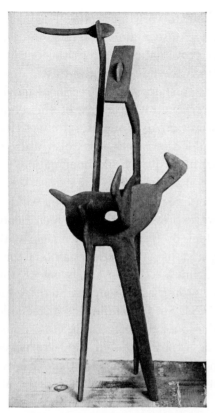 

22-26 (*left*). Isamu Noguchi, *Unknown Bird*, 1949. Stable Gallery, New York.   22-27 (*right*). Leo Amino, *Jungle*, 1950. Whitney Museum of American Art, New York.

Organically derived abstract forms dominate the sculptures of Isamu Noguchi (1904-   ). Noguchi's *Unknown Bird* (22-26) employs inter-locking forms which rest on one another much after the manner used in his handsome table (19-9), although here they are developed with more complexity and subtlety. The *Unknown Bird*, almost 5 feet high, is exe-cuted in green slate. The curiously tapered forms are endowed with both strangeness and grace. At the same time a monumental gravity character-izes the group, and it is this curious ability to invent and combine forms containing so many diverse qualities that distinguishes Noguchi's art. The rapidity with which modern art has developed away from traditional patterns is explicit in the fact that Noguchi studied with Gutzon Borglum.

Leo Amino (1911-   ) also creates what might best be described as "organic" abstractions, although more careful examination of *Jungle*

(22-27) reveals no direct borrowing from the organic world. This handsome and involved piece of sculpture is also almost 5 feet high. The subtle swelling ovoid shapes seem to grow naturally from the cutting, sanding, and polishing processes by which the fine-grained satiny mahogany is shaped. The amazing variety of the shapes and directional movements, the play of open spaces and interpenetrating forms, of encircling movements and sudden diverging gestures create a sculptural effect that is involved and demands thorough exploration. Amino has also utilized plastics and various synthetic stones with sensitivity and imagination.

An impressive group of young sculptors now working in welded metal can best be classified as abstract expressionists. These men bend, hammer, weld, and anneal their iron, steel, bronze, and silver images with the directness of the action painters, and like the action painters they achieve an earnest vehemence. David Smith (1906-   ) is one of the most energetic and imaginative of this group, as is demonstrated by his bronze and steel *Family Decision* (22-28). Smith handles his intractable materials with uninhibited freedom; the fantastic images which he pours forth can be whimsical, frightening, or astonishing, but they are never commonplace. Smith has been working with steel for more than twenty-five years, and his technical facility in handling metal equals his imagination.

David Hare (1917-   ) also works in steel. He frequently shows a predilection for a surrealist strangeness of form. His more than life-sized steel *Juggler* (22-29) is richly textured and full of somewhat ominous traplike forms and sharpnesses. Humor also plays a role in David Hare's sculpture.

22-28. David Smith, *Family Decision*, 1951. Willard Gallery, New York.

22-29 (*right*). David Hare, *Juggler*, 1950-1951. Whitney Museum of American Art, New York.   22-30 (*below*). Ibram Lassaw, *Procession*, 1956. Whitney Museum of American Art, New York.

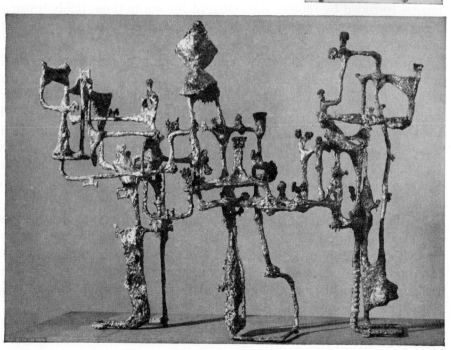

22-31 (*above*). Seymour Lipton, *Storm Bird*, 1954. Whitney Museum of American Art, New York. 22-32 (*right*). Theodore Roszak, *Specter of Kitty Hawk*, 1946-1947. The Museum of Modern Art, New York.

    Ibram Lassaw (1913-   ) works most frequently in brazed metal. His *Procession* (22-30) combines bronzes and silver in intricately involved forms that move through space in measured, continuous rhythms. The swellings and shrinkings, blisterings and drippings, the clusterings of small forms, and occasional larger masses provide the eye with involved and fascinating changes of form. There is something of the enigma of ancient images corroded by time or the action of the sea in these richly textured surfaces which have much sensuous beauty and yet, at the same time, a strangely repellent quality.

    Seymour Lipton (1903-   ) retains a preference for the more traditional sculptural quality of weight. His metal forms may be built up of thin sheets or bars of metal but they enfold one another to create a powerful sense of mass. *Storm Bird* (22-31), in nickel silver, is composed with forceful movements. The strong angular forms penetrate one another and define the voids by means of twisting rhythms, and the heavy surface texture intensifies the sense of drama. The dynamic emotionalism that is the goal of abstract expressionism is brilliantly achieved in the sculpture of Seymour Lipton and Theodore Roszak.

    Theodore Roszak (1907-   ) commenced his career using the severely geometric forms and cold impersonal surface finish of the constructivists. After World War II his style underwent a complete change, and he became engrossed in the use of forms which are "meant to be blunt reminders of primordial strife and struggle, reminiscent of those

22-33. Peter Grippe, *The City*, 1942. The Museum of Modern Art, New York.

brute forces that not only produced life, but in turn threatened to destroy it." Instead of employing smooth, reassuring, even slick surfaces he uses textures that are coarse, eroded, scarred, and pitted. The *Specter of Kitty Hawk* (22-32) is of welded and hammered steel, brazed with bronze and brass. Its spiked violence and anguished skeletal angularities express the terrors of the atomic age with unbridled eloquence. Though Roszak is an abstract artist, his sculptures are closely attuned to contemporary existence, but on a cosmic rather than a personal level, expressing the universal fears that beset our times.

Not all of the sculpture of our age is metal nor does it all reflect our trying times. Peter Grippe (1912-   ) has suggested the continuous flow of life that takes place behind the walls of the metropolis in his imaginative terra cotta *The City* (22-33). Walls and faces intermingle with hands, feet, cryptic symbols, and scrawled notations to create a sculptural form as evocative of the ever-present sense of humanity behind the city walls as the murmur of unseen voices. Digging deep within the unconscious recesses of his being, the contemporary artist finds meaningful symbols by which to communicate his most subtle intuitions and experiences to his fellow man.

Only a little over three centuries have passed since the settlers from Europe constructed the first rude dwellings on the shores of Virginia. In these three hundred years the world has undergone greater changes than during any comparable period in history. We now live in a world of almost inconceivable intellectual vigor, complexity, richness, and productivity. Such periods of vigorous development are inevitably full of conflict and confusion, for man is forging his way into new areas where there is no precedent or established pattern of behavior. The United States, more than any other country in the world, appears to be the heir of both the benefits and the conflicts inherent in this complex culture. America has always been the land of abundance; today this abundance extends itself to architecture, painting, sculpture, the crafts, and the allied arts. Institutions devoted to furthering the cause of the arts are well established in our national life and are flourishing. Architecture and the industrial arts, in particular, reflect the technical advance and the intricate social organization of our society both in their scale and in the discipline and refinement of their visual qualities. The best of our contemporary architecture and industrial design appears to reflect an integration between our advanced technology and a new scientific humanism. The journalistic arts are reassuring in their lively, perceptive, and entertaining variety. But the arts, like painting and sculpture, which express the philosophic goals and questionings of our society, frequently seem to reflect an atmosphere of pessimism, even anguish. Though we are energetic and productive, we are not certain where we are going, and though we may readily admit that life is an adventure and a quest, we frequently feel lost and without direction.

Because our society is one in which creative individuals are searching to find new directions and forward-looking values with which to identify themselves, our age is beset with well-grounded fears and confusing crosscurrents. Exploration and certainty cannot go hand in hand. But the very desire to adventure into the realm of the unknown speaks of optimism and assurance, and nowhere is this spirit more evident than in the arts. Along with the scientists who set out to investigate the structure of the molecule or to explore outer space, the artist too steps forward, gravely or gayly, into new forms of expression, intent on exploring what is without and expressing what is within.

SELECTED REFERENCES

for PART V Today: 1915-1960

General References

Cahill, Holger and Barr, Alfred H., Jr., *Art in America, a Complete Survey.* New York, Reynal and Hitchcock, 1935.
Larkin, Oliver, *Art and Life in America.* New York, Rinehart & Company, 1949.
McCurdy, Charles, editor, *Modern Art, a Pictorial Anthology.* New York, The Macmillan Company, 1958.

Architecture

Andrews, Wayne, *Architecture, Ambition and Americans.* New York, Harper & Brothers, 1955.
Fitch, James Marston, *American Building.* Boston, Houghton Mifflin Company, 1948.
Ford, Katherine M. and Creighton, Thomas, *The American House Today.* New York, Reinhold Publishing Corporation, 1951.
Gutheim, Frederick, *One Hundred Years of American Architecture.* New York, Reinhold Publishing Corporation, 1957.
Hitchcock, H. R., Jr., *In the Nature of Materials: The Buildings of Frank Lloyd Wright.* New York, Duell, Sloan and Pearce, Inc., 1942.
Mumford, Lewis, *Roots of Contemporary American Architecture.* New York, Reinhold Publishing Corporation, 1952.
Built in U.S.A. 1932-1944. New York, The Museum of Modern Art, 1944.
Built in U.S.A. Post War Architecture. New York, The Museum of Modern Art, and Simon & Schuster, 1952.

Painting and Sculpture

Baur, John I. H., *Revolution and Tradition in Modern American Art.* Cambridge, Mass., Harvard University Press, 1951.
Baur, John H., *New Art in America: Fifty Painters of the Twentieth Century.* New York, Frederick A. Praeger, Inc., 1957.
Boswell, Peyton, *Modern American Painting.* New York, Dodd, Mead & Company, 1939.

Brumme, C. Ludwig, *Contemporary American Sculpture*. New York, Crown Publishers, Inc., 1948.

Cheney, Martha C., *Modern Art in America*. New York, McGraw-Hill Book Company, 1939.

Craven, Thomas, *Modern Art, the Men, the Movements, the Meaning*. New York, Simon and Schuster, 1934.

The Eight. Brooklyn, N. Y., The Brooklyn Museum, 1943.

Eliot, Alexander, *Three Hundred Years of American Painting*. New York, Time, Inc., 1957.

Janis, Sidney, *Abstract and Surrealist Art in America*. New York, Reynal and Hitchcock, 1944.

Kootz, Samuel, *Modern American Painters*. New York, Brewer and Warren, 1930.

Mellquist, Jerome, *The Emergence of an American Art*. New York, Charles Scribner's Sons, 1942.

Richardson, E. P., *Painting in America*. New York, Thomas Y. Crowell Company, 1956.

Richie, Andrew C., *Abstract Painting and Sculpture in America*. New York, The Museum of Modern Art, 1951.

Schnier, Jaques, *Sculpture in Modern America*. Berkeley, Calif., University of California Press, 1948.

Sweeney, James J., *Younger American Painters, a Selection*. New York, Solomon R. Guggenheim Museum, 1954.

Watson, Forbes, *American Painting Today*. Washington, D. C., American Federation of Arts, 1929.

The New Decade, 35 American Painters and Sculptors. New York, Whitney Museum of American Art, 1955.

Wight, Frederick S., *Milestones of American Painting in Our Century*. New York, Chanticleer Press, 1949.

Interiors, Furniture, Crafts, and Industrial Design

Cheney, Sheldon and Cheney, Martha, *Art and the Machine*. New York, McGraw-Hill Book Company, 1936.

Dreyfuss, Henry, *Designing for People*. New York, Simon & Schuster, 1955.

Kaufmann, Edgar, Jr., *What Is Modern Design?* New York, The Museum of Modern Art, 1950.

Kaufmann, Edgar, Jr., *What Is Modern Interior Design?* New York, The Museum of Modern Art, 1953.

Kouwenhoven, John A., *Made in America*. Garden City, N. Y., Doubleday, 1949.

Lynes, Russell, *The Taste Makers*. New York, Harper & Brothers, 1954.

Nelson, George, *Interiors Library, Vol. I, Living Spaces*. New York, Whitney Museum of American Art, 1952.

Nelson, George, *Interiors Library, Vol. II, Chairs*. New York, Whitney Museum of American Art, 1953.

Nelson, George, *Interiors Library, Vol. IV, Storage*. New York, Whitney Museum of American Art, 1954.

Rogers, Meyric R., *American Interior Design*. New York, W. W. Norton & Company, 1947.

Teague, Walter D., *Design This Day*. New York, Harcourt, Brace & Company, 1949.

INDEX OF ILLUSTRATIONS

(Italic numbers show location of figures.)

INDEX